Tech and Crafts: Technology, Crafts and Innovation for Future Fashion

Guillermo García-Badell, María Luisa Calvo Frutos,
Diego Prieto López and Victoria Vásquez Pecile (eds.)

Tech and Crafts: Technology, Crafts and Innovation for Future Fashion

PETER LANG
Berlin · Bruxelles · Chennai · Lausanne · New York · Oxford

Bibliographic information published by the Deutsche Nationalbibliothek
The Deutsche Nationalbibliothek lists this publication in the Deutsche Nationalbibliografie; detailed bibliographic data are available on the Internet at https://dnb.dnb.de.

Library of Congress Cataloging-in-Publication Data

Names: García-Badell, Guillermo, 1981- editor | Calvo Frutos, María Luisa, 1985- editor | Prieto López, Diego editor | Vásquez Pecile, Victoria, 1984- editor
Title: Tech and crafts : technology, crafts and innovation for future fashion / Guillermo García-Badell, María Luisa Calvo Frutos, Diego Prieto López and Victoria Vásquez Pecile (eds).
Description: Berlin ; New York : Peter Lang, [2026] | Includes bibliographical references and index.
Identifiers: LCCN 2026023993 (print) | LCCN 2026023994 (ebook) | ISBN 9783631937822 hardback | ISBN 9783631937839 pdf | ISBN 9783631937846 epub
Subjects: LCSH: Clothing trade--Technological innovations | Fashion design--Technological innovations
Classification: LCC TT497 .T398 2026 (print) | LCC TT497 (ebook)
LC record available at https://lccn.loc.gov/2026023993
LC ebook record available at https://lccn.loc.gov/2026023994

Cover image by María Luisa Calvo Frutos and Guillermo García-Badell

ISBN 978-3-631-93782-2 (Print)
ISBN 978-3-631-93783-9 (ePDF)
ISBN 978-3-631-93784-6 (ePUB)
DOI 10.3726/b22900

Published by Peter Lang GmbH, Berlin, Germany

info@peterlang.com

This publication has been peer reviewed.

www.peterlang.com

Contact for General Product Safety Regulation (GPSR): gpsr@peterlang.com

Contents

Figures

Tables

Tech and Crafts

Technology, crafts and innovation for future fashion

The editors

"Tech and Crafts" is far more than just a book, it is a much broader project, an idea aimed at having many ramifications in the future.

"Tech and Crafts" represents the necessity of an agreement: just as progress must lean on technology, technology, in turn, must lean on tradition. These traditions materialize in production—whether craft-based or industrial—but also in the very conceptualization of designs. Ultimately, every object conceals a way of approaching problems and materializing solutions. Objects, therefore, express our culture and our heritage.

Thus, "Tech and Crafts" is a look to the future, but also an assertion of the past, of our history. Innovation and tradition are two sides of the same coin, two profiles that also serve to structure this book.

In the first part, we look from technology toward crafts, not with the aim of replacing them, but to explore them through new possibilities. Technologies such as artificial intelligence, virtual garment simulation, augmented reality, additive manufacturing, data analysis, bioelectronics, and generative design systems are transforming the ways we conceive, produce, and teach fashion.

Naturally, the initial chapters of this book present some applications of these advancements for the sector. However, the focus quickly shifts to the relationship between technology and tradition, explored through the lens of heritage. It is noteworthy the extent to which this Industry 4.0 is creating an opportunity to highlight the value of textile heritage. Clothes undeniably reflect our history and customs, but their preservation and presentation to the public are not always that evident. Consequently, thanks to technical advancements, museums, institutions, and even major luxury brands are breathing new life into their archives.

In the second part of the book, the approach is the opposite: innovation is viewed through the lens of tradition. Revisiting historical techniques, processes, and past innovations allows us to better understand contemporary fashion practices and to place current developments within a broader cultural and technical continuum. This idea underpins the following chapters, which adopt a historical perspective and explore the material, technical, and methodological foundations of fashion production across different periods.

Innovation within crafts is a linear and cumulative process, one in which ways of making inherently contain the identity of their time, the genius loci, and the technical knowledge that is transmitted across generations. These chapters reveal how such knowledge continues to inform present-day fashion, from design methodologies and pedagogical tools to the development of contemporary products, brand narratives, and spaces for fashion retail.

Design is fundamentally a process in which innovation is almost always present. The final chapters of the book further develop this perspective, focusing on how design processes are carried out, but also on how they are learned, documented, and transmitted. Every design responds to a specific problem within a particular context, where technology often acts as a powerful tool. Learning to design therefore means learning to integrate history, technique, material culture, and innovation.

"Tech and Crafts" is, as we have said, an idea—a necessity that cannot be fully encompassed in its breadth and complexity within a single book. It requires many more actions, some theoretical, some educational, but also practical. In reality, these texts offer only a first glimpse, aiming to highlight how closely fashion and technology have always walked hand in hand, and how consistently this partnership has maintained a distinctly humanist character.

Therefore, while this book has many limitations, we have strived to bring together experts and researchers from around the world to offer the broadest and most diverse perspective possible. Our goal has been to unite all viewpoints around a common interest: the future of fashion.

We hope you enjoy it.

PART 1

TECH and Crafts vs CRAFTS and Tech: Toward a Necessary Deal for Future Fashion

CHAPTER 1

Tech and Crafts

A necessary "new deal" and a strategic opportunity

*Guillermo García-Badell**

ABSTRACT
Industry 4.0 brings about changes at all levels. These changes are going to affect our production model, particularly the fashion system, and will modify society as a whole. To face this "revolution" with confidence in the future, a pact between tradition and innovation is necessary. This is the essence of the "Tech and Crafts" project as a whole, which finds a strategic location for its development in the Centro Superior de Diseño de Moda at the Universidad Politécnica de Madrid.

The objective of this text is to present this project, provide it with a historical and theoretical framework, first highlighting its background, and then systematically reviewing the texts that comprise it. Ultimately, it aims to contextualize and introduce "Tech and Crafts" as a project presented here in book format, but ensuring guidance to future scientific, technical, theoretical, and practical developments, all of them endowed with a much broader character where technology acts as a driver of progress in its most extensive sense.

Keywords: Technology, crafts, design, Industry 4.0, fashion, patrimony

Introduction: objectives, approach, and methodology

New technologies—with Artificial Intelligence playing a significant role, along with the Internet of Things, data analytics, virtual simulation, and advanced production processes that leverage advanced robotics and 3D manufacturing—are set to change the production system and society as a whole. This Fourth Industrial Revolution follows three others, moments in history where technical advancements necessitated much broader changes, and where a pact between the new and the old is more essential than ever to progress with confidence. The phrase "Tech and Crafts" (a clear allusion to the nineteenth-century Arts and Crafts movement) refers to this very pact.

"Tech and Crafts" also focuses on fashion. From a historical perspective, textile production has always been traditionally linked to early industrial

* Universidad Politécnica de Madrid.
(ORCID: https://orcid.org/0000-0002-3990-2744)

development. From that viewpoint, technological innovations have consistently impacted the sector, which alone would justify it as a field of study. Furthermore, from a contemporary perspective, if we look at the last 50 years, the fashion industry has undergone a complete transformation, turning clothing into a consumer good and consistently incorporating the latest technologies into its design, production, distribution, and communication.

In fact, the relationship between technology, craftsmanship, and fashion is a close one, as demonstrated by concrete examples throughout history. A notable case is that of logwood ("Palo de Campeche"), a natural dye discovered by the Spanish in Latin America in the sixteenth century, whose monopoly allowed the court of Philip II to project its technological and geopolitical power through fashion. Today, the latest trends once again turn to these natural dyes as markers of technological and cultural distinction (Chavlé-Vega et al., 2024).

This renewed interest in natural dyes responds to several factors. The first is cultural: the recovery of craftsmanship and its associated values. The second is the need for a more sustainable textile industry, in which water consumption and pollution demand concrete alternative solutions. Natural dyes and artisanal techniques are being reintroduced and combined with new technologies such as digital printing, 3D knitting, and waterless dyeing processes (Rahan & Kahn, 2025). In particular, when considering new technologies grounded in artisanal systems, digital textile printing stands out. Although it was introduced in the 1990s, it is only now experiencing scalable development capable of producing tangible effects within the industry (Tyler, 2025). Indeed, the current revolution in textile manufacturing is being driven by 3D printing technologies (Manaia, Cerejo & Duarte, 2023), which are also guiding advances in the integration of smart materials into the textile industry, enhancing the functionality of the latest wearables (Levitt et al., 2020).

Technology should not be understood as a barrier but rather as a tool that facilitates the convergence of the various functions within the industry, even at the design stage. Traditionally, designers were separated from production, including during pattern-making and prototyping phases. Simulation and 3D prototyping promote the integration of these stages, reinventing processes that were traditionally artisanal through the application of technology (Papahristou & Bilalis, 2017).

Actually, the aim of this text is to better understand the link between crafts and technology, between innovation and tradition through providing a comprehensive theoretical framework for the entire "Tech and Crafts" project, and to highlighting the opportunity of developing it within a prestigious technological university, such as the Universidad Politécnica de Madrid, specifically at its Centro Superior de Diseño de Moda.

From a methodological standpoint, this involves a systematic literature review to establish a prior historical context, but more importantly, to structure the subsequent texts around themes and bibliographical entries that link them. In any case, the essayistic nature of the text is not concealed, arguing, in fact, with data and references to justify the relevance of "Tech and Crafts" as both a concept and a future project.

As for the development, the first section aims to establish a historical context, ranging from the aforementioned "Arts and Crafts" movement to the current "Tech and Crafts" era. The industrial revolutions prior to the current one can help us understand the present as design has always served to unite innovation and tradition, therefore there are common grounds we should be aware of to face future changes with confidence.

The second section argues for the timeliness of the current moment. The spirit of the Bauhaus is more relevant than ever, the need for a humanistic and innovative approach in design is required, and this conjunction of tradition and technology precisely occurs at the Universidad Politécnica de Madrid, which would serve as a meeting point.

Indeed, the third section begins by arguing for the strategic position of the Centro Superior de Diseño de Moda de Madrid within that university, moving then on to structuring the texts that will follow this one in the present book. This structure is very clear, consisting of two parts: one that looks from technologies toward "crafts," where heritage presents a great opportunity for convergence while the other looks from the opposite side, from "crafts" toward technologies, concluding that design itself is a process, pure innovation methodology, which teaches us how to incorporate advancements into what is already known to ensure their success.

A necessary agreement between technology and craft from a historical perspective

Tech and Crafts: a necessary agreement

In December 2024, Google unveiled an experimental machine, a quantum computer capable of performing in five minutes what a traditional computer couldn't accomplish in 10,000,000,000,000,000,000,000,000 years (roughly seven hundred trillion times the estimated age of the universe).

A report from the International Monetary Fund (Cazzaniga et al., 2024) considers that Artificial Intelligence has the potential to alter the structure of the global economy—that is, to change the fabric of our social relationships, reportedly impacting 40 % of jobs.

We are in the midst of the Fourth Industrial Revolution, or Industry 4.0, where Artificial Intelligence plays a significant role. However, so do what's known as the "Internet of Things," cloud computing, 3D simulation, and advanced production processes that leverage advanced robotics and 3D manufacturing.

In the design sector generally, but particularly in fashion and retail, these industrial (and social) changes, coupled with increasing demands for greater sustainability, will undoubtedly revolutionize the sector. But who knows in what direction. In fact, change is a constant in the fashion industry, and trying to anticipate it can seem futile. It's certain that current successful formulas will die out in the near future, just as new ideas will emerge, leading to concepts we can't even imagine how will adapt to a new context full of opportunities.

Consequently, different states of mind, ranging from fear to enthusiasm (for the unknown), are logical. This text doesn't aim to assess whether the changes will be positive or negative, nor does it attempt to predict the future. We don't possess a crystal ball, but we do have the certainty that we are living in a context marked by change, largely driven by technology.

In the quest for certainties within an uncertain environment, we can always look to the past, where we have some experience. The challenges and opportunities are indeed new but previous to the Fourth Revolution since there are three previous industrial revolutions. Each of these generated that mix of distrust and optimism in the face of social changes, skepticism and faith in technical innovations. From this experience, we can learn several things. The first is that the future, though uncertain, is unavoidable, and in one way or another, it always incorporates new technologies. The second is that, thus far, in the medium and long term, technical advancements translate into social progress (it is undeniable that people have more prosperity, freedom, justice, and opportunities today than in the eighteenth century before the First Industrial Revolution). And the third is that the incorporation of so much new technology at once demands a pact, a social pact that is obviously achieved over time, but also a pact between the past and the future, between heritage and innovation, so that new ways of doing things incorporate the best of traditional approaches.

A pact between technology and craftsmanship is therefore more necessary than ever.

On Charles Frederick Worth and the origins of Arts and Crafts in Europe

Skepticism about technological advancements isn't new; it's arguably a constant in our society, and it becomes particularly intense during periods marked by an industrial revolution. The need for new models to preserve traditional *savoir-faire* within a completely new economic and social structure isn't new either. This invites us to look to the past to better understand the present and approach the future with perspective.

Charles Frederick Worth is a key figure in fashion history. Of British origin and based in Paris since the mid-nineteenth century (with a shop on Rue de la Paix since 1858), Worth is recognized as the founder of what we now call haute couture. Originally (in 1868), this was the *Chambre Syndicale de la Haute Couture*, a group of designers seeking business alternatives in response to the new systems emerging from the industrial revolution.

Worth is credited with originating what has now become the impressive luxury market, but what's often overlooked is the business vision behind his response. More importantly, people often forget how innovative his approach was within a very challenging context for dressmakers, a guild almost of artisans. To understand this context—the clothing business in the second half of the nineteenth century—we can turn to Émile Zola's novels, which describe French society during the Second Empire. In this case, we particularly focus on his *Au Bonheur des Dames* (originally published in 1883), which tells the story of a young immigrant moving from the countryside to the city in search of fortune as a department store saleswoman. With the Industrial Revolution, Paris grew, new businesses were established, and this rural exodus intensified. The Haussmann plan was proposed that, by breaking with the traditional urban fabric, laid out new, wide avenues intended to build the city of the future. Department stores (like *Printemps*, inaugurated in 1883, or *Le Bon Marché*, remodeled under a project by Boileau and Eiffel in 1879) offered quality, fast, and affordable commerce. This challenged all the guilds of artisans and designers, small merchants who largely went bankrupt, with exceptions like Worth, who proposed a quality alternative based on the prestige of design.

The Industrial Revolution didn't just bring opportunities; it also brought harsh consequences for the most disadvantaged and widespread skepticism among intellectuals and artists. Many painters, for instance, tried to escape, turning their gaze toward landscapes and rejecting the city, which they saw as contaminated by these new lifestyles. Only the impressionists truly reconciled with the changes, but distrust in the industrial city was more than prevalent in the nineteenth century, stimulating reactionary utopias.

In other disciplines, utopian movements also proliferated. Robert Owen (1771–1858), for example, concerned about the consequences of these changes, proposed an ideal factory in England. This model, intended for replication, featured good facilities, reasonable hours and conditions, and services like childcare to ease the lives of industrial workers. From there, his ambition grew, leading him to propose a necessary integration of agriculture—essentially, a pact between the rural and the urban, tradition and the new, after all.

Industrialization obviously brings social consequences of tremendous impact, but the material qualities of objects also seem to suffer. Mass production lowers costs, yet the average quality of products initially worsens. For this reason, in the second half of the nineteenth century, a movement emerged championing the value of what we now know as *applied arts*. Thus, one could speak of "major arts" and "minor arts"—or art and design, if you will—which must, indeed, establish strong ties for the benefit of both sides (Benevolo, 1963).

These are, then, the foundations of various movements, more or less reactionary against industrialization and in favor of tradition. Of course, John Ruskin stands out, advocating for the importance of artistic culture and serving as a reference for William Morris and the Arts and Crafts movement. This movement championed manual labor and proposed the exclusion of machines from the production of everyday objects.

From Arts and Crafts to Bauhaus: the search for balance between industry, art, and society in design

Industrialization continued its course and coincided with a period of peace that began after the Franco-Prussian War in 1871 and extended until the start of the First World War in 1914. This *Belle Époque* thus brought prosperity and social advancements in parallel with technical progress. New aesthetic languages were needed to respond to the new society across all artistic disciplines, leading to the emergence of *Art Nouveau* in architecture and decorative arts. Based in Belgium, Victor Horta championed this need for new forms in architecture and interiors, referencing nature with sinuous silhouettes and a distinct decorative character. This way, *Art Nouveau* was heavily influenced by the Arts and Crafts movement.

In reality, the aesthetic value and the ideas behind the Arts and Crafts movement are as undeniable as the fact that the path forward isn't to exclude technical advancements in the pursuit of new aesthetic principles. In fact, Morris himself eventually qualified his rejection, stating: "I do not say that we should do away with all machines [...], for soon, we shall be the masters of our machines, and not their slaves" (*On Art and Socialism*, 1888). Something similar lies behind the principles of Henry Van der Velde (another Belgian figure of *Art Nouveau* after Morris), who believed that the proposals of Arts and Crafts and its later followers were too elitist. He felt that the renewal of art would emerge only when it accepted new technologies, machines, and mass production.

However, Van de Velde's ideas are somewhat contradictory to his designs. His advocacy for machines and mass production contrasts with his embrace of individualism in objects. In a way, he trusted that twentieth century objects would incorporate new technologies in their production, but their conception—and perhaps even their marketing—would still be governed by older rules. In parallel, other ideals emerged, more openly embracing industry and the changes it brought to society. Hermann Muthesius, a Prussian diplomat stationed in London in 1896, experienced firsthand the British and Belgian approaches. Therefore, he returned to Germany convinced of the need for new forms—forms that would integrate the wisdom of crafts but definitively account for new techniques. Muthesius then founded the *Deutsche Werkbund* in 1907, an association where artisans were meant to trust industry and its new production systems.

Industry was the solution; it had grown enormously over the past 50 years and brought prosperity during this era of peace. What is more, the new machines were ready to mass-produce good and beautiful objects. Standardization was the aesthetic answer to individualism; this was Hermann

Muthesius's stance against Van der Velde, clearly demonstrated in a significant clash between the two during the last *Werkbund* conference in 1914.

Industrial growth was exponential during those years. Across Europe, and especially in Germany, growth seemed to demand more growth in a vicious cycle that, in a way, explains the outbreak of the World War in that very year, 1914. Of course, the political reasons for that conflict and its devastating consequences are far more complex, but at the end of the conflict in 1918, a certain skepticism toward technology returned. Naturally, reverting to a craft-based world was illogical. However, society, production, and design demanded a new balance between innovation and tradition, between technology and craftsmanship. It was this new need that explains the birth (in 1919) of the Bauhaus, the famous school whose principles and work were essentially about achieving that agreement between the old and the necessarily new.

A strategic opportunity

The Bauhaus spirit in a strategic moment

It seems natural that periods of peace and prosperity bring periods of optimism: welfare makes us more confident in our lifestyle, as opposed to fragmented confidence brought by wars. Thus, and once again without wishing to underestimate deeper political problems, it's logical that the rise of Nazism and its thirst for conflict led to the closure of the Bauhaus, which only lasted until 1933.

However, despite its short history, the Bauhaus remains the model for any design and architecture school, possibly due to its conviction that craftsmanship and industry, beauty and utility, and quality and mass production are not opposing concepts but quite the opposite.

Today, this confidence is more necessary than ever. We're living through a moment of crisis, of change brought about by the emergence of these new technologies guiding the Fourth Industrial Revolution, but also of social change, with a model (especially in the West) being called into question. The spirit of the Bauhaus is necessary and relevant; this is why the European Commission has championed it since its centenary in 2019, promoting what it has termed the "New Bauhaus"—a project for architecture and design in general to become part of the solution to the old continent's major challenges.

We are, therefore, in a strategic moment, a moment of opportunity where everything is going to be redefined. Technological changes will definitely help redefine social and even geopolitical relationships in the coming years. It is then time to use these changes to our advantage, with the confidence that the positive outcomes will far outweigh the negative consequences.

The UPM as a strategic location

We're living in a pivotal moment, but like all historical events, it needs a place to materialize these changes. From an academic perspective, the Universidad Politécnica de Madrid (UPM) seems like the ideal place to formalize the pact between tradition and innovation we are advocating for.

Starting with its history: the UPM is a "young" university integrated by Spain's "old" technical schools. Indeed, as a university, the UPM was "only" formalized in 1971, meaning it is not even 55 years old. However, this foundation integrated the major Higher Technical Schools of engineering and architecture, most of which were established during the reign of Carlos III in the eighteenth century. In essence, it is a university less than a century old, made up of schools over three hundred years old, consequently, tradition and innovation are in its DNA.

Considering its history, the Universidad Politécnica de Madrid (UPM) seems to be the ideal place to combine innovation and tradition. Regarding its global standing, its leadership as a Spanish university also helps build bridges in a complex geopolitical context. It's no coincidence that Spanish is the second most spoken native language on the planet, with 500 million speakers distributed worldwide, not only in Spain or Latin America. In fact, 40 million Americans are native Spanish speakers, and many Africans are as well (for example, around 75 % of Equatorial Guinea's population).

Furthermore, when it comes to technology, the UPM is undoubtedly a global leader. In this field, the UPM stands out as the best Spanish-speaking university in the world according to all prestigious international rankings. According to the QS 2025 ranking, it holds the 86th position globally in Engineering and Technology, excelling in categories such as Mechanical, Aeronautical, and Manufacturing Engineering (95th), Agricultural and

Forestry Engineering (79th), Civil and Structural Engineering (among the top 51–100), Mining and Mineral Engineering (among the top 51–100), and Data Science and Artificial Intelligence.

But beyond the convergence of tradition and innovation lies the essential pact between the technical and the humanistic which allows us to face the future with confidence. To this respect we must also highlight the strategic position of the UPM. In fact, the UPM excels in that same QS ranking in Architecture (at position 36 worldwide), in the Art and Design category (between 151 and 200), and even in History of Art (appearing among positions 21 to 50 globally).

Ultimately, the Universidad Politécnica de Madrid seems destined to play a significant role in the context defined in this text in order to become the meeting point where technology, conscious and respectful of the past, becomes a driving force for a better future. In particular, within the Universidad Politécnica de Madrid, its Centro Superior de Diseño de Moda (CSDMM) can be a key place in this narrative. On the one hand, as we will see in the next point, textiles are experiencing a pivotal moment within this period of change at all levels. On the other hand, fashion within the Universidad Politécnica, in contact with the most innovative technologies, represents an opportunity for the much-demanded union in this text.

The textile sector: a strategic industry

The textile sector is crucial for industrial development. If we look back to the First Industrial Revolution again, we'll see how manual production, driven by largely unskilled labor, transformed into a mechanized system with the advent of the steam engine. That workforce, as well as its machinery, became specialized. Consequently, many places worldwide that once had simple artisanal weaving operations are now leaders in more sophisticated industries like automotive.

Today, talking about textiles means talking about fashion and retail. Manufacturing, but especially distribution, is massive and global. Leadership in the sector isn't so much about quality or design, but rather the combination of these with a clear-sighted understanding of consumer demands and an effective supply chain. Once again, the pact between innovation and tradition is necessary if we want to move into the future with confidence.

If we look at success stories, the last 50 years have been marked (in the retail sector, but probably across the entire industry) by the rise of Zara and the Inditex group. Their manufacturing and distribution model has completely changed our habits, starting with how we dress. Clothes are definitely a consumer product, and their communication capacity now surpasses their practical dimension more than ever (with access to quality clothing at affordable prices being assured). Inditex's success is largely based on the incorporation of technology into its production, but also into its distribution (with sales points in the best locations worldwide) and stock management (with items always available where needed).

Inditex is an example, and its future success continues to depend on the accurate incorporation of technology. Global distribution is changing, the internet is becoming a common purchasing channel across all sectors as sending and collecting items from every home involves significant logistical challenges. The amount of data is multiplying exponentially, and its effective management can distinguish success from failure.

Artificial intelligence, the "Internet of Things," and advanced production processes that utilize advanced robotics and 3D manufacturing will be key for any industry, but especially for the textile sector, hence its strategic role as a case study.

Tech and Crafts vs Crafts and Tech: two project approaches

CSDMM: a "Tech and Crafts" project since its founding

We're living in a moment of unprecedented opportunities driven by the Fourth Industrial Revolution. In this general context, technological universities have a strategic chance to lead the changes. This is especially true for the Universidad Politécnica de Madrid (UPM), where its leadership in engineering is complemented by a humanistic sensibility that allows it to envision the future by integrating the best of the past. The textile industry, in particular, is undoubtedly one of the most active sectors in adopting these new technologies. Over the last half-century, its companies have thrived by embracing changes in production and consumption models. Today, there's no reason for them not to continue doing so.

The Centro Superior de Diseño de Moda de Madrid (CSDMM), a center within the aforementioned Universidad Politécnica, has therefore a dual opportunity: surrounded by cutting-edge technology, its field of study aligns with this strategic sector within the broader context. Furthermore, the CSDMM has effectively been a "Tech and Crafts" project since its inception. Founded in 1986, its genesis stemmed from several forces that, today more than ever, represent significant opportunities.

On the one hand, there is indeed the university itself, the UPM, which recognized the need to incorporate fashion into university degrees, a commitment that remains at the highest level today (it's no coincidence that it's the only university in Spain offering a full Bachelor's, Master's, and Doctorate program centered on fashion).

On the other hand, from its beginnings, the CSDMM understood the importance of "crafts" for their cultural significance. This understanding has been represented, since the center's early days, by the presence of Enrique Loewe on its board. Enrique Loewe, the fourth generation of the creators of the famous luxury brand, has held the belief since taking over leadership of the company (now part of the LVMH group) that design must have soul, and that this soul can only be achieved by incorporating artisanal work that reflects an entire culture of doing things. Enrique Loewe, current Honorary President of the Loewe Foundation, remains on the CSDMM's Board of Trustees, ensuring that respect for traditional design craftsmanship is embedded in the center's DNA and its way of working.

However, craftsmanship is only an opportunity if it is used to look to the future, allowing for the incorporation of cutting-edge technologies and industry into new designs. At its founding, the CSDMM was driven by INDUYCO, a Spanish garment manufacturing company that was part of the El Corte Inglés group, responsible for producing clothing for El Corte Inglés' own brands like Amitié, Tintoretto, Síntesis, etc. INDUYCO, as an industry, needed better and more technologically trained professionals to improve its systems. This relationship with the industry remains strong today. TENDAM Group (with brands like Cortefiel, Pedro del Hierro, Springfield, Women'secret, and Hoss Intropia), employing over 10,000 people worldwide, trusts the CSDMM to maintain a "classroom," conceived as a space for joint collaboration and research to improve future sustainability solutions.

In short, the CSDMM, within the UPM, seems to be the right place to lead this reflection on how to fit the past and the future, leading to technical advances into designs consistent with our identity (which is very much inherited from the past). Any agreement between two parties, "Tech and Crafts" in this case, can be viewed from either side. Of course, each party must move toward the other. Looking back at the historical summary, Van der Velde's disproportionate confidence in the individualization of designs was as extreme as Muthesius's faith in mass production and standardization at the time of their confrontation in 1914. Today, just as then, it seems necessary to listen to both sides: those who, as technology experts, seek humanistic solutions in its application (TECH and Crafts), but also those with a significant background of "know-how" who don't want to get stuck in nostalgia and wish to incorporate the new (CRAFTS and Tech).

Tech and Crafts: current state and future fashion

This section first aims to show how technologies are not parallel tools, incorporated after problems are defined and solutions proposed, but rather must be integrated in symbiosis with the system. Actually, the section focuses on new technologies in the production and conceptualization of fashion design. This is the idea put forth by Professor Mercedes Rodriguez in this text: "Artificial intelligence won't just change the way we produce, but designers are already incorporating it into the initial phases of creation."

Obviously, this incorporation will revolutionize everything and raise new issues. In this case, using Artificial Intelligence will present new challenges and doubts, especially regarding the concepts of authorship. Thus, intellectual property rights will be compromised in this new context (Yilmaztekin, 2023). Regarding production, as Rosa Deltoro points out in a second text in this section, industrial efficiency can lead to more excesses. Therefore, sustainability is undoubtedly one of the sector's challenges for the coming years. However, in this regard, it is worth noting that pollution is greater in the usage phase than in the production phase (Fletcher & Grose, 2012). This means we primarily need changes in models, rethinking from the outset, but also in how we use clothes and how they degrade. Thus, Professors Lorenzi and Grabowska continue with a chapter that offers material alternatives, considering bioelectronic materials that almost literally disappear after use, reinforcing the idea that designers today have the opportunity to work from the beginning with a planet-respectful orientation (Firstenberg, 2019).

New technologies should lead to new forms. Similarly, changing our approach to design also requires new tools. In the following text, Professor Calvo develops this idea, offering experimental pattern-making software that generates almost random shapes which are then adapted. This program would thus boost creativity, avoiding established practices and processes and, therefore, facilitating new ways of thinking and doing.

Experimentation on using new tools in iterative cycles as well as blending the physical and virtual in reverse-engineering systems that allow learning from existing designs presents an opportunity for designers (Ding & Liang, 2024). However, it is crucial to remember that incorporating new technologies might save time in the long run, but in the short term, it demands a training effort across the entire system and likely changes to established workflows (Papahristou, 2016).

Tech and Crafts is not only about how technology and design are two sides of the same coin but also about how new technologies offer new opportunities to preserve the patrimony. In any case, there's no doubt that integrating technologies for the preservation of textile heritage is not just timely, but necessary. Firstly, digitization can prevent excessive handling of old designs and ensure their proper maintenance (as discussed in the chapter by Professors Mohajer va Pesaran and Ponzoni). Furthermore, this digitization allows for a better study of traditional garments (text by Professor Portelli). Lastly, virtual reality can offer an alternative presentation method for exhibitions (Professors Koutsou, Stoikou, and Zoumaki).

The challenge with "dematerializing"—taking designs into a virtual reality—is the loss of context, and it demands more than ever intelligent technological integration if we are not to lose cultural specificities (Ribeiro et al., 2024). However, the benefits are clear, and numerous major museums and institutions are committing to digitization. Professors Bossenz, Behm, and Schnitt bring us the case of the Historisches Museum Hannover, and Professor Vásquez that of the Museo del Traje in Madrid (Ethnological Heritage Research Center of the Spanish Ministry of Culture, Government of Spain), the Azzedine Alaïa Foundation, and the Balenciaga Archive.

The Fourth Industrial Revolution isn't just virtual. 3D manufacturing is poised to play an important role, allowing for individualization without losing the benefits of mass production. This idea of "materializing" and "dematerializing" is at the core of the final text in this section. Professor Vandi proposes delving deeper into these back-and-forth approaches: 3D scanning and creating both digital twins of pieces, while also printing 3D manipulable replicas. It is in these iterative processes, in these combinations, where the real value likely lies—not just for heritage conservation, but generally for all the challenges facing the textile and fashion sector in these times of change.

Crafts and Tech: an historical overview of fashion techniques and production

Faced with the overwhelming emergence of new technologies, we might think we are witnessing an unprecedented event. However, from a historical perspective, this incorporation of technical advancements is much more common and natural than it seems, and, in this section, a first group of authors focus on how the past should be a reference for today.

Along these lines, Professor González Zymla's text reviews how innovations in spinning and weaving became more sophisticated as the physical need for clothing became nuanced, reinforcing the symbolic aspect of attire in accordance with Flügel's ideas (1964).

Moreover, the following chapters adopt this historical perspective, bridging the gap to the "here and now," from Classical Rome (in Professor Prieto's text) to twentieth century Spanish fashion (in Professor Salcedo's), passing through the eighteenth century and the formation and loss of what we could call Spanish haute couture (texts by Professors Bueno, Fernández, and Díaz respectively), and introducing historical techniques and historical approaches to costume design (Professor Montagna and professor Cucinotta respectively).

In fact, understanding the past is a way of looking toward the future, and the study of artisanal tradition seeks its incorporation into contemporary design practices. This is the approach adopted by the most recent research presented here.

First, there are more theoretical approaches that focus on methodology, documentation, and the transmission and teaching of fashion design as a design discipline. Texts by Professors Fortuna, Arcas, and Cagigas explore these issues in depth from diverse perspectives, supporting the idea that all creativity is grounded in a method (Munari, 1981). These perspectives are followed by more concrete approaches that propose specific solutions, clearly rooted in artisanal practices.

If anything defines haute couture from a technical standpoint, it is its commitment to craftsmanship (Vaquero Argüelles, 2007), which might lead us to believe it is stuck in the past. However, throughout this text, the persistent idea is that craftsmanship ensures continuous development, without major leaps—a linear progression, if you will. This type of development guarantees the immaterial transmission of values from each generation to the next (Amaya-Tellez, 2015). Looking at craftsmanship means looking at heritage since it incorporates the identity of techniques and the emotional memory of processes, which is why it's so appealing to today's brands. According to Rossellini (2024), Maria Grazia Chiuri, as Creative Director of Dior, leverages this very aspect by using local craftsmanship to approach (and incorporate) different cultures into her cruise collections. This is the starting point for Professor Serrano, and ultimately for the subsequent texts by Barrero, and Tinajero, who support this idea, from the study of trends to the enhancement of corporate image by major luxury brands through their store architecture.

In reality, integrating technological improvements through practice—the facto of learning and improving through repetition and adaptation—is pure innovation methodology. Actually, innovation was there, alongside traditional craftsmanship!

Conclusion and discussion

Industry 4.0 inherently brings change. However, it is widely recognized that technical advancements always lead to shifts in production and society. Looking back, the relevance of this topic and the need for a pact between tradition and innovation—a concept we can call "Tech and Crafts"—is undeniable. As we look to the future, the present moment seems especially vibrant, therefore, technological universities with a strong humanistic foundation could very well lead these transformations.

From a technological standpoint, the importance of artificial intelligence, digitization, and 3D scanning and manufacturing is paramount. From a historical viewpoint, the significance lies in heritage, particularly textile heritage, which finds an undeniable ally in technical advancements. Finally, from a design perspective, it is supported as an inherently innovative discipline that both naturally and unequivocally integrates new developments with tradition.

This text serves primarily as an introduction to other works, acting as a foundational thread to help build a common theoretical framework. As such, it has two limitations. On the one hand, it cannot delve into the depth of the issues as thoroughly as the original texts (which are presented later in the book). On the other hand, due to its introductory nature, parts of it may have an essayistic tone, differing from the purely scientific approach of many of the preceding research papers in this book. Consequently, we strongly encourage readers to read and study those works for a more concrete understanding.

References

Amaya-Tellez, H. (2015). Diseño y artesanía, un matrimonio con condiciones [Design and craftsmanship, a marriage with conditions]. *Actas de Diseño, 18*, 186–9.

Benevolo, L., Galfetti, M., & Puigvehí, A. P. (1963). *Historia de la arquitectura moderna* [History of Modern Architecture] (Vol. 2). Taurus.

Cazzaniga, M., Jaumotte, F., Li, L., Melina, G., Panton, A. J., Pizzinelli, C., Rockall, E. J., & Mendes Tavares, M. (2024). *Gen-AI: Artificial Intelligence and the Future of Work.* International Monetary Fund. https://www.imf.org/en/Publications/Staff-Discussion-Notes/Issues/2024/01/14/Gen-AI-Artificial-Intelligence-and-the-Future-of-Work-542379?cid=bl-com-SDNEA2024001.

Chablé-Vega, M. A., García-Hernández, E., Martínez-Heredia, J. E., Villalpando-Aguilar, J. L., Arreola-Enríquez, J., López-Rosas, I., & Alatorre-Cobos, F. (2024). The return of natural dyes: the case of logwood tree (Haematoxylum campechianum L.). Biotechnic & Histochemistry, 99(5), 269–277.

Ding, Q-K., & Liang, H-E. (2024). Digital restoration and reconstruction of heritage clothing: a review. *Heritage Science, 12.*

Firstenberg, A. (2019). *The Invisible Rainbow: A History of Electricity and Life.* AGB Press.

Fletcher, K., & Grose, L. (2012). *Sustainable Fashion and Textiles: Design Journeys.* Blume.

Flügel, J. C. (1964). *Psicología del vestido* [The Psychology of Clothes]. Paidós.

Levitt, A., Hegh, D., Phillips, P., Uzun, S., Anayee, M., Razal, J. M., Gogotsi, Y., & Dion, G. (2020). 3D knitted energy storage textiles using MXene-coated yarns. Materials Today, 34, 17–29.

Manaia, J. P., Cerejo, F., & Duarte, J. (2023). Revolutionising textile manufacturing: a comprehensive review on 3D and 4D printing technologies. Fashion and Textiles, 10(1), 20.

Munari, B. (1981). *¿Cómo nacen los objetos?* [How are objects born?]. Gustavo Gili.

Papahristou, E. (2016). *The effective integration of 3D virtual prototype in the product development process of the textile/clothing industry* [Doctoral dissertation, Technical University of Crete].

Papahristou, E., & Bilalis, N. (2017). 3D virtual prototyping traces new avenues for fashion design and product development: A qualitative study. Journal of Textile Science & Engineering, 7(2), 1–6.

Rahaman, M. T., & Khan, M. S. H. (2025). Green merchandising of textiles and apparel in a circular economy: recent trends, framework, challenges and future prospects towards sustainability. Journal of Open Innovation: Technology, Market, and Complexity, 11(1), 100457.

Ribeiro, M., Santos, J., Lobo, J., Araújo, S., Magalhães, L., & Adão, T. (2024). VR, AR, gamification, and AI towards the next generation of systems supporting cultural heritage: Addressing challenges of a museum context. *In Proceedings of the 29th International ACM Conference on 3D Web Technology (Web3D '24)*. ACM.

Rosellini, F. (2024). Proceso de diseño y artesanía [Design process and craftsmanship]. *Centro de Estudios en Diseño y Comunicación, 237*, 49–58.

Tyler, D. J. (2005). Textile digital printing technologies. Textile Progress, 37(4), 1–65.

Vaquero Argüelles, I. (2007). El reinado de la Alta Costura: la moda de la primera mitad del siglo XX [The reign of haute couture: fashion in the first half of the twentieth century]. *Indumenta 00, 155*. https://www.cultura.gob.es/mtraje-ndumenta/dam/jcr:0cd96564-482f-4d6c-9db8-8fd441f869b4/indumenta00-13-iva.pdf

Yılmaztekin, H. K. (2023). *Artificial intelligence, design law and fashion*. Routledge.

Zola, É. (1883/2012). *Au bonheur des dames* [The ladies' Paradise]. Le livre de poche.

PART 2

Tech and Crafts: Current State and Future of Fashion

New technologies in the production and conceptualization of fashion design

CHAPTER 2

From Savoir-Faire to Savoir-Tech

Generative AI and the new craft of fashion design

*Mercedes Rodriguez Sanchez**

ABSTRACT
This chapter analyzes the impact of generative artificial intelligence on the fashion industry, with particular focus on its application in product design and development. First, a context is provided for the role of generative AI within the digital transformation of the sector, then a review is undertaken of pioneering cases, designer/technology collaborations and new business strategies that show how the technology is being integrated into creative processes. The legal, ethical, and environmental challenges posed by generative AI, and its implications for authorship, intellectual property, and employment are discussed. Finally, the need to redefine the competencies of the contemporary designer is discussed in a discourse that underlines the importance of critical and cross-disciplinary training that combines creativity and technological literacy. *Savoir-tech* is proposed as the articulating axis of this new professional culture and the foundation for higher education in fashion design that critically and complementarily integrates human and digital aspects.

Keywords: artificial intelligence, generative AI, garment design, fashion industry, education, ethical use

Introduction

When news broke that in April 2023 the first AI Fashion Week would be held in New York (Schulz, 2023), most social media comments reflected concerns that artificial intelligence could eliminate human creativity and hijack designers' ideas. Similarly, Levi's announcement in March 2023 that it would test AI-generated fashion models raised concerns about the possibility of these replacing humans (Levi Strauss & Co, 2023). Since bursting onto the scene, artificial intelligence has established itself as a central issue in the cultural debate. A recent example is the case of H&M, which created strong controversy when it announced plans to use digital twins of real models in its advertising campaigns (Bain, 2025). The decision, presented as a way to reduce costs and streamline creative processes, has sparked criticism both

* Universidad Politécnica de Madrid.
(ORCID: https://orcid.org/0000-0002-9947-3865)

inside and outside the sector; it was seen as questioning the ethical limits of digital cloning, the representation of the human body and the future of work not only of models, but also of photographers, stylists, makeup artists and other professionals who have been—and continue to be—fundamental pillars in the aesthetic and symbolic construction of fashion brands.

Artificial intelligence (AI) involves the ability of a machine to exhibit the same capabilities as humans, such as reasoning, learning, adaptation, pattern recognition, creativity, planning, and natural language understanding. It has been said that AI is the attempt to understand and imitate human intelligence, so that computers can do the same kinds of things that the human mind can do (Boden, 2017; Bhargava & Sharma, 2022).

The history of AI dates back to the mid-twentieth century, when McCulloch and Pitts developed a first artificial neuron model (McCulloch & Pitts, 1943). Shortly after, Alan Turing suggested that machines could think, proposing his famous test as an evaluation criterion (Turing, 1950). In 1956, John McCarthy coined the term "the science and engineering of making intelligent machines" (McCarthy, 2007, p. 2) and the first attempts to develop programs capable of imitating human reasoning began (Arrestegui, 2012; Bonami et al., 2020).

In later years, AI development has oscillated between moments of great optimism and phases of stagnation, which Pamela McCorduck described as an "identity crisis" (McCorduck, 2004, p. 419), and which are commonly referred to as *AI winters* (AI Winter, n.d.). These stagnation periods, in the 70s and between 1987 and the mid-90s, while not entirely barren, were characterized by a slowdown in research due to unfulfilled expectations. However, over the last decade, the rise of deep learning and neural networks has driven advances such as generative models and computer vision systems.

A turning point was the launch of ChatGPT in November 2022, which reached one million users in five days and exceeded one hundred million in two months (Milmo, 2023). 2023 saw a rapid expansion of generative artificial intelligence with companies in various sectors, such as Microsoft, Amazon, Zoom and Moderna, incorporating it into their processes. Generative AI has the potential to substantially change our lives, interactions and all of human existence, to the point that it could drive a 7 % increase in global GDP, equivalent to almost seven trillion dollars (Tse, 2023).

Generative AI has been defined as a set of techniques capable of generating new and meaningful content from training data (Feuerriegel et al., 2023).

Tools such as DALL· E, Stable Diffusion and Midjourney generate images from textual descriptions; others, for example, ChatGPT, combine text generation with multimodal functions, such as image creation, voice interpretation and contextual interaction. Platforms such as Runway permit one to create and edit videos from text, images and clips. Written instructions, known as prompts, guide the model in creating content. The process is iterative: the user analyzes the model's results, adjusts the instructions and reruns the model to refine the content. This testing, adjusting and improving process, based on the creative and communicative objectives of the project, is essential for personalizing results.

Generative AI applications in the fashion industry

Generative AI, an emerging and evolving technology, faces challenges and limitations. Nonetheless, it is predicted to have a significant impact on the fashion industry, given its potential to increase business productivity and improve the customer experience. McKinsey estimated that, in the years between 2024–2028, it could generate between 150,000 million and 275,000 million dollars in additional operating profits in the clothing and luxury sectors (Harreis et al., 2023). Given that AI can be applied at all stages of the value chain, companies that integrate the technology could gain competitive advantages by accelerating product innovation, optimizing marketing efforts and delivering more personalized experiences. Table 1 lists the main application areas and the most important technology providers:

Table 1. Applications of generative AI across the fashion value chain

Stage	Application	Provider / tool
Product development	- Trend forecasting - Design briefs - Moodboards and visual inspiration - 3D design + tech packs - Automated patternmaking - Sustainable material simulation - Design optimization for waste reduction	Adobe Firefly, Cala, DALL·E, Google AI, Midjourney, Runway, Stable Diffusion

(Continued)

Table 1. *(Continued)*

Stage	Application	Provider / tool
Supply chain and logistics	- Supplier research - Real-time demand forecasting - Route optimization - Inventory management - Return personalization	C3.ai, Google AI, Project44, Fourkites, Blue Yonder
Marketing and communication	- Campaign segmentation and strategy - Behavioral analysis - Automated content creation - Adaptive social media - Hyper-personalized offers and content - Generative video avatars	Copy.ai, Jasper, Writesonic, Runway, Persado, Dynamic Yield, Yotpo, HeyGen
Retail and customer experience	- E-commerce product descriptions - Advanced virtual assistants - Size recommendation - Real-time virtual try-on - Personalized product suggestions - Hyperrealistic fitting	Gladly, Google AI, Shopify, Vue.ai, Emarsys, Luma AI, Revery AI
In-store operations	- Accelerated 3D store design - Optimized layout and visual merchandising - Real-time store analytics - Facial recognition for VIP clients	RetailNext, StoreForce, Trax, InContext Solutions
Internal operations and support	- Personalized training materials - Administrative task automation - Talent acquisition - Performance analysis	Beamery, Genie AI, SAP, Workday, HireVue

Note: Adapted and updated by the author from McKinsey & Business of Fashion, The State of Fashion 2024, p. 66.

Within this wide range of applications of artificial intelligence in the fashion industry, this chapter focuses on the impact of generative AI on the most creative phases of the design process, particularly product development. The technology not only introduces new tools and workflows but can also profoundly transform the professional activities of the fashion designer.

Generative AI in fashion: from experimentation to industry adoption

Although the media and commercial explosion of generative AI occurred in 2023, the fashion industry had been exploring its possibilities for several years. From experimental initiatives to structured collaborations, players in the sector have been testing the technology in the most creative processes of fashion design.

In 2017, Amazon announced that it was developing AI technologies to detect, interpret, and even start fashion trends, with the aim of automating processes such as product recommendation and garment design. This research included style evaluation, algorithms developed from a few tags and generative adversarial networks (GANs) capable of creating new pieces from scratch (Knight, 2017). A year later, students from the Fashion Institute of Technology collaborated with IBM to analyze runway images and Tommy Hilfiger sewing patterns, creating new design proposals (Fashion Institute of Technology, 2018). In 2019, Massachusetts Institute of Technology students launched the AI-powered Coven.ai brand (Peng, 2019), and startup Cross & Freckle used AI not only to design t-shirts, but also to create its name, logo and website (Pardes, 2019). Although some of these initiatives did not prosper due to the entities' lack of experience in fashion, other companies, such as Myntra and Levi Strauss & Co., managed to successfully incorporate AI into their creative processes (Cazares, 2021).

Unlike conventional AI, generative AI has a direct impact on the sector's creative core. It allows designers to quickly turn sketches and moodboards into detailed representations, customize products at scale, and expand conceptual exploration from brand files, trend data and/or aesthetic references. Approaches and strategies that illustrate how generative AI has been introduced into fashion design and development are set out below.

Pioneering AI-based creative experimentation projects

Project Muze, Zalando and Google: Fashion inspired by You, designed by Code

Launched in 2016, Project Muze (see Figure 1) was an experiment developed by Zalando and Google to "explore the creative use of machine learning in the field of fashion" (Google, 2017). The neural network was trained using style data from more than 600 experts, Google's Fashion Trends Report and Zalando historical sales. To create their own customized model, respondents had to answer a questionnaire on, among other variables, age, gender, style, color, mood and musical preferences. Based on the responses, Zalando then created 3D designs which they put up for sale on the web. The project resulted in the creation of more than 40,000 designs in the first month and had a total reach of 19 million people and 3.4 million social media-based organic interactions (#projectmuze).

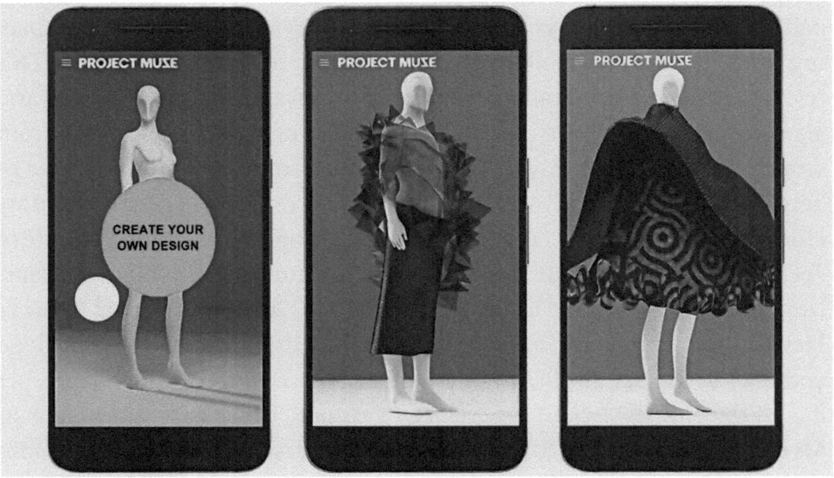

Figure 1. Project Muze.
Google and Zalando.

Finesse: Zara meets Netflix

The Californian startup Finesse presents itself on social networks as "the first AI-led fashion house where you decide what we produce. No overproduction. No waste" (Finesse, n.d.). Replacing designers and buyers with algorithms, it seeks to eliminate overproduction and resolve the inefficiencies of the traditional fashion system. Its founder, Ramin Ahmari, describes Finesse as a combination of Zara and Netflix, merging fast-fashion speed, customer focus and efficient operations driven by the platform economy (Roberts-Islam, 2021). Its goal is to transform the conventional paradigms of fashion design and production, completely redefining the value offered to its customers. Its mission is clear: to create designs that meet the desires of Gen Z, at the right time and in the right quantities.

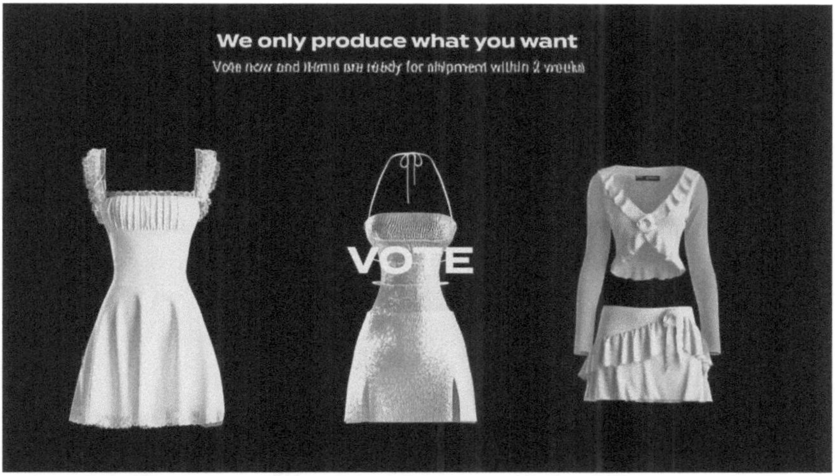

Figure 2. Finesse's voting system for selecting AI-generated designs.
Finesse.

Before the production process, to identify emerging trends, Finesse applies a time series analysis, natural language processing applied to social networks, computer vision and proprietary machine learning algorithms. Based on the information this process provides, the AI system generates three design proposals for consumers to vote on (see Figure 2). Only the design with the most votes goes into production. A distinctive feature of this process is that a single, physical sample is manufactured at a partner plant in China for final validation, thus avoiding the usual intercontinental exchange of prototypes. Using this methodology and advanced 3D modeling software, the company is able to significantly shorten time to market, reduce costs and minimize the waste associated with sample creation. The entire cycle takes less than 25 days, and results in the production of a range of sizes from XS to 3XL.

Collaborations between designers and generative models

Robbie Barrat and Acne Studios

"I'm doing something with fashion and AI but I don't know what yet" (Barrat, 2018), wrote artist and programmer Robbie Barrat on his Twitter account during the summer of 2018. This statement marked the beginning of an experiment in which Barrat began to explore the creative possibilities of AI applied to fashion design, combining generative techniques with the visual archives of great houses such as Balenciaga. Although the proposed creations did not materialize into actual garments, the project attracted industry attention and led to a collaboration between Barrat and the Swedish firm Acne Studios.

Generative AI debuted on the runway during Paris Fashion Week Autumn-Fall/Winter 2020, with this collaboration by Barrat and Acne Studios (see Figure 3). The artist first fed an AI system with thousands of the brand's archive images. Then, he introduced intentional errors to generate unusual visual proposals to serve as a starting point for the design team. This approach

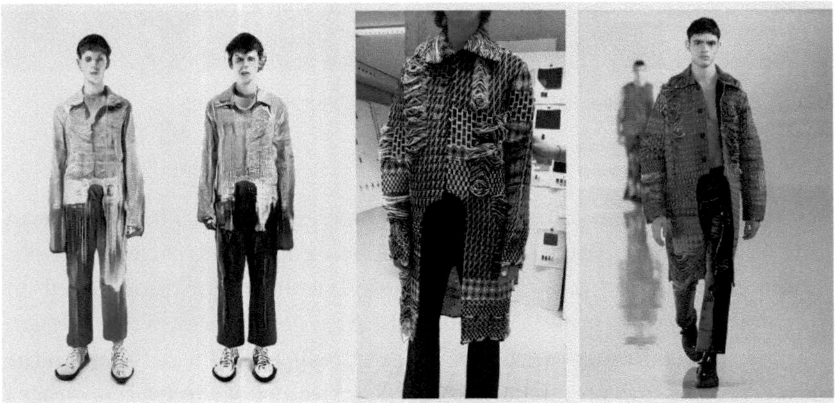

Figure 3. Images generated by Robbie Barrat using AI (left) prototype inspired by these images (center) and final coat from Acne Studio's Fall/Winter 2020 menswear collection (right).

Robbie Barrat @videodrome.

revealed one of the most powerful paradoxes of generative-based AI fashion: when the technology fails to understand the functional meaning of its output, it can provide unexpected results that expand creative possibilities. While such "hallucinations" might be problematic in other sectors, in design they can be a valuable resource. As Barrat acknowledged, many of the images created were not usable garments, thus the real challenge was to turn those abstract sketches into marketable pieces.

The collection was met with mixed reviews. Vogue described it as a "math-crunched amalgam of all previous Acne Studio collections" (Leitch, 2020). However, creative director Jonny Johansson argued that AI was a valuable liberating tool in the creative process (Brain, 2020), and that designers can refine it to balance functionality and innovation without losing the aesthetic richness of the unexpected.

Collina Strada and Midjourney

In 2023, designer Hillary Taymour announced that she had used Midjourney for Collina Strada's Spring/Summer 2024 collection (Bain, 2023). The AI system was fed with archive images of the brand, and the results were refined using textual prompts. This approach addressed creatives' concerns about intellectual property rights and maintained the brand's distinctive style. Taymour highlighted the challenges of transforming generative proposals into physical garments. The shapes and textures generated by the AI were sometimes difficult to reproduce, to the extent that it took four weeks to figure out how to construct the sleeve of one dress. Although the results preserved the visual identity of the brand, Taymour explained that transforming generative images into real garments was a significant technical challenge. She insisted that AI does not replace creativity but rather complements it.

Norma Kamali and Maison Meta

This ability of AI to decode a brand's visual DNA is being explored by New York designer Norma Kamali, who is collaborating with the Maison Meta agency on a pioneering project aimed at preserving its creative legacy. Together they developed a customized AI model—an AI Design CoPilot—trained with more than 40 years of designs from the agency's copyrighted archive (Maison Meta, 2023). This system, developed together with the company's creative team, aims to test whether technology is capable of producing designs faithful to the brand's stylistic identity. Beyond its experimental dimension, the project points to a possible use for AI in resolving a key challenge for many fashion houses: the change of creative director. Guiding the founding designer's transition toward an artistic direction consistent with the brand's identity is one of the most complex challenges facing the industry.

New scenarios for fashion: catwalks and brands that are committed to generative AI

AI Fashion Week and Revolve

Fashion weeks are undergoing a notable transformation, ranging from traditional in-person fashion shows—which continue to be held in major cities—to new forms of digital presentation. During the pandemic, the virtual format consolidated itself as a temporary alternative, later giving way to launches set in video games, presentations in the metaverse and, more recently, collections in which the designers themselves openly acknowledged having used generative AI tools. A paradigmatic example of this evolution is Artificial Intelligence Fashion Week (AIFW), organized by Maison Meta in New York in spring 2023, where 133 AI-designed virtual collections were presented. The three winning proposals were transformed into physical garments by the Revolve brand in Los Angeles, and marketed through its online platform, with prices ranging from $228 to $1,598 (see Figure 4). To date, two editions of AIFW have been held, in April and November 2023.

Adoption by brands and recent developments

2023 was the year in which it was confirmed that the fashion industry was using generative AI, both commercial brands and designer-led projects. G-Star Raw, for example, developed a collection of 12 denim designs using the AI tool Midjourney. From these, the brand selected a denim cape with a sculptural silhouette and futuristic details for production in its Amsterdam-based workshop. The production process was particularly challenging, as the tailors worked from a single AI-generated image, with no patterns, and had to interpret and adapt complex and illogical details that would not have emerged from conventional human design (G-Star, 2023). In a second example, Desigual took a dual approach, launching its first on-demand collection created with AI, and focusing its Awesome Lab incubator on generative model-based startups. Subsequently, the Spanish brand reinforced its commitment to

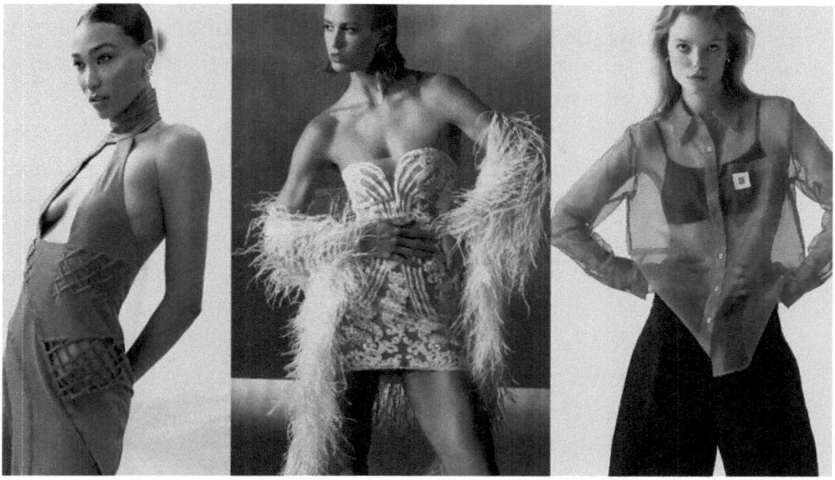

Figure 4. Revolve and Maison Meta transformed AI-generated designs from the first edition of AI Fashion Week into physical garments available for purchase on revolve.com. Pictured: looks by Paatif (left), Opé (center) and Molnm (right).
Maison Meta.

AI with successive generative "on-demand" collections, produced exclusively to order (Desigual, n.d.).

In 2025, other luxury brands began to integrate the technology into their processes. Using AI, Burberry reinterpreted its historical archive to create immersive experiences; Hugo Boss launched AI-generated product content for e-commerce; and Tapestry (parent company of Coach and Kate Spade) worked with AI-based Adobe tools to design digital twins (Ryder, 2025). These cases demonstrate that generative AI has ceased to be an experiment, that it has become a tool with the potential to exert a great impact on fashion design innovation, and that it is redefining creative processes, traditional notions of authorship and aesthetics in the age of the algorithm.

Challenges of AI adoption by the fashion industry

In recent years, the integration of artificial intelligence into the fashion industry has been progressive and functional, especially in areas such as logistics, personalization and trend analysis. However, its move into creative territories has raised concerns inside and outside the sector. As algorithms begin to be used in processes traditionally reserved for human intuition and sensitivity, new questions arise about authorship, ethics, sustainability in its various forms and the future of work.

Critics suggest that copyrighted designs might be replicated, without compensation or recognition for the original creators. As the images and texts created are not exactly the same as the original material developed, the new system providers argue that they belong to the prompt creators. However, generative content is clearly derived from the previously developed images and texts used to train the models, which has intellectual property implications (Davenport & Mittal, 2022). AI-generated fashion designs come with two fundamental issues that need to be addressed by national and international regulatory authorities. On the one hand, should these designs be protected by copyright legislation? If the answer is yes, who are the authors/owners of the intellectual property rights? On the other hand, who is liable for infringing the use of third-party material in these generative designs (Yılmaztekin, 2023)?

Regionally based legislative differences are setting the course for the use of generative AI in fashion. While in the United States copyright has been denied to works created without direct human intervention, in China some courts have recognized copyright. In the UK, the Getty Images vs Stability AI case illustrates the debate over using protected works to train AI models and raises the need to clarify responsibility for generated content (Curtis & Moss, n.d.). The European Union is moving forward with the AI Act, which, although it does not consider that most uses of AI in fashion are high-risk, introduces new transparency obligations and requires brands that do not want their data to be used for training purposes to explicitly say so in a machine-readable format (Znaty, 2024). These differences indicate a fragmented legal scenario, where international harmonization will be key to ensuring legal certainty and fostering ethical and responsible adoption of AI in the industry.

Beyond the legal implications, the incorporation of AI into the fashion industry also poses significant challenges in terms of social, environmental and economic sustainability, employment and the transformation of creative work. Some experts have drawn attention to the high energy consumption associated with training AI models, an important concern in a sector that is increasingly committed to environmental sustainability (Mzizi, 2024).

At the same time, fears persist that automation will replace human designers and other professional profiles. As with previous technological revolutions, new tools often profoundly change the nature of employment: certain jobs disappear, others are transformed and new opportunities arise. In the context of fashion, the tasks most susceptible to automation are office-based—such as writing product descriptions or managing databases—while the manual tasks linked to clothing remain less susceptible (Bain, 2023). In this scenario, resisting AI adoption doesn't seem like an effective strategy. On the contrary, brands, professionals and employees must learn to live with, and adapt to, AI to maintain their competitiveness in an industry in continuous transformation.

Training the future: *savoir-tech* and ethical design education

From savoir-faire to savoir-tech: key competencies in contemporary design

Fashion companies are demanding their employees have skills different to those required in the past. Just as artisanal fashion demands *savoir-faire*, new designers will need to master *savoir-tech*. The industry is looking for professionals who not only stand out for their creativity, but who can also master new technologies. For example, the ability to customize prompting techniques into generative AI tools is becoming a highly valued competency. Companies are hiring both prompt engineers and generative fashion designers, who consider their prompts as their secret formula: the competitive advantage of *savoir-tech*. The core concept was first outlined in Rodriguez Sanchez (2024) and is expanded here with new industry cases.

A particularly important example of this transformation is Mango's strategic commitment to AI as a cross-cutting driver of innovation. Since 2018, the brand has developed more than 15 proprietary platforms based on machine learning, integrated at different points in its value chain: from dynamic pricing (Midas) through the personalization of the shopping experience (Gaudí) to its multilingual customer service (Iris). One of its most significant creativity-focused initiatives is Inspire, a platform that assists the design team through a system of trend recommendation and visual references, which reinforces their ability to make informed and agile aesthetic decisions. This integration of AI into the conceptual phase of design reflects a paradigm shift: the designer no longer starts solely from intuition or subjective inspiration but can be nourished by intelligent tools that expand his/her field of creative exploration. This approach is reinforced by an internal virtual assets team, composed of 3D engineers, AI specialists, blockchain, and digital artists, with a focus on producing immersive content and consolidating the link between physical, digital and virtual channels.

Finesse, among a growing number of companies, has a successful model that, far from being based on the authentic creativity of a designer/design team, is based on data analysis. These brands are less focused on design, and more on the market. While this strategy may make sense for this type of company, it cannot, and should not, be the solution for designers and creative brands, which run the risk of losing that innovative essence that differentiates them from the competition and forms the bases of their DNA and positioning in the market.

To strike a balance between creativity and data, designers must integrate their creative and digital skills from the earliest stages of the design process. This will ensure that technologies are adapted to the particular needs of each brand. Tomorrow's designers will not only be creators of beauty, but experts in technology, merging the traditional with the digital. Those who manage to balance design expertise with *savoir-tech* will be better positioned to be at the forefront of a rapidly evolving industry.

In addition to individual competencies, the effective implementation of AI in fashion will involve organizations undergoing cultural transformations. Before incorporating AI into their operations, companies need to invest in talent, culture and training; for example, by developing internal training programs for the acquisition/improvement of technological skills. Nike uses AI-powered tools that provide its leadership team with access to personalized analytics that support decision-making. Estée Lauder and Microsoft have collaborated on the creation of an AI innovation lab to train the beauty group's employees. Germany's Hugo Boss has worked with the consultancy company Metyis to build a data science-dedicated campus. Moreover, companies must complement their internal training programs by selecting highly adaptable candidates, that is, with the ability to learn, unlearn and relearn.

Fashion managers shouldn't prioritize opportunities for quick wins at the expense of the human factor. While AI has great potential, too rapid adoption could result in layoffs, job displacements and job terminations among creative agencies and freelancers. Companies using AI tools must maintain human connection and creativity. They should embrace a culture that integrates technology with a human-centric approach, ensuring that AI enhances—rather than replaces—the unique value that only people can bring. People and purpose are the most powerful pillars of any brand, the key to its success.

Higher education, critical thinking, design ethics and AI

This transformation challenges the educational field, where how to train the designer of the future is being redefined. The evolving industry demands that future generations of designers be prepared for a constantly changing job market that demands *savoir-tech*. AI has found its place in the education field, with teachers, researchers and students exploring its application in the creative process and other areas. The inclusion of AI in academic programs and hands-on workshops allows students and educators to work with generative models, encouraging experimentation and inspiration in design.

It is essential that educators teach students how to use technology as a means, and not as an end in itself, promoting a comprehensive approach that develops innovative and adaptive skills. We propose that only when students have acquired sufficient design skills, and developed the essential critical thinking, can AI be an exploratory tool that triggers new creative ideas and, as an auxiliary, transform ideas into tangible results, from conception to realization.

Educators can play a crucial role in fostering creativity and critical thinking, and by guiding students to use AI ethically to explore new frontiers in fashion design. The progressive integration of AI into curricula can equip students and teachers with the skills needed to thrive in a dynamic industry.

To ensure the responsible and sustainable use of AI in the field of fashion design, *savoir-tech* education must address its ethical and legal implications. Fostering an ethical and discerning mindset will be critical in differentiating between derivative and transformative work, which will prepare everyone involved to face the future with confidence, and can avoid the use of AI as a quick fix.

Conclusions

Generative AI is driving a profound change in the fashion industry, not only in its technical, logistic and communicative processes, but particularly in its creative dimension. As noted throughout this chapter, AI not only optimizes solutions to complex tasks and accelerates data-driven decision-making, but it also has become a tool that expands the expressive potential of the designer and redefined traditional creative practices.

Instead of replacing the human designer, AI invites us to rethink his/her role. Fashion designers have increasingly evolved toward carrying out more conceptual and strategic functions, relying on technical teams to materialize their ideas. Cases such as Virgil Abloh, Raf Simons, Miuccia Prada and Rei Kawakubo show that mediation through images, words and visual references were part of the creative process long before the advent of generative AI. The difference today is that the designer can work directly with an intelligent system that interprets and transforms his/her ideas into immediate visual representations, opening up a new field for experimentation.

Looking to the future, the true differential value of the designer will not lie so much in mastering each tool, but in knowing how to combine them with aesthetic criteria, critical thinking and strategic vision. The challenge is not to compete with the machines, but to collaborate with them using human intelligence. In a context of increasing automation, the ability to imagine the possible, question the given and design with purpose can be the foundation of the new *savoir-tech* that will define the next generation of creators.

References

AI winter. (n.d.). In *Wikipedia*. Retrieved May 31, 2025, from https://en.wikipedia.org/wiki/AI_winter

Arrestegui, L. B. (2012). Fundamentos históricos y filosóficos de la inteligencia artificial [Historical and philosophical foundations of artificial intelligence]. *UCV-HACER. Revista de Investigación y Cultura, 1*(1), 87–92.

Bain, M. (2023, May 3). Should fashion fear AI? *Business of Fashion*. https://www.businessoffashion.com/articles/technology/should-fashion-fear-ai/

Bain, M. (2023, September 13). Why Collina Strada's Hillary Taymour thinks generative AI is a "game changer." *Business of Fashion*. https://www.businessoffashion.com/articles/technology/how-collina-strada-used-ai-to-design-its-new-collection/

Bain, M. (2024, March 25). H&M plans to use AI models. *Business of Fashion*. https://www.businessoffashion.com/articles/technology/hm-plans-to-use-ai-models/

Barrat, R. (2018, July 15). I'm doing something with fashion and AI but I don't know what yet [Tweet]. *Twitter*. https://x.com/videodrome/status/1018612770084753408

Bhargava, C., & Sharma, P. K. (Eds.). (2022). *Artificial intelligence: Fundamentals and applications*. CRC Press.

Boden, M. (2017). *Inteligencia artificial*. Turner Publicaciones.

Bonami, B., Piazentini, L., & Dala-Possa, A. (2020). Education, big data and artificial intelligence: Mixed methods in digital platforms [Educación, Big Data e Inteligencia Artificial: Metodologías mixtas en plataformas digitales]. *Comunicar, 65*, 43–52. https://doi.org/10.3916/C65-2020-04

Brain, E. (2020, January 20). Acne Studios is inspired by artificial intelligence in progressive FW20 show. *Hypebeast*. https://hypebeast.com/2020/1/acne-studios-fall-winter-2020-collection-runway-paris-fashion-week

Cazares, M. (2021, November 10). How AI is shaping design at Levi Strauss & Co. *Levi Strauss & Co.* https://www.levistrauss.com/2021/11/10/ai-shaping-design-levi-strauss/

Curtis, L., & Moss, S. (n.d.). The impact of AI on IP law in the world of fashion. *Chartered Institute of Trade Mark Attorneys*. https://www.citma.org.uk/resources/the-impact-of-ai-on-ip-law-in-the-world-of-fashion-mb24.html

Davenport, T. H., & Mittal, N. (2022, November 14). How generative AI is changing creative work. *Harvard Business Review*. https://hbr.org/2022/11/how-generative-ai-is-changing-creative-work

Desigual. (n.d.). *On demand*. https://www.desigual.com/es_ES/ondemand/

Fashion Institute of Technology. (2018, February 1). Students team with IBM and Tommy Hilfiger to use AI. *FIT Newsroom*. https://news.fitnyc.edu/2018/02/01/students-team-with-ibm-and-tommy-hilfiger-to-utilize-ai-to-elevate-design-manufacturing-and-marketing/

Feuerriegel, S., Hartmann, J., Janiesch, C., & Zschech, P. (2023). Generative AI. *Business & Information Systems Engineering, 66*(1), 111–26.

Finesse. (n.d.). *Finesseusstudios* [Instagram profile]. Retrieved May 18, 2025, from https://www.instagram.com/finesseusstudios/

G-Star. (2023, March 28). Our first denim couture piece designed by AI. *G-Star*. https://www.g-star.com/en_us/stories/art/artificial-intelligence-fashion

Harreis, H., Koullias, T., Roberts, R., & Te, K. (2023, March 8). Generative AI: Unlocking the future of fashion. *McKinsey & Company.* https://www.mckinsey.com/industries/retail/our-insights/generative-ai-unlocking-the-future-of-fashion

Knight, W. (2017, August 24). Amazon has developed an AI fashion designer. *MIT Technology Review.* https://www.technologyreview.com/2017/08/24/149518/amazon-has-developed-an-ai-fashion-designer/

Leitch, L. (2020, January 19). Acne Studios Fall 2020 menswear. *Vogue.* https://www.vogue.com/fashion-shows/fall-2020-menswear/acne-studios?_sp=3f6431e1-479b-4c4b-911d-75f237a9478a.1725447550627

Levi Strauss & Co. (2023, March 28). LS&Co. partners with Lalaland.ai. *Levi Strauss & Co.* https://www.levistrauss.com/2023/03/22/lsco-partners-with-lalaland-ai/

Maison Meta. (2023, October). Norma Kamali—Gen AI custom solution. *Maison Meta.* https://maisonmeta.io/portfolio-item/norma-kamali-gen-ai-custom-solution/

Maison Meta. (2023, November 24). AI Fashion Week winners collections just dropped on Revolve. *Maison Meta.* https://maisonmeta.io/ai-fashion-week-winners-collections-just-dropped-on-revolve/

McCarthy, J. (2007). What is artificial intelligence? *Computer Science Department, Stanford University.* https://www-formal.stanford.edu/jmc/whatisai.pdf

McCorduck, P. (2004). *Machines who think: A personal inquiry into the history and prospects of artificial intelligence* (2nd ed.). A K Peters.

McCulloch, W., & Pitts, W. (1943). A logical calculus of ideas immanent in nervous activity. *Bulletin of Mathematical Biophysics, 5,* 115–33. http://dx.doi.org/10.1007/BF02478259

McKinsey & *Business of Fashion.* (2024). *The state of fashion 2024: Finding pockets of growth as uncertainty reigns.* https://www.mckinsey.com/industries/retail/our-insights/state-of-fashion-2024

Milmo, D. (2023, February 2). ChatGPT reaches 100 million users two months after launch. *The Guardian.* https://www.theguardian.com/technology/2023/feb/02/chatgpt-100-million-users-open-ai-fastest-growing-app

Mzizi, Y. (2024, July 3). Fashion's AI dilemma is getting worse. *Business of Fashion.* https://www.businessoffashion.com/articles/technology/fashion-ai-dilemma-is-getting-worse/#:~:text=Baggu%20and%20Collina%20Strada%20are,the%20innovation%20with%20open%20arms%3F

Pardes, A. (2019, July 11). AI's latest job? Designing cool T-shirts. *Wired.* https://www.wired.com/story/artificial-intelligence-in-fashion-design/

Peng, T. (2019, April 4). Is the fashion world ready for AI-designed dresses? *Synced.* https://syncedreview.com/2019/04/04/is-the-fashion-world-ready-for-ai-designed-dresses/

Roberts-Islam, B. (2021, January 27). Zara meets Netflix: The fashion house where AI removes designers and overstock. *Forbes.* https://www.forbes.com/sites/brookerobertsislam/2021/01/27/zara-meets-netflix-the-fashion-house-where-ai-replaces-designers-eliminating-overstock/

Rodriguez Sanchez, M. (2024). Savoir tech: El impacto de la inteligencia artificial en el diseño de moda [Savoir tech: The impact of artificial intelligence on fashion design]. In T. Hidalgo-Marí & J. Herrero-Gutiérrez (Eds.), *La cuestión de la comunicación desde las universidades: Enfoques multidisciplinares*, pp. 12–27. Dykinson.

Ryder, B. (2025, January 26). How will luxury use AI in 2025? *Jing Daily.* https://jingdaily.com/posts/how-will-luxury-use-ai-in-2025

Schulz, M. (2023, April 5). What to expect at the first AI Fashion Week. *Vogue Business.* https://www.voguebusiness.com/technology/what-to-expect-at-the-first-ai-fashion-week?status=verified

Tse, C. (2023, August 7). An AI on the future. *Goldman Sachs.* https://am.gs.com/en-int/advisors/insights/article/2023/an-ai-on-the-future

Turing, A. (1950). Computing machinery and intelligence. *Mind, 59*(236), 433–60.

Yılmaztekin, H. K. (2023). *Artificial intelligence, design law and fashion.* Routledge.

Znaty, B. (2024, November 11). Fashion meets the AI Act: Low-risk systems with important transparency requirements. *Taylor Wessing.* https://www.taylorwessing.com/en/interface/2024/ai-act-sector-focus/fashion-meets-the-ai-act

Exploring the Relationship Between Technology and the Development of Textile Printing

*Rosa Deltoro Cremades**

ABSTRACT

This paper provides an overview of the advancements in printing systems employed by the textile industry. It analyzes the relationship between the development and implementation of new technologies, the acceleration of production processes, and their environmental consequences. The emergence of Indian chintz in Europe was a decisive factor in the entrepreneurial development that transformed the artisanal printing process into an industrial method. The mechanization of processes and new technologies has improved graphic registration on fabric and has accelerated production, generating significant economic benefits as well as leaving a notable environmental footprint. Increased production speed has led to the mass and continuous consumption of non-renewable resources, contributing directly to climate change. In light of this new paradigm marked by the climate crisis, this paper reflects on the urgency of integrating new concepts into the fashion industry's production chain, such as eco-efficiency, eco-innovation, and eco-design. It examines the new role of technological innovation and the scope of change required to address the textile industry's difficulties in implementing sustainable production and consumption practices.

Keywords: Indian chintz, textile industry, fashion, textile printing, sustainable development goals, printing methods

Since the First Industrial Revolution, when systems still retained certain artisanal components, technological development and innovation have contributed to the improvement and evolution of printing processes. The European arrival of Indian chintz, printed fabrics imported from the East, led to the birth of what we now know as the textile industry. In order to replicate these fabrics, the first chintz factories were established, at which a constant pursuit to improve all processes involved in printing production was established. In so far as obtaining a base for printing—thus improving weaving—, creating a variety of solid colors which adhere vibrantly to fabrics, and finally the mechanization of the process of printing designs onto textiles so as to enhance productivity and meet increasing demand.

* Universidad Politécnica de Valencia.
(ORCID: https://orcid.org/0009-0007-9302-1781)

The evolution of printing methods is crucial to the industrial development of textiles as it has led to increases in production speeds and is a key factor in the substitution of original Eastern products with European counterparts. The progression was swift, transitioning from domestic production to workshops, then to manufacturing facilities, and finally to factories. From 1780 to 1880, significant technological innovation ushered in the extensive production of printed fabrics (Ginsburg, 1993, p. 55). This change in technical systems aimed to achieve a high volume of colorful, intricate, and delicate prints to meet society's growing demand. As Agustín Nieto-Galan states:

> En efecto, las indianas han sido identificadas por algunos historiadores como un objeto técnico clave para explicar la transformación del trabajo artesano y gremial en un nuevo sistema fabril centralizado y de alta división de funciones y especialidades [Indian chintz has been identified as a key technical artifact to explain the transformation of artisanal and guild-based labor into a new, centralized factory system with a high division of roles and specialties.] (Nieto-Galan, 1996, p. 18)

Textile printing in Europe at its inception was an artisanal system in which block printing with wooden molds was the predominant technique. This system, which was used almost exclusively until 1770 (Schoebel Orbea, 2003), sped up the manual process of hand-painted printing but was nevertheless slow and failed to meet productivity goals. A 30 m length of cotton fabric required over 400 applications of the molds (Nieto-Galan, 1996, p. 18), yielding designs of lower quality which were crude in comparison to Eastern fabrics. The need to produce more in less time to meet the demand for these fabrics drove this nascent industry to seek new processes. In 1699, the wooden roller printing machine was invented. This new technology accelerated production, transitioning from a discontinuous printing process to one that printed on lengths of fabric continuously by virtue of the cylinder's rotation. However, the results, when it came to their graphic quality, left much to be desired and as a result, this method did not endure.

By 1770, the use of copper plates for printing became widespread. This discontinuous system, similar to wooden blocks, enabled artists to design without the technical limitations associated with drawing, while also allowing for printing on larger surfaces due to the greater size of copper plates compared to wooden blocks (Robinson, 1969, p. 17). To boost production and refine the first attempts at continuous printing, the copper roller printing method was introduced. In 1783—or possibly 1785, as some sources suggest—Thomas Bell revolutionized the process by creating a technique that enabled the seamless printing of a single color which soon increased to six in a continuous flow, marking a pivotal moment in textile manufacturing (Ventosa, 2011).

Alongside advancements in mechanized printing, significant progress was also made in the chemistry of colors. During the nineteenth century, knowledge about natural dyes and mordants for fixing them was solidified. The discovery of aniline by William Perkin in 1856 marked the beginning of a true revolution in printing colors (Postrel, 2021, p. 167). Synthetic dyes entered the textile industry, offering an infinite number of colors to choose from and excellent colorfastness, allowing for vibrant and colorful designs.

Refocusing on the mechanized printing processes, in 1834 Louis Jérôme Perron invented the Perrotine, a machine that mechanized the printing process using wooden blocks. This represented an important step forward from the manual block printing method on fabric. The Perrotine could print up to three colors simultaneously (Robinson, 1969, p. 106). Although the motifs printed using this system were not highly complex, it offered a significant advantage: time efficiency. "It takes four minutes to machine-print the design of a cotton fabric, while two people would need six hours to do the same work by hand" (Rhiannon, 1993, p. 61). The copper roller system and the Perrotine accelerated production, ensuring the success of these new systems. It also increased printing speed and production to meet growing demand, resulting in greater economic benefits for these industries.

In 1850, a new printing system was introduced, one which is still in use today: the *Lyonnaise*. This method allows for the reproduction of intricate designs, the attainment of vibrant colors, and minimal restrictions regarding the dimensions of a repeating pattern (*rapport*). Later, during the 1950s, machinery manufacturers developed fully automated flat plate printing, significantly reducing the time required for printing. Driven by the goals related to technological innovation within the fashion industry—improving processes and increasing productivity—a new industrial printing machine prototype, the rotary Lyonnaise, was unveiled in Germany at the 1963 International Textile Machinery Exhibition (I.T.M.A). The rotary machine is a system capable of printing large amounts of fabric in a short time with high definition. It has proven to be the simplest and most cost-effective means of achieving continuous printing with high precision in designed motifs (Storey, 1974, pp. 139–141). This type of printing remains one of the most widely used systems in the textile sector for large volumes of fabric, alongside a new printing method: digital printing.

Digital printing emerged from the introduction of new reproductive graphics techniques on paper. A considerable amount of time elapsed before this new technical reproduction system could be implemented, as research was needed to develop suitable inks and industrial-level machinery capable of printing large amounts of fabric at widths between 1.5 and 3 m. This new method requires less water than rotary printing, resulting in a lower environmental impact. It can reproduce any design or full-color image with less ink waste, as it uses the exact amount necessary for printing, leaving the remaining ink in the feed system for future prints. This printing system not only increases productivity but is also a more sustainable alternative to previous printing methods (Bisht et al., 2025, p. 5).

This brief overview of textile printing milestones reveals the evolution of a system initially based on artisanal and manual practices to one that has become industrialized and automated, thanks to research, innovation, and the use of new technologies. These fundamental tools have accompanied the development of the textile industry in its goal of producing higher quantities in less time with optimal graphic results, thereby generating greater economic benefits.

The twenty-first century textile industry still requires innovation, development, and the implementation of new technologies to improve printing systems and the design and production of garments. However, within today's context, the focus must shift. A starting point for sustainability-focused innovations could involve decoupling commercial success and the overconsumption of materials and resources to reduce pollution and its associated consequences. Currently, the acceleration of production systems has led to the mass and continued consumption of non-renewable resources, directly contributing to climate change, aquifer depletion, and contamination, biodiversity loss, and the "colonialism" of fashion. This acceleration has taken place in such a way that regions far from the so-called First World bear the consequences of excessive production (Toboso, 2017). Sustainability appears to be an almost unattainable goal for a sector such as fashion, whose structure is rooted in an economic growth model in which market expansion and profit generation rely on constantly creating new products.

The new role of technology within this paradigm should not be about the acceleration or production processes or the improvement of graphical precision—which are already at optimal levels—but rather should be about contributing to the creation and implementation of tools that reduce resource consumption and support the sustainable development of the textile industry. The aim should be to meet today's society's needs while ensuring that future generations' can also be met without compromise.

Until recently, advanced technology has been considered that which maximizes resource extraction in the shortest time possible. However, this model is short-sighted and obsolete. The challenges faced by today's textile industry cannot be resolved using the same systems by which they were created.

Achieving sustainability in the textile industry is a complex issue requiring the concerted actions of industry entities, government institutions, and consumers. The required transformations must encompass environmental perspectives, governance, and societal commitment. The new sustainability-focused model should be based on maximizing benefits while minimizing the use of resources. To achieve this, it is crucial to integrate concepts such as eco-efficiency, eco-innovation, and eco-design into the production chain of the fashion industry. These concepts are directly linked to research and the development of new technologies.

It is understood that eco-efficiency and eco-innovation technologies aim to derive a wide range of applications and products from minimal natural resources. For instance, the print preparation of fabrics, the printing process itself, and subsequent washing and finishing processes consume significant amounts of water and energy. Techniques to achieve finishes such as the "washed" or "worn" look on denim require high energy and water use and have negative health impacts on factory workers. Incorporating eco-efficient and innovative technologies into the production process will contribute to reducing overconsumption and occupational hazards.

One example of eco-innovation is the Valencian company Jeanologia, which develops technologies such as laser, ozone, e-Flow, SmartBoxes, and H2 Zero technology to enhance productivity, reduce water and energy consumption, and eliminate harmful emissions and waste. Another example of eco-efficiency and innovation is the advancement of digital printing, a technology that has been in ongoing development for over three decades. This method allows designs to be directly printed on fabrics using inkjet printers, eliminating the need for plates or cylinders. This technique significantly reduces material waste, ink consumption, and water usage, as it does not require intensive washing to set colors.

A more recent advancement is dry digital textile printing, which predominantly relies on pigment-based inks. A representative example is the FOREARTH digital textile printer, developed by Kyocera Document Solutions Inc., which applies pigmented inks using a specialized dry inkjet head, thereby significantly reducing water consumption by avoiding conventional aqueous pre- and post-treatment stages (Kyocera Document Solutions Inc., 2023). In parallel, innovative textile dyeing technologies, such as DyeCoo, replace water with closed-loop supercritical CO_2 systems, enabling dye dissolution and fiber penetration without aqueous processing (DyeCoo Textile Systems B.V., 2021). This method utilizes the solvent properties of pressurized CO_2 to dissolve dye and deeply penetrate fibers, achieving vibrant colors while saving up to 85 % of energy and avoiding 95 % of wastewater. Other patents, like Alchime-Endeavour™ and Twine, adopt similar processes. While sustainable, these technologies still face high implementation costs, limiting their industrial adoption.

Designing from a new perspective is another key factor. Anticipation and evaluation of the environmental impact before designing a garment are fundamental. Eco-innovation and eco-design aim to reduce the environmental impact of products throughout their entire lifecycle, from conception to disposal. For instance, to minimize the environmental impact during the course of the "use phase" of a garment's lifecycle, specific fabric finishes can reduce the impact of washing. Scotchgard™ and Teflon®, two of the most well-known finishes, impart stain-repellent properties to fibers. Similarly, antibacterial finishes help keep clothing clean for longer periods, reducing water consumption (Fletcher & Grose, 2012, p. 93).

One of the core strategies of eco-design is the circular economy. Modern economic systems primarily operate on linear principles: use and dispose. Circularity, on the other hand, aims to keep resources circulating for as long as possible. One of the textile industry's challenges is designing with sustainability and circularity in mind, using materials and ingredients sourced from responsibly managed resources, such as certified organic farming or livestock, and produced by using minimal resources. This avoids materials derived from intensive agriculture or livestock farming, which have significant environmental impacts.

Examples of sustainable raw materials include renewable fibers like cotton, linen, and hemp, as well as new alternatives such as Pyratex, derived from pineapple leaves, or others from materials such as nettle and algae. Creating garments where both the product and its components can be reused is also crucial. For instance, avoiding the mixing of fibers like polyester and cotton—common in the industry—facilitates recycling and its conversion into new fibers.

Educational institutions play a pivotal role in this shift. Preparing future designers to approach design from its earliest conceptual stages, where options are weighed, and decisions are made, is vital. Providing students with knowledge, tools, and critical thinking skills is essential to transforming the way design has been approached over recent decades. Designers must consider environmental aspects during the design process and think about ecological waste management throughout a product's lifecycle. Reducing waste through planning, reuse, recycling, and repair are four crucial elements to new design practices.

Fostering the adoption of new technologies that allow the visualization of a product without taking it into production may not be a determining factor, but it does contribute to a reduction in unnecessary textile production. For instance, the creation of fabric samples by textile suppliers to showcase their collections to various brands is a widespread practice in the textile industry. Software such as Clo3D enables the rendering of a designed garment using its pattern, applying the intended fabric or print thereby avoiding printing, sewing, and transporting garments across the globe. These garments, often destined for disposal, serve no purpose beyond presenting a collection.

While the industry is making progress toward achieving sustainable development goals, the high costs, insufficient regulatory support, and evolving technology present significant challenges, making it appear nearly impossible to sustain environmentally friendly production and consumption practices.

There are numerous examples of how the concept frequently surpasses the industry's ability to implement change. Patagonia designed a new footwear model called *Sugar and Spice*, intended to be dismantled and recycled. However, it failed to achieve its goal because the necessary industrial infrastructure was not available (Fletcher & Grose, 2012, p. 87). The lack of economic incentives, insufficient financial investment in the development of new technologies (Wearme Fashion, 2021, p.26), and the absence of sustainable infrastructure in developing countries—where most of the textile industry is concentrated—for companies with a lower environmental impact make the goal of change an almost herculean task.

In recent years, driven by the goal of sustainability and growing environmental awareness, a renewed appreciation for craftsmanship has emerged within parts of the fashion industry. This approach embraces values such as time, quality, and intentionality—qualities that stand in stark contrast to today's high-speed, productivity-driven economic systems. Craftsmanship places the focus on the product itself rather than the volume of output, emphasizing care and attention to detail over mass production.

Interestingly, there seems to be a growing opportunity for innovation, the very force that once pushed industries away from artisanal methods, now intersects and harmonizes with the principles of craftsmanship. This convergence could pave the way for a more thoughtful and balanced approach to fashion production.

Slow fashion proposes the return to a model where time, dedication, and quality take precedence over the accelerated pace of fast fashion. It prioritizes the product over productivity, valuing quality and design over quantity, and finding a balance between innovation and tradition. This involves a shift toward producing fewer garments but ensuring high-quality production using sustainable materials, low-impact processes, and timeless designs that encourage a more conscious and respectful relationship with the clothing we consume.

This return to craftsmanship not only addresses the current climate crisis but also offers the opportunity to establish a textile industry that prioritizes respect for the time required to design and produce, natural resources, and, consequently, the impact on the planet on which we live.

Governance, in conjunction with society, is one of the fundamental aspects of change necessary to encourage sustainable practices, the drafting of regulatory frameworks, and the monitoring of compliance. As individuals, we are active agents in this transformation. The way we consume and care for our clothing has a significant impact on sustainability. Studies reveal that the use phase of a garment has four times the environmental impact of the production phase.

From the study and investigation of ecological impact, new initiatives have emerged such as the British government's Sustainable Clothing Roadmap program, which funds research into washing technology and strategies to promote clothing sustainability (Fletcher & Grose, 2012, p. 92). This approach brings together institutions, industry, and society to achieve sustainable development goals.

Each individual action may not yield an immediate positive effect, but combining efforts through new initiatives and adopting habits that include the technological innovations at our disposal will foster change. By anticipating the impact of processes, evaluating alternatives, and understanding that development must seek new productive and long-term committed avenues, we can ensure the textile industry's survival and progress as well as the conservation of our environment, flora and fauna, and human communities. Governance, society, and industry must unite to make a future possible.

Awareness, analysis, reflection, and evaluation of our actions will drive change thereby aligning technology with the sustainable development of the textile industry.

References

Bisht, A., Singh, R., & Kumar, P. (2025). Digital textile printing technologies and sustainability: Recent advances and future perspectives. *Journal of Textile Engineering*, *71*(1), 1–12.

DyeCoo Textile Systems B.V. (2021). *BNiD – DyeCoo technical specifications.* https://dyecoo.com/pdf/BNiD-DyeCoo-Techspec-cor-210120-Online.pdf

Fletcher, K., & Grose, L. (2012). *Sustainable fashion and textiles: Design journeys*. Laurence King Publishing.

Ginsburg, M. (1993). *The history of textiles*. Libsa.

Kyocera Document Solutions Inc. (2023). *Sustainability summary report 2023*. Kyocera Document Solutions. https://www.kyoceradocumentsolutions.com/en/company/csr/csr_report.html

Nieto-Galán, A. (1996). Textile industry and the history of technology: European chintz of the early nineteenth century. *Revista de Historia Industrial*, *(11)*, 11–37.

Rhiannon, R. (1993). *Printed textiles in the Industrial Revolution*. Thames & Hudson.
Schoebel Orbea, A. (2003). La estampación textil en Europa. En *Textil e indumentaria: materias, técnicas y evolución* (pp. 44–60). Universidad Complutense de Madrid.
Storey, J. (1974). *Manual of textile printing*. Chapman and Hall.
Toboso Chavero, S. (2017). Colonialismo ambiental y globalización: impactos de la industria textil. *Revista de Estudios Sociales, (61)*, 45–58.
Ventosa, S. (2011). Les indianes, un regal per als sentits. Notes sobre els processos de producció. *Barcelona Quaderns d'Història, (17)*, 51–65.
Wearme Fashion. (2021). *Sustainable fashion: Responsible consumption, design, fabrics, and materials*. Bloomsbury Academic; Promopress; Hoaki Books.

CHAPTER 4

Solar Cells You Can Eat: The Future of Bioelectronics

Developing bioelectronics: edible solar cells for compostable organic photovoltaic systems

Elisabeth Lorenzi, Paulina Grabowska***

ABSTRACT
Electricity is the main force that powers all the processes in nature. Nowadays, we rely on electricity in almost all aspects of our lives. However, traditional electronic devices are made of non-renewable resources, such as metals, silicone, and synthetic plastic. The idea behind renewable electronics is to create batteries and photovoltaic solar cells from mostly organic materials that are accessible, sustainable, and capable of being renewed.

This article is based on the collaboration research conducted by Elisabeth Lorenzi, a material researcher, textile technological artist, and professor from Fashion Design University of Madrid (CSSDM-UPM) and innovator and bio-designer P. Grabowska, who conducted this research together with a group of students at SWPS University in Warsaw.

The joint effort resulted in the prototypes of a compostable DSSC (Dye Sensitized Solar Cell) solar cell made from renewable materials and also based on food waste criteria. This article points to the making process of a new type of cOPV (compostable Organic Photovoltaics) system that can prevent non-recyclable e-waste production and lessen the ecological footprint of electronics, which currently relies mostly on mining and fossil fuels. This creates new electronic materiality with a planet-oriented design.

The materiality and energy produced by these prototypes offer interesting opportunities for application in wearables or interactive projects when fashion is connected with principles of sustainability.

Keywords: bioelectronics, bioplastic, DSSC, edible, electronics, organic, photocell, wearables

Introduction

Faced with the environmental emergency caused by the vast use of synthetic plastics and non-recyclable fast electronics, it is crucial to develop alternative

* (ORCID: https://orcid.org/0000-0002-9518-6666), Universidad Politécnica de Madrid.
** (ORCID: https://orcid.org/0009-0007-0178-319X), NASDRA Sp. z o.o., Design Department, SWPS University in Warsaw.

bioplastic materials from abundant natural elements, such as vegetables, algae, animals, and bacteria. In this research project, we investigate the possibilities of using so-called *biomaterials* to create alternative energy sources for bioelectronics. This transition can empower and support local makers who use local materials to avoid non-renewable material dependencies for technological innovation.

Bioelectronics examines traditional electronics from the perspective of organic chemistry. It is connected to the concept introduced by Arthur Firstenberg (2019) in his book *The Invisible Rainbow*: that electricity was originally a field of experimentation on life and the body before it became the engine of the Industrial Revolution, represented by ferrous materials.

Nowadays, the innovative focus on the potential of biomaterials for their electronic properties has led to a growing wave of research. Bonné, R., Meysman, F. J. R., and Hermans, L. (2022) provided an insightful overview, highlighting ongoing research into organic semiconductors, particularly their applications in Organic Photovoltaic (OPV) systems.

Traditionally, the development narrative has relied on science and technology as the engine that makes us go further. In the face of climate change and the concept of the Anthropocene epoch as defining the role of humans on a dying planet, the development of new technologies continues to be part of the narrative of human and planetary salvation. As Tironi et al. (2022) propose, designers have the opportunity to promote a technologically viable present and future to the extent that we can avoid user-centric designs and embrace planet-oriented ones. Therefore, our proposal aims to prototype renewable energy resources using natural, compostable materials that support the circular economy.

By applying some scientific principles, this project was promoted by designers and artists with backgrounds in anthropology, fashion, biomaterials, and ecology. This collaboration resulted in prototypes of solar cells and biotic batteries that can produce a low income of volts (around 0.5 V voltage by each sample). The work results from a cross-disciplinary collaboration among two designers who mentored design students' work to develop and test functional prototypes.

The origin of this process began in 2017 when Elisabeth Lorenzi, a Spanish artist and researcher interested in applying bioplastics to generate energy, began experimenting with solar cells. Her idea was to replicate the operation of a Graeztell solar cell with compostable materials, which was activated with natural dyes but built initially with mineral crystals. Publishing this experiment on networks, it caught the interest of the artist and popularizer from the United States, Jeffrey Yoo Warren, who offered to illustrate the process of making a fanzine (Lorenzi & Warren, 2020).

Once the fanzine was published, Paulina Grabowska, a Polish bio-designer and teacher at SWPS University in Warsaw, used this recipe and other examples of energy generation with living processes to be tested and developed by her students in dialogue and collaboration with Elisabeth Lorenzi to improve its electronic properties and develop a total edible prototype.

The principles of the research methodology are: to build a functional prototype, replicate the experiment in different contexts with low-tech technology and easily replaceable material, measure electronic properties and compare different versions, and search for the possibilities of using edible and compostable materials.

Renewable materials, renewable electronics

Photovoltaic systems are an attractive and common solution for obtaining renewable energy. silicone solar panels on roofs, farms, and small devices are already part of our imagination of a better future. However, the materials from which traditional PV cells or wind turbines are made are non-renewable.

Solar cells have a relatively long service life (around 30 years), but their rigidity makes them vulnerable to manipulation. On the other hand, standard solar cells are complicated to recycle because their inorganic components are challenging to separate. The spread of traditional photovoltaic technology as a renewable energy solution will be a huge problem when it becomes e-waste.

Globally, renewable energy aims to reduce reliance on fossil fuels as an energy source. Yet, its production and infrastructure development depend heavily on fossil fuel-based energy and non-renewable materials such as silicone, fossil-derived polymers, iron, and rare-earth elements. As a result, renewable energy currently has a substantial ecological footprint. In *The Rare Metals War*, Guillaume Pitron (2019) explores the environmental impacts of rare-earth element extraction and processing, which are critical for renewable energy and digital technologies. He also highlights the geopolitical tensions arising from global competition for these strategic resources. Therefore, it is crucial to consider principles other than the current ones when creating future solutions for photovoltaic technology. Because, Photovoltaic energy sources are the future, but not as they are developed.

On a smaller scale, photovoltaic energy could be a very interesting solution for powering on smaller dispositives that dominate our imagination about how we interact with machines and nature in the future. In this way, the inspiration toward wearables and interactive devices is a starting point to think in more plastical and organic solutions for solar panels.

Our research aims to incorporate a sustainable perspective into the material design of solar cells, aligning with zero-waste principles. We are exploring compostable and even edible solutions as alternatives for the materials used in this energy resource.

For the development of this perspective, we were inspired by the increasing attention toward bioplastics, materials with plastic properties that are synthesized from renewable organic sources and varying degrees of biodegradability. A large part of these natural polymers are synthesized from agricultural residues, such as cellulose, potato, or corn starch. But they can also be derived from algae, animals (such as collagen-gelatin) fungi, and bacteria. The most interesting thing about biopolymers is that in each place it can be extracted sustainably and in accordance with its socio-cultural context. Another layer of the benefits of these materials is their water solubility during the processing, which allows them to be made in low-tech environments, such as a kitchen, making them easily replicable. This also connects with our focus on incorporating food waste materials into the ingredients. The experimentation around these materials has experienced a great impulse since they can be synthesized from nearby materials and very simple tools.

Organic electronic or polymer electronics, is a branch of electronics that deals with the study of organic materials, such as conductive polymers, for the creation of electronic circuits and devices. It is given the name of *organic electronics* because the polymers or molecules of which the devices are composed, are based on carbon molecules. In contrast to traditional electronics that use inorganic conductive and semiconductor materials, such as copper, germanium, or silicone. Most of this development is based on synthetic materials with a long term of degradability.

Our contribution to this field is prototyping electronic devices with fully compostable and renewable materials as bioplastic. In this way, we use these biomaterials to build solar cells inspired by the building procedure and functionality of Graeztell solar cell (dye-sensitized solar cell, DSSC, DSC o DYSC) a photoelectrochemical system based on the potential difference generated by the reaction to light of dyes of natural origin, in contact with a semiconductor. We get inspired by this solar cell model because of the potential to incorporate colors from nature into compostable materials.

Circularity of resources in edible solar cells

Our work consists of replicating an already proven energy source, such as DSCC cells, but using materials that align with circular economy principles. Therefore, we will define more clearly the principles we are pursuing:

- Edible means compostable but with several restrictions (no zoonotic materials)
- Bioelectronics can be a step between using food waste from industrial-scale production and composting.

Globally, approximately one third of all food produced is wasted. This equates to about 1.3 billion tons annually, impacting resources like water, land, and labor. Strategies to reduce food waste include improving supply chain efficiency, raising consumer awareness, enhancing food recovery programs, and encouraging sustainable consumption practices. Governments and organizations also play a key role in implementing policies and incentives to reduce food waste at all stages of the food chain OECD (Bagherzadeh et al., 2014). Our work points to the possibility of the collecting of some food waste as vegetable peels for producing the dye, eggs and mollusk shells for sourcing the calcium carbonate semiconductive layer. Also, we collected biomass-based activated charcoal for the carbon layer.

The use of food waste materials highlights a significant opportunity to develop edible and compostable alternatives. It emphasizes the potential to responsibly integrate these materials into the circular value chain, allowing them to be transformed into soil or natural gas, thus promoting sustainability.

The DSSC solar cell made from renewable materials

Photovoltaic cells are devices that manage to transform light energy into electrical energy. Crystalline silicone photovoltaic cells are the most used in the manufacture of solar panels. In 1991 the first dye solar cell was developed by O'regan and Grätzel (1991), which inaugurated the turn toward the use of organic materials to produce photovoltaic energy.

The functionality of their DSSC cell lies on the interaction among different layers of organic/non-organic materials. The device is based on a transparent film of titanium dioxide particles, coated with a monolayer of a dye to sensitize the film for light harvesting. This solar cell is composed of two electrodes, at least one of them is transparent for light (in most cases it is made of conductive glass). This transparent conductive glass covers a semiconductor, usually made from the anatase modification of titanium (IV) oxide (TiO2) which contains excess free electrons. A dye pigment is attached to the TiO2 surface and should assemble an electrically homogeneous dipole layer. Photoexcitation of the pigment from the ground leads to the injection of an electron into the conduction band of TiO2. The oxidized pigment is restored by electron transfer from the electrolyte. A widely used liquid electrolyte is the iodide-triiodide and reduces the positively charged pigment whereby. The inner surface of the cathode used to contain either graphite or platinum particles as an attractor of the electrons (Hug et al., 2014).

The first experiments were performed mainly with synthetic dyes, but further developments exchanged the synthetic dyes of the setup of DSSCs with vegetal based ones. The potential of this schema is huge because it is based on how plants transform solar energy based on a photosensitive dye as chlorophyll and this concept inspired later developments of this solar cell.

Hubert Hug et al. (2014) summarize current available knowledge on natural dyes that have been used in DSSCs which should provide reasonable light harvesting efficiency by each color spectrum.

Bioplastic solar cell

Our contribution to the development of DSSC cells is the replacement of inorganic materials with organic materials from renewable sources. The purpose of this change is to try to replace materials that come from extractive industries. These types of materials unfortunately mean that photovoltaic energy, despite its advantages, also has a negative impact on the environment and promotes geopolitical inequality, due to the struggle for resources, or the rising market price of resources. In our study, we are looking for materials that can be easily substituted, grown, or built with little specialized technology. We based our technology primarily on dyes of natural origin (derived from flowers, vegetables, and fruits), which are relatively widely available.

The first step was to replace the conductive glass with a transparent, conductive, and organic material. To do this, we experimented with different materials, such as gelatin and agar. In the end, we choose agar for its properties and cruelty-free extraction. To increase its conductive properties, we add NaCl (table salt) and glycerin.

To create a compostable solar cell, it was important to eliminate all toxic materials, such as TiO2 (Titanium dioxide). Therefore, we successfully experimented with other materials, such as calcium carbonate (derived from eggshells) or natural indigo pigment.

The experiment used different types of pigments, derived from edible plants such as beets, onion peels, pomegranates, or turmeric. Each pigment (color) generated a different electric current outcome.

Another advancement from the original prototype was that it was designed as a single module with layers of different functionalities bonded together to enhance the photovoltaic reaction. In this case, separate and stackable modules were created for each layer, making them interchangeable, which simplifies the comparison of each layer's efficiency. For example, it was possible to observe the difference in potential across dyed layers (orange, red, yellow) and the functionality of semiconductor substitutes (titanium dioxide replaced by eggshell-derived calcium carbonate) without the need for separate experiments.

The composted batteries can become fertilizer for growing vegetables and herbs from which pigments can then be extracted to create bioelectronics. Therefore, creating a circular and regenerative method for new types of devices.

Conclusion

Through our research, testing, and prototyping, we can conclude that it is possible to create a fully organic, compostable, and edible solar cell using renewable materials. The cells do not have a long lifespan (up to two weeks), which is also a big value of the solution. Since the solar cells are made of organic and some food-grade mineral materials are safe to be composted.

The composting process will produce biogas as well as fertilizer. The biogas can be used as a heat source for example for off-grid solutions. In turn, fertilizer can be used to nourish plants from which dyes are extracted to create photovoltaic cells.

The results of our research so far are working prototypes and samples. Ultimately, we aim to create fully functioning devices. Therefore, the research will need to continue and evolve to become more technologically advanced. In this article, we have highlighted one of our research focuses, but we also maintain other areas of work that we hope to have the opportunity to publish in the future, such as prototyping with biotic batteries made from food waste and fermentation processes. Our work demonstrates the possibilities of cross-disciplinary thinking between science and circularity, aimed at achieving compostable materials made from food waste.

We want to draw attention to the great potential of this research direction as an opportunity to move away from finite resources to create energy sources. To be able to free up energy sources from relying on materials such as silicone, metals, or rare-earth elements.

In conclusion we would put on the table the power to imagine and prototype possible futures from artistic and design backgrounds. This has allowed us to develop a prototype of a solar cell that we consider viable in a future framework in which energy sources are oriented not only to satisfy the needs of humans but also generate a positive impact on the diversity of the environment.

Acknowledgments

We would like to thank the SWPS University's students who contributed to the development of the prototype under the supervision of their professor for their dedication, effort, and creativity in this project. Their collaboration was essential to the realization of this work: Karolina Gerschmann, Amelia Kucińska, Helena Rytwńska, Inga Turska.

References

Bagherzadeh, M., Inamura, M., & Jeong, H. (2014). Food waste along the food chain. *OECD Food, Agriculture and Fisheries Papers, 71*. OECD Publishing. https://doi.org/10.1787/5jxrcmftzj36-en

Bonné, R., Meysman, F. J. R., & Hermans, L. (2022). Diversity and metabolic potentials of microbial communities associated with pollinator and cheater fig wasps in fig-fig wasp mutualism system. *Frontiers in Microbiology, 13*. https://doi.org/10.3389/fmicb.2022.906363

Firstenberg, A. (2019). *The invisible rainbow: A history of electricity and life*. AGB Press.

Grätzel, M., & O'Regan, B. (1991). A low-cost, high-efficiency solar cell based on dye-sensitized colloidal TiO_2 films. *Nature, 353*(6346), 737–40. https://doi.org/10.1038/353737a0

Hug, H., Bader, M., Mair, P., & Glatzel, T. (2014). Biophotovoltaics: Natural pigments in dye-sensitized solar cells. *Applied Energy, 115*, 216–25. https://doi.org/10.1016/j.apenergy.2013.10.055

Lorenzi, E., & Warren, J. Y. (2020). *Gelatin solar cell* [Zine]. https://issuu.com/elisabethlorenzi/docs/gelatin_solar_cell_issu

Pitron, G. (2019). *La guerra de los materiales raros: El lado oculto de la transición energética y digital* [The war of rare materials: The hidden side of the energy and digital transition]. Taurus.

Tironi, M., Albornoz, C., & Chilet, M. (2022). Problematizing human-centred design: Notes on planet-oriented design open debate. *DIID-Disegno Industriale Industrial Design, 77*, 22–9. https://doi.org/10.30682/diid7722c

CHAPTER 5

Toward a New Paradigm

Integrating generative pattern-making software into fashion design practice

*María Luisa Calvo Frutos**

ABSTRACT

In the fashion industry, the roles of the pattern maker and designer have traditionally been well differentiated. In the conventional workflow, design precedes patternmaking. However, with the widespread adoption of digital technology in the garment development process—particularly 3D virtual simulation—this traditional role separation and workflow are being re-examined. This article presents a new framework for garment design, where digital technology not only serves as a tool for virtually presenting a product but also functions as a generative entity. This study proposes a software, [Re]gPD, that generates unconventional bodice blocks based on user-input measurements. The code uses algorithms grounded in traditional pattern-cutting rules, which the software itself breaks. Design science research methodology was followed taking a problem-centered approach. During the demonstration and evaluation phase [Re]gPD was used in combination with digital sampling software CLO. First, 24 sets of blocks were generated with [Re]gPD and virtually simulated. From these, three were further developed into virtual garments. The research demonstrated that [Re]gPD can be easily integrated with virtual sampling technologies making the design and development process fully digital. This new approach to fashion design fosters the evolution of garment design and development by challenging established industry practices and processes.

Keywords: pattern cutting, digital design, fashion software, fashion design, fashion technology

Introduction

Fashion has adopted digital technology as a tool to facilitate and speed up the design and production process. Computer-Aided Design (CAD) software programs are widely used in industry to help visualize the designer's idea. With regards to the garment development process, the proliferation in recent years of digital pattern-making programs with different price points finally spread their use from large fashion chains to smaller brands. In recent years, the adoption of 3D garment simulation tools by fashion brands has increased

* Universidad Politécnica de Madrid.
(ORCID: https://orcid.org/0009-0000-5507-6916)

significantly, driven by improvements in user-friendliness, precision, and overall performance (Lee & Park, 2017; Baytar, 2018; Wang & Zhang, 2007). However, all these software programs have been designed so that they replace, in quite a literal way, traditional manual processes.

In the traditional workflow of the fashion industry, designers begin by sketching their ideas, usually first as conceptual drawings and later as technical flat sketches, which are then passed on to the pattern maker. Pattern makers frequently rely on basic blocks as starting points, applying a series of transformations to them in order to create patterns that can then be used to construct a specific design. In this conventional model, particularly prevalent in the ready-to-wear sector, the roles of designer and pattern maker are clearly defined, with design almost always preceding pattern development.

The aim of this research is to present an example of how the design of generative digital technologies specific to garment development could lead to a rethinking of the traditional workflow and roles in the industry. This project focuses on the development of a digital tool named [Re]generative Pattern Design ([Re]gPD) that generates unconventional bodice blocks based on a set of body measurements. In this case, digital technology is not used to help visualize an idea, but to generate the idea by using and, at the same time breaking, traditional pattern-cutting rules. This challenges the traditional perception of technology as merely a tool to control a process and its results. The appropriateness of [Re]gPD to be used in conjunction with 3D simulation programs was also considered, as this combination would entail a fully digital garment design and development process which could present several advantages, which will be discussed later.

This work builds upon the study conducted in the master's thesis titled [Re]generative Pattern Design: a generative digital tool for creative pattern cutting (Calvo Frutos, 2018) but certain methodological and theoretical aspects have been updated to reflect technological advancements since then.

Literature review

Digital technologies can be incorporated nowadays in every step of the garment design and making. There are software and hardware solutions to aid the design, pattern making, lay planning, and cutting process. Furthermore, in this field, we are currently experiencing a flourishing use of artificial intelligence, either as a tool to assist in the ideation process or as a tool to generate realistic images of designs, for a variety of purposes.

With regards to pattern cutting, for many years pattern design software use was the reserve of large fashion chains, who could afford the costly programs and hardware associated (digitizer or scanner and plotter). As an alternative to the pattern drafting systems that the main CAD/CAM companies supplied (Gerber AccuMark, Lectra Modaris, Assyst Bullmer, Optitex, or Vetigraph), others appeared (PAD Pattern, Pattern Maker, Fashion CAD, Cameo, Poly Pattern or Telestia Creator, etc.) that offered more affordable alternatives and that allowed smaller fashion brands to be able to use digital pattern making.

Around 2015, the virtual simulation of garments became an area of increasing interest in the fashion industry. A study by Kalypso and Indiana University (2017) about retail industry found that digital product creation—particularly in the areas of 3D sampling, visualization, and approval—had become the focus of significant investment within retail product development practices. Despite the availability of 3D prototyping tools (such as Lectra Modaris 3D, Gerber AccuMark 3D, and CLO), the adoption of such software was initially slow due to resistance from fashion companies. This reluctance was largely due to a lack of trust in 3D technology (Seo, 2018), as well as concerns over its accuracy and efficiency, which were seen as barriers to broader industry adoption (Porterfield, 2014; Wu et al., 2011). While 3D simulation tools can save time and resources in the sampling process, other factors such as the time required for training, and the fear of disrupting established design workflows (Papahristou, 2016; Seo, 2018) slowed their implementation. However, today, virtual garment simulation is widely adopted within the fashion industry.

All the digital technologies mentioned were designed for the fast-fashion context. The aim was to substitute manual processes with software to make them more cost-effective, increasing accuracy, and speeding up productivity. The combination of these digital technologies disrupts the traditional fashion product development, production, and marketing models, which has ironically opened the door to a more sustainable practice and to models, as mentioned in Mattila (2016), that could enable mass-customization and localized manufacturing in the near future.

Aims and objectives

Software programs are used in product development as a tool to control and speed up each individual process, mimicking the traditional workflow. However, there is a lack of research on the development of software, specially created for garment designers and pattern cutters, that facilitate creativity and that could be employed for any design concept and market. In this context, there are no tools in which digital technology acts as a generative entity that encourages alternative thinking. That does not mean that pattern design software cannot be used to implement creative ways to pattern cut, but they do not offer or encourage an alternative or more creative approach to pattern making.

This research proposes a different but supplementary way of using digital technology in pattern cutting with the development of a software program, [Re]generative Pattern Design ([Re]gPD), that creates unusual bodice blocks. [Re]gPD was conceived as a block generator that would provide pattern cutters with starting shapes intended to be further developed and fitted for them to become garment patterns. The software had to allow for an easy integration with existing digital technologies as well as present pattern making not as an over-complex task, but as a creative activity. For these reasons, ensuring good usability was considered essential.

The chosen generative design framework offers an approach to pattern cutting that cannot be replicated manually. Its purpose is to challenge the traditional separation of roles between designers and pattern cutters, rethinking the conventional garment creation workflow. Additionally, it aims to foster creativity among fashion professionals and students, encouraging innovation within pattern-cutting discipline.

Methodology

In this project, coding is used as a form of research and enquiry. To address the research problem, a design science research approach was adopted, as it supports the creation of innovative artifacts and the generation of knowledge through their design, use, and evaluation. Design science research is particularly suited to problem-centered studies that aim not only to understand existing practices but to propose and assess new ones (Gregor & Hevner, 2013; Vaishnavi, 2017).

Given the lack of a methodology for the production and presentation of design science research in information systems, Peffers et al. (2007) developed design science research methodology (DSRM). DSRM consists of six activities: problem identification and motivation, definition of the objectives for a solution, design and development, demonstration, evaluation, and communication.

In the work on this project, procedures were designed under a DSRM. Design science research has a dual mission: "to design applicable IT artefacts and to develop theories for design and action" (Kloör et al., 2018). With regards to the latter, the generative framework, under which [Re]gPD was designed, disrupts the traditional design workflow and presents technology as a creator and not as a tool that mimics individual manual tasks. Moreover, the generative nature of the program was an essential quality in order to present a method exclusively digital, that could not be implemented manually.

As the project takes a problem-centered approach, every step of the methodology was implemented, as explained below:

Phase 1: Problem identification and motivation

The lack of innovative digital pattern-cutting methods was identified through a literature review. The development of software that implements alternative ways to pattern cut would allow for the immediate integration of new methods with the ubiquitous 2D and 3D digital technologies used for garment development.

Phase 2: Definition of the objectives for a solution

A method of generating patterns that could not be performed manually was created to prove the singularity and exclusive possibilities of using a computer to generate the blocks.

Phase 3: Design and development

To break the rules, it is important to know the rules. A simple way to translate this requirement and ideas into computational thinking was to use a generative design framework in which algorithms based on traditional pattern-cutting rules are used; rules that the software itself breaks.

Phase 4: Demonstration

Simulation was used as a research method to demonstrate that the artifact created met the main objectives. This phase focused on the testing of the general wearability of the blocks, the variety of shapes generated, the correct generation of pieces, the correct saving of the patterns, and their compatibility with other software.

The simulation involved the 3D virtual sampling of 24 distinct sets of block patterns generated using [Re]gPD, all based on the same set of body measurements. The number 24 was selected to ensure a sufficiently wide variety of shapes to test the functionality of [Re]gPD. It is worth noting that the generative rules are not gender-specific; however, for demonstration purposes, a female avatar corresponding to UK size 8 in the Alvanon Standard Global women's size chart (Alvanon, 2018) was utilized.

Phase 5: Evaluation

Simulation was further used to observe and evaluate how well [Re]gPD performs when compared with the rest of the objectives. Within the 24 sets of blocks that were generated for the previous phase, three were selected to be fitted on an avatar and developed into a virtual garment. The three sets chosen were representative of different 3D volumes that can be obtained when assembling [Re]gPD patterns and using different settings for their generation.

The main objective of this phase was to evaluate whether [Re]gPD blocks can be used as a starting point for the development of different types of garments.

Phase 6: Communication

To communicate the utility and novelty of the artifact created (Peffers et al., 2007), this article was presented.

Design and development

User interface

The interface was designed as a single, very simple screen where the user is required to input a series of body measurements and press the "Generate" button, upon which a front bodice block and a back bodice block are automatically generated. These blocks are polygons consisting of a total of eight sides, corresponding to: neckline, left shoulder, left armhole, left side seam, hem, right side seam, right armhole, and right shoulder. All sides of the polygon are straight lines except for the neckline and armholes which are quadratic curves.

Before generating the blocks, the user can select the "symmetrical" and/or "sleeves" options. If the "symmetrical" option is selected, the front and back bodice patterns will be generated as symmetrical shapes. If the "sleeves" option is selected, in addition to generating a front bodice block and a back bodice block, one or two sleeve patterns are also generated. A single sleeve pattern is created if the bodice blocks are symmetrical, while two sleeve patterns are generated if the bodice blocks are asymmetrical.

The program requires the user to input only three body measurements: neck circumference, shoulder, and bust circumference. If the user has chosen the option to generate sleeves, the sleeve length measurement must also be provided. All measurements must be entered in centimeters.

Once the patterns have been generated, the user can save them at full scale as DXF files, a file format that can be imported into most 2D and 3D software available on the market.

Generative rules

The position of each vertex of the generated bodice blocks is calculated based on the algorithms traditionally used for drafting bodice patterns, with an added random component. This random component is a variable that is allowed to take different values within a range for each execution. The inclusion of aleatory elements in the generation of the vertices of both symmetrical and asymmetrical bodices makes the chance of obtaining the exact same set of patterns twice close to zero. The range set for each variable is broad enough to generate a wide variety of shapes, yet narrow enough to prevent the blocks from resulting in excessively large garments.

For the generation of the sleeve blocks a different approach has been taken. The main objective was to create sleeves that fit the bodice blocks that they have been created for. Therefore, there is no random component built into the algorithms that define the sleeve points. The sleeve head curve was created using two cubic curves, one for the front and one for the back armhole. To determine the sleeve cap height a series of formulas that calculate the front and back armhole and shoulder lengths for each side of the garment, and others that estimate how much the shoulder and armholes are dropped in relation to the body, were developed. For a particular bodice, it is easy to define rules for the generation of sleeves. However, it proved difficult to determine the rules that define the generation of sleeves for an infinite number of unusually shaped blocks. The final rules generate sleeves that fit the generated bodice blocks but they might need to be altered for an optimal fitting depending on how the blocks are positioned on the body and the type of garment being made.

Results

Following initial experimentation to adjust the ranges of the random variables, the generation and 3D simulation of 24 [Re]gPD blocks were carried out using CLO software. These simulations proved that the overall dimensions of the virtual garments created using blocks generated with [Re]gPD were correct and that a variety of shapes could be achieved. The compatibility of [Re]gPD patterns with various 2D and 3D software, including Adobe Illustrator, Gerber AccuMark, and CLO, was verified by saving the pieces' coordinates as DXF files. These files could be imported into all of the mentioned software without any issues.

Discussion

For the evaluation of the ability of [Re]gPD to generate blocks that can be developed into different types of garments, three sets of blocks were chosen from those presented in Figure 5. The selection was made based on their prospective suitability to be used in the development of one of the following: a vest, a shirt, and a pullover; as well as trying to represent a variety of the different volumes obtained.

In addition to showcasing a variety of garments, these examples aim to illustrate different possible degrees of transformation applied to the initial blocks. Figures 6 to 8 present a visual comparison of the original [Re]gPD blocks and their altered patterns, alongside images of the resulting virtual garments. The shape generated by [Re]gPD is represented as a gray shaded area, while the final patterns are outlined in black.

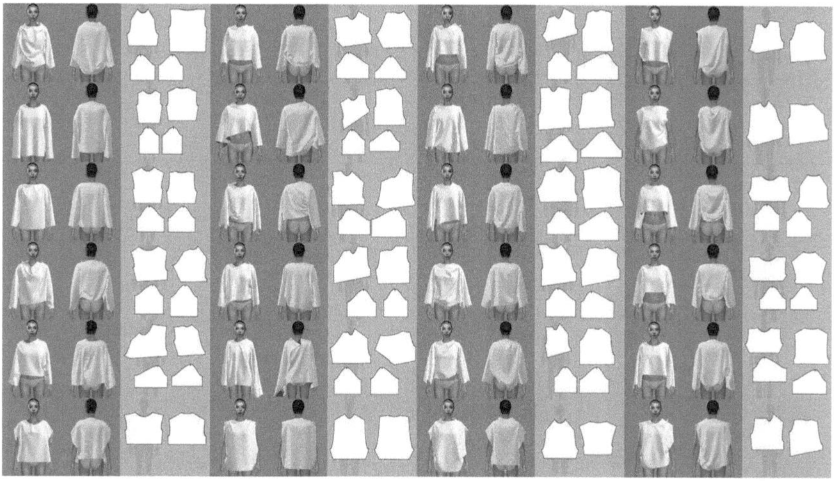

Figure 5. Virtual simulation of twenty-four [Re]gPD blocks.
Image by the author.

In some cases, additional pattern pieces were drafted and incorporated into the garments (vest and shirt), whereas the pullover was created with only minor alterations to the original [Re]gPD blocks. Various methods of fitting and transforming garments are demonstrated, including pleats, gathering, paneling, and darts.

Figure 6 presents a specific example of the proposed working methodology. As observed, asymmetrical bodice blocks were generated, with slight modifications applied to the shoulder and neck areas to improve fit. Additionally, for aesthetic purposes, the pieces were divided into multiple panels, and a button placket was incorporated at the center front, allowing the patterns to be assembled into a vest.

Figure 7 illustrates another example, in which a shirt was created. In this case, the patterns underwent further modifications, utilizing excess fabric on one side of the back to generate an exaggerated volume through the use of darts. An asymmetrical generation with sleeves was selected. The sleeves were subsequently adjusted to more closely resemble traditional shirt sleeves in terms of length and width. This modification was made to establish a contrast between the conventional aesthetic of the sleeves and the unconventional volume of the body.

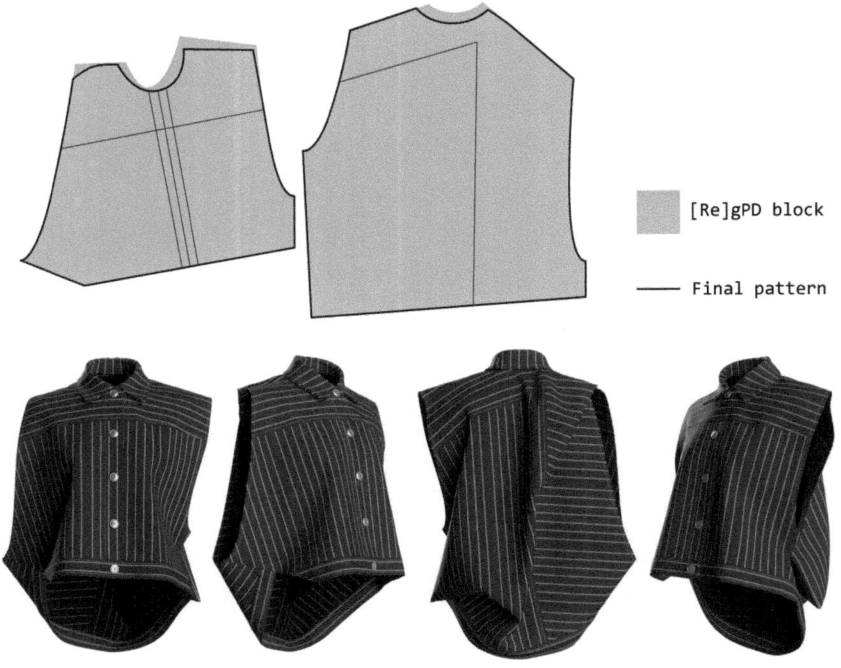

Figure 6. [Re]gPD blocks developed into a virtual vest.
Image by the author.

Finally, Figure 8 presents an example in which a pullover was developed by generating symmetrical bodice pieces and sleeves using [Re]gPD, with minimal modifications applied. The front and back bodice remained unchanged, while the sleeve length and width were adjusted for aesthetic purposes.

Conclusion

This study proposed a generative design framework in which digital technology is used for the development of new creative pattern-cutting methodologies that enhance creativity; it demonstrates that technology can be used in a different way within the discipline, presenting it as a creator and not as a tool to mimic manual ways of doing.

The proposed creative pattern-making methodology challenges the traditional garment design process, as it alters the order of the design and

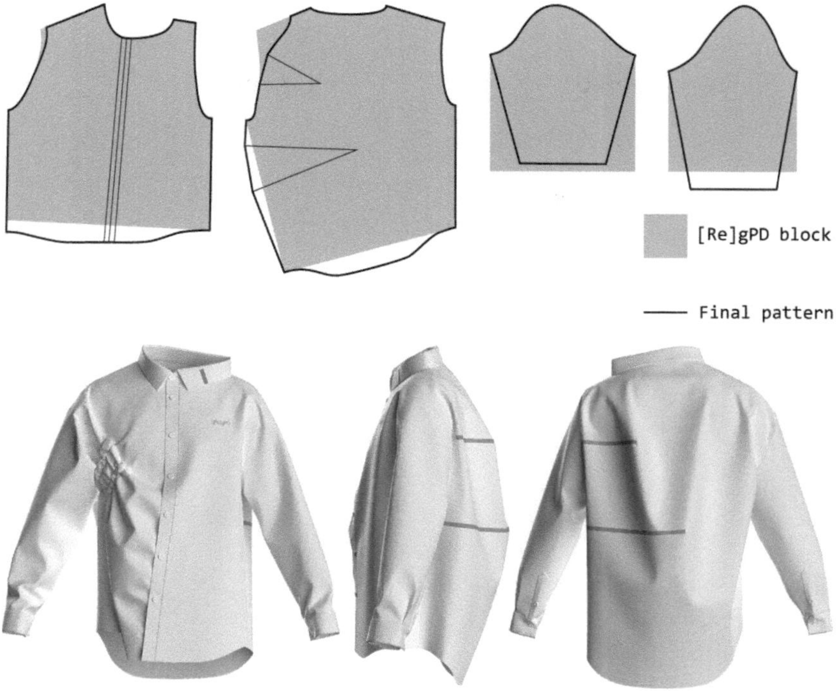

Figure 7. [Re]gPD blocks developed into a virtual shirt.
Image by the author.

development phases of a garment and completely eliminates the lines that traditionally separate the tasks of the designer from those of the pattern maker.

A software called [Re]generative Pattern Design was designed and developed under a design science research methodology (DSRM) as an example of how this framework could be implemented in practice. The software can generate infinite bodice blocks for a single set of measurements.

The three-dimensional shape that [Re]gPD blocks produce when sewn is difficult to envisage by simply looking at the flat shapes. Therefore, although the software generates two-dimensional shapes, it encourages a subsequent 3D draping process. A traditional draping-on-the-stand process could be used, but in this case, a total of 24 sets of blocks were generated with [Re]gPD and virtually simulated to check the correct functioning of [Re]gPD and its interoperability. This allowed to visualize the type of 3D volumes

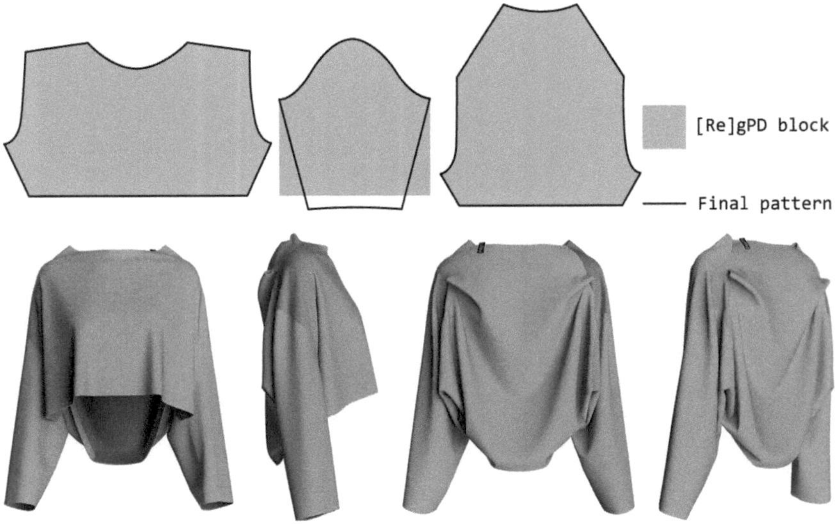

Figure 8. [Re]gPD blocks developed into a virtual pullover.
Image by the author.

that the software is able to generate. Three of those 24 sets of blocks were developed into virtual garments to check the possibilities and limitations of the software.

[Re]gPD was created for pattern cutters and focuses on usability but it is a tool that could facilitate the design process. Although the shapes are generated with some embedded design features, these are meant to be interpreted by the user and the possible interpretations are endless. Any design concept could be applied to them, just as a design concept can be applied to a traditional bodice block. The software does not replace the designer or the pattern cutter, but merges both design and pattern making.

Limitations and future research

This research focused on the design and development of a software that exemplifies the use of digital technology as a key element in the development of innovative creative pattern-cutting methods. The procedures, designed under a DSRM, focused on prototype testing to inform the design activity.

However, it was not within the scope of this project to evaluate [Re]gPD's effect on creativity. Therefore, subsequent testing and evaluation of [Re]gPD is recommended in order to measure how the use of the software impacts on creativity. Future studies could assess this impact in the fashion industry or in an educational context. In a work environment, an evaluation of how the use of [Re]gPD alters the traditional garment design and development process could be carried out. Considering Hardingham's (2016) evidence that alternative teaching approaches to creative pattern cutting can be beneficial for students, research could be undertaken in education to evaluate how this novel approach to pattern making can benefit the students' learning and whether [Re]gPD can help students engage with the discipline.

[Re]gPD could serve as a model for the development of similar systems that fulfill specific business or educational needs. Furthermore, [Re]gPD has the potential to open the way for the development of other digital pattern-cutting methodologies, within or outside the proposed generative design framework, which contribute to the field of innovative pattern cutting.

References

Alvanon. (2018). *Alvanon Standard Global / Women: AlvaFORM*. https://alvanon.com/wp-content/uploads/2018/06/AF-SPECS_ASD-GLOBAL-Women_v4.0__06MAR2015.pdf

Baytar, F. (2018). Apparel CAD patternmaking with 3D simulations: Impact of recurrent use of virtual prototypes on students' skill development. *International Journal of Fashion Design, Technology, and Education, 11*(2), 187–95. https://doi.org/10.1080/17543266.2017.1378731

Calvo Frutos, M. L. (2018). [Re]generative pattern design: A generative digital tool for creative pattern cutting [master's thesis, University of the Arts London, London College of Fashion].

Gregor, S., & Hevner, A. R. (2013). Positioning and presenting design science research for maximum impact. *MIS Quarterly, 37*(2), 337–55.

Hardingham, L. A. (2016). How can a box become a garment? *International Journal of Fashion Design, Technology, and Education, 9*(2), 97–105.

Kalypso & Indiana University Kelley School of Business Center for Education and Research in Retail. (2017). *Adoption of leading product development practices in a digital world*. http://kalypso.com/downloads/media/Retail_Innovation-_A_Study_of_Leading_Product_Development_Practices_27011741.pdf

Kloör, B., Monhof, M., Beverungen, D., & Braäer, S. (2018). Design and evaluation of a model-driven decision support system for repurposing electric vehicle batteries. *European Journal of Information Systems, 27*(2), 171–88. https://doi.org/10.1057/s41303-017-0044-3
Lee, E., & Park, H. (2017). 3D virtual fit simulation technology: Strengths and areas of improvement for increased industry adoption. *International Journal of Fashion Design, Technology, and Education, 10*(1), 59–70. https://doi.org/10.1080/17543266.2016.1194483
Mattila, H. (2016). Digital fashion—how and when? *Tekstil, 65*(9–10), 334–9.
Papahristou, E. (2016). *The effective integration of 3D virtual prototype in the product development process of the textile/clothing industry* [Doctoral dissertation, Technical University of Crete].
Peffers, K., Tuunanen, T., Rothenberger, M. A., & Chatterjee, S. (2007). A design science research methodology for information systems research. *Journal of Management Information Systems, 24*(3), 45–77.
Porterfield, J. A. (2014). *Exploring 3D garment simulation as a prototype validation tool for costume design* [MPhil thesis, North Carolina State University].
Seo, D. (2018). Addressing resistance to 3D virtual prototyping in apparel design and product development. *Apparel*. https://apparelmag.com/addressing-resistance-3d-virtual-prototyping-apparel-design-and-product-development
Vaishnavi, V., Kuechler, W., & Petter, S. (Eds.). (2017). Design science research in information systems. *Association for Information Systems*. http://www.desrist.org/design-research-in-information-systems/
Wang, J. P., & Zhang, W. Y. (2007). An approach to predicting bra cup dart quantity in the 3D virtual environment. *International Journal of Clothing Science and Technology, 19*(5). https://doi.org/10.1108/09556220710819546
Wu, Y. Y., Mok, P. Y., Kwok, Y. L., Fan, J. T., & Xin, J. H. (2011). An investigation on the validity of 3D clothing simulation for garment fit evaluation. In *Proceedings of the IMProVe 2011 International Conference on Innovative Methods in Product Design* (pp. 1–6). http://www.improve2011.it/Full_Paper/99.pdf

The future in the past: technology as an opportunity for fashion heritage conservation

CHAPTER 6

Reverse-Engineering Fashion Objects

Object-based research and 3D reconstruction of paper garments in the collection of ATOPOS CVC

Daphne Mohajer va Pesaran, Martina Ponzoni***

ABSTRACT
The digitization of ephemeral fashion archives is crucial for preserving, providing access to, and studying historical fashion. By converting fragile physical materials into high-resolution digital records, institutions, researchers, and designers can safeguard the knowledge of rare garments, textiles, sketches, and documents from deterioration while making them widely accessible to a global audience. This chapter discusses a documentation and reverse-engineering project related to paper garments using historical research and digital tools. Through a case study of a residency undertaken at ATOPOS CVC, a nonprofit cultural organization in Athens, Greece, the authors explore how digital technologies such as Clo3D can preserve and disseminate knowledge of the material history of fashion and textiles, particularly through the reverse-engineering, 3D rendering, and analysis of paper garments.

Keywords: fashion, archive, paper, 3D replica, reverse-engineering

Introduction

The digitization of fashion archives plays a critical role in preserving and studying historical garments and material culture. By translating fragile and ephemeral physical objects into high-resolution digital records, institutions and researchers can safeguard knowledge embedded in rare garments, textiles, sketches, and documents that are vulnerable to deterioration, while enabling broader access beyond the constraints of physical archives. As Ding and Liang (2024) argue, digital tools are particularly urgent for the reverse-engineering of garments and objects that are too delicate to repair or handle, allowing their material, structural, and technical qualities to be documented and analyzed without further damage. Through processes of digitization, reverse-engineering, and digital recreation, fashion archives can support

* (ORCID: https://orcid.org/0000-0001-5775-1487), RMIT University.
** d_archive, and RMIT University.

research and education, deepen understanding of historical construction techniques, enhance research opportunities, support education, and foster innovation by allowing future generations to explore and learn from past designs, materials, and construction techniques.

Additionally, digitization can contribute to the democratization of fashion history, ensuring that diverse narratives and cultural heritage are preserved and shared beyond the limitations of access to physical archives. Digital methodologies can reveal aspects of garments that are typically inaccessible—such as internal structures, patternmaking, and methods of assembly—thereby expanding historical narratives and shifting attention from designers toward makers and material processes. The Exploding Fashion project, led by Caroline Evans and funded by the Arts and Humanities Research Council (2018–2020), demonstrates this potential through its use of digital storytelling and immersive technologies to make otherwise invisible elements of historic garments perceptible. Evans' initiative focused on the patternmaking involved in producing a garment, thereby reinterpreting historic artifacts and shifting the lens from the designer to the maker. This cultural perspective was experienced using digital interventions, ensuring wider accessibility and public engagement. By using digital storytelling and immersive technologies, the *Exploding Fashion: From 2D to 3D to 3D Animation* project provided new ways of interacting with historical objects, demonstrating the relevance of digital methodologies in fashion heritage preservation and contextualization (Evans, 2025).

This chapter contributes to ongoing discussions on the role of digital technologies in fashion heritage preservation by discussing the documentation and reverse-engineering of paper garments using a hybrid model involving digital skills and object-based historical research. It draws on a case study from a 2024 residency at ATOPOS CVC, a nonprofit cultural organization in Athens, Greece, which houses one of the world's largest archives of garments made from paper. Paper garments present particular challenges for preservation and display due to their extreme fragility and rarity, making them especially well-suited to digital documentation. The research emerged from a collaboration between ATOPOS CVC, Daphne Mohajer va Pesaran, and d_archive, and demonstrates how digital tools can support the analysis, interpretation, and dissemination of vulnerable fashion objects. This reinforces the value of object-based histories in dialogue with emerging digital practices.

Methodology

The integration of digital technologies into heritage preservation has led to innovative approaches in documenting and understanding fashion artifacts. Recent studies have emphasized the importance of digital restoration and reconstruction, particularly for delicate and ephemeral textiles. Ding and Liang's (2024) comprehensive review of the field highlights the emergence of digital methods such as 3D digital reconstruction, digital restoration and virtual display as useful tools for restoring and reconstructing heritage clothing. They discuss various digital techniques and their applications in preserving textile artifacts, and note that "in recent years, three-dimensional (3D) reconstruction of historical clothing, 3D modeling, virtual simulation, and reverse-engineering have become important research hotspots in the fields of clothing and archaeology, demonstrating the feasibility of restoring and inheriting heritage costumes by digital means" (Ding & Liang 2024). Their findings highlight the need for further methodological advancements in this field.

The digitization of cultural heritage in fashion and textiles encompasses several technologies, including laser scanning or photogrammetry and digital rendering using CAD software. These methods facilitate the accurate documentation and analysis of heritage objects, including fashion artifacts, thereby aiding in their preservation and study.

This chapter discusses a collaborative project with researcher Daphne Mohajer va Pesaran and members of d_archive, a platform for digital fashion. The aim of the project was to digitize very delicate and damaged historical pieces, thereby making them accessible to a wider audience and also reverse-engineer them to recreate their original state without the damage present on the pieces.

This research project was undertaken at ATOPOS CVC, which is a unique cultural organization based in Athens, Greece, dedicated to exploring and promoting the expression and adornment of the human body through innovative and unconventional approaches. Founded in 2003 by Stamos Fafalios and Vassilis Zidianakis, ATOPOS CVC derives its name from the ancient Greek word *άτοπος* meaning strange, eccentric, or unclassifiable qualities that reflect the organization's commitment to challenging traditional norms and embracing the unusual in visual culture.

The organization's mission is deeply rooted in interdisciplinary collaboration, bringing together diverse fields such as art, architecture, fashion, and anthropology. This convergence of disciplines allows ATOPOS CVC to foster a dynamic platform where contemporary visual culture is researched, curated, and celebrated. By focusing on the body as a canvas for artistic and cultural expression, ATOPOS CVC positions itself at the intersection of historical exploration and forward-thinking innovation.

A central element of ATOPOS CVC's work is its extensive and eclectic collection of design objects, particularly its remarkable archive of paper garments. These garments, ranging from 1960s disposable paper dresses to traditional Japanese clothing and contemporary experimental paper designs, form the core of ATOPOS CVC's research and curatorial practice. The collection not only serves as a resource for scholarly investigation but also as a catalyst for creative exploration, inspiring new interpretations and applications of historical materials.

Through residencies, exhibitions, and public programs, ATOPOS CVC engages with artists, designers, and researchers from around the world. The ATOPOS CVC collection was developed to stimulate research into the culture of dress and the history of design, focusing on innovative and less familiar themes (Pichou, 2020). ATOPOS CVC has a library, a curatorial practice, and a residency program to achieve this aim—it also has an archive of design objects that were the focus of this fellowship and the reason the authors conducted a residency on site. At the core of the ATOPOS CVC collection is a collection of roughly 400 1960s disposable paper dresses, produced during a 'fad' for disposability at the height of the optimism of the space age. In addition to these pieces, the collection houses paper clothing artifacts that stretch back into history, and some more recent from contemporary fashion designers and artists. The former includes paper Japanese garments, and the latter includes experimental paper fashion designs from Martin Margiela, A. F. Vandevorst, and others.

Pieces for digitization were selected based on their rarity and in discussion between the co-founder and artistic director of ATOPOS, Vassilis Zidianakis,

Mohajer va Pesaran, and d_archive. To reverse-engineer the garments, the researchers used primary object-based research (Mida & Kim, 2015), secondary literature, contextual and historical review in tandem with digital restoration and rendering. Finally, they offered a public workshop to discuss some of the initial findings of the fellowship with a local community of artists and fashion and textile designers. Mohajer va Pesaran approached each piece from a cultural, structural, and material point of view. She examined each piece physically and provided written descriptions that encompassed the production methods, potential context, and materiality. These descriptions were added to the digital archive of reverse engineered garments on the d_archive website.

The d_archive team approached the pieces in the ATOPOS collection from a technical point of view, reverse-engineering the patterns by taking detailed photographs and measurements, then using traditional pattern-making techniques to collect the necessary data from each piece. This information was then imported into a 3D fashion design CAD software with patternmaking and cloth simulation capabilities, to build 3D replicas of each piece. Each fabric or material was also photographed in high resolution for later use in reconstructing PBR (physically based rendering) textures for the 3D replica. Surface texture and surface designs such as handwriting and motifs were photographed, as well as small parts such as buttons and trims were also measured to allow their 3D reconstruction in the CAD software.

Case studies: digitized paper garments from the ATOPOS collection

The pieces studied are as follows: a set of *tabi* shoe patterns, a *sodenashi* (vest), a *kappa* (cape), a woven kimono overcoat, a padded *hanten*, a kimono made of recycled ledger paper, and a Filipino military cape. Three of the item descriptions are included below.

Kimono made of recycled ledger paper

This rare piece is a full kimono made from recycled paper from a *daifuku-cho* (accounting book). The kimono consists of a single layer and was likely worn to provide warmth or collect sweat beneath an outer kimono. Made from recycled accounting books, fragments of text such as "quote" and "revised" can still be seen on its surface. It shows some signs of staining, and there may be evidence of repair work. The garment is both hand-sewn and glued, suggesting careful assembly, and over time, it has likely developed natural wrinkles without the typical *momigami* (wrinkled paper) treatment, as it was likely made never to be seen. This piece offers a glimpse into the resourceful techniques employed in its creation (see Figure 9).

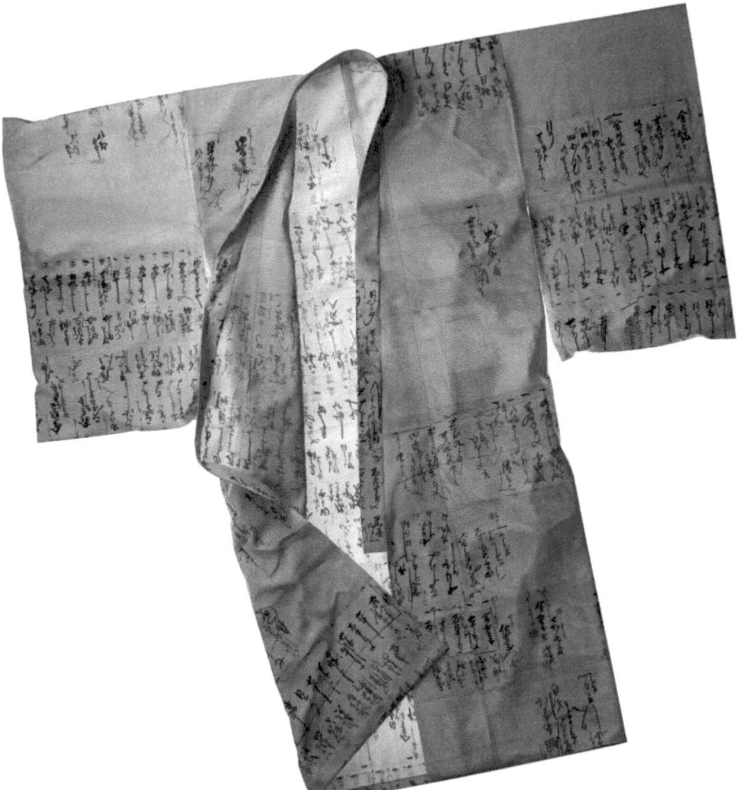

Figure 9. Render of 3D replica of kimono made of recycled ledger paper. *d_archive 2024.*

Padded hanten with bamboo motif

A padded *hanten* made of printed handmade washi paper. A *hanten* (袢纏) is a traditional Japanese short winter coat worn over kimono or casual clothing for warmth. It is a unisex garment with a history dating back to the Edo period (1603–1868). *Hanten* are typically made from thick, quilted cotton fabric and are characterized by a straight-cut body, wide sleeves, and a simple collar. This garment, which is a padded or *wata-iri hanten*, often has a padded interior for insulation, making it ideal for colder weather. The entire garment is padded, likely with cotton or silk wadding. The design of a *hanten* is similar to that of a *haori*, but it is more casual and functional. While a haori can be formal and part of ceremonial attire, a *hanten* is primarily worn over other clothes at home or in more relaxed settings. Traditionally, it was used by commoners as a practical, everyday garment, and it continues to be popular in modern Japan for its comfort and warmth in colder seasons.

This *hanten* features a velvet collar, applied unevenly at the center front, a lining, padding, and is made of small sheets of paper. The entire garment has been sewn by hand. *Hanten* often feature simple, bold patterns or family crests, as does this example held in the collection at ATOPOS CVC. Three different printed papers have been used in the construction of this garment: The printed blue outer paper, the brown floral-printed paper facing the neck and lining the sleeves, and the printed paper used to bind the opening at the hem of the side seams and the armpit. The orientation and placement of the motifs indicates that the sheets were printed before being pieced together to make a bolt of paper "cloth." This "cloth" was then cut to make the *hanten*.

The sheets of paper composing the outer shell have been stenciled/printed in blue with floral bamboo and lily motifs and a striking right-slanting diagonal stripe composed of a grouping of abstract shapes. These sheets have been glued together, likely using a rice or seaweed-based glue. Some glued seams have been printed, leading to the conclusion that single sheets were attached to form a roll of paper, which was then printed. In some areas, the patterns don't match, though, so perhaps this garment was made of leftovers (see Figure 10).

Some staining appears on the paper, but overall, the vibrancy of the blue pigment remains bright. The print, interestingly, seems to not have a top or bottom; it has no determined orientation, as one of the two rows of bamboo printed on each sheet grows according with gravity, and the other row is upside-down. This is a clever and useful way of designing a print as it means it can be used continuously in either direction, especially in the case of a kimono-style garment that has no shoulder seam and the fabric is used continuously from front, across the shoulder, to the back. A single-orientation motif would appear upside-down on the back.

It was purchased from Morita antiques, a well-established antique shop in the Aoyama neighborhood of Tokyo.

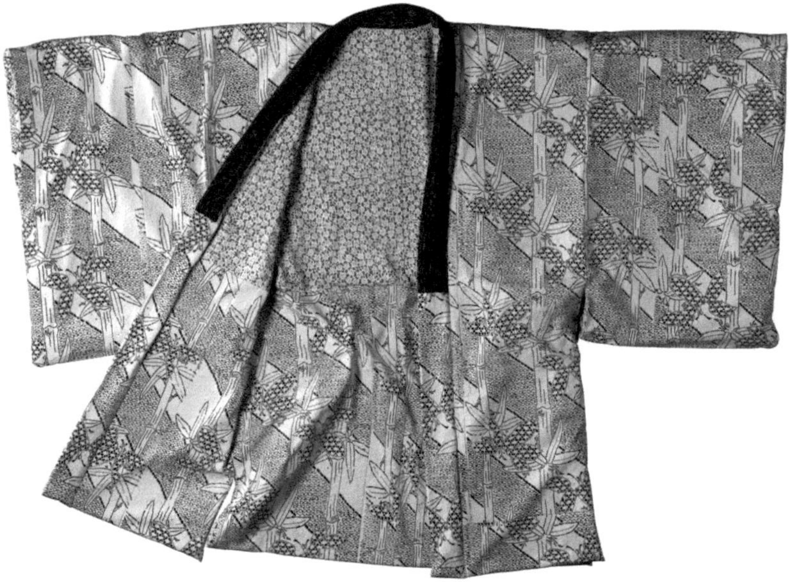

Figure 10. Render of 3D replica of Padded hanten with bamboo motif. *d_archive 2024.*

1960s paper caper dresses

These two 1960s paper dresses by Scott Paper Company were part of a novelty line introduced in 1966 as a marketing experiment in disposable consumer goods. They were designed to match the company's current line of disposal tableware at the time and offered to customers who sent in a coupon and $1. Made from "paper," that was really a cellulose and rayon material called

Dura-Weave that more closely resembles disposable facemasks, these dresses were intended to be inexpensive, single-use garments. The collection included two main styles: a red bandana print that captured the playful, bohemian spirit of the decade and a striking black-and-white optical print, which resonated with the decade's pop-art and mod fashion influences. These dresses ignited a short-lived fad in mainly the USA and the UK for printed disposable "paper" dresses, and they represent the somewhat short-sighted optimism of the Space Age that directly contrasts with a twenty-first century trajectory away from irresponsible disposability and instead toward circularity and knowledge of material origins (see Figure 11).

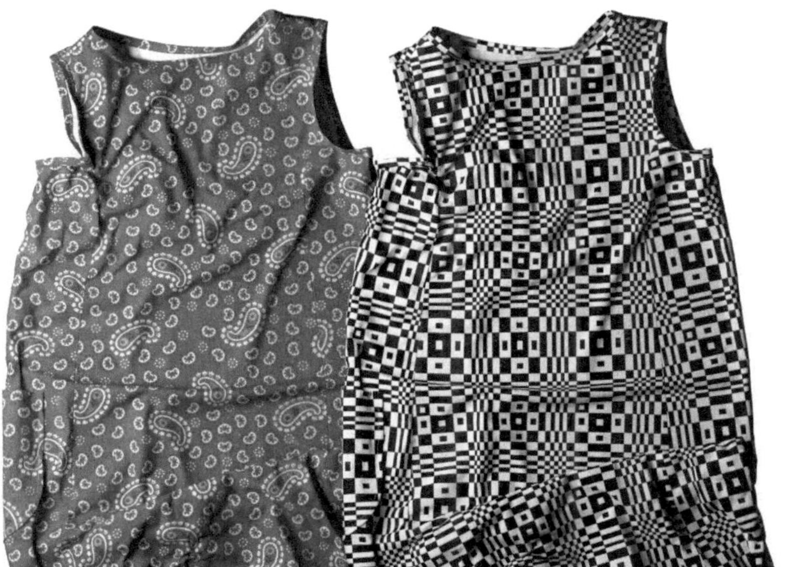

Figure 11. Render of 3D replica of two Scott Paper dresses.
d_archive 2024.

Public engagement and knowledge dissemination: the workshop experience

The researchers were invited to conduct a public workshop to disseminate some of the findings of the fellowship and residency. This was done over the course of one day, and 15 participants were selected to participate. The workshop first introduced the paper garments digitized during the residency with the addition of one from the collection of the National Gallery of Victoria in Melbourne, Australia. Participants were invited to learn about the garments and the research process by trying to reverse-engineer them themselves using cheap paper. This process allowed participants to understand what a replica means (how accurate it should be and what characteristics to record and reproduce), the material limitations and possibilities of paper (by examining the physical artifact and manipulating the digital object), and understand the research methods employed by the researchers. The participants were split into two groups, one working from the digital rendering of the NGV archival piece, and one observing a physical garment in the ATOPOS collection, which in this case was the ledger-book kimono. Participants working from the digital rendering spent their time trying to accurately create a half-size reproduction, while those working from the real artifact spent their time reinterpreting and recreating the surface of the ledger-book kimono as a textile.

Discussion: the role of digital technologies in augmenting fashion heritage

Digitizing cultural heritage objects offers benefits in preservation, accessibility, and education. The availability of high-resolution 3D replicas minimizes the need for physical handling, thereby reducing wear and tear on delicate artifacts and ensuring their longevity. These digital surrogates can be disseminated globally, allowing scholars, students, and the public to access and study cultural assets without geographical constraints. In this way, digital archives serve as resources for educational initiatives, enabling interactive learning experiences that can enhance cultural appreciation and understanding.

A structured approach to digitization is crucial for ensuring efficiency and long-term usability. *Flowchart for 3D Digitisation*, introduced by Debra Knoop from Modemuze during the European Fashion Heritage Association

Members Workshop 2024 on 3D Digitisation, proposes a systematic framework that can guide institutions to choose the right tools for their needs, ensuring 3D fidelity and data longevity. These structured workflows are particularly beneficial for smaller archives with limited resources, helping them navigate the technical and logistical challenges of 3D digitization (Knoop & Ernst, 2024).

However, all digitization processes can present challenges. Technical limitations can impede the accurate capture of an object's intricate details or tactility, leading to potential losses in fidelity. The process is often resource-intensive, requiring specialized equipment and expertise, which can strain institutional budgets. Additionally, the rapid evolution of digital technologies poses risks to the longevity of digital formats, necessitating ongoing efforts in digital preservation to prevent obsolescence.

Further, the connection of traditional craftsmanship with digital innovation has opened new avenues for preserving and reimagining fashion heritage. This synergy allows for the documentation of endangered crafts, providing a platform for their transmission to future generations. 3D tools allow us to digitally restore garments and accessories to what is assumed to be their original state, without having to intervene on the physical piece. In case of mistakes or newfound information around the original piece, 3D replicas can be updated accordingly. This iterative restoration process opens new possibilities for restoration efforts, without putting at risk the physical artifact.

However, the digital translation of historical pieces alone is not sufficient—so-called digital craftsmanship techniques play a crucial role in ensuring the accuracy, artistry, and depth of 3D replicas. Just as traditional artisans refine their skills over years of practice, digital creators must master techniques such as precise 3D modeling, texture reconstruction, and virtual tailoring to replicate the intricacies of physical objects. The process of reverse-engineering fashion patterns, refining digital drapery, and simulating fabric behavior requires a level of skill that mirrors traditional handcraft, and it is based on its knowledge. Without this expertise, digital reproductions risk appearing overly mechanical or losing the nuanced details that define heritage artifacts. The digital practice will not replace craftsmanship but rather evolve as a new form of artistry alongside it—one that demands the same dedication, refinement, and attention to detail as its physical counterpart.

Conclusion

This study highlights the significance of digital technologies in fashion heritage preservation, emphasizing their role in recording, reconstructing, and disseminating knowledge about historical garments. Through the examination of various digital techniques, including 3D modeling and virtual reconstructions, the research has demonstrated how these tools can aid in preserving fragile and ephemeral textiles. Two additional pieces from the archive were recorded for future digitization, despite their original use and context being unknown. The potential for digital manipulation on the body—or on the body of a horse, in the case of one item—presents new avenues for understanding their historical significance, particularly as their fragile nature prevents physical experimentation.

Beyond the immediate implications for textile conservation, this study contributes to broader discussions on the intersections of fashion heritage and digital technologies. The ability to digitally archive and manipulate garments provides researchers and the public with unprecedented access to historical artifacts, ensuring their continued relevance in contemporary discourse. Furthermore, such advancements pave the way for more sustainable approaches to heritage preservation, minimizing the physical degradation of delicate materials while maximizing their educational and cultural impact.

The authors remain committed to advancing the field of digital heritage preservation, fostering collaborations between fashion historians, digital technologists, and cultural institutions. By promoting innovative methodologies and interdisciplinary partnerships, they aim to ensure that historical garments are not only preserved but also remain active components of cultural dialogue. Their ongoing efforts seek to bridge the gap between traditional conservation techniques and emerging digital tools, reinforcing the importance of accessibility and engagement in heritage studies.

Finally, this research highlights the essential role of interdisciplinary collaboration in fashion heritage preservation. The intersection of digital technologies, material studies, and historical analysis creates a dynamic space for innovation, enabling new ways of interpreting and engaging with the past. As the field continues to evolve, the integration of diverse expertise will be crucial in shaping the future of heritage conservation, ensuring that fashion's rich history is safeguarded for generations to come.

References

Ding, Q-K. & Liang, H-E. (2024). Digital restoration and reconstruction of heritage clothing: a review. *Heritage Science 12*(225).

Evans, C. (2025, May 2). *Exploding fashion: Cutting, constructing, and thinking through things*. Retrieved from https://gtr.ukri.org/projects?ref=AH%2FP009085%2F1

Knoop, D., & Ernst, M. (Eds.). (2024). *Unlocking fashion heritage: A manual for digitising collections.* Modemuze and Unlocking Fashion Heritage Project. https://modemuze.nl/sites/default/files/2024-12/MM%20Flowchart%20Digitalisering%20v06.pdf

Mida, I. E. & Kim, A. (2015). *The dress detective: A practical guide to object-based research in fashion*. Bloomsbury Academic.

Pichou, M. (2020) The ATOPOS cvc RIPPING Project: A 'new' life for dress objects? *Costume* 54 (2), 242–64.

CHAPTER 7

Uncovering Hidden Heritage

Digitizing the Maltese traditional costume for cultural preservation

*Lorraine Portelli**

ABSTRACT
Digitization plays a vital role in uncovering and disseminating the often-hidden knowledge embedded in traditional costume heritage, enhancing accessibility for researchers, textile professionals, and the general public. This paper highlights the importance of digitally preserving one of Malta's iconic traditional garments, the *Għonnella*. Through digital preservation and analysis, deeper insights are gained into the garment's historical significance and cultural context.

The intricate materials, patterns, and techniques employed in the creation of historical garments offer significant value for historians, academics, and designers, serving as a rich source of inspiration for contemporary and future design practices. This study adopts a multi-method approach, combining physical artifact analysis with advanced 2D and 3D digital imaging techniques. High-resolution imaging captures the fine details of construction, patterning, and material composition, while 3D modeling and digital photography facilitate accurate visualization and scaling. These tools enable reinterpretation, preservation, and innovation in the field of fashion and textile design.

Keywords: digitalization, 2D and 3D imaging, X-ray imaging, Għonnella, traditional costume, cultural preservation

Introduction

Historical garments are rich cultural artifacts that offer designers and artists a valuable source of inspiration and innovation. These garments embody the aesthetics, craftsmanship, and socio-cultural values of their time, providing insights into materials, construction techniques, and symbolic meanings. By studying historical costumes, contemporary designers can reinterpret traditional motifs, silhouettes, and textile techniques to create new, contextually enriched designs that bridge past and present (Taylor, 2002). This process not only fosters creative innovation but also promotes cultural continuity and appreciation for heritage (McSweeney et al., 2025).

* University of Malta.

Studying fragile traditional costumes can be difficult, and in some cases, nearly impossible, even for fashion and costume researchers (Csanák, 2019). An increasing number of scholars have explored the virtual restoration of traditional costumes within this field of study (Kuzmichev et al., 2018; Moskvin et al., 2019).

Digital documentation and archiving of costumes are vital for studying materials that have deteriorated or are at risk of being lost. The adoption of 2D and 3D digital technologies has become increasingly prevalent in efforts to preserve cultural heritage. The transition from 2D to 3D digitization further enhances detail and accuracy, offering more comprehensive preservation, though it entails methodological and resource challenges (Cassar, 2025). Moreover, reliable digital assets—including high-precision 3D models—serve as crucial preservation tools, ensuring cultural objects remain accessible even if the physical originals deteriorate or perish.

Digital technologies enable researchers to closely study how a garment interacts with the human form, including its drape, volume, structural elements, color, materials, embroidery techniques, and methods of construction. Furthermore, digital archives make traditional garments from diverse cultures accessible to a global audience, allowing them to be explored and studied anytime and from anywhere (Villareal, 2020).

To achieve successful digitalization, it is crucial to have a well-defined vision of the intended outcome. A fundamental step in this process involves exploring various digitalization methods and assessing how they align with the specific objectives (Mulder, 2024).

In recent years, advancements in 3D imaging have significantly enhanced the study of traditional garments. Researchers now digitally reconstruct historical clothing, enabling the recovery of lost elements and the integration of new design features. High-precision 3D scanning technologies, particularly structured-light and laser scanning, facilitate the creation of detailed digital replicas, which can be used to replace damaged or missing components of original garments—revealing previously obscured construction techniques and structural nuances (Żyła et al., 2021). Moreover, through virtual restoration and 3D modeling, scholars can simulate how garments originally appeared, including their drape, fit, and decorative details, offering deeper insights into historical fabrication practices and enabling informed conservation and reinterpretation efforts (Costello et al., 2023).

Digital preservation through 2D and 3D technologies plays a vital role in safeguarding cultural artifacts while keeping traditional costumes intact within archival collections. By creating high-fidelity 3D models, conservators can evaluate the effects of various preservation methods and environmental conditions—such as temperature, humidity, and light exposure—on textile materials, in ways that would be unfeasible with the original, delicate garments (Ilies, et al., 2020). Moreover, these digital records serve as invaluable references for restoring deteriorated or damaged pieces, ensuring precision and historical accuracy during reconstruction.

The Għonnella, also referred to as the faldetta, is a traditional Maltese garment recognized for its distinctive shape and complex construction. Its evolution spanned centuries, gradually adopting its unique form through influences from various cultural and historical elements. Despite its significance, there remains a limited body of research on this extraordinary costume, making its study particularly valuable for understanding Malta's sartorial and social history. The Għonnella featured a voluminous, cape-like covering that extended over the head and shoulders, draping down to ankle length. Its structure was reinforced with materials such as whalebone and thick cardboard, providing it with a rigid yet elegant appearance. Initially, the garment was predominantly black or dark in color, commonly worn by women across different social classes (Portelli et al., 2024).

A defining characteristic of this attire was its upper half, which was stiffly constructed to maintain its distinctive shape. The circular frame, created through a combination of cardboard and whalebone, gave the garment its recognizable silhouette. This unique construction not only influenced the way the Għonnella was worn but also contributed to its practicality, providing protection from the sun while maintaining a sense of modesty and elegance (Portelli et al., 2024).

To date, the *Għonnella* has never undergone a formal process of digitization. Despite its cultural and historical significance as a symbol of Maltese identity, this traditional garment has remained largely undocumented in digital formats. The absence of digital preservation means that access to detailed visual and structural information about the *Għonnella*—such as its construction techniques, fabric composition, and decorative elements—has been extremely limited. This lack of digitization not only hinders academic research and public awareness but also poses a risk to the long-term preservation of the garment, especially as physical artifacts are susceptible to deterioration over time. Digitizing the *Għonnella* for the first time represents a crucial step toward safeguarding its legacy and making it accessible to a broader audience, including future generations of researchers, designers, and cultural historians.

The preservation and digitalization of the Għonnella are crucial for safeguarding Malta's rich textile heritage. Given its intricate design and historical relevance, efforts to study, document, and digitally reconstruct the garment can provide deeper insights into its cultural significance. By utilizing modern technology, such as 3D modeling and virtual exhibitions, researchers and historians can offer new perspectives on the Għonnella's construction, societal role, and aesthetic evolution. These advancements ensure that future generations can appreciate and engage with this traditional Maltese costume, even if physical examples become increasingly rare.

This research seeks to enhance understanding, promote awareness, and preserve the Għonnella, a traditional Maltese garment, as an important part of cultural heritage. It also aims to examine the unique features of this historical attire. To achieve new insights into the Għonnella, object-based research methods and digitalization techniques were employed. This paper presents the findings from the digital documentation of the costume, covering its materials, production techniques, and distinctive characteristics.

Methodology

Prior to the digitization process, a thorough analysis of the *Għonnella* was conducted to examine the materials used, its sewing construction techniques, and details that were not immediately visible. To facilitate this investigation, a worn and damaged *Għonnella* was acquired at an auction, allowing for its deconstruction in order to document and understand its components thoroughly. This initial step was essential for informing the subsequent stages of the project, including the digitization of the garment's patterns.

A 1920s Għonnella donated for the scope of the study was used for the digitalization process. Accurate measurement of the *Għonnella*, followed by its digitization, during which technical sketches and patterns were digitally developed using Adobe Illustrator (2023 and 2024). To investigate the garment's construction techniques non-invasively, X-ray imaging was also utilized (Yahaghi et al., 2024). The analysis of the garment's patterns enabled the creation of digital replicas, which were archived for documentation and preservation purposes.

The creation of 2D patterns

The pattern-making process for the Għonnella began with the creation of full-scale templates on paper and cardboard. Precise measurements were taken directly from the original garment to ensure accuracy in scaling the patterns. The Għonnella, which includes the fabric of the headpiece and six supporting cardboard elements, along with the fabric back piece, were carefully outlined at full scale. These physical patterns served as the foundation for developing digital 2D versions using Adobe Illustrator (AI) (2023).

A comprehensive digital pattern of the Għonnella was created, incorporating all individual components within a single large layout (see Figure 12). Different colors were assigned to distinguish the various cardboard elements, ensuring clarity in the pattern structure. Additionally, multiple layers were utilized within AI to facilitate easy identification and organization of each pattern piece. The finalized 2D patterns were saved in both AI and PDF formats for documentation and further use.

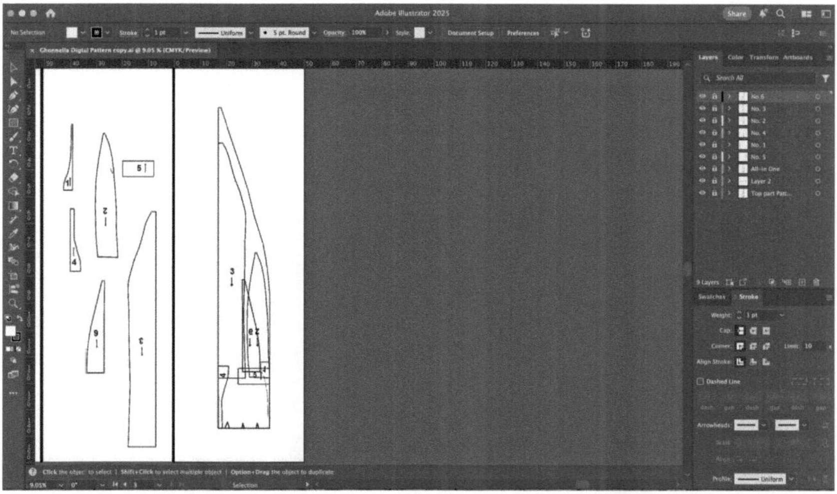

Figure 12. Adobe Illustrator (2023) was used to create the 2D patterns of the Għonnella.

Image by the author.

To ensure precision in the digitization process, the patterns were printed using a plotter to produce full-scale hard copies. These printed versions were then compared against the original garment to verify that the measurements and proportions were accurately transferred. This validation step was essential in confirming the reliability of the digital patterns, ensuring that they faithfully represented the original Għonnella's construction.

Since the Għonnella is made up of multiple layers of thick materials, X-ray imaging (see Figure 13) was utilized to thoroughly examine its construction. The main objective was to determine the composition of the headpiece and uncover the distinctive techniques used in its assembly. X-ray imaging is a highly effective method for researchers, as it allows them to see beneath an object's surface, revealing concealed details about its internal structure, material composition, and craftsmanship (Pantea et al., 2023).

During the imaging process, X-rays pass through the object, with different materials absorbing the radiation at varying levels. Materials with higher density absorb more radiation, creating shadowed areas, while the remaining radiation that penetrates the object forms an image on the film positioned behind it (Victoria and Albert Museum, 2018). This technique provided valuable insight into the hidden layers of the Għonnella's structure.

The X-ray imaging was conducted at the Metropolia University of Applied Sciences in Helsinki, Finland, using a Shimadzu MobileArt Eco (Shimadzu, Japan) system. The scanning parameters were set at 40 kV and 2.0 mAs, with a scanning distance of 90 cm to ensure precise and detailed imaging of the garment's internal layers.

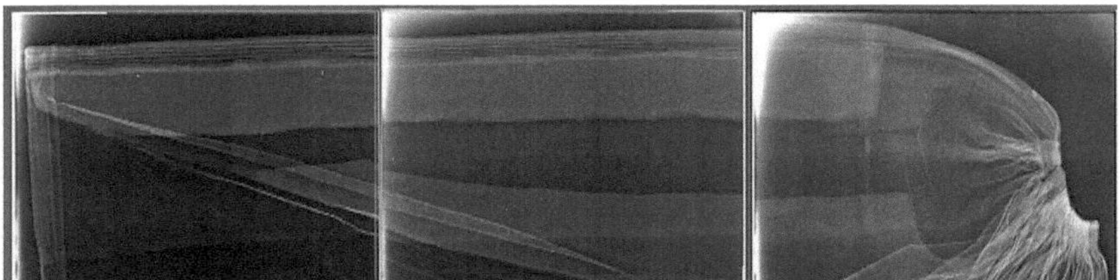

Figure 13. X-ray image of the Għonnella.
Metropolia University of Applied Sciences.

3D photogrammetry

Another digitalization process was conducted on the Għonnella using 3D photogrammetry, a technique that involves capturing a series of high-resolution images from multiple perspectives around the object. These images are then processed and combined to generate a detailed three-dimensional model, which reveals essential information about the costume's physical characteristics and structure (Saiki et al., 2017; Ch'ng et al., 2018). This method of creating 3D models significantly enhances access to culturally significant costumes, enabling their examination by a wide range of individuals globally. Artists, educators, students, and the general public can now explore and study these objects of cultural heritage remotely, expanding the potential for learning and appreciation across different disciplines and geographical locations.

The 3D photogrammetry (see Figure 14) of the Għonnella was developed through a collaborative effort between a specialized team from the Conservation and Digitalisation Department at Heritage Malta. To facilitate the process, the Għonnella was carefully placed on a mannequin specifically created to provide additional support, ensuring the costume maintained its shape and structure. A series of high-resolution photographs were captured from multiple angles around the costume to gather all the necessary visual data. Subsequently, a software tool was then used to process these images

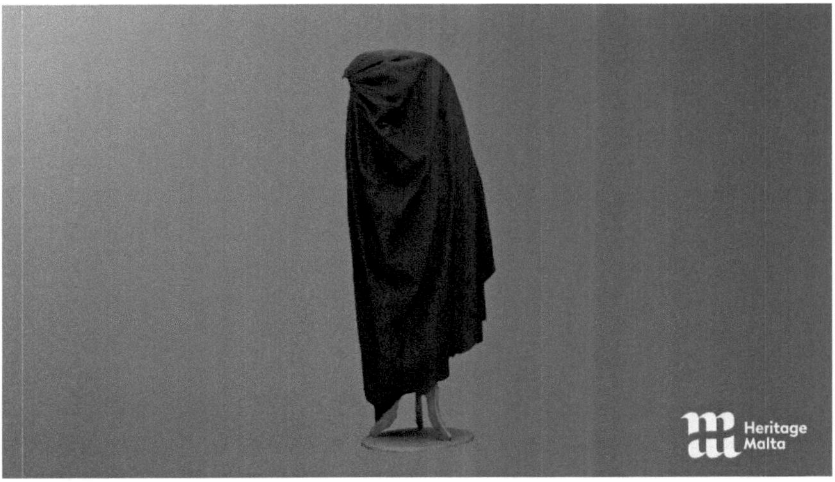

Figure 14. 3D Photogrammetry of the Għonnella.
The Conservation and Digitalisation Department at Heritage Malta, Kalkara.

and create a detailed 360-degree digital 3D model of the Għonnella, allowing for a comprehensive and immersive virtual representation of the costume (Politecnico di Milano, 2023).

CLO 3D

The integration of sophisticated digital technologies in fashion design boosts both accuracy and efficiency. The design software commonly used in the field generally falls into two main categories. First, there are professional auxiliary drawing tools like CAD (Computer-Aided Design) software, known for their strong computational power and seamless integration capabilities. These tools are indispensable in key aspects of fashion design such as garment creation, pattern scaling, and virtual fitting. With CAD, designers can better control production costs, enhance precision, and minimize the errors often associated with traditional hand-drawn methods.

The second category includes multidimensional image editing software, which complements CAD systems by offering advanced tools for image manipulation, color application, and garment visualization. Programs like CLO 3D and Photoshop are widely used in this area, particularly in the later stages of design, helping designers bring their ideas to life with refined visuals and detailed renderings. Moreover, 3D fitting simulations provide valuable insights into how a garment behaves on the body, enabling designers to evaluate both static and dynamic aspects of their creations before production (Cao & Wang, 2023).

Additionally, CLO 3D software (CLO Virtual Fashion, 2024) was employed to visualize how the Għonnella would appear when worn (see Figure 15). This advanced virtual fashion design platform allows researchers to examine garment structure, fit, and motion using a digital avatar, providing valuable insights into its real-world appearance and behavior. The primary goal was to closely examine the Għonnella through its virtual representation. To begin, the 2D patterns of the Għonnella were imported into the CLO 3D software, which serves as a digital workspace for garment creation. These 2D patterns were then mapped onto the digital avatar, effectively transforming the virtual figure into a representation of the traditional Maltese national costume. This process allowed for a detailed analysis of the costume's appearance, functionality, and behavior in a virtual environment, offering insights into its fit and how it would interact with the wearer's movements.

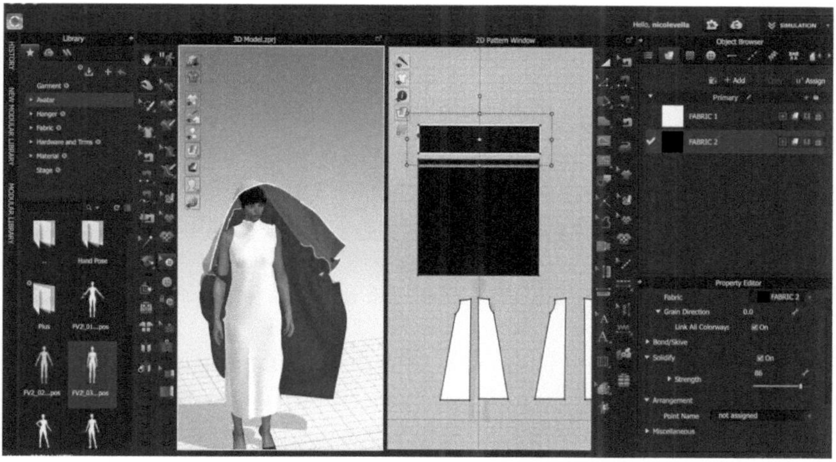

Figure 15. Digital recreation process of the Għonnella in CLO 3D.
Image by the author.

Europeana and Google Arts & Culture

Europeana, the European Union's digital platform for cultural heritage, and Google Arts & Culture were utilized to showcase and promote the digital cultural heritage of the Għonnella, ensuring wider accessibility and engagement with this unique aspect of Maltese history. By leveraging digital technology, these two platforms serve as a bridge between cultural heritage and modern audiences, allowing researchers, educators, heritage professionals, and history enthusiasts to explore and gain fresh insights into historical artifacts.

This initiative plays a vital role in preserving and disseminating cultural knowledge by offering a vast collection of digitized materials from museums, libraries, and archives across Europe. Europeana collaborates with over 2,000 institutions, providing an extensive and diverse digital repository that spans various cultural disciplines. Through this platform, historical garments such as the Għonnella can be analyzed in detail, fostering a deeper understanding of tailoring, societal influences, and the evolution of fashion.

Moreover, the Europeana platform encourages interactive learning and research by integrating digital tools that enhance engagement. Users can access high-resolution images, historical documents, and 3D representations, allowing them to examine artifacts from multiple perspectives. This approach not only supports academic studies but also makes heritage more accessible to the general public, inspiring new interpretations and creative applications.

In addition to the 3D photogrammetry video, four high-resolution digital patterns in JPEG format were uploaded on the Europeana platform. These digital files provide a detailed look at the garment's design and structure, making them useful tools for scholars, fashion designers, educators and students. The designs disclose the intricate procedures and materials used to create the Għonnella, allowing the study of this costume accurately. Three high-resolution X-ray images of the costume were also uploaded on Europeana.

By incorporating the Għonnella into this digital archive, its historical significance is safeguarded for future generations, ensuring that this traditional Maltese garment continues to be recognized and appreciated globally. Through initiatives like Europeana, cultural heritage is not only preserved but also revitalized, enabling people to connect with history in innovative and meaningful ways (Europeana, n.d.).

Findings

The upcoming section presents the findings of a detailed analysis of the Għonnella, focusing on its textile structure, construction techniques, and overall design. These analyses involve a thorough examination of the materials and construction methods employed in its creation. The findings offer valuable insights into the complex design elements and techniques involved in the making of the Għonnella, highlighting both its functional and aesthetic dimensions. It seeks to provide a comprehensive understanding of the garment's composition, and the methods used in its creation.

Technical drawings

A thorough investigation of the garment's construction and the techniques employed in its design and stitching was essential for understanding its elaborated details. The technical drawing highlights the distinctive characteristics of the Għonnella, such as the use of pin tucks and tightly gathered fabric, which contribute to the costume's volume and shape. Pin tucks are decorative features that create narrow, parallel folds in the fabric, often used to add texture or structure to a garment. The findings along with the technical image of the Għonnella, is presented in Table 2.

Table 2. Features and technical drawing of the Għonnella

Measures (cm)	Materials and techniques
Length: 1.50 Width: 180: double width of fabric (90 + 90)	Fabric: 100 % corded silk. Mercerized cotton and silk thread. Hem: blind catch stitch. Pin tuck with inserted whalebone.

Source: Lorraine Portelli (personal archives)

Four or five pin tucks were machine stitched along the outer edges, producing a crisp, firm border. Achieving the precise effect of these pin tucks required consistent, even topstitching, ensuring uniformity throughout. Additionally, strips of whalebone were carefully inserted into the delicate folds of the pin tucks, a detail that is clearly revealed in the X-ray image (see Figure 13). The combination of the pin tucks and the whalebones not only add structural integrity to the costume but also enhances its flexibility and texture, creating both visual interest and dimensionality in the overall design. These elements are crucial in giving the Għonnella its characteristic form and aesthetic appeal.

The gathered section of the Għonnella is a defining and intricate element of the costume. To achieve the desired fullness and volume in this area, five horizontal rows of stitching were carefully sewn across the fabric using a robust cotton thread. This thread was specifically selected for its strength and resilience, ensuring it could endure the tension exerted during the gathering process without breaking. The stitching lines were essential in controlling the fabric's shape and volume, and they played a key role in structuring the garment.

The gathering itself was performed by hand, requiring significant precision and skill. The process involved making small, evenly spaced stitches along the fabric's width, with each stitch placed deliberately to maintain uniformity across the entire section. These hand-sewn stitches were not simply functional but required careful measurement to ensure the gathers would be even and balanced throughout the fabric. Once the stitching was complete, the threads were gently pulled tight, causing the fabric to scrunch up evenly. This pulling action was done gradually to avoid uneven bunching and to maintain a controlled, smooth gather. As a result, the fabric formed tight, uniform folds that contributed to the iconic, voluminous silhouette that is characteristic of the Għonnella and other traditional Maltese costumes (see Figure 13).

This gathering technique was instrumental in creating the distinctive shape of the garment, giving it a sense of fullness and movement that enhances the visual impact of the costume. In addition to the gathers, the hem of the Għonnella was finished with a blind catch stitch, a subtle yet important detail in the garment's construction. This hand-stitched technique allows the hem to remain discreet and neatly finished, ensuring the hemline doesn't detract from the overall aesthetic.

Digitalization results

2D patterns of the Għonnella

The creation of a Għonnella involved the use of multiple patterns, as detailed in Table 2 and illustrated in Figure 12. These patterns served as templates from which various sections of the garment were cut, using fabrics such as cotton or corded silk, depending on the design requirements. Upon examining the construction process, it became evident that specific cardboard pieces, as shown in Figure 12, played a crucial role in shaping the costume. These pieces were layered and strategically placed to form the distinctive arched structure of the Għonnella, particularly the front section, which is one of its prominent features. These cardboard pattern pieces were carefully sandwiched between layers of fabric, helping to maintain the integrity and shape of the arched part while providing additional support and structure to the overall design of the garment. This layering technique was essential in achieving the stiff, structured appearance of the costume.

X-ray imaging

An X-ray scan of the Għonnella provided a detailed and insightful examination of its internal structure, revealing hidden layers, stitching techniques, and the methods employed during its construction (see Figure 13). The X-ray images clearly depicted the cardboard patterns used to shape the costume, particularly the arched feature. These patterns were visible as distinct layers inserted into the fabric, forming the sturdy structure that characterizes the costume. Additionally, the X-ray revealed the strips of whalebone running through the precisely sewn pin tucks, highlighting how these features contributed to the costume's overall texture, structure, and flexibility.

The gathered section of the garment was also distinctly visible in the X-ray, showing how the entire width of the fabric was meticulously gathered to create the characteristic fullness of the Għonnella. This revealed the carefully controlled gathering process, ensuring that the fabric was evenly distributed across the garment. The hemline, complete with its facing, was also clearly outlined in the X-ray image, providing a closer look at how the edges were finished. Even the individual hemming stitches used to secure the hem were discernible in the scan, showcasing the precise craftsmanship involved in every detail of the garment's construction. This in-depth imaging technique provided a comprehensive view of the Għonnella's intricate design and sewing methods that would otherwise remain hidden from the naked eye.

3D photogrammetry

The 3D photogrammetry of the Għonnella provided a highly detailed and comprehensive view of its fabric folds and drapes, offering valuable insights into how the costume fits and behaves when worn by women in Maltese society. Through this advanced imaging technique, the precise details of the garment's construction, including the intricacy of its gathers and folds, were clearly captured. The 3D model revealed how the fabric was manipulated, with particular emphasis on the fullness generated by the gathering process, which plays a crucial role in shaping the costume.

The results of the 3D imaging were exceptional, as they provided a virtual representation of the Għonnella that allowed for an in-depth examination of its structure. The photogrammetry made it possible to observe how the fabric's weight and texture contributed to the visual appeal of the costume, and how these elements influenced its fit. The digital model provided a deeper understanding of how the costume draped over the body and adapted to the wearer's form, offering valuable insights into the design decisions and practical considerations underlying its construction.

In addition to illustrating the overall aesthetic and fit of the costume, the 3D model also highlighted the garment's movement. It showed how the folds and drapes shifted and adapted to the wearer's posture and actions, providing a clearer understanding of how the Għonnella functioned in everyday life and within the cultural context of Maltese traditions. This digital examination not only helped preserve the visual aspects of the Għonnella but also shed light on its role in reflecting the status, identity, and cultural practices of the women who wore it. Through the 3D model, we were able to engage with the costume in a way that traditional photography or physical examination could not, gaining a more holistic view of its design, function, and significance.

The Għonnella in CLO 3D

To digitally recreate the Għonnella in CLO 3D (version 2024), the first step was to design a virtual mannequin. The mannequin's skin tone, gender, style, and pose were carefully selected to ensure a realistic and accurate representation (see Figure 15). Once the avatar was generated, a simple white dress was specifically designed to serve as a contrasting background against the Għonnella. This dress played a dual role: it complemented the garment's aesthetics and facilitated a smoother digital simulation within the software.

Using CLO 3D, the white dress was rendered in an interactive 3D format, allowing for real-time adjustments and modifications. This stage ensured that the virtual garment draped naturally and realistically on the avatar, enhancing the overall accuracy of the representation.

The two-dimensional patterns of the Għonnella were imported into the CLO 3D software to eventually transform them into the three-dimensional costume. The advanced features of CLO 3D enabled the garment to be displayed dynamically, offering an immersive 360-degree view, which allowed for a thorough examination of the costume from multiple angles.

Through 3D modeling technology, the software effectively showcased the structural integrity of the Għonnella, providing insights into its form, fit, and overall construction. One of the key advantages of using CLO 3D was its ability to manipulate fabric types, colors, and structural adjustments with scientific precision (Cao & Wang, 2023).

This flexibility allowed for detailed experimentation, ensuring an accurate and highly customizable digital representation. By integrating traditional construction with cutting-edge digital technology, this process resulted in a highly detailed, visually dynamic recreation of the Għonnella. The digital model was rendered on an interactive avatar, offering a realistic representation of how the garment would appear and function in real life. The ability to explore the garment's design, fit, and movement in such depth provided an immersive experience, bridging historical costume techniques with modern fashion technology.

Europeana and Google Arts & Culture

The integration of the Għonnella into European[1] and Google Arts & Culture[2] illustrates the powerful role of digitalization in preserving and sharing cultural heritage. These platforms enhance access to Malta's iconic traditional garment, overcoming the physical limitations posed by its fragile nature. Through high-resolution imaging, digital cataloging, and interactive features, users can closely examine the garment's construction and cultural meaning, encouraging new interpretations and wider engagement.

Digitization also supports comparative studies, allowing researchers to analyze the Għonnella alongside other European garments, uncovering insights into historical fashion, tailoring practices, and socio-cultural influences. The collaboration among historians, designers, and digital experts has fostered interdisciplinary innovation and highlighted themes such as sustainability, craftsmanship, and women's roles in textile production.

Moreover, the use of 3D modeling and virtual reality has enriched the viewing experience, offering immersive perspectives and the ability to simulate how the garment was worn. This enhances both academic analysis and public appreciation without compromising the original piece. The success of this collaboration highlights the need for ongoing investment in cultural heritage technologies, with a focus on improving metadata accuracy, digital preservation, and user experience to ensure continued access to valuable historical artifacts.

Overall, the results affirm that digitalization is a transformative force in heritage preservation. By digitizing the Għonnella and integrating it into a globally accessible platform, Europeana has not only safeguarded a vital element of Maltese history but has also demonstrated how technology can revitalize interest in cultural heritage, making it relevant and engaging for future generations.

---

1 https://www.europeana.eu/eu/item/1227/europeana_fashion_0.

2 https://artsandculture.google.com/story/pAUxRowhola4dg.

Discussion

The in-depth analysis of the Għonnella presented in this study reveals not only the technical mastery involved in its construction but also the garment's significant cultural, historical, and technological relevance. By combining traditional garment analysis with modern digital tools, this research provides a holistic understanding of a complex cultural artifact whose design, function, and symbolism transcend its physical form.

Artisanal precision and cultural identity

The construction techniques revealed through technical drawings and X-ray imaging illustrate an exceptional level of sewing construction techniques. Features such as pin tucks reinforced with whalebone and meticulously hand-stitched gathers demonstrate both the technical expertise of the maker and the garment's dual purpose: structural function and aesthetic sophistication. These details point to a deeper cultural narrative. The precision involved in producing the Għonnella speaks to the value placed on modesty, femininity, and social decorum in historical Maltese society. Far from being purely decorative or practical, the garment becomes a canvas for cultural expression, embedded with symbolic meaning about gender roles and communal identity.

Integration of traditional and digital techniques

One of the most compelling outcomes of this study is how it bridges traditional textile skills with contemporary digital methods. The use of CLO 3D, photogrammetry, and X-ray technology offers a multi-layered examination that would have been impossible through conventional methods alone. These digital tools not only uncover the hidden structure of the costume but also simulate its behavior in motion, offering insights into its function and wearability.

Such a multidisciplinary approach elevates the Għonnella beyond an artifact to be preserved—it becomes a living document of past lives, allowing both researchers and the general public to interact with it in immersive and educational ways. The virtual reconstruction and digital modeling serve as vital instruments in preserving this knowledge for future generations, particularly as traditional making techniques face the threat of being forgotten.

Digital heritage and democratization of access

The inclusion of the Għonnella in platforms like Google Arts & Culture and Europeana marks a significant advancement in cultural heritage dissemination. Digitization ensures that this unique garment, once restricted to archives or local exhibitions, becomes accessible to a global audience. It facilitates not only greater appreciation but also academic comparison across cultures and epochs.

Moreover, the integration into these platforms illustrates the importance of digital heritage projects in reshaping how we perceive and interact with the past. High-resolution imagery and interactive features break down barriers of geography and exclusivity, inviting a more democratic and participatory model of heritage consumption.

Implications for fashion studies and sustainable design

The construction details and material choices offer valuable lessons for contemporary fashion design. Techniques such as pin tucks for structure, strategic gathering for volume, and minimal visible stitching speak to an economy of means—achieving maximum visual impact with restrained yet highly skilled methods. These principles resonate strongly with current conversations around slow fashion and sustainable design.

Furthermore, the durability of the materials and the multifunctionality of structural elements (e.g., whalebone in pin tucks for both shape and texture) suggest a design ethos deeply connected to longevity and utility—an ethos often lacking in fast-fashion paradigms. Studying historical garments like the Għonnella thus contributes not only to heritage preservation but also to reimagining a more sustainable fashion future rooted in refined sewing skills and care.

The Għonnella as a socio-technological artifact

Finally, the Għonnella emerges from this analysis as more than a traditional costume. It is a socio-technological artifact—a garment constructed through a fusion of design, accurate construction principles, and evolving cultural values. The cardboard and whalebone inserts, the mathematical precision of the gathers, and the strategic layering techniques all point to a sophisticated understanding of material science and form.

In this light, the digital reconstruction becomes more than a reproduction; it is an interpretive tool, allowing us to explore not just how the garment was made, but why it was made in such a way, and what it meant to those who wore it. In doing so, it contributes to a broader dialogue on the intersections between fashion, identity, technology, and history.

Conclusion

This study examines how digitalization is transforming the preservation, study, and appreciation of traditional garments such as the Għonnella. Owing to their fragility, these costumes have traditionally been restricted to archives, limiting both scholarly access and public engagement. The application of technologies such as high-resolution imaging, X-ray analysis, and 3D modeling now enables detailed examination of construction techniques, materials, and historical context without risking physical damage.

Equally important is the insight this research offers into the sustainability practices inherent in historical garment-making. Traditional Maltese costume-making, as demonstrated through the Għonnella, reveals a resourceful approach to materials—maximizing fabric use, incorporating leftover textiles, and designing garments for longevity and adaptability. These strategies reflect an early form of what today is understood as zero-waste and slow fashion, offering valuable lessons for contemporary discussions on ethical and sustainable design.

The Għonnella, therefore, stands as more than a historical artifact; it is a testament to cultural identity, craftsmanship, and ecological mindfulness. By combining traditional textile research with digital innovation, this study not only safeguards a vital aspect of Maltese heritage but also contributes to a global discourse on how fashion intersects with history, technology, and sustainability. As digital tools continue to evolve, they will remain essential in ensuring that garments like the Għonnella—and the cultural knowledge they embody—are preserved, understood, and celebrated for generations to come.

Acknowledgments

The author wishes to express sincere gratitude to Heikki Häyhä of Metropolia University of Applied Sciences, Helsinki, for his invaluable assistance in the

X-ray imaging of the Għonnella. Special thanks are also extended to Nicole Vella for her contributions to the technical sketches, as well as the 2D and 3D imaging of the costume. Appreciation is due to Claire Bonavia and Francesco Vella from the Conservation and Digitalisation Department at Heritage Malta for their support and collaboration throughout this research.

References

Cao, Y., & Wang, S. (2023). Research on the application of CLO3D technology in the structure design of national costume. (n.d.-b). https://madison-proceedings.com/index.php/aemr/article/view/1223/1222

Cassar, A. (2025). Digitising the National Collection. In: M. Ioannides, D. Baker, A. Agapiou, P. Siegkas (Eds.), *3D Research Challenges in Cultural Heritage* V. *Lecture Notes in Computer Science*, (pp. 184–95). Springer, Cham. https://doi.org/10.1007/978-3-031-78590-0_16

Ch'ng, E., Cai, S., & Zhang, T. E. (2018). Crowdsourcing 3D cultural heritage: Best practice for mass photogrammetry. *Journal of Cultural Heritage Management and Sustainable Development*, 9(1): 24–42.

Costello, A., Kingsland, K., Jones, B., & Tanasi, D. (2023). Virtualization and 3D visualization of historical costume replicas: Accessibility, inclusivity, virtuality. In *Lecture Notes in Computer Sciences*, (pp. 122–30). Springer nature Switzerland. http://dx.doi.org/10.1007/978-3-031-37731-0_10

Csanák, E. (2019). Craft & tradition: Challenges of reinterpreting national heritage in fashion and textile design. In *Proceedings of the 10th International Scientific-Professional Conference Textile Science and Economy.*

Europeana. (n.d.). About us. *Europeana*. https://www.europeana.eu/en/about-us

Ilieş, D. C., Herman, G. V., Caciora, T., Ilieş, A., Indrie, L., Wendt, J. A., Axinte, A., Diombera, M., Lite, C., Berdenov, Z., & Albu, A. (2020). Considerations regarding the research for the conservation of heritage textiles in Romania. In A. Körlü (Ed.), *Waste in textile and leather sectors* (pp. 88–93). IntechOpen. https://doi.org/10.5772/intechopen.91393

Kuzmichev, V., Moskvin, A., Moskvina, M., & Pryor, J. (2018). Research on 3D reconstruction of late Victorian riding skirts. *International Journal of Clothing Science and Technology, 30*(6), 790–807. https://doi.org/10.1108/IJCST-12-2017-0192

McSweeney, K., Portelli, L., Räisänen, R., Kosunen, M., Arvanitidou, Z., Fernström, P., & Hyrsky, K. (2025). Looking, experimenting, creating, telling—Testing a pedagogical model for design learning. *Design and technology Education: An International Journal, 30*(1), 102–28. https://doi.org/10.24377/DTEIJ.article2805

Moskvin, A., Kuzmichev, V., & Moskvina, M. (2019). Digital replicas of historical skirts. *The Journal of the Textile Institute, 110*(12), 1810–26. https://doi.org/10.1080/00405000.2019.1621042

Mulder, S. (2024, October 24–5). *EFHA Workshop 24. 5D culture and 3D digitisation of fashion heritage* [Video]. *Vimeo*. https://vimeo.com/showcase/11461163/video/1031607512

Pantea, E., Petcu, C., Gemici, M. S., & Mitrofan, G. (2023). Heritage textiles—an integrated approach for assessment and future conservation. *Textile and Leather Review, 26*(3), 221–34. https://doi.org/10.35530/TLR.2023.26.3.56

Politecnico di Milano. (2024, July 16). *Gianfranco Ferré Research Center at Politecnico di Milano* [Video]. *YouTube*. https://www.youtube.com/watch?v=07mD3UvgMPo

Portelli, L., Arvanitidou, Z., McSweeney, K., & Räisänen, R. (2024). Tradition in action-traditional costume innovations. *Heritage, 7*(10), 5307–18. https://doi.org/10.3390/heritage7100250

Saiki, D., Stratton, T., Birk, V., & Sanchez, M. (2017). Exploring methods to make 3-D images of historic clothing using photogrammetry. In *Proceedings of the International Textile and Apparel Association Annual Conference, 74*(1).

Taylor, L. (2002). *The study of dress history*. Manchester University Press.

Victoria and Albert Museum (2018). Revealing hidden structures through X-rays. *Victoria and Albert Museum*. https://www.vam.ac.uk/articles/revealing-hidden-structures-x-rays

Yahaghi, E., Madrid García, J. E., Movafeghi, A., & Mirzapour, M. (2024). Improving X-ray images of historically significant textiles, *Journal of Cultural Heritage*, 66 (March–April), 415–425. https://doi.org/10.1016/j.culher.2023.12.020

Żyła, K., Kęsik, J., Santos, F., & House, G. (2021). Scanning of historical clothes using 3D scanners: Comparison of goals, tools, and methods. *Applied Sciences, 11*(12), 5588. https://doi.org/10.3390/app11125588

CHAPTER 8

The Story Behind

VR technologies as a powerful tool for preserving and exhibiting fashion

*Venetia Koutsou, Eleftheria Stoikou, and Maria Zoumaki**

ABSTRACT
The manufacturing process of a garment has been proved to be linked to its added value, when this process is based on reference that connects the garment with art, tradition, and the personal heritage of the designer. The process of inspiration and the transfer of the idea into the creation of the garment, requires a pathway to understanding the field from which it is drawn. Behind the garment and its production, there is always a story, which is revealed through its individual components: the fabric, the color, the weaving techniques, etc. This narrative is the guarantee for the emotional durability of the garment and its longevity, as a link between man's everyday sartorial performance and his culture.

This paper aims to present the development of a digital narrative of the work of the graduates of the Department of Creative Design and Clothing, International University of Greece. In particular, it will highlight the design methodology, the traditional techniques that were revealed and the short story behind each creation. To serve this purpose, a continuously updated VR exhibition was created, demonstrating the students' creations, accompanied by audiovisual material from previous exhibitions. The exhibition includes an AI-guided tour, offering detailed information about the students' works, the artistic concept behind them, as well as their cultural and sustainable aspects.

Keywords: art and fashion, economy, cultural heritage, digital humanities, VR Museum, AI tour guide

Introduction

The relationship between the manufacturing process and the added value of a garment lies in how production influences its economic, emotional, and cultural significance. Key factors such as the origin of materials, production techniques, and attention to detail play a crucial role in determining a garment's quality, functionality, and value. Handmade garments, for instance, often feature unique elements (such as traditional weaving techniques, intricate patterns, or high-quality fabrics) that are challenging to replicate in

* (V. K.: ORCID: https://orcid.org/0009-0001-6610-6401) (M. Z.: ORCID: https://orcid.org/0009-0006-8538-8754), Department of Creative Design and Clothing, School of Design Sciences, International Hellenic University.

modern fast-fashion models (Ahuvia, 2005). Studies show that when production incorporates traditional techniques or cultural references, garments transcend their utilitarian purpose, becoming meaningful connections to the history and identity of a culture (Ahuvia, 2005; Chapman, 2009; Cooper, 2010; D'Alisa et al., 2014; Hoskins, 1998). Yet these layers of meaning, process, context, and narrative are often difficult to communicate in conventional fashion exhibitions, where garments are typically encountered as static, fragile objects that cannot be handled, worn, or viewed "in motion." This is precisely where virtual reality (VR) and extended reality (XR) can enhance fashion exhibition practices: by enabling visitors to experience garments as story-bearing artifacts through immersive environments, interactive interpretation, and contextual reconstruction that exceed the constraints of physical display (Angeletti et al., 2024).

Recent fashion-heritage scholarship highlights that garments require forms of display that communicate movement, detail, and cultural environment, needs that VR can address through immersive visualization and interaction (Angeletti et al., 2024). Beyond visualization, social VR approaches have been shown to support richer "behind-the-garment" engagement by introducing interaction, context-building, and co-present exploration (e.g., visiting with others), while also offering a conservation-friendly way to "access" fragile pieces via digitized surrogates (Wylezek, 2024; Wylezek, 2025). In parallel, museum-focused VR research emphasizes that interaction and presence are central mechanisms through which virtual exhibitions increase immersion and user satisfaction, important considerations when the goal is not only to display fashion, but to communicate meaning, memory, and making (Chang & Suh, 2025).

A powerful medium for showcasing and enhancing the cultural and emotional value of a garment is the integration of art into its production process. Art not only reflects the personal expression and inspiration of the artist but also conveys the narrative of the design and construction process, as well as the culture of the designer and their era. Through the artist's perspective, the combination of colors, patterns, and fabrics transforms the garment into a carrier of cultural heritage and memory (Ahuvia, 2005; Hoskins, 1998).

The role of art, when combined with respect for tradition and the designer's personal narrative, is essential in creating garments with distinct cultural, emotional, and artistic value. By drawing inspiration from artistic creations (such as painting, sculpture, or installations), designers can incorporate elements like patterns, colors, shapes, symbols, and even entire narratives. This process creates a bridge between art and fashion, transforming the garment into a profound expression of human creativity. The result is a piece that serves as a canvas for art, giving the wearer a sense of connection to a unique and meaningful creation (Miller, 2007; Mida, 2015; Suh et al., 2013).

Building on this, VR can function as a narrative exhibition medium (storyliving), where documentation of making (materials, technique, trials), designer intention, and cultural references can be integrated around each garment as a guided, explorable experience rather than a label-bound summary (Angeletti et al., 2024; Stacchiotti, 2025). The goal of this project is to present a digital narrative of graduates' work, emphasizing their design methodology, the traditional techniques they utilized, and the cultural storytelling behind their creations. The case study presented here consists of two sequential course exhibitions and demonstrates how VR exhibition design can make these behind-the-garment stories accessible and engaging by connecting the final artifact to process evidence and personal/cultural references captured in the students' portfolios.

This study specifically highlights two exhibitions conducted as part of the courses Artistic Dimension of Design and Garment Creation and Portfolio which are sequential courses spanning two different semesters. In the first course, students explored the field and expressive means, while the second focused on developing the design process and storytelling. These two courses were selected for virtual presentation because the students' portfolios documented not only the construction process but also the stories that connect the final garments to their creators and sources of inspiration.

The exhibitions were also displayed in a museum setting, forming the foundation for the creation of a virtual museum. In recent years, artificial intelligence and virtual reality technologies have gained prominence in efforts to preserve and promote cultural heritage. Museums and cultural institutions are increasingly adopting these technologies to provide visitors with more interactive and immersive experiences. Virtual reality allows for the creation of virtual spaces to host exhibitions or to accurately replicate museums and archaeological sites (Zhang et al., 2018; Wang et al., 2021). Through VR, users can explore the past, visit distant locations, or experience the daily life of previous eras. By making cultural heritage more accessible to a global audience, these technologies not only enrich in-person experiences but also ensure the preservation and transmission of cultural treasures to future generations (Zhang et al., 2018; Sooai et al., 2017; Aiello et al., 2019; Margetis et al., 2021).

To give the works a global dimension, free from geographical or temporal limitations, they were presented on a digital platform featuring multimedia and virtual reality. The platform, designed as a virtual reality museum, allows for the continuous addition of new material, ensuring the presentations remain dynamic and relevant (Sooai et al., 2017; Spyrou et al., 2025). It includes an AI-guided tour that provides visitors with an immersive experience, showcasing the unique personal and cultural references of each designer, as well as the symbolism and meanings behind their garments.

This approach not only highlights the graduates' creations but also emphasizes the processes and stories behind them. Through digital storytelling, their design methodologies, traditional techniques, and cultural connections are brought to life, giving their work a new dimension that seamlessly blends fashion with cultural and artistic expression.

Theoretical background

The theoretical framework underpinning the project's methodology centers on contemporary trends in garments and their sustainability, particularly through the lens of Deconstruction principles. Researchers such as Chapman introduced the concept of *emotional durability* in product design, emphasizing the importance of creating objects that foster lasting emotional connections.

Amid the issues of the modern "throwaway society" characterized by the increased rate of product consumption due to the loss of emotional value, contemporary production leads to excessive and continuous waste generation with heightened environmental costs. The creation of products with enhanced emotional durability is deemed necessary and can be achieved through the production of objects that tell stories or are connected to personal memories, making them more emotionally valuable. These objects evolve with the needs of their users, develop a bond of trust through high-quality craftsmanship and timeless aesthetics, and, by fostering a strengthened user-object connection, also create a sense of commitment (Chapman, 2019; Errázuriz & Müller, 2022).

Through a reevaluation of how we perceive progress and social prosperity, many other researchers, such as D'Alisa, Giacomo et al., have also addressed these issues. Their work presents a multidimensional approach to an alternative concept of production that embraces different organizational models, such as the commons economy and sustainable local development (D'Alisa et al., 2014).

Using these multidimensional theoretical frameworks, the project transitioned into practical applications, incorporating voices from different fields and focusing on Greek culture, art, and heritage. It aimed to inspire students to participate, through their creations and designs, in the ongoing and increasingly intense dialogue within the academic field of garments (and beyond) about a change in lifestyle and production methods. This change is based on values such as equality, sustainability, and cooperation.

Methodology

The methodology focused on thoroughly documenting the students' creative processes while integrating art, tradition, and technology to create a unique presentation experience through the VR exhibition. The exhibitions were structured around the story of each garment, both individually and collectively, reflecting the shared cultural and creative inspiration behind them.

In the *Wear is Art* and *Small Stories of Revolution* exhibitions, the designer's portfolio accompanied each garment. For example, in the first exhibition, visitors could observe the artistic techniques studied by the students and how these techniques were transformed into their garments. In the second exhibition, the portfolios included photographs and textual references to the Greek revolution, the central theme of the exhibition. Each story highlighted historical figures or events, with the garments serving as tangible representations of moments or attire from the revolution. Characteristics such as fabric, color, pleating, and stitching were used to bring these stories to life, with personal narratives emerging from the archival materials included in the portfolios (Koutsou & Stoikou, 2022 and 2019).

Data collection process

The initial stage of the project involved selecting works for inclusion in the virtual museum to provide a comprehensive understanding of the students' creative journey. Stories, sources of inspiration, techniques, and narrative approaches were documented to interpret each student's unique process. The completed works were then analyzed in detail, including their presentation methods, design characteristics (e.g., colors, materials, geometries), and the narratives behind their creation.

Collection of multimedia material

After the works and creative processes were thoroughly examined, representative pieces were digitized for inclusion in the virtual museum. Videos, photographs, and audio from previous exhibitions were collected to enrich the narrative of the AI tour guide. The students' creations were digitized using detailed 3D scanning (Reality Capture by Epic Games, Unreal Engine 5.4). Initial sketches and prototypes were also included to showcase the transition from concept to completion. Phases of the construction process (such as material selection and final detailing) were recorded to fully document the creators' efforts.

Virtual reality and in-person-digitalizing the in-person experience

To present and promote the exhibitions, a virtual museum was developed using a VR platform. The three-dimensional design of the virtual museum was created with Rhino 7 software and the parametric plugin Grasshopper. After conducting several design studies, the most functional design, a traditional museum layout, was selected to align with user expectations. Visitors begin their journey in a central hall, where they are greeted by an AI tour guide. The guide provides an overview of the museum's contents, answers questions related to the exhibitions and directs visitors to specific exhibits while offering an interactive tour (see Figure 16).

The virtual building's floor plan was designed radially for two main reasons: to facilitate the future addition of new rooms and exhibitions, and to ensure user-friendly navigation. During user testing, which involved individuals with little to no experience using VR headsets, layouts with multiple staircases caused confusion, nausea, and dizziness. A single-story layout proved more intuitive and comfortable for users to explore (Catton & Smith, 2021).

The artificial intelligence system was trained to focus exclusively on the exhibition's content. It was designed to reject offensive or derogatory

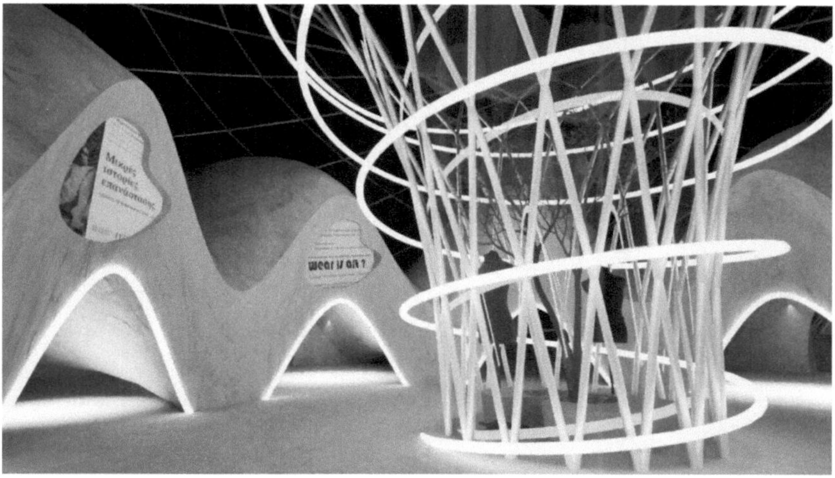

Figure 16. "The Story Behind" VR Museum. The central hall of the museum, in which the visitor starts the museum tour.

Image by the authors.

comments and to avoid providing irrelevant information. For example, during testing, when users asked about unrelated topics such as political events, the guide appropriately responded that these were outside its scope. The AI system was developed using Unreal Engine 5.4.1 and the Unreal Metahumans Plugin.

The three-dimensional geometry of the museum was imported into Twinmotion 2023 to enhance photorealism and incorporate materials. In keeping with the exhibition's theme, earthy materials such as clay and glass were used. The final twinmotion file was then transferred to Unreal Engine 5.4.1 to create the VR environment. The garments were 3D scanned to ensure precise representation within the virtual space, and multimedia elements, such as images, videos, and sound, were added to provide a multidimensional experience.

User tests were conducted with Meta's Oculus Quest 2 headsets. Visitors could freely explore the virtual space, interact with specific works for a closer examination, and view related multimedia content, creating an immersive and engaging experience.

Results and discussion

Design methodology. From inspiration to garment

Students draw inspiration from various sources, such as nature, art, cultural heritage, or personal experiences. Within the framework of collective research and study, a common source of inspiration is selected for the entire group. This shared focal point allows for collaborative research, the exploration of resources, and their sharing among the group, fostering discussion and interaction throughout the semester. Additionally, it highlights materials related to sewing techniques and fabric processing, ensuring consistent references and coherence in their understanding. In this way, a unified framework is built, encompassing both a collective and personal narrative.

Inspiration is first captured on paper, through photographic material or written elements, in a manner that each component serves as both evidence and expression of inspiration. Subsequently, this material is developed into sketches, techniques, and prototypes, which evolve as ideas and come to life through experimentation with colors, fabrics, and shapes.

The selection of fabrics and weaving or knitting techniques is guided by the source of inspiration. For instance, in the exhibition *Small Stories of Revolution* the garments featured pleats (referencing the fustanella of the Evzone) or sewing techniques and details from nineteenth-century women's attire. In the *Wear is Art* exhibition, the study of artistic media (color, coloring techniques, forms) was reflected in the garments as volumes, sewing techniques, or color palettes (see Figure 17).

The final garment embodies the essence of the designer; the creator's originality and initial idea are reflected through it. The designer's personal perspective acts as the filter and the point where material and intangible elements merge, giving rise to a personal narrative and connecting the garment to its story.

Narrative elements. The story behind each creation

Fashion serves as a medium of expression, bridging artistic creativity with cultural narratives or personal stories. Each garment carries a story, making it a unique and emotionally durable creation. These narratives enhance the emotional bond between the garment and its wearer, transforming it from a mere product into a carrier of history and culture.

The works presented in the exhibitions reflect the innovative perspectives of young designers, who successfully integrate art, culture, and tradition

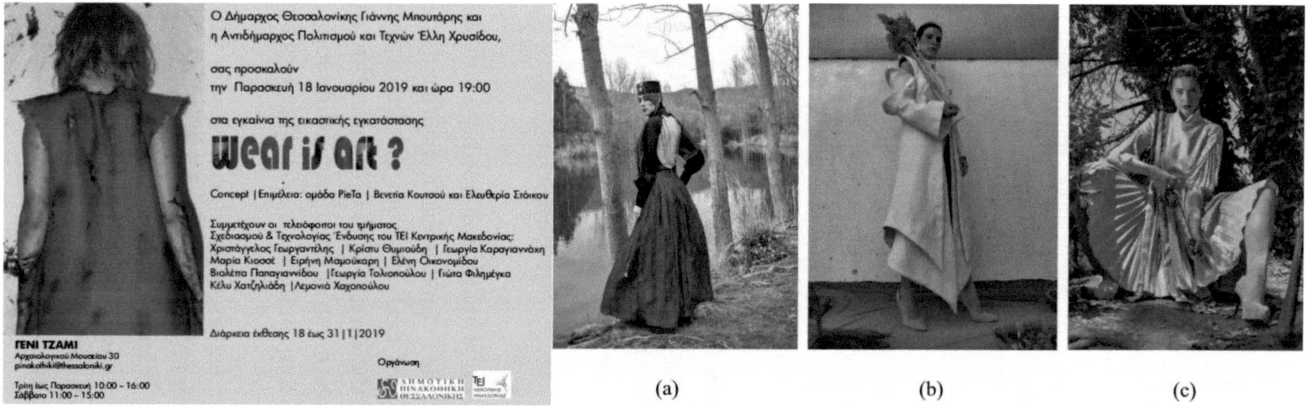

Figure 17. Left: "Wear Is Art" Exhibition Poster. Presented at Geni Tzami in Thessaloniki, this exhibition explored the fusion of fashion and visual art, inspired by iconic Greek artists. Right: a) "Frosyni" by Elena Tsalikidou, b) "Women of Clay" by Eleni-Maikanti Paliochoriti, c) "Matomenes (Bloodstained)" by Athanasios Vassiliadis. Images by the authors.

into their creations. Their designs redefine cultural heritage with a modern aesthetic, creating emotionally impactful pieces that honor the past while embracing the future.

Indicative examples of student creations

1. *Frosyni* by Elena Tsalikidou. The designer states about her work: "*Frosyni* was executed by drowning by Ali Pasha, along with other women of Ioannina. The story is unclear whether it was a political act or an act of revenge within the framework of the strict patriarchy that prevailed in the societies of that time." (see Figure 17).
2. *Women of Clay* by Eleni-Maikanti Paliochoriti. The creator noted the following about her work:
   "Colors from emotions. Ochre and clay merge with the white bodies of women enduring hard lives and daily struggles, as depicted in the paintings of Nikiforos Lytras and Theodoros Rallis." (see Figure 17).
3. *Matomenes (Bloodstained)* by Athanasios Vassiliadis. The designer provided a profound narrative for his symbolic work:
   "The bloodstained are the fustanellas of the warriors wounded in battle. But they are also the bloodstained women who stayed behind and endured torture." (see Figure 17).

The significance of narrative in cultural heritage and sustainability

Narrative plays a pivotal role in linking fashion with cultural heritage and sustainability. The works of students from the Department of Creative Design and Clothing at the International Hellenic University exemplify this connection, as each garment in the digital exhibition is accompanied by a unique story drawn from traditions, personal experiences, and artistic influences.

Through narrative, garments are imbued with identity. The stories behind each creation establish a connection between the designer and the consumer, as the latter selects pieces based on personal psychological and social affinities. This interaction attributes value to both the designer's creativity and the consumer's choice, elevating the garment beyond its physical form. As a result, garments gain cultural and emotional resilience, fostering a strong bond between the creator, the wearer, and the inspiration, whether rooted in tradition, history, or personal vision (Niinimäki et al., 2013).

The VR exhibition's digital storytelling offers viewers an opportunity to delve into the inspiration behind each design and appreciate its cultural significance. By embedding emotional resilience into each garment's story, the exhibition contributes to sustainability. A garment tied to a rich narrative holds greater value for the wearer, reducing the likelihood of disposal and promoting long-term use (Ribeiro et al., 2024). This dynamic highlights fashion's potential as a medium for preserving cultural diversity while creating meaningful connections between consumers and garments as carriers of memory and culture.

The narrative is further enhanced through the creators' use of expressive media, such as traditional weaving techniques, patterns, and color palettes. These elements, reinterpreted and presented in the students' portfolios, preserve cultural heritage while reframing it through a modern, creative lens. The use of VR technology expands access to these cultural narratives, reaching a broader audience and ensuring their relevance in a contemporary context.

In this work, narrative is more than a promotional tool for fashion or exhibitions; it is a catalyst that connects clothing to sustainability, cultural identity, and technology. By integrating narrative processes into the digital exhibition, this project bridges the past with the present and lays the foundation for a sustainable and culturally enriched future for fashion (Niinimäki et al., 2013; Niinimäki, 2010; Liu & Kwon, 2019; Meier et al., 2021).

Digital exhibition: features of the VR exhibition

The results demonstrate how the integration of design methodology, narrative elements, and digital media creates a comprehensive experience that showcases fashion as both cultural and artistic expression. The VR exhibition leverages advanced technologies to offer an innovative presentation method that connects audiences to the art and history behind each creation.

This interactive space enables visitors to freely explore the digital environment, allowing them to examine each creation in three dimensions at their own pace. The experience is enriched with multimedia content, including videos and audio clips, as well as AI-guided tours that provide real-time interaction and respond to visitors' questions, making the exhibition both engaging and immersive (see Figure 18).

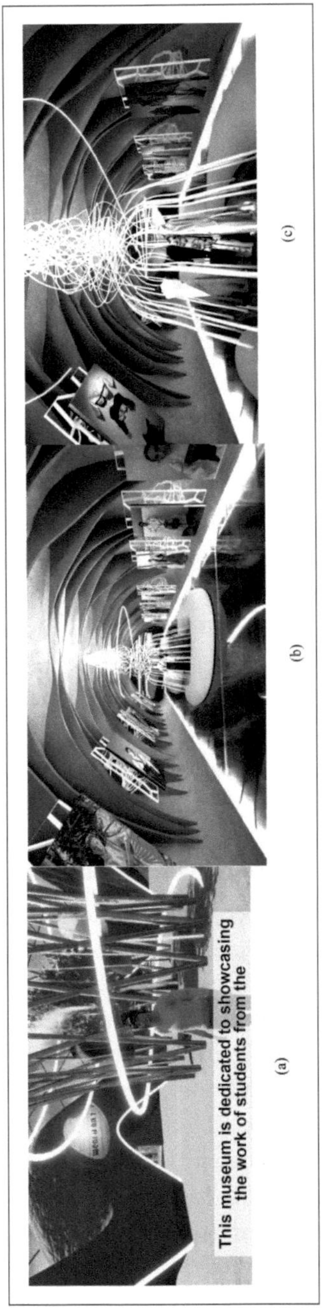

Figure 18. a) AI Tour Guide welcoming the visitor to "The Story Behind" Museum, b) "Little Stories of Revolution" Virtual Reality Exhibition. All Images and 3D Scanned Clothes were reprinted with permission from the designers, c) "Wear Is Art" Virtual Reality Exhibition. Images by the authors.

The ultimate goal of the VR exhibition is to help visitors recognize the profound connection between fashion, art, tradition, and sustainability. Through this innovative medium, the exhibition creates a meaningful and lasting impression, demonstrating the transformative power of fashion as a cultural and artistic form (see Figure 18).

The goal is for the visitor, through the experience, to grasp the emphasis on the connection of fashion with art, tradition, and sustainability.

Challenges in the integration of technologies

The integration of technologies into the design and promotion of traditional techniques poses challenges that require careful consideration and sensitivity. Tools such as 3D scanning, virtual reality, and artificial intelligence enable the global dissemination of local traditions. However, to appeal to broader audiences, there is a risk of altering or diluting the cultural authenticity of these traditions. To mitigate this, technological integration must be approached with respect for cultural specificities, ensuring that the authenticity of the traditions is preserved as much as possible (Ribeiro et al., 2024).

Another challenge lies in the potential weakening of the connection between a design and its original inspiration during the transfer process through technological means. This can reduce the narrative value of the garment, shifting focus toward its technological aspects rather than its cultural and artistic significance. To address this, critical evaluation must be applied at every stage of technological integration, mirroring the scrutiny used during the design process (Ribeiro et al., 2024; Yang et al., 2024; Magdalena, 2023).

Expert guidance is essential in preserving authenticity. Input from traditional craftsmen or individuals who have firsthand experience with the cultural elements inspiring the artist is invaluable. However, a pressing challenge of our time is the decline in skilled artisans familiar with traditional garment production methods, as these processes are often time-consuming. This decline makes it increasingly difficult to find experts capable of teaching or applying these techniques.

Opportunities in the integration of technologies

While these challenges are significant, they are outweighed by the opportunities that technological integration offers for preserving cultural heritage and promoting sustainability. Combining traditional techniques with modern technologies can lead to innovative and unique creations. In this project, students offered a contemporary perspective on tradition and Greek art, using 3D scanning, virtual reality, and artificial intelligence to create an immersive exhibition that transcends geographical and temporal boundaries, reaching a global audience (Ribeiro et al., 2024; Magdalena, 2023; Dragicevic & Bagarić, 2019; Martin & Vacca, 2018).

The project successfully contributed to the revival of Greece's cultural heritage, a goal that has also been pursued by other designers and researchers in the past. Its broader ambition is to attract works from other cultures and countries, creating a shared virtual museum space where diverse traditions and treasures at risk of being lost can be preserved. By celebrating multiculturalism and diversity, the project highlights both the shared and unique characteristics that connect and unify different peoples. These technologies, combined with local storytelling, provide a platform for preserving and promoting cultural diversity in fashion, countering the uniformity of mass production.

The promotion of these technologies by both the scientific and artistic communities stems from their global potential and their ability to support sustainability. Traditional techniques, often more environmentally friendly, offer an alternative to the resource-intensive practices of mass production. Modern technologies like 3D scanning and 3D visualization further reduce waste and consumption, while virtual reality exhibitions promote the works of local designers, strengthening local economies (Liu & Kwon, 2019; Meier et al., 2021; Ahn et al., 2023; Martin & Vacca, 2018). Moreover, technologies like virtual reality exhibitions contribute to promoting the products of local designers and strengthen the local economy. A core goal of this project is to showcase emerging designers and their personal perspectives, promoting values of sustainability and cultural preservation. By leveraging these technologies, designers can transform the industry, creating products that are meaningful, long-lasting, and unique. In this way, technology not only enhances storytelling but also fosters a sustainable future for fashion and design (Meier et al., 2021; Wu et al., 2022; Addis, 2005; Martin & Vacca, 2018).

Conclusions

The results of this project underscored the critical connection between design methodology, narrative elements, and digital media in promoting fashion as a powerful medium of cultural and artistic expression. The design process showcased by the students of the Department of Creative Design and Fashion extended beyond the creation of garments, evolving into a multifaceted journey that combined artistic inspiration, cultural heritage preservation, and sustainability.

Guided by the department's professors, the students designed garments that transcended functionality. They incorporated traditional techniques, artistic geometries inspired by Greek culture, and traditional patterns and color palettes that reflect Greek art, history, and reality. Each creation was accompanied by a narrative that strengthened its identity, not as a mere decorative element but as a bridge between the past and the future, between culture and art.

The use of virtual reality as a medium for showcasing the students' creations further amplified this connection, merging Greece's rich tradition and culture with technology and the future. The VR platform provided an innovative and practical solution, offering global accessibility and creating an interactive, immersive experience. Visitors could engage with the art, history, and cultural significance of each piece, while artificial intelligence provided interactive tours that allowed them to explore the designers' creative processes and form emotional connections with the exhibits.

By integrating traditional elements, modern technologies, and storytelling, the project created a comprehensive experience that enriched the understanding of the relationship between art, culture, and fashion. This approach opens new possibilities for promoting cultural heritage and sustainable creation, laying the foundation for a future where fashion serves as a bridge between innovation, tradition, and sustainability.

References

Addis, M. (2005). New technologies and cultural consumption: Edutainment is born! *European Journal of Marketing, 39*(7/8), 729–36.

Ahn, D. K., Bae, B. C., & Kim, Y. (2023). User experience of a digital fashion show: Exploring the effectiveness of interactivity in virtual reality. *Applied Sciences, 13*(4), 2558.

Ahuvia, A. C. (2005). Beyond the extended self: Loved objects and consumers' identity narratives. *Journal of Consumer Research, 32*(1), 171–84.

Aiello, D., Fai, S., & Santagati, C. (2019). Virtual museums as a means for promotion and enhancement of cultural heritage. *International Archives of Photogrammetry, Remote Sensing and Spatial Information Sciences, XLII-2/W15*, 33–40.

Angeletti, E., Gaiani, M., Palermo, R., & Garagnani, S. (2024). Beyond the physical exhibit: Enhancing, showcasing and safeguarding fashion heritage with VR technologies. *Digital Applications in Archaeology and Cultural Heritage, 32*, e00314.

Catton, F., & Smith, L. (2021). Museums without walls: A temporal analysis of virtual exhibitions in GLAM institutions. *Pathfind: Canadian Journal of Information Science Studies Early Career Professionals, 2*, 72–85.

Chang, S., & Suh, J. (2025). The impact of VR exhibition experiences on presence, interaction, immersion, and satisfaction: Focusing on the experience economy theory (4Es). *Systems, 13*(1), 55.

Chapman, J. (2009). Design for (emotional) durability. *Design Issues, 25*(4), 29–35.

Cooper, T. (2010). *Longer lasting products: Alternatives to the throwaway society* (1st ed.). Routledge.

D'Alisa, G., Demaria, F., & Kallis, G. (Eds.). (2014). *Degrowth: A vocabulary for a new era* (1st ed.). Routledge.

Dragicevic, M., & Bagarić, A. (2019). Virtual technology in museums and art galleries business practice: The empirical research. In *7th International OFEL Conference on Governance, Management, and Entrepreneurship: Embracing Diversity in Organisations* (pp. 175–83), April 5–6, 2019, Dubrovnik, Croatia.

Errázuriz, T., & Müller, E. (2022). "My cherished garment": Rethinking fashion, attachment and durability. *Fashion Theory, 27*(3), 327–54.

Hoskins, J. (1998). *Biographical objects: How things tell the stories of people's lives*. Routledge.

Koutsou, V., & Stoikou, E. (2022). Μικρές ιστορίες επανάστασης [Small stories of revolution]. *Archaeological Museum of Thessaloniki.* https://www.amth.gr/exhibitions/temporary/mikres-istories-epanastasis

Koutsoy, V., & Stoikou, E. (2019, March 8). Wear is art? *Department of Creative Design and Clothing, IHU.* https://cdc.ihu.gr/wear-is-art-thessaloniki-archaiologiko-moyseio-geni-tzami-ianoyarios-2019/

Liu, S., & Kwon, M. J. (2019). A study on spatial aesthetic characteristics in modern fashion converged with virtual reality technology: Focusing on fashion shows, fashion exhibitions, and fashion design apps. *Journal of Fashion Business, 23*(5), 96–110.

Magdalena, P. S. (2023). Artificial intelligence in the context of cultural heritage and museums: Complex challenges and new opportunities. *European Parliamentary Research Service (EPRS).* Belgium.
Margetis, G., Apostolakis, K. C., Ntoa, S., Papagiannakis, G., & Stephanidis, C. (2021). X-reality museums: Unifying the virtual and real world towards realistic virtual museums. *Applied Sciences, 11*(1), 338.
Martin, M., & Vacca, F. (2018). Heritage narratives in the digital era: How digital technologies have improved approaches and tools for fashion know-how, traditions, and memories. *Research Journal of Textile and Apparel, 22*(4), 335–51.
Meier, C., Berriel, I. S., & Nava, F. P. (2021). Creation of a virtual museum for the dissemination of 3D models of historical clothing. *Sustainability, 13*(22), 12581.
Mida, I. (2015). Animating the body in museum exhibitions of fashion and dress. *Dress, 41*(1), 37–51.
Miller, S. (2007). Fashion as art; is fashion art? *Fashion Theory, 11*(1), 25–40.
Niinimäki, K. (2010). Eco-clothing, consumer identity, and ideology. *Sustainable Development, 18*(3), 150–62.
Niinimäki, K., & Armstrong, C. (2013). From pleasure in use to preservation of meaningful memories: A closer look at the sustainability of clothing via longevity and attachment. *International Journal of Fashion Design, Technology, and Education, 6*(3), 190–9.
Ribeiro, M., Santos, J., Lobo, J., Araújo, S., Magalhães, L., & Adão, T. (2024). VR, AR, gamification, and AI towards the next generation of systems supporting cultural heritage: Addressing challenges of a museum context. In *Web3D '24: Proceedings of the 29th International ACM Conference on 3D Web Technology.* ACM.
Sooai, A. G., Nugroho, A., Azam, M. N. A., Sumpeno, S., & Purnomo, M. H. (2017). Virtual artifact: Enhancing museum exhibit using 3D virtual reality. *TRON Symposium (TRONSHOW)*, Tokyo, 2017, 1–5.
Spyrou, O., Hurst, W., & Krampe, C. (2025). A reference architecture for virtual human integration in the metaverse: Enhancing the galleries, libraries, archives, and museums (GLAM) sector with AI-driven experiences. *Future Internet, 17*(1).
Stacchiotti, E. (2025). From interpretation to immersion: XR and the transformation of fashion heritage storytelling. In S. Campana, D. Ferdani, H. Graf, G. Guidi, Z. Hegarty, S. Pescarin, & F. Remondino (Eds.), *Digital Heritage 2025.* The Eurographics Association. (Paper dh.20253181).

Suh, S. H., & Kim, Y. I. (2013). Fashion as art through the expansion of aesthetic concept of contemporary art and fashion. *Journal of the Korean Society of Clothing and Textiles, 37*(4), 577–89.

Wang, Y., Sun, Y., & Zhou, C. (2021). Research on the development and application of museum cultural resources display based on virtual reality technology. *E3S Web of Conferences, 236*, 01048.

Wu, Y., Jiang, Q., Liang, H., & Ni, S. (2022). What drives users to adopt a digital museum? A case of virtual exhibition hall of National Costume Museum. *SAGE Open, 12*, 1–17.

Wylezek, K. (2024). *Reaching behind the glass: Fashion exhibition and social virtual reality* (master's thesis). Centrum Wiskunde & Informatica (CWI).

Wylężek, K., Viola, I., & Cesar, P. (2025). Curating with technology: How to bring old fashion back to life in museum exhibitions. In *Proceedings of the 3rd International Workshop on Interactive eXtended Reality (IXR '25)* (10 pp.). Association for Computing Machinery (ACM).

Yang, L., Cheng, N., Jiang, P., & Noriega, P. (2024). Virtual museums: State of the art, trends, and challenges. In C. Stephanidis, M. Antona, S. Ntoa, & G. Salvendy (Eds.), *HCI International 2024 Posters. HCII 2024. Communications in Computer and Information Science* (Vol. 2119). Springer.

Zhang, L., Qi, W., Zhao, K., Wang, L., Tan, X., & Jiao, L. (2018). VR games and the dissemination of cultural heritage. In N. Streitz & S. Konomi (Eds.), *Distributed, ambient and pervasive interactions: Understanding humans* (Lecture Notes in Computer Science, vol. 10921). Springer.

CHAPTER 9

Moritz From Buxtehude

Bridging past and future by digitally preserving cultural heritage

*Sylvia Bossenz, Carsten Behm, and Timo Schnitt**

ABSTRACT
This article explores the innovative use of digital technologies in preserving cultural heritage, focusing on the *Moritz from Buxtehude* research project. This interdisciplinary project, a collaboration between Hanover University of Applied Sciences and Arts and the Historical Museum Hanover, aims to digitally preserve and bring to life the unique sixteenth century wardrobe of Duke Moritz of Saxony-Lauenburg. By employing cutting-edge technologies like photogrammetry, 3D scanning, 2D digitization, and cloth simulation software (CLO3D), the project team created digital twins of Moritz and his attire, offering new avenues for research, education, and public engagement with history. This article details the project's process, highlighting the challenges and opportunities encountered in digitally preserving delicate textile artifacts and creating a historically accurate and engaging representation of Duke Moritz and his environment.

Keywords: digital tailoring, cultural heritage, 3D scanning, photogrammetry, cloth simulation, Moritz von Buxtehude

Introduction

The preservation of cultural heritage in the digital age presents a compelling intersection of tradition and innovation. While museums and archives have long served as guardians of our past, the delicate nature of historical artifacts, particularly textiles, often restricts physical access and limits public engagement. Digital technologies offer a transformative solution by enabling the creation of accurate and accessible digital replicas, safeguarding these precious objects from further deterioration while simultaneously democratizing access for research, education, and the public. This article delves into the *Moritz from Buxtehude* project, a pioneering initiative that exemplifies the potential of digital tailoring to bridge the gap between past and future, ensuring that cultural heritage remains a vibrant and integral part of our shared human experience.

* Hanover University of Applied Sciences and Arts.

Who we are

The *Moritz from Buxtehude* project is the result of a dynamic collaboration between Hannover University of Applied Sciences and Arts and the Historical Museum Hannover. At the forefront of this initiative are three key individuals: Sylvia Bossenz, teacher for special tasks with expertise in costume, fashion, media, and product design with a focus on the development of forms in the design process; Carsten Behm, a professor of fashion design specializing in digital pattern development and clothing simulation and Timo Schnitt, a professor of 3D animation, visual effects, and media design informatics. Their combined knowledge forms the foundation for this innovative project, which seamlessly blends historical research with cutting-edge digital technologies.

Beyond this core team, the project benefits from the contributions of specialists in various fields, including 3D animation, photogrammetry, textile restoration, and museum curation. This interdisciplinary approach ensures a comprehensive understanding of the historical garments, their cultural significance, and the technical challenges involved in their digital preservation. The team's shared passion for history and dedication to innovation drives the project forward, pushing the boundaries of what is possible in the realm of cultural heritage preservation.

Preservation of cultural heritage

Cultural heritage encompasses the tangible and intangible legacies of past generations, shaping our understanding of the world and our place within it. These legacies include monuments, artifacts, traditions, and knowledge systems that define the identity and history of communities. Preserving this heritage is crucial for maintaining cultural diversity, fostering a sense of belonging, and providing continuity between past, present, and future. However, the task of preservation is fraught with challenges. Textiles, due to their organic nature, are highly susceptible to degradation. Light, humidity, and even the slightest touch can cause irreversible damage. How can we preserve them and make them visible at the same time?

Traditional methods of preservation, while invaluable, often face limitations. Moreover, access to these artifacts is frequently restricted to protect them from further deterioration, limiting public engagement and educational opportunities. This is where digital technologies offer transformative potential, opening up new avenues for research and education. Digital preservation involves the use of technology to capture, store, and share cultural heritage in digital formats. This approach not only safeguards artifacts from physical damage but also democratizes access, allowing people worldwide to engage with cultural heritage in new and meaningful ways. Digital replicas can be studied, shared, and even manipulated without risking harm to the original artifacts. Digital tools enable the reconstruction of missing or damaged parts, providing a more complete understanding of the garment's original form and function.

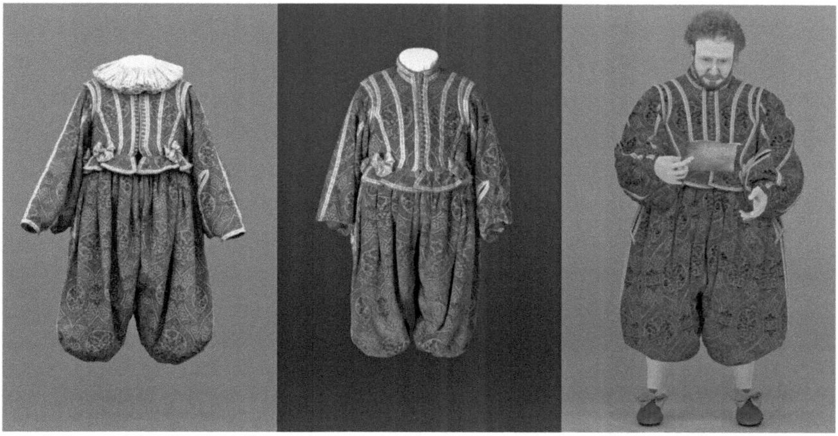

Figure 19. Photogrammetry of the artifact (left), original photograph from the Museum (center), Moritz from Buxtehude Avatar (right).
Images by the authors.

Research project: Moritz from Buxtehude

The research project *Moritz from Buxtehude* stands as a testament to the power of digital innovation in the field of cultural heritage preservation. This initiative focuses on the unique collection of garments belonging to Duke Moritz of Saxony-Lauenburg, a historical figure whose life and attire offer a fascinating glimpse into the past. The project aims to not only preserve these delicate textiles but also to bring them to life through digital reconstruction and animation, creating an engaging and immersive experience for audiences.

As the younger brother of Franz II, Duke of Saxony-Lauenburg, Moritz was excluded from the line of succession. He resided in Buxtehude with his mistress and her husband. However, as insignificant and chronically penniless he may have been for his time, this insignificance is the reason that an extraordinary, unique collection of clothing from his possessions around 1600 has survived the centuries and is preserved in Hanover's museums. This collection, comprising 24 objects, is a rare and invaluable resource for historians and researchers. It offers an almost complete representation of the clothing and life of a nobleman from the period around 1600, a time from which clothing is rarely preserved in such a comprehensive manner.

The project began with a meticulous examination of the collection, selecting eight key garments that would best illustrate a typical day in Moritz's life. The Historical Museum Hannover undertook the crucial task of art-historical reappraisal and textile restorative examination. This involved researching the provenance of the objects, analyzing their construction and materials, and carefully documenting their condition. Using traditional analog methods, textile conservator Carmen Markert took the 2D patterns from the garments, which then served as the basis for the digital reconstruction (see Figure 19).

Recognizing the importance of public engagement, the museum team developed a website to document the research process and share findings with a wider audience. This website provides a transparent and accessible window into the project, allowing the public to follow the journey of digital preservation and learn more about Duke Moritz and his unique wardrobe.

Two ways to get a digital replica

Photogrammetry to create a digital 3D-image

Scanning is a crucial component in the creation of a 3D digital image and forms the basis for creating accurate and detailed digital replicas of historical artifacts. In this article we focus on the Red Doublet, an object to best illustrate our approach.

Scanning the red doublet begins with careful preparation. This involves ensuring that the doublet is in optimal condition for scanning, taking into account factors such as lighting and positioning. The aim is to capture the garment in its entirety, including intricate details such as seams, fabric

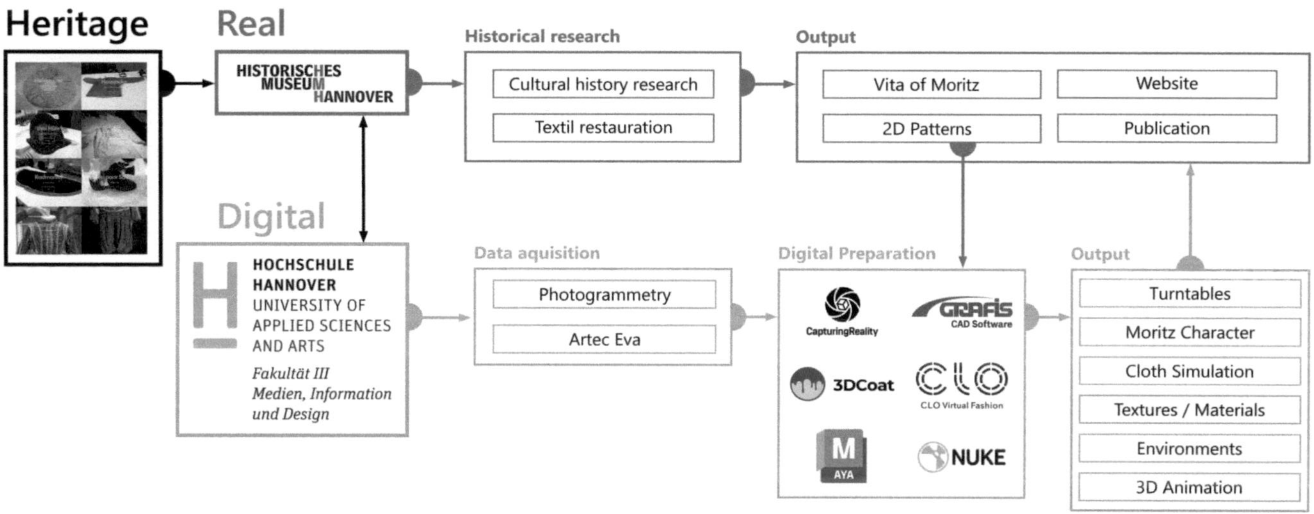

Figure 20. Flow chart of our processing and collaboration with the Historical Museum Hanover.
Image by the authors.

structure, and color variations. Advanced scanning technologies such as photogrammetry and structured-light scanning are used to capture the fine details required for an accurate digital representation.

To establish a uniform lighting configuration within the museum setting, we constructed a light cube with LED strips and affixed marker points to the walls, ensuring greater precision in subsequent calculations. The Red Doublet was retrieved from the museum depot, carefully unpacked, and placed on a test dummy.

First, the Artec Eva scanner was used, a lightweight and fast device that uses structured light to create precise, high-resolution 3D models. This was followed by the utilization of photogrammetry technology, whereby a multitude of high-resolution images of the garment were captured from different angles. The images were captured using a bespoke tripod with wheels, which enabled us to move in concentric circles around the object. This setup allowed for mounting the camera at five distinct heights, enhancing the efficiency of the photogrammetry process. A Macbeth Color Checker Chart was used to ensure consistent color reproduction. This dual approach ensured that a backup was available in case one method did not produce the desired results (see Figure 20).

The scanning process required two complete working days. After data acquisition, the data was meticulously reviewed and processed. The Artec Eva scanner provided rapid and high-resolution 3D geometry, but its photo textures were lower in resolution than those obtained through photogrammetry. To achieve the highest possible resolution, the objects were photographed with a high-resolution digital camera.

Once the scanning of the Red Doublet was completed, the next crucial phase in the digital preservation process was digital preparation and processing. This stage transforms the raw data collected during scanning into a coherent and accurate digital model for analysis, research, and educational purposes. The process is both technical and creative, requiring precision and artistry to ensure the digital representation faithfully captures the essence of the original artifact.

Digital preparation begins with aligning the data from the various scanning methods. This involves carefully matching the 3D models generated by the Artec Eva scanner with the high-resolution images captured through photogrammetry. This alignment process ensures that the digital model accurately reflects the garment's shape, dimensions, and surface details. Specialized software packages were used to merge the data, creating a composite model that combines the high-resolution mesh and the high-resolution photos to a combination of both worlds.

When processing the photogrammetry data, it turned out that this process enabled us to create very high-resolution geometries. In addition, the high-resolution photos are automatically congruent with the geometry in this step, allowing us to achieve significant time savings. Photogrammetry provided us with the geometry and texture data we needed. We therefore discarded our first step of combining both techniques and only continued to work with the photogrammetry model.

The next step is refining and enhancing the digital model. This involves correcting discrepancies from the photogrammetry process, such as geometry outgrowth, shadows, highlights, and reflections, to ensure accurate geometry, texture, and color depiction. The goal is to create a lifelike digital representation that captures the intricate details of the Red Doublet, from stitching patterns to fabric texture.

In addition to refinement, the process involves enhancing the model for various applications, optimizing it for platforms like virtual reality environments or online exhibits. The digital model must be versatile and adaptable, suitable for a range of educational and research contexts. This requires careful consideration of different file formats and resolution to meet the needs of diverse audiences for research and publication.

Digital tailoring to create a digital simulation

Digital tailoring represents a revolutionary approach to the preservation and study of historical garments. By leveraging advanced digital technologies, we can recreate, analyze, and preserve clothing artifacts with a level of detail and accuracy that was previously unattainable. In the context of cultural heritage preservation, digital tailoring offers numerous advantages, transforming how we engage with historical textiles and garments.

The transition from the real world to the digital realm in our project involves the use of CLO3D, a cutting-edge software that allows for the creation of highly detailed and accurate digital models of garments. This process begins with the 2D patterns obtained from the textile restorer's work, which are then digitized and imported into the software. CLO3D enables us to simulate the garments in a virtual environment, providing a lifelike representation that captures the essence of the original artifacts.

In the case of Duke Moritz's wardrobe, the digital tailoring process allows to recreate the construction and materials of the garments in an unprecedented level of detail. Through the digital models, we can emulate the sewing techniques, fabric composition, and design elements that characterize the wardrobe. This level of analysis provides insights into the craftsmanship and fashion trends of Duke Moritz's era, enriching our understanding of the historical context.

Moreover, digital tailoring facilitates the preservation of garments that are too fragile or deteriorated to be handled physically. By creating digital replicas, we ensure that the garments' details are preserved for future generations, even if the original artifacts continue to degrade. This approach not only safeguards the garments but also democratizes access, allowing people worldwide to engage with cultural heritage in new and meaningful ways.

Moritz comes to life

The culmination of our digital preservation efforts is the creation of a 3D character of Duke Moritz, dressed in the meticulously recreated Red Doublet. This digital avatar brings history to life in a dynamic and interactive way. By animating Duke Moritz, we bridge the gap between static artifacts and living history, offering a unique opportunity to engage with the past.

The creation of an animated 3D Moritz figure involves several steps, each of which requires a mixture of historical accuracy and creative interpretation. The process begins with research on Moritz and the digital model of the Red Doublet, which serves as the basis for the character's clothing. This is supplemented with further details like a story, a Moritz character, a rig for the character, the 2D patterns, the textures, and colors, such as the pomegranate velvet, that reflect the original appearance of the garment, the clothing simulation, the environment, a room in his house in Buxtehude, assets, and finally the animation. The goal is to create a lifelike representation that captures the essence of the doublet and its historical context.

Developing the character of Duke Moritz presents unique challenges, as no painted portrait of him exists. Instead, we rely on historical records and descriptions to ensure accuracy. Remarkably, there is only one coin on which the face of Duke Moritz is recognized, providing a rare glimpse into his appearance. This coin and the portraits of his relatives served as a crucial reference for the design. To further enhance the realism of the figure, the team meticulously researched the habits of the nobility in the sixteenth century. To this end, historical reports and portraits of contemporaries were studied and even hairstyles from the period were analyzed. Based on this research, the digital Moritz was given a hairstyle and beard that accurately reflects the fashion of his time. The adding of a well-told story completed his digital likeness, reflecting his physical features and demeanor.

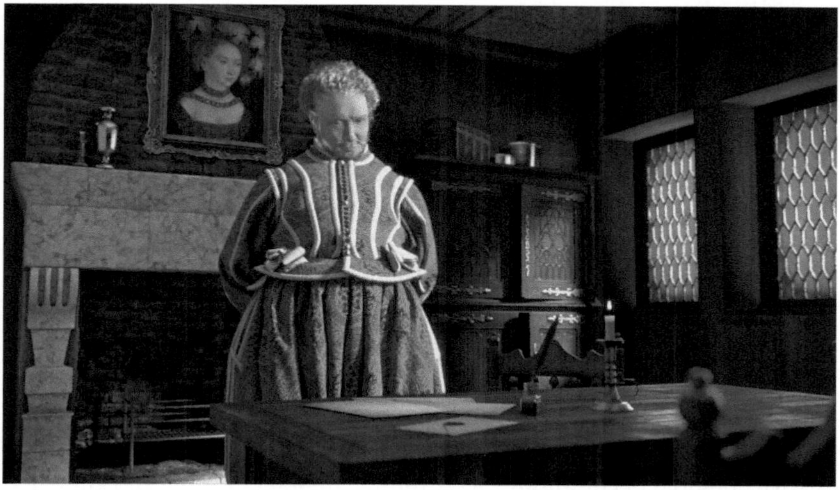

Figure 21. Our animated Moritz in his recreated cabinet. Image by the authors.

The character is then animated, allowing for movement and interaction within digital environments. This animation adds a layer of realism, enabling users to explore the character in a more immersive way (see Figure 21).

The journey goes on

The journey of digital preservation is an ongoing endeavor, filled with opportunities for further exploration, innovation, and collaboration. Our work with Duke Moritz and the Red Doublet is just the beginning, serving as a foundation for future projects that aim to preserve and revitalize cultural heritage through digital means. As technology continues to evolve, so too do the methods and possibilities for engaging with history in meaningful ways.

One of the most exciting aspects of digital preservation is its potential for expansion. Imagine you could virtually step into the chamber of a sixteenth century nobleman and experience the clothing from that period. Through our research, we could significantly improve the quality of cultural heritage visualization.

Collaboration is key to the success of digital preservation efforts. By partnering with museums, educational institutions, and cultural organizations, we can enhance the reach and impact of our work. These collaborations can lead to the development of innovative educational programs, virtual exhibits, and interactive experiences that engage audiences worldwide. By working together, we can ensure that cultural heritage remains accessible and relevant to people of all ages and backgrounds.

Advancements in technology also offer exciting new possibilities for digital preservation. Emerging technologies such as Augmented Reality (AR) and Virtual Reality (VR) provide immersive ways to experience and interact with historical content. By integrating these technologies into our projects, we can create engaging and interactive experiences that bring history to life in unprecedented ways.

Conclusion

In conclusion, the *Moritz from Buxtehude* project exemplifies the transformative potential of combining 3D scanning, digital tailoring, and animated storytelling in the field of cultural heritage preservation. Through collaboration with the Historical Museum of Hanover and their meticulous historical research, our project team has succeeded in creating a dynamic and engaging representation of a historical figure and his clothing using state-of-the-art digital technologies. This digital recreation not only preserves fragile artifacts but also offers new avenues for research, education, and public engagement with history.

The project's success highlights the importance of continued exploration and innovation in the field of digital preservation. As technology evolves, we can expect even more sophisticated and immersive ways to experience and learn from our shared cultural heritage. By embracing these advancements and fostering collaboration across disciplines, we can ensure that the stories and artifacts that define our collective identity continue to inspire and educate for generations to come.

CHAPTER 10

Digitization of Clothing as a Conservation Methodology for Heritage Preservation

The collections of the Museo del Traje CIPE in Madrid

*Victoria Vásquez Pecile**

ABSTRACT
The creation of new digital collections to support the conservation of art objects in a museum is one of the goals aimed at safeguarding cultural heritage. Over the years, this activity, supported by technological advancements, has improved digitization processes tailored to each type of format, whether it be books, paintings, or sculptures.[1] However, when it comes to clothing, its specific characteristics have delayed its digitization. Thanks to 3D technology, its digitization and recreation can now be faithfully reproduced. But, to what extent can the *digital twin* be accepted as a documentary source? What processes need to be improved? How should each methodology be designed in relation to the garment being digitized? This article presents various studies applied to pattern objects, mock-ups, and finished garments to address these questions. The studies begin with the collections of patterns and mock-ups from the Museo del Traje CIPE in Madrid, as well as the Balenciaga Archive and the Azzedine Alaïa Foundation in Paris.

Keywords: clothing, pattern, methodology, digitization, digital twin, 3D

Insides

The profession of patternmaking has developed within the technical field, following a formal education structure today, complemented by workshop hours and the attentive learning of apprentices from their mentors. Thanks to this guidance, apprentices can understand the processes involved in constructing and finishing garments. For years, these apprentices copy and repeat processes to perfect their muscle memory. This type of oral and theoretical training is further enhanced through practice and repetition until the hand,

* Universidad Politécnica de Madrid.
(ORCID: https://orcid.org/0009-0006-0703-3018)

1 Factum Foundation. (2024, November). Books and Publications. Retrieved from https://factumfoundation.org/resources/books-and-publications/. One of the major companies dedicated to the reproduction of artworks, located in Madrid.

eye, and mind develop a memory that is challenging to trace in books. But what about garments?

While the transmission of knowledge in other sciences is achieved through reading and study, in this field, it is acquired through imitation, error, correction, and time. These elements are interconnected by gestures, hands, and objects. Even though these techniques are applied to different designs, their sources of reference are the garments previously created. The act of unpicking a garment to understand its construction is one of the most common methods for studying and improving assembly techniques and fabric handling. Therefore, it can be said that the primary documentary source for this craft is the garment itself—whether it be historical, traditional, familiar clothing, or pattern-making books and notes.

As this research began, manuals explaining these processes were sought. However, aside from pattern drafting manuals, there is currently no traceable documentation of the activity of the creators themselves, making it difficult to understand their prior training or locate any text where their technical thought process might have been recorded.

Studying a historical garment involves valuing the methodology of visually analyzing all its elements. Consequently, the mere description of the object transforms and becomes the guide that establishes the different stages it underwent, defining the level of training of the hands that created it.

Returning to the idea of tracing the historiography of pattern making—which seeks to establish schools, trends, and the development of manuals, always in relation to how technological changes impact fashion—, the aim of this study focuses on presenting a proposed methodology for preserving clothing heritage through the digitization of patterns, mock-ups, and finished garments. This is achieved using Clo 3D in its initial phase, beginning with the digitization of the mock-ups and patterns held in the collections of the Museo del Traje CIPE in Madrid to preserve and later recreate all the elements involved in the construction of a garment, whether or not it is complete. The study is complemented by several practical cases from the Balenciaga Archive and the Azzedine Alaïa Foundation in Paris.

How did the idea and materialization of this project come about?

For many years, the fields of the garment industry and historical and theoretical studies on fashion have remained separate, each focusing on different objectives despite being closely related.

While the industrial world developed tools that have been in use for over 30 years, academia fostered a formalist type of study, which was expanded by only a few academics who prioritized technical aspects—although this was not the mainstream approach.[2] The study of the history of techniques involves a closer relationship with understanding an object. Following the premises of Bertrand Gille (1920–2005):

> The study of technique, as a way of knowledge, offers a new approach of understanding the world. It invites us to consider that the history of technique is not only a history of tools and machines but also a history of ideas and of human relationships with their environment. Technique, being transformative, also transforms knowledge, as it introduces new ways of thinking and understanding. (Gille, 1978)

Moreover, textile technicians rarely ventured into this research path, except in the realm of costume designers for cinema or theater. For them, the primary documentary sources have been paintings, literature, and—most critically—the collections of historical garments preserved in institutions worldwide.[3]

Both public and private collections, which have made great efforts to preserve such clothing, have traditionally grown with a focus more aligned with the collecting of finished garments. Consequently, in some cases, due to the absence of a technical perspective to guide or complement these efforts, elements like mock-ups, patterns, fabric samples, construction trials, and many other workshop-related objects have been discarded. This was because there was no significant interest in these items or their collection.

It is true that establishing criteria for what is important to preserve is essential to classify what is distinctive and worthy of conservation. However, the emergence of new technologies for data collection, as well as improvements in digitization and 3D recreation, has provided significant momentum toward valuing this group of objects.

As previously mentioned, all these factors have kept two distinct paths in the field of clothing separate, paths that can indeed be combined. However,

---

2 Studies on the history of technique reflect on the premise that technical advancements imply a modification in knowledge, in the way a community conceptualizes its environment and its significance (Nieto-Galan, 1996).

3 Among other institutions, we can mention costume museums, fashion museums, private collections, and companies such as Sastrería Cornejo or Peris Costume located in Madrid.

it was not until technological and cultural changes occurred that this new way of thinking about heritage conservation could be developed.

The first change is the advent of industrial digitization processes in textile production, which led to the development of 3D software.[4] The second involves a generational shift and advances in technical training, as well as their professional applications, which enabled researchers with technical expertise to enter the academic world.

Regarding the first point, in the fashion industry, these digitization systems began to be applied to maximize efficiency and profitability in response to the type of production, supply, and demand that needed to be addressed. The increasing variety of garments being produced led to the development of systems that required minimal physical storage for preservation. As a result, digital archives and databases were created, initially for internal use only. In some cases, these digital files were preserved as intellectual property and heritage assets, while in others, they were not.

On the other hand, more than fifteen years ago, there was growing consideration of how to create production systems that maintain economic viability without exceeding social and environmental limits. These digitization systems aimed to improve processes without eliminating the profits essential to any business. At this point those new technologies began to expand, and 3D was introduced to enhance these conditions. This opened the door to the creation of new tools that we can now apply to other fields, such as research and conservation.

Regarding the second aspect, the growth of academic offerings in the fashion industry has led to an increased demand for technical professionals to provide the training required within universities, not just vocational education programs. Consequently, many technically trained graduates have begun their research careers as members of teaching staff in various institutions.[5] When it comes to focusing on doctoral theses, new premises and

---

4 Gerber, founded in 1968, and Lectra, established in 1973, both pioneers in the implementation of digitalization systems in the industrial production of garments.

5 A singular and pioneering example in Spain is the doctoral program *Arquitectura, Diseño, Moda y Sociedad*, offered by the Polytechnic University of Madrid. The program is directed by Guillermo García-Badell.

questions emerge, marking a shift in research methodologies. When a technical profile applies garment digitization methodologies—originally used in production—to the data collection of studied objects, it demonstrates how both worlds can enrich each other.

Thus, by applying digitization and 3D recreation processes to clothing collections, this project was initiated, specifically through the ongoing study of mock-ups and patterns from the Museo del Traje CIPE in Madrid (see Figure 22).

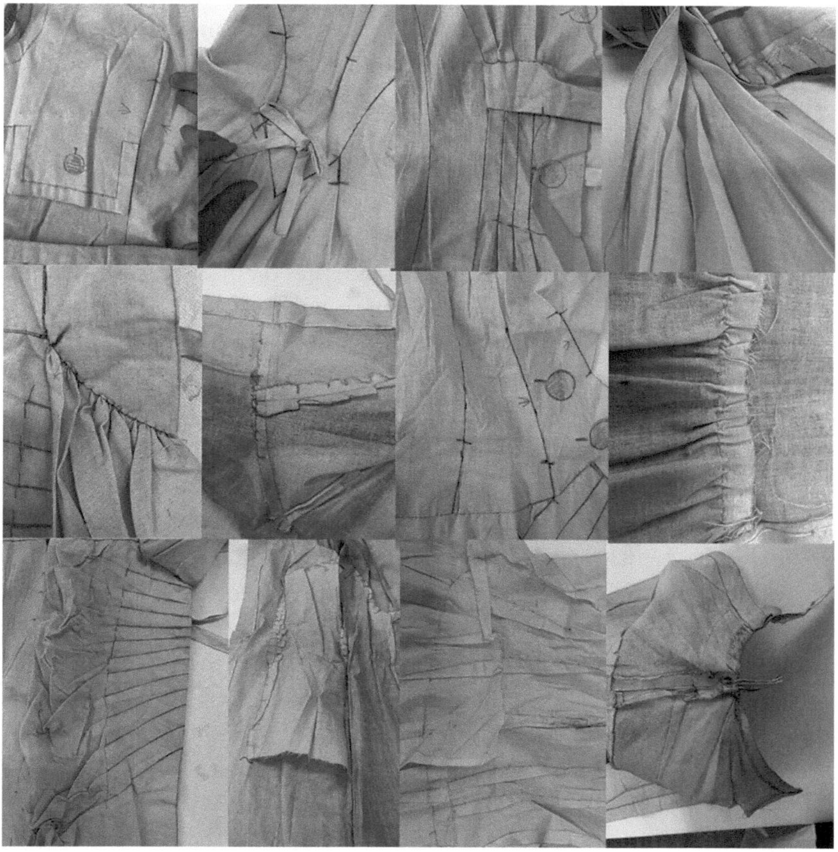

Figure 22. Muslins, 2023, Museo del Traje (details).
Image by the author.

In this case, digitization began as a tool for cataloging, describing components, and measuring the pieces to create a comparative database. However, this same process later evolved into digitization for preservation and the creation of a digital archive of garments—transforming from a tool into a subject of study.

Steps: steps

The Museo del Traje CIPE houses a diverse array of garments that offer significant potential for study within the framework of technical history. These pieces contain untapped data that remains largely unexplored. A substantial collection of patterns and muslins is being uncovered, with digitization emerging as a pivotal tool for extracting and analyzing diverse forms of information. This research draws extensively on original sources, with garment construction techniques embodied precisely in these patterns and mock-ups. Furthermore, it is crucial to acknowledge that the materials used for these sources are predominantly plant-based, rendering them susceptible to rapid and varied deterioration. As their condition becomes increasingly fragile, access for consultation is restricted, ultimately leading to their inaccessibility.

Patterns represent the blueprint for the pieces that will make up the garment, while mock-ups/ muslins (toiles) serve as the initial test where all the elements for construction are adjusted. They are the foundation for preliminary work on the final garment, and they are used to test assemblies, structures, types of joins, seams, or the machinery to be employed.

Their documentary significance lies in the fact that each workshop prepared these materials in different ways. By conducting a detailed study, it is possible to trace the methodology and techniques applied in each house. It could even lead to research on the composition of the fabrics and threads, providing additional information about the origin of these materials and their connection to the internal operations of the workshops.

The hand

The documentary sources for the history of garment-making techniques are based on three types of objects that form the foundation for mapping these historical-technical processes:

- Paper patterns.
- Mock-ups or toiles made from muslin.
- Finished garments.

A different methodology is designed for each type of object, as it is necessary to consider the material, handling methods, and the state of preservation of the pieces. Textile materials, being among the most sensitive and delicate, are subject to various types of damage. Below are some characteristics of these objects based on their material:

For patterns:

- Differences in paper thickness, color, and type.
- Variations in manual annotations made with different types of pencils and markers.
- Differences in line thickness and cut-out sections.
- Surface damage, wrinkles, tears, and external elements like adhesive tape.

For muslins:

- Variations in fabric construction types.
- Different types and compositions of basting threads.
- Assemblies of mock-ups following diverse criteria.
- Annotations and labels.

All these elements provide data about the workshop where they were created, the hands that assembled them, and how those hands manipulated the materials to apply the craftsmanship that ultimately resulted in the creation of the garment.

One intriguing aspect of these objects is that many of them are copies of the originals, as there was a hidden market for these patterns. All workshops sought to reproduce, with slight modifications, the designs of major fashion houses. These patterns often include notes that provide additional information for their recreation and tracing. Workshops would make small changes to avoid accusations of plagiarism, while others would directly purchase the patterns. For the major couture houses, this was both a form of advertising and, in some cases, a direct or indirect way of maintaining quality in tailoring processes.[6]

The patterns and mock-ups housed at the Museo del Traje CIPE have various origins—among them, the most significant are highlighted below:

- The Millán Group of paper patterns: Originating from a Barcelona-based company that specialized in the manual reproduction of designs for sale and distribution. These patterns are often accompanied by their half-sized mock-ups and fashion illustrations, which served as assembly guides.
- Paper patterns from Givenchy: Featuring numerous annotations related to the workshop and the head seamstress responsible for creating the garment. These also include technical details about construction and fabrics, making them a valuable source of information.
- Patterns and illustrations from Philippe Venet: These include the design and pattern drawn on tissue paper. These items also bear the model number and, in the lower-left corner, the firm's seal. Many of these patterns later became part of the workshop of dressmaker Amalia Cortés Hernández, located in Madrid, which was highly active from 1941.

The same situation applies to the mock-ups. These are thought to originate from workshops such as Balenciaga's or from other designers who worked with him. Some are reproductions that accompanied the paper patterns. They are linked to dressmakers such as Amalia Cortés and Hubert de Givenchy. Others could represent models purchased by a dressmaker from Balenciaga's Paris workshop or copies of mock-ups that another designer replicated from Balenciaga. There are also reproductions attributed to Antonio Castillo, Dior, Balmain, Cardin, and others.

The dating of these examples falls between 1950 and 1980, helping to situate and complete the collections to which these tests belonged.[7] Major fashion

---

6 It is also important to mention the collections of toiles from private collections, such as the Antoni de Montpalau collection. One is the collection of Ana López, a seamstress for Balenciaga and Rodríguez, who, along with her sisters, was the main copyist of Balenciaga in the Catalan capital. The other collection is from the dressmaker Carme Lladó, who had works from Lanvin, Balenciaga, Dior, and more, and established an extensive network for exchanging patterns.

7 A reference work that highlights these objects, materialized in a collection and exhibition catalog, is the study conducted by the Antoni de Montpalau Foundation.

brands have considered this preparatory work as a heritage worth protecting, which has allowed the preservation of numerous examples. Thus, it is argued that their custody and handling require rethinking methods to maintain the physical characteristics of these textile objects in the best possible condition.

The movement

The digitization methodology begins, for all three groups of clothing objects, with the measurement of all their component pieces. Therefore, the first phase involves collecting data on all the areas and surfaces of the pieces that make up the pattern object, the muslin/mock-up object, and the garment object.

By obtaining these measurements and the fabric's cutting directions, the approach aligns closely with the drafting systems used by dressmakers and tailors. However, it is still necessary to verify to what extent this data contributes to understanding, as some information has been lost or has limited content.

Description and comparison are made possible thanks to digitization using specific software for pattern drafting, in this case, Clo3D. By compiling this data, it becomes possible to create a valid recreation while respecting the actual metric information (see Figure 23).

The key elements to document for each object are as follows:

- The paper pattern: Including its measurements, shape, and original boundaries.
- Cutting direction: To understand the correct fabric orientation and ensure proper assembly, which will subsequently influence its 3D recreation and animation.
- Type of fabric: To preserve and recreate its physical properties and actual behavior (e.g., drape, sheen, sound). If such information exists, it can be used or studied further to enhance recreation through analyses of fabric composition.

This point is crucial and distinguishes this methodology from others, as the digital records available for clothing and their collections are predominantly

---

VV.AA Museu de Historia de Catalunya. (2019). *Mode i Modistes. Col·lecció Antoni De Montpalau* [Exhibition Catalog].

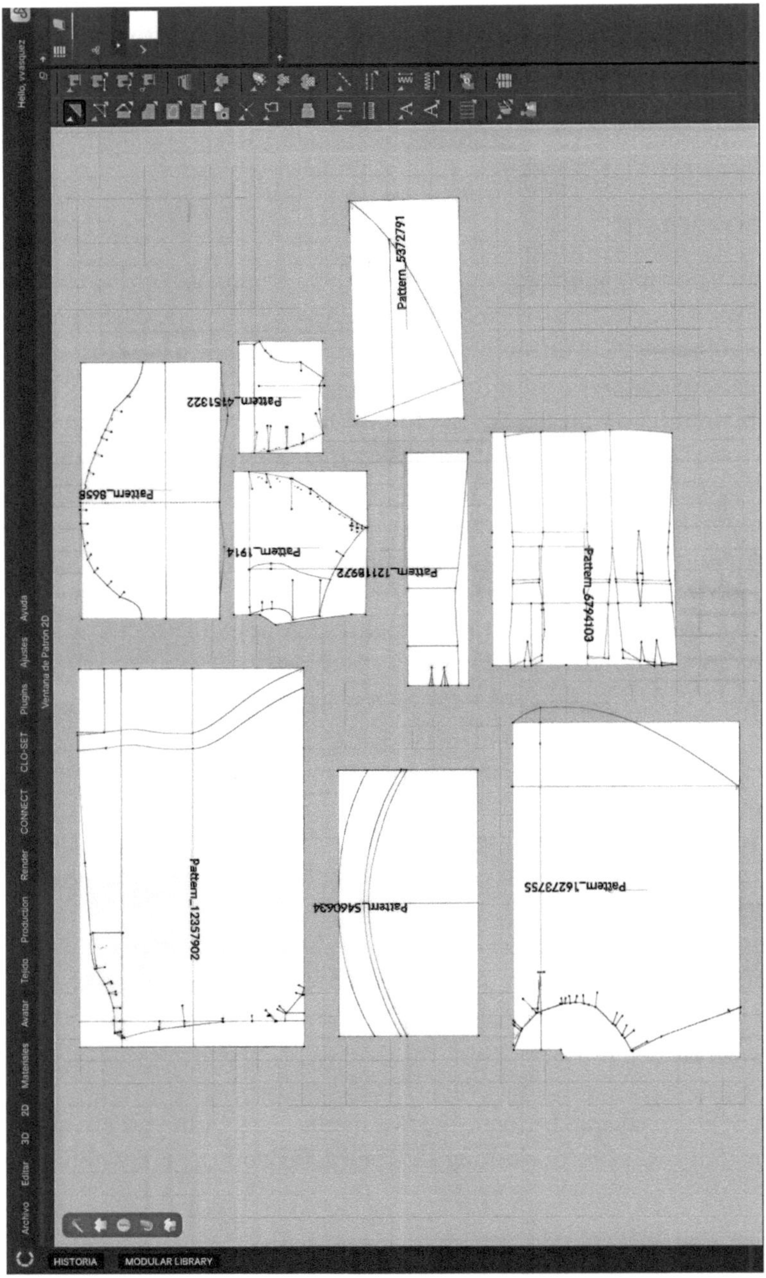

Figure 23. 2D Process, Clo3D.
Image by the author.

limited to photographs or panoramic views. While technological advancements have facilitated the recreation of objects through photogrammetry, achieving high-quality reproduction, the challenge persists in the continued production of static digital objects.[8] These do not address the fundamental questions posed by many technicians, researchers, and specialists in the history of fashion: How are the garments assembled? What insights does the assembly process provide?

By breaking down each layer of a garment's construction, we can understand the process in a more global way. The method of reverse-engineering (Vandi, 2023) has been understood as an appropriate process to unravel and understand the initial structural systems practiced in each workshop. When combined with the application of technological advancements, reverse-engineering provides the perfect vehicle for preserving and managing accurate data of each pattern piece, enabling the recreation of its construction (Vacca & Vandi, 2023).

This moment is now. The process of garment digitization is currently being studied by numerous teams from various perspectives.[9] The goal is to develop a methodology where the principles of conservation, restoration, handling, and digitization coexist for the benefit of maintaining the object, its exhibition in museums, and its dissemination to the community.

Each research center (Lance, 2022)[10] is trying to find the most suitable way to reconstruct and recreate these objects.[11] Institutions to which these

---

8 Giravolt, 3D digitization of Catalan cultural heritage, is one of the projects undertaking this type of digital recording, delivering high technical quality, and providing training to the broader research community. (2025) https://patrimoni.gencat.cat/es/giravolt.

9 The team formed by Sylvia Bossenz, Carsten Behm, and Timo Smith leads a complete recreation not only of the garments but also of the collections belonging to the Historisches Museum Hannover.

10 Alistair O'Neill and his team from Central Saint Martins recreated five garments displayed in the "Exploding Fashion" exhibition at MoMu Antwerp, 2022.

11 The *Pattern-A-Thon* project, led by Dieter Suls at MoMu Antwerp in 2022, is an initiative focused on the digitalization and study of fashion patterns. The project brings together experts from different fields to work on fashion history, technology, and design. The goal of the *Pattern-A-Thon* is to digitally recreate fashion patterns and explore the ways in which they can be preserved and shared for future generations. https://commons.wikimedia.org/wiki/Category:MoMu_Pattern-a-thon.

researchers belong must increase financial and infrastructural support so these teams can apply the technology needed to prove if the designed methodologies work, allowing validation of digital objects as documentary collections for internal use within institutions and for consultation by the wider community. From this point, numerous digital objects can be created based on their intended purpose.

Following the measurement phase, the obtained outline can be edited. Editing refers to verifying the measurements against the original pattern to ensure the information is respected. This process is enriched by the methodology used in industrial production, as its development led to the creation of all the software that enables better and faster data management.

By laying out the pieces flat and stretched, the entire area is mapped for it to be registered. But what happens when the paper pattern is very deteriorated or has missing pieces? The difference between the two processes, production digitization and conservation digitization, is that in the second case, the digitization of historical patterns may not allow us to stretch the pattern properly. Therefore, the measurement process must be much more thorough and detailed, always following the criteria and best practices established by the restoration teams.

All digitized patterns undergo a second phase of 3D construction, without incorporating details about the fabric or its finishes. This phase is understood as an initial assembly, where silhouette information predominates, enabling recognition in relation to the collection or designer to which the garment belongs. Using programs such as Clo3D, the assembly process is largely automated, resulting in a visualization of the garments that allows for immediate recognition of the object in its three-dimensional form.

When applied to the study of historical clothing, 3D assembly becomes an essential tool as it helps in finding garments that were thought to be lost, improving the dating of collections, authenticating others … countless functions that justify treating these elements as documentary sources. With their digitization, they can be preserved and consulted more efficiently and closely, without damaging their physical condition.

This initial assembly stage, where the value of the silhouette predominates, must respect aspects that will later be recreated in 3D. As mentioned earlier, the garment holds significance, among other elements, due to the behavior of the fabric. The physical characteristics of a fabric are what enable its selection by the designer, so if the possibility of recreating these characteristics is not respected, the 3D object would not achieve the same documentary value. Therefore, it is essential to consider the way the pattern is traced and cut in relation to the selected fabric. For example, a piece cut on the bias (at a 45-degree angle) does not fall or behave the same way as the same piece cut along the grain or vertically. This effect on the drape is a design element that, if it was sought after at the time, must be respected now (see Figure 24).

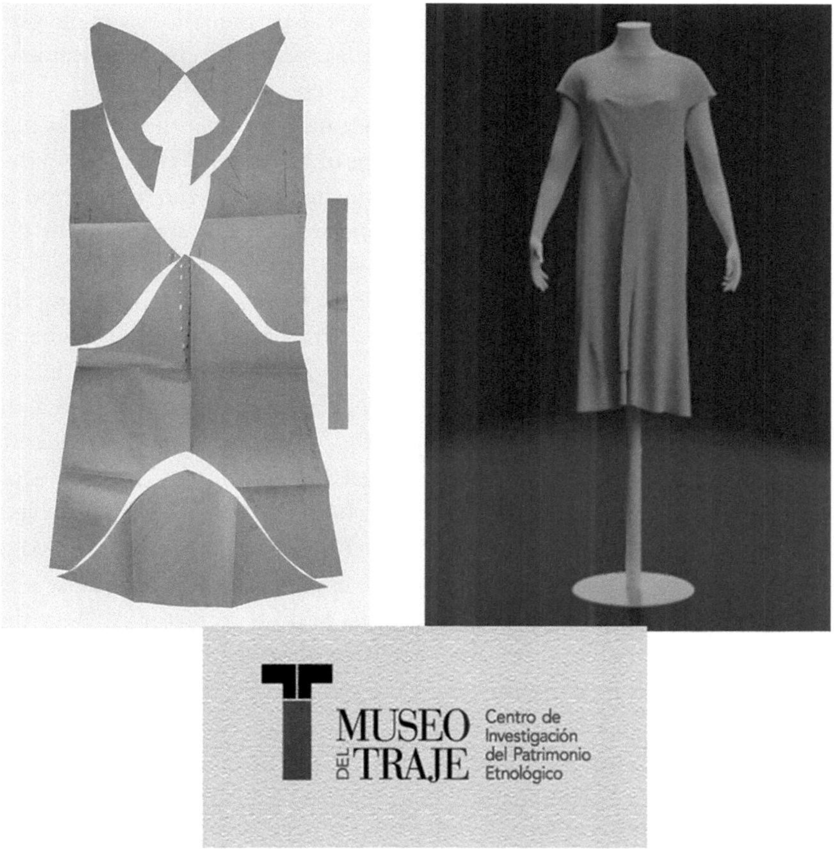

Figure 24. Paper Pattern, Millán, Model No 485. MTCE093930, Museo del Traje, Madrid. *F. Javier Maza Domingo.*

The measurement process related to the group of muslins or toiles[12] must be more rigorous since the volume of the constructions is achieved, and the placement of the patterns on the fabric must be absolutely respected in relation to its cutting direction or grain. The passage of time and the conditions in which the fabrics have been preserved may have affected them detrimentally. Therefore, if we do not have a paper pattern with which to verify the measurements, we must consider that they may vary. This brings up the question of whether a margin of error should be accepted, and if so, how much. This is a task that should be studied by the research community. We must not forget that fabrics stretch, harden, lose their qualities and physical characteristics, or may have missing parts that prevent precise measurement. When fabric is lost, the surface area may change.

In the case of studying the mock-ups, we must consider the contribution they offer regarding the texture and the type of fabric used. Therefore, in this methodology, we add the collection of information and the registration of all the physical properties they possess, which can later be applied as texture on the same model in the next phase of digital object editing.

This new phase in the digitization process, which involves applying the fabric texture and decorative elements, is performed to complete what is known in the research community as the *digital twin*. This concept is currently being discussed, particularly regarding the degree of authorship (Gupta et al., 2024). This becomes a crucial point for discussion that emerges with these new working methods. From a legal standpoint, the digital object, although a copy, is also a creation. This is because creating a digital object requires specialists and many hours of work where not only knowledge and experience in using the software are applied but also sensitivity and care when selecting the criteria to ensure a faithful recreation.[13] Thus, the object—whether public or private—has this authorship, belongs to a specific creator, and holds its significance.

---

12 Medium essay of a garment, made of muslin. It is used to test the design, fit, and construction before cutting in the final fabric. The term "*toile*" comes from the French and means "cloth" or "canvas."

13 The work carried out for MoMu in the recreation of a horsewoman's outfit from its collection, conducted by d_archive, demonstrates that these aspects must take precedence in the execution of such digitization.

The measurement of patterns and toiles is focused on the measurement of components that only have a single layer, whether it is a pattern or fabric. There are no elements such as linings, interlinings, decorations, or additions. If these elements exist (as may be the case with paper patterns), they are all recorded independently to facilitate assembly. But when dealing with a finished garment, is this methodology still useful?

The last group of objects that can be digitized using this methodology is the most interesting: the digitalization of finished garments. Data collection and measurements are done in reverse (Vandi et al., 2024). This system has been practiced for several years, as mentioned in the introduction, since it is the only way to understand the entire assembly without the possibility of disassembling the garment.[14]

Finished garments are much more complex but also more enriching, as they greatly assist museums. There are specimens that cannot be displayed, handled, or consulted. The methodology has been applied to three specific cases from the following institutions:

- 1949 dress by Cristóbal Balenciaga, belonging to the Balenciaga Archive in Paris.
- 1935 red dress by Madelaine Vionnet, belonging to the Azzedine Alaïa Foundation.
- 1989 Spring-Summer dress by Yves Saint Laurent, belonging to the Yves Saint Laurent Museum in Paris.

These three garments, still in the process of digital construction, were selected by the institutions based on different criteria. The aim was to apply the methodology to specific cases that addressed the following issues:

- A state of conservation that prevents the garment from being consulted or exhibited to the public.
- Lack of patterns for all parts of the garment.
- The garment only appears as a partial piece.

---

14 You can consult the beginnings of this methodology, prior to digital systems, in the work carried out by Janet Arnold and continued by *The School of Historical Dress* in London, through courses and publications.

- The garment has significant losses.
- The assembly of the garment on a mannequin is unknown.
- The type of mannequin used to give meaning to the garment is unknown.

All the cases mentioned above responded to one of these conditions. The application of digitalization to garments that have deterioration that may continue to grow and require urgent attention has also helped to reconsider old restoration criteria. This occurred with the Balenciaga case, which led to the design of a new restoration intervention, as the previous one had become outdated and was causing more harm to the garment.

This type of methodology for finished garments recommends that digitalization and recreation be carried out in parts, which will later be assembled into a complete model. Examples of this approach were successfully carried out by the company d_archive[15] in collaboration with the MoMu collection or Athopos in Athens.[16]

For each of these cases, a specific digitalization methodology and handling were designed. The procedures must be studied in advance to establish a protocol that addresses and provides answers to the best way to take the garment's measurements and to digitize the fabric and its components. Once these actions are established, measuring and recording fabric textures are performed similarly to the method used for toiles.

In all three garments, the initial principles have been maintained:

- Respect for the fabric grain and cutting direction.
- Verification of patterns and the effects that use and the passage of time have had on the fabric, enabling the reproduction of the original patterns.
- Reproduction of fabric texture and its physical properties and behavior. This included weighing and measuring, as well as recording the surface to generate it in 3D.
- Reproduction of decorative elements. Each of them has been digitized and recreated to present the thesis.

---

15 Martina Ponzoni, Daniele Scarante, Erisa Ibrahimi and Virgile Biosa d_archive (2023). https://darchive.io/

16 2024. https://atopos.gr/open-call-how-to-reverse-engineer-a-kamiko-%e7%b4%99%e8%a1%a3/

A report has been created for each of these three examples, which belong to the respective institution, so they can use the digital object internally and begin bringing these collections to life. Once work begins on creating a digital wardrobe archive, these methodologies can vary depending on the professionals involved and the team assembled, making 3D recreation a completely versatile tool to achieve this goal: the protection of fashion heritage. It is a process that is part of a project that can serve as a key to blend more traditional disciplines with the most innovative ones.

The train

In conclusion, several benefits of this methodology are presented, as once the digital twin is achieved, its applications and conservation system are vast:

- The valorization of pattern objects and muslins as documentary sources within research will facilitate the creation of numerous easily accessible digital archives, eliminating the need for physical handling. This approach will help prevent further deterioration of the materials from which they are made.
- Thanks to the methodologies applied to each group of objects, studies can be developed from various perspectives, improving the maintenance and dissemination of these objects, which can then be discussed and progressed.
- The digital archive will facilitate the expansion of collections through new discoveries and the comparison of documents with other archives or institutions, which have not been previously valued or studied in detail.
- This internal archive will be managed by each institution and its staff, enabling various actions to be carried out depending on the specialized professionals responsible for these projects.
- Records and digitizations of garments from before the twentieth century, as well as garments for which the original is unavailable, but a pattern exists, will be collected. This will enable the creation of an archive encompassing ancient, modern, and contemporary patterns to support research and exhibition narratives of fashion collections.
- The recreated digital twins will serve as exhibition resources for cultural dissemination organizations or for exhibition design purposes.

- The design and development of workshops for the dissemination of these institutions' collections.
- Objects available for consultation within internal cataloging systems at state museums.
- Economic benefits arising from the reproduction and sale of digitized patterns, while preserving all reproduction rights.

We must take advantage of digitalization as a methodology for acquisition, custody, and dissemination, ensuring the preservation and respect for traditional work alongside the application of new technologies. This will enhance the protection of heritage. By combining different viewpoints, but recognizing that neither can progress without the other, we can modernize the most classic aspects of the great ateliers through digitalization. Thanks to the understanding of technique, 3D recreation will be able to complete the history of fashion.

References

Fahl, A., Fugensi, F., Kammann, C., Prüser, J., Huntebrinker, J. W., & Brockhaus, M. (Eds.). (2024). *Moritz aus Buxtehude: Der Kleidernachlass des Herzog Moritz von Sachsen-Lauenburg 1551–1612* [Moritz of Buxtehude: The clothing estate of Duke Moritz of Saxe-Lauenburg, 1551–1612]. Schnell & Steiner.

Gille, B. (1978). *Histoire des techniques* [History of techniques]. Gallimard.

Gupta, S., Iyer, R., & Kumar, S. (2024). Digital twin: Theory and concepts (pp. 1–17). *Springer Nature Switzerland.* https://doi.org/10.1007/978-3-031-76564-3_1

Lance, J. (2022). Alistair O'Neill et al., *Exploding fashion: Making, unmaking, and remaking twentieth century fashion. Costume, 56*(2), Article 2. https://doi.org/10.3366/cost.2022.0237

Nieto-Galan, A. (1996). Industria textil e historia de la tecnología: Las indianas europeas de la primera mitad del siglo XIX [Textile industry and history of technology: European printed cottons in the first half of the nineteenth century]. *Revista de Historia Industrial, 9,* 11–37.

O'Neill, A. (2021). *Exploding fashion: Making, unmaking, and remaking twentieth century fashion.* Lanoo.

Vacca, F., & Vandi, A. (2023). Fashion archive as metamedium: Unfolding design knowledge through digital technologies. In K. Vaes & J. Verlinden (Eds.), *Cumulus Antwerp 2023. Connectivity and Creativity in Times of Conflict,* (pp. 74–84). Academia Press. https://doi.org/10.26530/9789401496476-074

Vandi, A. (2023). Dealing with objects, dealing with data: The role of the archive in curating and disseminating fashion culture through digital technologies. *ZoneModa Journal, 13,* 155–68.

Vandi, A., Bertola, P., & Suh, E. (2024). Human-computer interactions to rematerialize fashion heritage artefacts: A collaborative project between the Gianfranco Ferré Research Center Politecnico di Milano and the Massachusetts Institute of Technology. *Fashion Highlight,* 68–77. https://doi.org/10.36253/fh-2702

CHAPTER 11

Dematerializing and Rematerializing Archival Fashion

Analytical approaches to unravel fashion knowledge

*Angelica Vandi**

ABSTRACT
The paper explores how digital technologies facilitate new methods of representing and visualizing culture-intensive knowledge belonging to fashion archival artifacts. Archives and collections often preserve a rich intangible dimension—comprising manufacturing techniques, socio-cultural meanings, and cultural values—that can be ephemeral and difficult to access. By dematerializing these implicit aspects, technologies such as virtual prototyping enable users to understand the complexity of fashion artifacts. Additionally, these technologies allow for the rematerialization of these artifacts through processes like 3D printing. In light of this, the concepts of dematerialization and rematerialization are examined and contextualized within the existing literature, then illustrated through case studies of research pilots developed by the Gianfranco Ferré Research Center at Politecnico di Milano. In this framework, the paper examines the evolving role of archives as active repositories of Intangible Cultural Heritage, shifting from a focus on conservation and preservation toward one focused on activating the preserved knowledge and values for the development of contemporary applications.

Keywords: fashion archive, digital technology, augmented heritage, knowledge representation

Introduction

Extelligence, a term coined by Ian Stewart and Jack Cohen in *Figments of Reality* (2009), refers to cultural capital stored externally and available through external media like folklore, traditions, books, and digital formats. The term contrasts with intelligence, which is an internal cognitive knowledge. The interplay between *extelligence* and intelligence, termed *complicity*, highlights their interdependence in developing individual and collective consciousness. In this context, they describe a shared *extelligence space*—an accessible pool of human knowledge—shaped by tacit understanding and cultural learning,

* Gianfranco Ferré Research Center, Design Department, Politecnico di Milano. (ORCID: https://orcid.org/0000-0002-3627-0059)

that each individual can access the parts with which their intelligence is complicit.

Fashion archives and collections are fundamental parts of the *extelligence* space, as they hold a set of meanings, stories, and cultural values that connote a very articulated domain, represented by not only garments and accessories but also by a wide range of documentation related to design creativity: studies on shapes, textiles and color variants, sketches, paper patterns and fabric prototypes, studies for the design development, embroideries, but also advertising campaigns, runway pictures, and fashion magazines. This heritage often remains ephemeral and challenging to access (Casciani & Vandi, 2022; Peirson-Smith & Peirson-Smith, 2020; Vacca, 2012; Vandi, 2023), preventing the understanding of the actual value and meaning of the artifacts preserved inside archives (Angeletti et al., 2024, p. 1). As a matter of fact, conservation strategies have always focused on preserving fashion artifacts by suppressing the very nature that brings them to life: tactility, the movement of the body, and the interaction between fabric and skin as well as the opportunity to interconnect different artifacts and consult them together as part of the same design process. The standard display methods reflect this same caution: the garment is exhibited solo and exists only confined, immobile, draped over a mannequin, or locked inside plexiglass cases (Schnapp et al., 2024). Indeed, from a curatorial standpoint, fashion heritage displays remain deeply tied to an object-centered tradition firmly grounded in the history of costume and style (Vandi et al., 2024). While digital technologies have broadened the range of media available for forms that are not tied to physical objects (Kenderdine, 2015), curators still experiment with the traditional exhibition format, exploring the evocative yet silent potential of objects to create complex meanings and experiences that not often are understood by visitors (Healy, 2013). Even when using digital media, fashion exhibitions still rely on traditional presentation methods, emphasizing the final aesthetic of the preserved garment and celebrating its form and visual impact, yet rarely exploring in depth the creative process and design intentions behind its creation. Focusing on the latter, these curatorial practices can now be rethought in light of the opportunities arising from digital technologies that enable new forms of visualization and representation of what stands behind the physical artifact. Through the codification of new methods that hybridize the physical dimensions of fashion-related cultural heritages (Vacca & Vandi, 2023), these approaches significantly expand the performative space of objects, developing curatorial narratives that start with the object itself and then open up to cross-cutting analytical perspectives (Clark, 2017). Integrating digital elements into a fashion exhibition allows access to a wealth of archival information about the behind the scenes of the exhibition and the aesthetics of the garments on display, transcending the boundaries of materiality related to the physical environment (Pecorari, 2019). This perspective is leading to a rethinking of what Staniszewski (2000) refers to as the "power of visualization," in which the medium used for exhibition installations not only shapes the meanings of artworks but also generates specific ways of interacting with the content, giving rise to immersive experiences that redefine the concept of curating as we have understood it so far.

In light of the depicted scenario, the article aims to understand how integrating technologies into research and curatorial practices makes archives improve their accessibility to the *extelligence* space, representing the knowledge behind artifacts in innovative, engaging ways. Indeed,

> The new animated archives of fashion history are transporting us beyond the preservationist paradigm towards new horizons where garments again become objects of interaction, where their secret architectures can be explored even as we honor their physical integrity, and where their materiality and movement in time and space become integral to the web of stories that they tell, whether on the scale of individuals or society as a whole. (Schnapp et al., 2024, p. 165)

Methodology

The methodology followed by the article falls within qualitative research (Creswell, 2009; Creswell & Poth, 2016) that by nature is exploratory and holistic, aiding the construction of a comprehensive understanding of social phenomena within their natural setting, considering social and cultural contexts. The qualitative methodology is well-suited for exploring and interpreting the meanings individuals or groups ascribe to social and human problems, ultimately contributing to reframing theories or practices (Newman & Ridenour, 1998). For the purpose of the article, a systematic literature review in the field of cultural studies, fashion heritage, and fashion design has been conducted through the main digital academic channels and platforms to define the agencies that digital technologies have on the representation and visualization of tacit knowledge belonging to fashion heritage. Part of the literature panorama was arranged and informed by the doctoral thesis of the author completed in 2024 titled *Archiving Fashion Futures. Design-driven Curatorial Practices Fostering Digital Innovation in Cultural and Creative Industries* which contributed to identifying gaps in current knowledge and establishing the current state of understanding of the topic. Consequently, the Results section proposes a thorough analysis and interpretation of the literature review primarily related to the two central technological agencies on Fashion Heritage: *dematerialization* and *rematerialization*. Those two trajectories have been exemplified by two best practices in the field, belonging to research and dissemination activities of the Gianfranco Ferré Research Center at Politecnico di Milano where the author is part of the research team. The Center was built around Gianfranco Ferré's archival heritage, and funded in 2022 with the aim to:

> Investigate, develop, and experiment with advanced techniques for the visualization, representation, and use of material artifacts with a high cultural content, typical of the creative and cultural industries that represent a distinctive identity element of Italian Culture and its recognition and positioning in the international arena. (Gianfranco Ferré Research Center, n.d.)

Discussions of the present paper revolve around the consequent redefinitions of curatorial practices in fashion contexts.

Results

Dematerialization of fashion knowledge

As discussed above, unlike static artworks such as sculptures, garments demand to be experienced with the observation of details in their entirety, enabling a comprehensive 360° exploration of all the collateral materials preserved that compose the whole creative process aimed at the realization of the final garment or accessory. Moreover, tactility and movement are, by nature, singular characteristics of a fashion artifact. As discussed by Angeletti et al. (2024, p. 1), "clothes must be experienced in motion, when worn, facilitating the observation of their details as a complete entity, within the cultural and environmental context in which they were originally conceived, as opposed to the stillness of a rigid mannequin." Simultaneously, the growing adoption and integration of the technologies belonging to the reality-virtuality continuum (Milgram & Kishino, 1994), such as VR, AR, and Digital Twins, within design practices have led first the fashion industry and then heritage sectors to recognize the importance of incorporating digital fashion into their operational and curatorial frameworks. Indeed, whether initially designed as an alternative solution for sample development to reduce the amount of fabric used, shorten time-to-market, speed up vendor feedback delivery, and improve sustainability efforts within the fashion industry, these technologies are increasingly embraced by heritage actors to deconstruct and then to digitize and disclose knowledge from already assembled garments. This digitalization process aligns with the concept of fashion's dematerialization (Schauman et al., 2023; Spagnoli & Fabro Cardoso, 2023), enabling the creation of new experiences through an enhanced visualization of fashion's cultural capital. Thanks to technology-driven processes, such as Reverse-Engineering (Vacca & Vandi, 2023), which reconstruct the step-by-step development of fashion artifacts through acquisition, simulation, and restitution phases, it becomes possible to represent the design thinking and creative processes that culminate in the final garment through the design of the Digital Twin of the garment (O'Neill, 2021). In these circumstances, the Digital Twin technology, already adopted by other industries, is now starting to consolidate its place in fashion curatorial contexts since the process used to prototype a digital twin of a physical garment allows at the same time to unfold and represent all the steps digitally—meaning the design of the paper pattern, the choice of a specific fabric, the renderization of embellishments, and embroideries, until the model running the catwalk—that made that garment culturally relevant, otherwise impossible to access physically.

In light of this, new practices enabled by digital technologies are emerging within cultural contexts focused on heritage preservation, aiming to extract and represent the intrinsic knowledge associated with the intangible and implicit values stored in archival artifacts (Nissley & Casey, 2002). Although attempts to use digital tools for in-depth studies of the creative processes and technical craftsmanship that make up fashion heritage remain rare, new interdisciplinary contexts focused on researching and activating fashion heritage through technologies are starting to showcase the deconstruction of archival artifacts with dematerialization processes inside exhibitions.

This is the case of the exhibition *Gianfranco Ferré. Tra Ragione e Sentimento*, promoted by the Legnano Municipality in Milan in October 2024 and curated by the Gianfranco Ferré Research Center for the designer's 80th anniversary. The exhibition aimed to explore Gianfranco Ferré's unique approach to fashion design through a selection of designs and white shirts, his iconic garment, with the particularity of offering the visitor an experience enriched by the digital connection with the Ferré archive via QR Code. Each shirt on display had been appropriately studied in its geometric and textile composition through paper patterns and fabric cards. This allowed an augmented understanding of these shirts, communicated to visitors through a mobile application that acted as an augmented guide. Through this guide, all materials related to the garment—such as the illustration, technical sheet, fashion show photos, and advertising photos—were made accessible to the public, as well as the ability to see the garment take shape from the paper pattern and then in motion through the development of Digital Twins. This guide, while elementary in its technology and intuitive in its use, made possible an augmented exploration of Ferré's archival garments, visualizing and representing the curatorial thinking behind the exhibition process with the study of the garments on display, showing digital twins and immersive animations to allow visitors to explore the creative process behind some of the pieces on display. This dematerialized approach provides an analytical perspective on the composition of artifacts, unfolding archival knowledge and making it accessible and interactive through the thoughtful use of technology-driven processes. This approach presents scalability potentials for every archival garment and accessory preserved within archives and different didactic applications within Galleries, Libraries, Archives, and Museums (GLAMs) paths.

Rematerialization of fashion knowledge

In the transition from reality to virtuality, we are witnessing a loss of materiality in objects, prioritizing the informational aspect of data over the sensory experience (Esposito, 2022). This is primarily due to the dominance of vision-based interfaces in digital interactions, which somehow consolidate the notion that the object's materiality is subordinate to its logical or semiotic structures (Vandi et al., 2024, p. 70). In light of these circumstances, the split between the real and virtual versions emphasizes the necessity of introducing the idea of materiality within dematerialized processes. Haptic technologies and related tactile robotic applications aim to combine the tactile connection of the physical world with the augmented agencies of the virtual world (Silverstone, 2002). However, these technologies still fail to replicate the complicated tactile qualities that define our interaction with fashion artifacts (Ornati, 2019), which are characterized by particular sensorial queues related to a variety of textiles and materials that characterize the complexity and richness of meaning that fashion holds.

In this context, it has been demonstrated that since multi-sensory experiences are fundamental to comprehending the object, additive manufacturing technologies, especially 3D printing techniques, are suitable technologies to represent while reintegrating materiality and other non-visual senses into cultural experiences (Neumüller et al., 2014, p. 121). Although most 3D printers are still limited in material variety and color palette, printing out replicas of heritage objects allows first (i) to have an enhanced multisensorial experience of the heritage object that cannot be touched otherwise, and (ii) to reinterpret and actualize technical heritage through a 4.0 reassessment of traditional techniques, while completing the analog-virtual-analog continuum by acting as a rematerialization technology (Rizzi et al., 2024; Vandi et al., 2024). Regarding the first point, future innovation frontiers in additive manufacturing need to be focused on rematerializing physical attributes like weight texture, as well as mechanical features, especially regarding soft materials like fabrics and textiles, which would allow for a more comprehensive appreciation of the objects produced (Neumüller et al., 2014). Concerning the second aspect, considering the scaling applicability opportunities in fashion, the interest in multi-sensory experiences coincides with the promise of additive manufacturing and advanced robotic systems to revolutionize how research and the industry approach manufacturing processes and techniques. This is because recent innovations could also play an essential role in extracting and codifying knowledge from small-scale artisanal production processes, progressing toward cultural sustainability, and preserving and enhancing ICH (Casciani & Vandi, 2022, p. 254). Besides modifying and reassessing fashion production and operational processes, technological innovation toward rematerialization is profoundly affecting how archival objects are exhibited, especially prototyping new communication experiences that enhance artifacts' value by allowing audiences to immerse in production processes and design details, eventually contributing to a reconsideration of the role of GLAMs for the society. In truth, the emphasis has been shifting from the typical museum visit toward a multi-layered, multi-sensory experience, following the idea that we need to experience reality through all the senses we have at our disposal (Ballarin et al., 2018, p. 56). This is due to the increasing trend among contemporary museums to incorporate interactive supports that facilitate novel didactic forms of engagement alongside artworks traditionally displayed in conventional cases. Beyond merely providing information, monitors, projections, and tangible replicas reshape how viewers engage with the archival piece. Furthermore, recent studies have shown that the use of 3D-printed replicas within museum spaces provides a more accessible means for individuals to learn and engage with reality (Neumüller et al., 2014), particularly when involving children or individuals with sensory disabilities in the educational process (Ballarin et al., 2018, p. 56). Thus, GLAMs are transforming their primary role, shifting from conservators and preservers of cultural knowledge to vehicles—a medium through which this knowledge is conveyed to a broader audience.

In the context of the residency program *Rematerialising Fashion Cultural Capital through Additive Manufacturing Techniques* conducted in collaboration with the Gianfranco Ferré Research Center and MIT and in collaboration with the Design and Mechanical Engineering Departments of Politecnico di Milano, research focused on understanding how to apply additive manufacturing technologies to rematerialize the production process of a heritage object have been conducted. These studies involved 3D scanning, 3D design, and 3D printing methodologies in jewelry and garment design, leveraging on previously successfully demonstrated results that used analog and digital tools belonging to *post-digital design* (Pereira & Fernandes, 2021; Rizzi et al., 2024) in order to return again to the physical dimension once the primary form of the archive has been dematerialized for understanding its original manufacturing process. The studies involved one jacket made of a golden cord belonging to the Ready-to-Wear FW 1993 collection and a bronze galvanized brass bracelet from the Ready-to-Wear SS 2003. After a Reverse-Engineering approach to unlock the cultural-historical meanings belonging to their manufacturing processes that brought the objects into the digital form, the artifacts were then managed to be replicated through 3D printing. While the jacket was produced using small printed sections with materials that fell short of replicating the original fabric, researchers encountered a broader range of successful experiments with the bracelets, particularly in terms of materials and 3D printing techniques. 3D printers have proven effective for creating and recreating jewelry (Spahiu et al., 2021). However, certain steps in the analog-virtual-analog Reverse-Engineering process—especially those involving 3D scanning—highlighted the technological limitations of Industry 4.0 tools, which could not fully capture and dematerialize the intricate technical heritage embedded in both pieces. Despite these challenges, as discussed in (Rizzi et al., 2024; Vandi et al., 2024), these findings hold significant research value, as they contribute to developing a new process to extract and representing the implicit and tacit knowledge embedded in culturally significant artifacts through advanced digital techniques. Furthermore, the newly 3D-printed artifacts enhance the original pieces' value, allowing individuals to touch, explore, and interact with them without the constraints typically associated with archival heritage objects. In this way, designers served as mediators of meaning to facilitate a seamless transition between the scanning, modeling, and 3D printing stages of artifact 4.0, using their technical expertise to address the remaining flaws in the technological tools under investigation.

Discussion

Results fall into the debate on how curatorial practices have been reinterpreted and reframed by technology-aided processes augmenting the representation agencies of the tacit knowledge preserved inside fashion cultural artifacts. Curation has always been the practice adopted to represent fashion knowledge, being a method of "critically thinking over, investigating, and analyzing fashion as an expression of contemporary culture which anyway was initially fostered by elements of secrecy and rarity" (Vandi, 2024, p. 103). We are currently witnessing the emergence of a new curatorial paradigm grounded in multidisciplinary approaches, where the application of Reverse-Engineering (RE) methodologies to historical fashion garments has the potential to foster a dynamic ecosystem of actors engaged in the process of "visualizing the thinking through things" (O'Neill, 2021, p. 20) a hallmark of the fashion design process. In this context, the curator's role is no longer exclusive but relies on collaborative, multidisciplinary teams who co-design and utilize tools that combine expert knowledge in fashion with tech-driven practices. As a result, the fashion archive transforms from a symbol of historical authority and ownership into what can be considered a "metamedium" (Vacca & Vandi, 2023)—a relational, ever-evolving repository that encompasses various methods of cultural creation, manipulation, and interaction, alongside a constantly expanding array of data formats. No longer confined to institutional boundaries, the archive becomes fluid, adapting and shifting over time. This shift goes beyond the straightforward content of records and collections; it encompasses managing, curating, and preserving fashion archives, including decisions about access, the methods of access, and the motivations behind their use (Peirson-Smith & Peirson-Smith, 2020). This emerging model inverts the traditional archival hierarchy: while materials remain central, the base is occupied by communities that actively produce content, interpretations, and associated data. These contributions gradually rise within the archival structure, becoming part of the archive only after undergoing increasingly open and flexible processes. As a result, the archive's concept is redefined—not merely as a place of preservation but as a space where dynamic activities take place (Schnapp et al., 2024) to inform future literacy on fashion production and communication patterns. This shift enables multiple layers of engagement, diverse methodological approaches, and novel perspectives on research and learning (Rossi, 2020), transforming the archive into an "animated archive" (Schnapp, 2013).

References

Angeletti, E., Gaiani, M., Palermo, R., & Garagnani, S. (2024). Beyond the physical exhibit: Enhancing, showcasing, and safeguarding fashion heritage with VR technologies. *Digital Applications in Archaeology and Cultural Heritage*, *32*. e00314. https://doi.org/10.1016/j.daach.2023.e00314

Ballarin, M., Balletti, C., & Vernier, P. (2018). Replicas in cultural heritage: 3D printing and the museum experience. *The International Archives of the Photogrammetry, Remote Sensing, and Spatial Information Sciences*, 55–62. ISPRS TC II Mid-term symposium towards photogrammetry 2020 (Volume 42–2), 4–7 June 2018, Riva del Garda, Italy. https://doi.org/10.5194/isprs-archives-XLII-2-55-2018

Casciani, D., & Vandi, A. (2022). Hyper-Sensing creative acts. The role of design in transmitting intangible cultural heritage through digital tools. *Digital Memories*, *23*, 227–52.

Clark, J. (2017). Props and other attributes: Fashion and exhibition making. In *Fashion Curating: Critical Practice in the Museum and Beyond* (1st ed., pp. 91–104). Bloomsbury Publishing.

Creswell, J. W. (2009). *Research Design: Qualitative, Quantitative, and Mixed Methods Approaches* (3rd ed.). SAGE Publications.

Creswell, J. W., & Poth, C. (2016). *Qualitative Inquiry and Research Design* (4th ed.). SAGE Publications. https://uk.sagepub.com/en-gb/eur/qualitative-inquiry-and-research-design/book246896

Esposito, E. (2022). *Comunicazione artificiale. Come gli algoritmi producono intelligenza sociale* [Artificial communication: How algorithms produce social intelligence]. Bocconi University Press.

Gianfranco Ferré Research Center. (n.d.). *Gianfranco Ferré Research Center.* Dipartimento di Design, Politecnico di Milano. https://dipartimentodesign.polimi.it/en/research-groups/gianfranco-ferre-research-center

Healy, R. (2013). Immateriality. In *The handbook of fashion studies* (pp. 325–43). Bloomsbury Academic.

Kenderdine, S. (2015). Embodiment, entanglement, and immersion in digital cultural heritage. In S. Schreibman, R. Siemens, & J. Unsworth (Eds.), *A new companion to digital humanities* (pp. 22–41). John Wiley & Sons. https://doi.org/10.1002/9781118680605.ch2

Milgram, P., & Kishino, F. (1994). A taxonomy of mixed reality visual displays. *IEICE Trans. Information Systems*, E77-D, 12, 1321–9.

Neumüller, M., Reichinger, A., Rist, F., & Kern, C. (2014). 3D printing for cultural heritage: Preservation, accessibility, research, and education. In M. Ioannides & E. Quak (Eds.), *3D research challenges in cultural heritage: A roadmap in digital heritage preservation* (pp. 119–34). Springer. https://doi.org/10.1007/978-3-662-44630-0_9

Newman, I., & Ridenour, C. (1998). Qualitative-quantitative research methodology: exploring the interactive continuum. *Educational Leadership Faculty Publications*. https://ecommons.udayton.edu/eda_fac_pub/122

Nissley, N., & Casey, A. (2002). The politics of the exhibition: Viewing corporate museums through the paradigmatic lens of organizational memory. *British Journal of Management, 13*(S2), S35–S45. https://doi.org/10.1111/1467-8551.13.s2.4

O'Neill, A. (2021). *Exploding fashion: making, unmaking, and remaking twentieth century fashion* (1st ed.). Lannoo.

Ornati, M. (2019). Touching the cloth: Haptics in fashion digital communication. In N. Kalbaska, T. Sádaba, F. Cominelli, & L. Cantoni (Eds.), *Fashion communication in the digital age* (pp. 254–8). Springer International Publishing. https://doi.org/10.1007/978-3-030-15436-3_23

Pecorari, M. (2019). Fashion archives, museums, and collections in the age of the digital. *Critical Studies in Fashion & Beauty*, *10*(1), 3–29. https://doi.org/10.1386/csfb.10.1.3_7

Peirson-Smith, A., & Peirson-Smith, B. (2020). Fashion archive fervour: The critical role of fashion archives in preserving, curating, and narrating fashion. *Archives and Records*, *41*(3), 274–98. https://doi.org/10.1080/23257962.2020.1813556

Pereira, S., & Fernandes, M. A. (2021). Post-digital fashion: The evolution and creation cycle. *ZoneModa Journal*, *11*(1), Article 1. https://doi.org/10.6092/issn.2611-0563/13121

Rizzi, G., Gallitto, A., & Vacca, F. (2024). Augmenting cultural heritage through 4.0 technologies: A research on the archival jewelry of the Gianfranco Ferré Research Center. *World Academy of Science, Engineering, and Techn*ology https://publications.waset.org/10013917/augmenting-cultural-heritage-through-40-technologies-a-research-on-the-archival-jewelry-of-the-gianfranco-ferre-research-center

Schauman, S., Greene, S., & Korkman, O. (2023). Sufficiency and the dematerialization of fashion: How digital substitutes are creating new market opportunities. *Business Horizons*, *66*(6), 741–51. https://doi.org/10.1016/j.bushor.2023.03.003

Schnapp, J. (2013). Animating the archive. *Design & cultural heritage, archivio animato*, 63–80.

Schnapp, J., Vandi, A., & Rizzi, G. (2024). L'archivio dal vivo. Dal progetto all'algoritmo [The live archive: From project to algorithm]. In *Gianfranco Ferré dentro l'obiettivo* (1st ed., pp. 149–71). Forte di Bard Editore.

Silverstone, R. (2002). Complicity and collusion in the mediation of everyday life. *New Literary History*, *33*(4), 761–80.

Spagnoli, A., & Fabro Cardoso, G. (2023). Dematerializing fashion. Improving design-led sustainable and hybrid retail experiences via digital twins. *Cumulus Antwerp 2023. Connectivity and Creativity in Times of Conflict*, 372–8.

Staniszewski, M. A. (2000). Museum as web site, archive as muse: Some notes and ironies of the conventions of display. *Convergence*, *6*(2), 10–16. https://doi.org/10.1177/135485650000600202

Stewart, I., & Cohen, J. (2009). *Figments of reality: The evolution of the curious mind*. Cambridge University Press.

Vacca, F. (2012). Silent witnesses. Innovation through tradition in Italian fashion companies. *Research Journal of Textile and Apparel*, *16*(4), 48–58. https://doi.org/10.1108/RJTA-16-04-2012-B006

Vacca, F., & Vandi, A. (2023). Fashion archive as metamedium. Unfolding design knowledge through digital technologies. *Cumulus Antwerp 2023. Connectivity and Creativity in Times of Conflict*, 379–83. https://doi.org/10.26530/9789401496476

Vandi, A. (2023). Dealing with objects, dealing with data. The role of the archive in curating and disseminating fashion culture through digital technologies. *ZoneModa Journal*, *13*(1S), Article 1S. https://doi.org/10.6092/issn.2611-0563/17935

Vandi, A. (2024). *Archiving fashion futures. Design-driven curatorial practices fostering innovation in CCIs* [Doctoral dissertation, Politecnico di Milano]. POLITesi.

Vandi, A., Bertola, P., & Suh, E. (2024). Human-computer interactions to rematerialise fashion heritage artefacts: A collaborative project between the Gianfranco Ferré Research Center Politecnico di Milano and the Massachusetts Institute of Technology. *Fashion Highlight*, *3*. https://doi.org/10.36253/fh-27

PART 3

Crafts and Tech: A Historical Overview of Fashion Techniques and Production

The past as a reference: a historical overview

The Technical Basis of Textile Creation and the Construction Process of the Second Skin

*Herbert González Zymla**

ABSTRACT
The evolution of textile technology must be studied within the general framework of the hominization process. Born as a consequence of the need to construct a second skin to protect the human body from cold and prevent dehydration, the strategies for doing so have been as varied as complex: covering the body with sewn skins, painting the body, covering it with mud, with grease, with braided vegetable or animal fibers, until finally covering it with fabric. This article contextualizes the appearance of thread and fabric as well as the different procedures for spinning and weaving, within this process.

Keywords: tattoo, second skin, thread, loom, spinning wheel, spindle, ponderal

Introduction and purpose

The emergence of textile technology must be studied within a broader cultural and evolutionary landscape than has been traditionally done, given that it was a fundamental part of the hominization process. In fact, this process is none other than the set of physical and psychological changes by virtue of which higher primates evolved into hominids, colonized the entire planet, and became the predominant species alongside ants and spiders (Jaiswal, 2007). The purpose of this article is to relate the emergence of textile technology to the hominization process by establishing as a theoretical foundation the premise that the increasing complexity of human social relationships led, in parallel, to an increasing complexity in spinning, weaving, cutting, and sewing techniques.

Methodology and initial discussion

This article has been developed by supporting the claims made within it with the working methodologies of different disciplines. Archaeology has been used to analyze human material culture, then anthropology to analyze

* Universidad Complutense de Madrid.
(ORCID: https://orcid.org/0000-0002-8578-3272)

human relationships between dominant and dominated groups, and, finally, iconography to study the visual arts. These three disciplines are understood as a mode of nonverbal communication whose messages can be read in order to achieve a better understanding of the past. The ultimate objective of this article is to analyze the emergence of textile technology—thread and the loom—in its most basic primitive forms, from the earliest material evidence to the appearance of the mechanical loom at the end of the eighteenth century. The broad scientific debate within which this study is framed seeks to answer the following questions: How can the emergence of textile technology be explained within the framework of the hominization process? What strategies did hominids use in this process? What role did thread and the loom play in this process? What were the looms like and how were they used?

The creation of a second skin in the context of the hominization process

In 1859, the naturalist Charles Robert Darwin (1809–1882) postulated in his book *On the Origin of Species*, following ideas formulated by the Frenchman Jean Baptiste Lamarck (1744–1829), that all species of living beings on the planet have evolved from a common ancestor through a process he called natural selection, which establishes the mechanism of evolutionary change (Boyd, 2021). Those species that adapt to the geo-climatic changes occurring in their environment, with the most varied survival strategies, perpetuate themselves by reproducing, while those that remain static or are unable to adapt and do not reproduce become extinct (Cameron, 2004). These adaptive changes are usually grouped into two broad categories. Within the physical changes are: increasing cranial capacity, the arrangement of the vocal cords that allowed the emergence of articulated language, the position of the hip that led to bipedalism, the prehensile hand with the opposable thumb that allowed the manufacture of tools and utensils for self-sufficiency, frontal copulation, the redistribution of pheromones and testosterones in parallel with the hyper-development of sight compared to the almost total atrophy of smell, the disappearance of the tail, the loss of body hair … The second category encompasses psychic changes, among which should be studied: the emergence of reflective thought, spiritual and religious thought, the ability to cook, the first artistic manifestations, and the ability to transform the environment with the help of diverse tools and technologies, so that these transformations generate positive living conditions that make physical changes, always slower, unnecessary (Leakey, 1994).

The hominization process began in East Africa (Ethiopia and Tanzania) at a date prior to 4,500,000 BC, and from there, in successive migrations and in a continuous process of morphological and psychic change, hominids populated the five continents. One of the most significant physical changes was the progressive loss of body hair. Hominids abandoned their hairy appearance, common to that of other mammals, and acquired a distinct appearance with a substantially smaller amount of body hair. In mammals, hair serves a triple function: to protect, maintain temperature, and prevent dehydration. The loss of body hair forced hominids, in order to survive, to generate different adaptation strategies, whose successive appearance does not necessarily make them mutually exclusive.

The first adaptation strategy was to cover the body with animal hides, that is, to construct a second skin with which to wrap and protect the body, also used to visually express status and hierarchy (Martínez, 1998, pp. 381–408). In the Upper Paleolithic (40,000–10,000 BC), the appearance of needles in archaeological contexts of human occupation, usually made of bone, suggests that the hides of the animals that hominids hunted were used to make bodily coverings by joining them together, in the manner of a protective second epidermis, capable of maintaining temperature and preventing dehydration. Wooden and bone needles are documented as early as the Gravettian (33,000–22,000 BC), Solutrean (22,000–17,000 BC), and Magdalenian (17,000–10,000 BC) periods. Needles are the oldest material evidence of sewing technology. They have a perfectly recognizable shape when compared to modern needles: a cylindrical filament, sharpened at one end and with an eye at the opposite end that allows threading and sewing (Wilkinson, 2000). The different sizes, thicknesses, and hardness of the needles suggest functional diversity; that is, harder needles would allow for sewing more rigid hides, while thinner, and therefore more brittle, needles would only be useful for softer and more flexible materials. It is certain that the hides would have been pierced with awls to facilitate their joining in this kind of stitching. It is more difficult to know what material they would have used to facilitate such joins: Tendons? Leather strips? plant or animal fibers held together by hand? If we accept the third hypothesis, which to this day is only a supposition, these hand-twisted fibers would be the most primitive precedents of thread (Corbishley, 1994). The oldest identified needle was found in Potok Cave (Slovenia). Its dating is around 41,000 BC. A magnificent example of a Magdalenian needle is the one found in the Gourdan Cave, measuring 59x3x2 mm, in the Upper Garonne, dated to around 17,000–10,000 BC, and preserved in the Museum of Toulouse.

The extinction of large animals as the last glaciation retreated, or their drastic decrease in number, led hominid communities to generate new evolutionary strategies when it came to covering the body with a protective second skin. This is how the second great adaptation strategy appeared, which consisted of painting a second skin on the body with clay or other materials. The body painting that we currently think prehistoric humans might have done on their bodies is often studied heavily influenced by the considerations that sociology and anthropology have made about the societies we now call aboriginal and that Edward Burnett Tylor labeled in 1871 with the term *primitive peoples*. Fortunately, this terminology is outdated as it has been surpassed by the Eurocentric view of material cultures that are different from Western ones and are not necessarily peripheral (Caplan, 2000). Above the possible protective value of body painting, its ornamental character emerges, bringing it closer to a kind of semiotics based on nonverbal communication. By using different colored clays, a second epidermis is added to the body, which constitutes an embellishment, an adornment of attractive colors, similar to the plumage of the most striking birds when they dance and court. Ornamentation distinguishes the individual within the group. We find a magnificent example of the semiotic use of body painting in the current Ethiopian Karo tribe, who paint their bodies using white clay that stands out against the melanin of their skin, along with necklaces of beads and multicolored feathers.

Fixing body paint to the skin with the help of stable coloring pigments and needles to allow the ink to penetrate the epidermis would be the next step. Tattooing is nothing more than body painting done with the intention of being stable and lasting over time, combining custom, ritual, aesthetics, identity, prophylaxis, healing, and, in certain societies, a distinctive sign of having received punishment or living in a situation of marginalization (Gilbert, 2000). Flügel analyzes tattooing from the perspective of body decoration and beautification, and it can act as a psychological equivalent of clothing (1964, p. 46). The oldest preserved evidence of tattooing dates back to 4000 BC, one of the most interesting being the mummy of Amunet (2134–1991 BC), a priestess of Hathor (Deter-Wolf, 2016, pp. 19–24). In the Hermitage Museum in Saint Petersburg, several tattooed human skins are exhibited, originating from the bodily remains of several Scythian men, likely tribal chiefs of the Iron Age, who expressed their social pre-eminence with the help of tattoos. These Scythian princes lived around 500 BC, and their burial mounds were found on the Ukok Plateau. Of particular interest is the Pazyryk man, whose perfectly preserved arms, pectorals, and legs are tattooed with animals, fish, and monsters intertwined with plant motifs that surely served to signify his qualities as a warrior and as a leader (Rudenko, 1970, pp. 110–4) (see Figure 25).

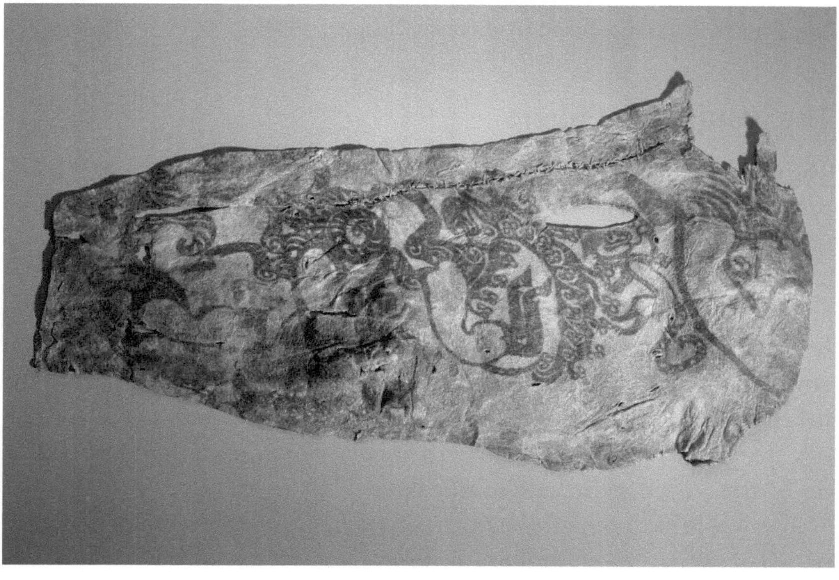

Figure 25. Tattooed skin from the shoulder of a Scythian chief whose tomb was found in Pazyryk, Ukok Plateau, c. 500–400 BC.
Hermitage Museum, Saint Petersburg.

Another strategy to protect the body was to cover it with dry plant fibers or to layer tree bark over it, understanding that such fibers regulate temperature and waterproof the surfaces they cover. In the mask festival of Dédougou, in

Burkina Faso, ritual dances are performed by men with their bodies completely covered in ceremonial costumes made from dry or freshly cut plants. The women of the Molo tribe in Kenya make skirts from stripped and dried plant fibers. Unequivocal proof that the technological strategies we have outlined so far were not mutually exclusive but perfectly compatible with each other is the archaeological discovery in 1991 of the mummy of Ötzi, the Iceman, whose date is estimated to be between 3370 and 3100 BC. His body was tattooed, he wore warm clothing made from sewn hides, and he had a kind of raincoat made from plant fibers similar to the *corozas* of traditional Galician clothing (Fleckinger, 2009) or to the Japanese *Mino* armor. In Béjar (Salamanca), a tradition of distant medieval origin is preserved in which men dressed in moss accompany the Blessed Sacrament in the Corpus Christi procession to commemorate that Christian soldiers took the city from the Muslims in 1208 disguised in this way (López, 1996).

The conquest of fibers

The climate change toward a progressively greater aridity from 10,000 BC onwards is what explains the emergence of the Neolithic period, perhaps the greatest revolution humanity has known and undoubtedly the most significant. Humankind ceased to be nomadic and predatory to become productive and sedentary, thanks to two new activities: agriculture and livestock farming, from which three new artistic techniques derived. First, architecture, which arose from the need to settle in one place. Second, ceramics, born from the necessity to successfully store food surpluses. Third, textiles, a new technology that made it possible to cover the body with as many layers of skin as necessary: second, third, and fourth skins.

The Neolithic, with all the differential nuances one wishes to establish, occurred approximately at the same time, between 10,000 and 4,000 BC, in three unconnected places on the planet: the Fertile Crescent, the valleys of the Indus and the Yangtze. This fact suggests that it was a similar response to a change in the material conditions of human existence that equally affected all of humanity (Demoule, 2009).

Thanks to agriculture and the domestication of certain animal species, humans came to understand that some animal fibers, such as sheep's wool tufts, and plant fibers, such as wicker and esparto grass, can be worked by interlacing them (Alfaro Giner, 1984). Esparto grass was, surely, the first plant material used to manufacture utensils such as baskets for storing food surpluses, sacks for storing seeds, mats for the floor, and clothing (Baró, 1923). Wicker and broom grass must have quickly caught the attention of humans due to the flexibility and resistance of their stems. Esparto grass could be cut into bundles and softened in water. Once the fibers were prepared, they could be separated according to their quality and size. The coarsest could be used in the manufacture of baskets and mats, braiding them with the hands to form a solid mesh. The finest, also braided, could be used to construct a second skin to protect the body. In both cases, braiding requires the ability to differentiate even and odd rows when counteracting and relating them to each other. Did humans imitate the ability of spiders to weave or of birds to connect the straws and twigs with which they build their nests in these works? The surely did. Perhaps the findings from the Bat Cave in Albuñol, now in the National Archaeological Museum in Madrid, are the oldest examples in Europe. It is in the braiding of dehydrated fibers that we must look for the genesis of the technology that would lead to textiles proper, based on the interlacing of warps and wefts. An example that demonstrates how solid the products made with this kind of fiber could become can be found in the Penitent Magdalene, carved in 1664 in polychrome wood by the Baroque sculptor Pedro Mena for the professed house of the Jesuits in Madrid, currently in the National Sculpture Museum of Valladolid. The saint wears a wicker sackcloth that covers the nudity of her body and accentuates the contrast between the softness of the skin and the roughness of the plant fibers (Anderson, 1988).

Textile technology was the most complex of all the strategies conceived by humankind to construct a second skin with which to protect and shelter the body. It must have emerged when, in parallel, some animals were domesticated and animal hides became a scarce commodity. As the number of hunted animals drastically decreased, the possession and use of hides became associated with the social status of those who had them and the exercise of power. The basic work, prior to the existence of fabric, is the manufacture of threads from fibers of animal (wool) or vegetable origin (linen or cotton), bound together by a twisting process aimed at resolving the problem of their reduced length in their natural state. Although thread can be made manually with the fingers or hands, in antiquity, mechanical twisting techniques were developed to ensure that the dimensions and thickness of the threads were homogeneous, their resistance proven, and the technical manufacturing process was fast, convenient, and with yielded quality results as uniform as non-standardized artisanal technical processes might have allowed.

The basic spinning techniques are twofold: spindle spinning (with a spindle whorl) and the mechanical pedal spinning wheel. The spindle whorl, which can also be called a *malacate*, flywheel, or *fusayola*, is a weight made of stone, ceramic, bone, or wood with a hole in its center so that it can be used as a counterweight by attaching it to the lower end of a spindle, which is simply a cylindrical rod of wood or other material. When the spindle and the whorl are joined, the lower part of the spindle is called the nut. From a typological point of view, spindle whorls can be cylindrical, truncated conical, spherical, conical, or polyhedral. Propelled by hand, the spindle whorl maintains the inertia of the rotational spin, in a manner similar to how a spinning top works, facilitating with this movement the cohesion by twisting various kinds of fibers and turning them into thread. The different sizes of the spindle whorls must be related to the creation of threads of very different thicknesses and levels of resistance. For the thread to be of quality, it is essential that the spindle whorl is balanced and symmetrical with respect to the spindle or twister and that the impulse with which it is moved is uniform (Franquemont, 2009). Spindle whorls have been found in archaeological excavations of the Neolithic settlement of Çatalhöyük in occupation layers dating from 6500 BC, which demonstrates the existence of an incipient textile industry that arose in parallel with the domestication of certain animals and the emergence of livestock farming (Mallett, 1990, pp. 1–27).

Iconography allows us to affirm that the making of thread was one of the essential activities of women in the domestic sphere (López-Cordón, 1996, pp. 175–98). Proof of this is that Christian iconography imagines Eve, after her expulsion from paradise, making thread (Reau, 1995, pp. 111–8), the Virgin Mary spinning during the Annunciation (Reau, 1996, pp. 182–202), and that popular culture equates feminine intelligence with the skill to spin fine thread. The Fates, goddesses of destiny, spin the thread of human life, and Atropos determines its end by cutting the thread with scissors (Barba, 2008, pp. 317–9). These same iconographies show the method of use. Holding the spindle vertically at waist height with the left hand, it was made to spin using the force of gravity, while, with the right hand, the fiber located above on the distaff of the spinning wheel was drawn out. In this way, by twisting the fiber on itself, the thread was gradually formed while it was wound along the spindle. We could cite hundreds of examples of spindle whorls and spindles preserved in archaeological and ethnographic museums and illustrate them with representations of women spinning. Examples include the vaporous-toned Attic oinochoe, attributed to the Byrgos Painter, executed between 490 and 470 BC, now in the British Museum; the paintings of the International Gothic style representing the cycle of Adam and Eve executed by Master Bertran around 1375–1383, now in the Kunsthalle Hamburg; the reliefs representing Eve spinning and caring for Cain and Abel, carved by Jacopo della Quercia on the portal of San Petronio in Bologna; the village spinner painted by William Adolphe Bouguereau in 1873, now in the Art Renewal Center Museum; or the fantastic photograph published in the Diario de Burgos in 1915 showing women making thread, sitting on stools, at the door of their house.

The spinning wheel, strictly speaking, is the rod on which the raw fiber is placed from which the thread will be made (see Figure 26). Over time, this term came to name what is actually a mechanical spinning machine, which is nothing more than a machine born from the traditional spindle, usually made of wood, in which the work of spinning is facilitated by mechanizing this action with the help of a wheel whose movement is activated by a pedal or a crank operated respectively with the foot or by hand. The spinning wheel is usually located on the opposite side to the wheel. In this way, the rotational movement of the spindle is much more uniform, allowing the hands to be free and, as a consequence, exponentially multiplying the amount of thread produced per minute. This way its quality is substantially better because the fibers are interlocked with a more cohesive twist (Derry, 1977, pp. 117–9). The spinning wheel includes a small reel or a rotating support, often in the shape of a blade and flywheel, which allows the thread to be wound onto it, forming a skein, a spool, or a bobbin. Although there is much debate on this matter, it is now accepted that the hand-operated mechanical spinning wheel originated in India around 500 BC from a hand-operated wheel that was already used by the Chinese to spin silk thread from silkworm cocoons. The spinning wheel is so transcendental to Indian identity that it was incorporated into its independence flag from 1931. The hand-operated mechanical spinning machine began to be used in Europe at the beginning of the thirteenth century, and, in the fifteenth century, it incorporated the pedal. When manufacturing is done by winding the thread onto a reel, before using the thread, it is necessary to ball it by hand to prevent tangling (Ruíz, 2023, pp. 1–12). We also have magnificent iconographic examples of mechanical spinning wheels that can be compared with spinning wheels preserved in ethnographic museums. Examples include the photograph of the elderly Irish woman working with a spinning wheel taken around 1900, preserved in the Library of Congress of the United States; the elderly Athena depicted spinning on a fast-moving spinning wheel and the young Arachne winding thread depicted in the foreground of Velázquez's *Las Hilanderas* (The Spinners), an oil on canvas painted in 1657, now in the Museo del Prado (Stoichita, 2021, pp. 257–74); or the image consecrated by the animated drawings of Heidi interacting with Peters's blind grandmother.

The loom was, undoubtedly, the greatest technical achievement in the process that led to the construction of the second skin. A loom is a machine for weaving, normally made of wood or metal, in which a series of parallel threads, called the warp, are arranged and tensioned by various procedures so that they can be separated, individually or in groups, to form an opening, the shed, through which parallel threads running in the opposite direction, called the weft, are successively passed, generating a more or less dense network of threads related to each other perpendicularly and secantly (Forbes, 1987). The warp threads are the ones that must be kept taut, while the weft, which is what is woven, is inserted by passing over and under the warp in order to create the relationship between the two. Although the interlacing can be done manually, it is more efficient to do it with the help of a machine, the loom, which facilitates establishing the interlacing relationship of the warp and weft threads in a homogeneous and regular manner. The shape of the loom and the mechanism that facilitates the interlacing of the threads vary depending on whether we are talking about traditional artisanal looms, in which the operator makes the fabric by manipulating the machine, or industrial mechanical looms, in which the machine makes the fabric and the person monitors and controls the manufacturing process or assists the machine at specific times (Broudy, 1979). The ends of the warp threads must be held in tension on the beams. Only in this way do the warp threads remain parallel, taut, and approximately the same length. The fabric is made by weaving at one end of the warp threads and advancing toward the opposite end. In many

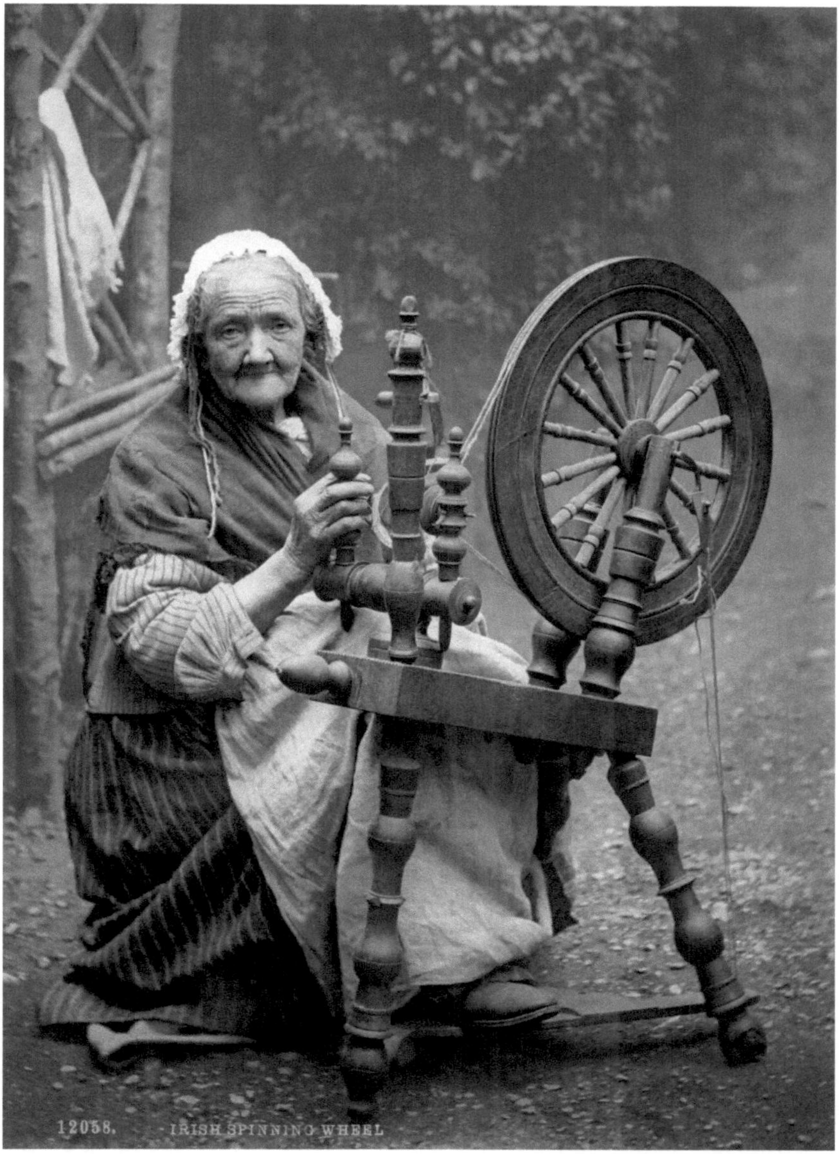

Figure 26. Photograph of an Irish woman around 1900 making yarn with a spinning wheel.

Library of Congress, United States.

languages, the first beam is called the warp beam and the other is called the cloth beam. In Spanish, the most frequent term is *enjulio*. Often, *enjulios* are used as rollers to make it easier for the weaver to work a longer piece of fabric. In this way, as the weft threads are woven, the manufactured fabric is rolled onto the *enjulio*, called the take-up roller, and work continues. The part of the fabric being worked on is called the fell (Marín, 1999).

Any loom, regardless of its various types, must facilitate the execution of three main movements: shedding, picking, and battening. Textile technology may have originated from the mimesis of nature, particularly the observation of how spiders secrete and interlace the silk thread with which they make cobwebs. This is suggested by the myth of Arachne's punishment, the weaver of Lydia who dared to challenge the Goddess Athena in her skill in the art of weaving and was punished to live suspended from the thread of her craft, weaving eternally, transformed into a spider (González, 2020, pp. 560–6). Shedding consists of separating a part of the warp threads to form a sufficient space between them, which is called the shed, distinguishing raised threads from unraised ones, in order to insert the weft thread through that space. Simple shedding is limited to alternately separating even and odd threads, with taffeta resulting from this type of interlacing. Complex shedding separates non-alternating threads, generating twill. Depending on the relationship of the warp and weft threads, we can identify different types of taffeta, such as the basic, cross, mat, ribbed, or seersucker taffeta. As for the twill, we would refer to *batavia*, roman, sateen, broken, compound, and virginia twills. Picking is the crossing of the weft thread from one side to the other of the outermost warps, passing it through the shed, usually with the help of a flying wooden shuttle where the spool of thread is often housed. Battening is the final action. After the pick, each new weft thread must be pressed against the other parallel threads in order to give consistency to the woven fabric. The more threads there are per cm^2, the tighter they are and, the finer they are, the higher the quality of the fabric will be achieved. Done with the help of wooden, bone, or metal combs, battening is a fundamental part of the manufacturing process and the final quality of the woven product.

Although looms can come in a wide variety of forms depending on the type of fabric to be produced and the lifestyle of the weaver or the society that produces and consumes the textile, we can study the types of looms in four basic categories: belt looms, frame looms, vertical looms, and horizontal looms. Often, the type of society in which the weaver lives determines the type of loom they use. Thus, among nomadic peoples, the most common looms are belt looms, frame looms, and portable looms. The looms of sedentary urban societies are usually vertical, as they are conditioned by the lack of space, while in rural areas, the predominant loom is the horizontal one.

The belt loom is the simplest type and perhaps the first type of loom. It consists of two parallel wooden or metal bars, used as beams to arrange the warp. One of the bars is attached to a fixed object, such as the trunk of a tree or a wall, and the other to the weaver, attached to their waist with the help of an anchor or ring to a belt or sash. In this way, the tension of the warp is established by the weavers themselves with the force of their body, sitting or squatting while leaning backward. This type of loom has two important limitations: only narrow fabrics can be made with it, since the width of the fabric is limited by the weaver's wingspan. On the other hand, in each work session, the warps are tensioned with a different force, and this causes the final result to be uneven.

The frame loom is a structure whose wooden frame is adjusted to a geometric section: square, rectangular, triangular, hexagonal, or circular (mesh), which allows for arranging and tensioning a warp from which to interlace the weft. The main drawback of this type of loom is that, due to its size, it only allows the production of small fabrics. Its small size does, however, allow for an extraordinary level of detail in the ornaments, which explains why its use was very frequent in aristocratic circles. In fact, the technique of frame embroidery, in which designs are embroidered onto an already manufactured fabric with its warp and weft by sewing overlapping colored threads, derives from the frame loom.

The vertical loom is one of the oldest forms of loom. Instead of two beams to tension the warps, vertical looms have an upper beam, and the warp threads are kept taut thanks to a series of weights attached to the lower ends of the threads, so that the force of gravity is what keeps the warp tensioned. These weights are called *pondus* or *ponderales* and should not be confused with spindle whorls (Hoffmann, 1974). For the beam to remain parallel to the ground, there are three strategies: supporting it against the trunk of two parallel trees or to a tree by using a post; supporting it on two uprights or wooden posts driven into the ground by fixing the beam parallel to the ground on the top of both supports; finally, supporting the beam against a wall as if it were the beam of a building. The warp tension required in a vertical loom is proportional to the diameter of the yarn used. The loom weights must be identical in shape, weight, and size and should be placed uniformly, in a row and leveled. As the shape of the loom weight limits the number of threads it tensions and determines the final number of threads per cm^2, the type of fabric being produced, its properties, and resistance can be calculated from a loom weight. In the vertical loom, there is a second horizontal bar, transverse and parallel to the ground, which is called a heddle or *lizo* and which, placed in a certain way in relation to the warp threads, allows them to be organized, separating them into even and odd groups, in order to interlace the weft. The heddle makes it easier to create the shed and counter-shed and allows the shuttle to pass through the shed. If the beam and the heddle of the vertical loom are large, the weaver must work standing, walking from side to side of the warp ends, or work in pairs, as seen in the black-figure *lekythos* called the Weavers' Vase, painted by Amasis between 550 and 530 BC, which is preserved in the Metropolitan Museum of New York (Carrol, 1983, pp. 96–9). In it, one of the weavers, after hours of activity, puts her hands on her lower back in a gesture that seems to express the back pain suffered by weavers.

In order to make working on the vertical warp-weighted loom more comfortable, the relationship of the upper beam to the lower beams, from which the weights hung, could be established with the plane slightly inclined. Typically, weaving was done from top to bottom, and the upper beam allowed the woven fabric to be rolled up to continue making the cloth, which freed the weaver from the limitation imposed by the height of the uprights. The only limitation, therefore, was the size of the upper beam, determined by the height of the wooden trunk from which it was made, which horizontally limited the dimension of the fabric. The oldest vertical looms have been documented in the Neolithic period in the Starčevo culture, dating back to around 4000 BC, located in Serbia and Hungary. In the Bronze Age, vertical looms have been documented in Miletus from 2500 BC onwards (Barber, 1991). One of the oldest testimonies of the vertical loom, with two women squatting and working together, next to another who is spinning, is found in the tomb of Khnumhotep, discovered in the Egyptian necropolis of Beni Hasan, whose dating is set between 1911 and 1870 BC (see Figure 27).

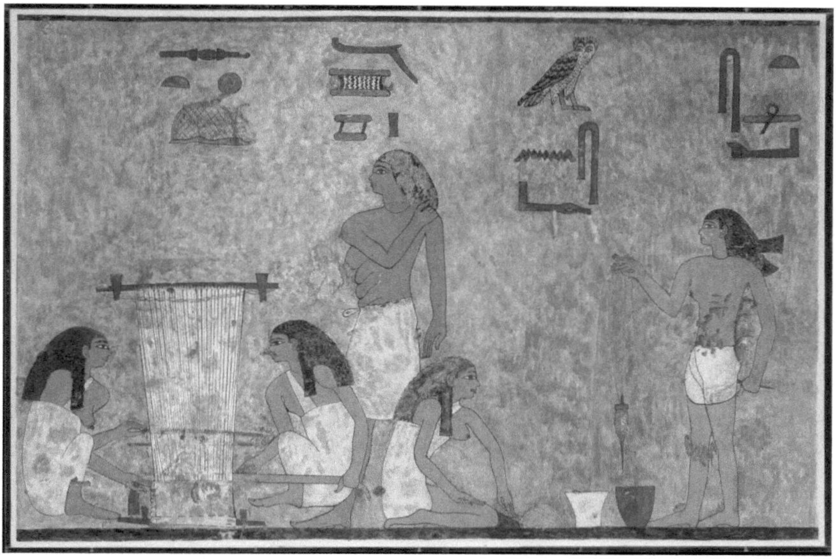

Figure 27. Drawing made by the archaeologist Garis Davies of the reliefs from the tomb of Khnumhotep, Egyptian necropolis of Beni Hasan, 1911 and 1870 BC. *Metropolitan Museum of New York.*

Tapestries and carpets can have extraordinarily complex wefts since threads of different colors and materials are used to form the desired design and decoration. The manufacturing speed of tapestry is always slower, and the shedding and pick devices are usually manual. Looms for making tapestries are divided into two large groups: high-warp looms, which produce large tapestries or carpets, and low-warp looms, which are smaller. In all of them, the warp is usually vertical, and they are woven from bottom to top, with the master tapestry maker who knots the threads squatting or sitting on a bench. The ultimate goal in both tapestries and carpets is not to create a second skin for the body, but to paint on the fabric with colored threads, without resorting to the technique of embroidery, and to build a second skin to overlay the architecture. Since antiquity, just as we have dressed the body and adorned it for festive days, architecture with tapestries and the furniture within it have also been dressed in tapestries, hangings, curtains, sheets, bedspreads, tablecloths, etc. (Harris, 2020).

Horizontal looms come in two distinct types: the stake loom or ground loom, and the horizontal or treadle loom (Endrei, 1968). In stake looms, the beams are staked to the ground with wooden wedges or ties that allow adjustment of the warp tension, whose threads are parallel to the ground. From a technical point of view, it is very easy to assemble and disassemble, given that it is very light, and therefore it is also very easy to transport, being one of the most common types of loom among nomadic peoples. Weavers work squatting to create the shed that separates the warp threads and to make the pick and the threading. The treadle loom is a loom built from a wooden frame in the shape of a parallelepiped with a square or rectangular cross-section, within which a loom is installed. The warp or this loom is parallel to the ground, and its shed is controlled by pedals that allow the even threads to be separated from the odd ones when interlacing the weft. Although there is much debate about its antiquity, the oldest horizontal loom known is depicted on a ceramic dating to around 4400 BC and is associated with Pharaonic Egypt. The advantage of this type of loom, of which many examples are preserved in ethnographic museums such as the González Santana Museum of Olivenza, lies in the fact that, when the pedals are operated, the even and odd threads are separated automatically, leaving both hands free, so that it can be operated by a single person and the fabric manufacturing process is faster.

Looking to the past to envision the future

The landscape of textile material culture changed radically with the mechanization of labor. The Industrial Revolution of the eighteenth century, first applying hydraulic power, then the steam engine in the nineteenth century, and finally electricity, allowed for the standardization and homogenization of spinning and fabric manufacturing. Humans no longer produced either the yarn or the cloth; instead, machines manufactured the textiles, with humans assisting them only at specific points in the production process. Order, reason, and applied sciences led to a productive universe that accelerated the consumer system we have inherited today.

The Arts and Crafts movement, followed by the historical avant-gardes and Dadaism, understood that this ordered, rational, and productive world had led to alienation in the workplace, stemming from the undeniable fact that machines were manufacturing the final product. The alternative proposed by the artists who embraced Arts and Crafts was to recover primitive production techniques and processes, particularly those regulated by the guild system of the Late Middle Ages. Their aim was for the artisan and the artist, without a clearly defined boundary between them, to once again be the masters of their creations, understood as the personal product of an individual. From this approach stem the current schools of arts and crafts, where some students train to become independent artisans and open their own workshops, while another, equally important, train to become art restorers, whose work requires expertise in traditional techniques. This approach is also reflected in contemporary artistic practices such as María Jesús Manzanares's (Figure 28).

The historical avant-garde movements, and Dadaism in particular, understood that rationalism and positivism had led to the great World Wars. If this world of reason and order had led to the chaos of war, humanity had to look back to everything that preceded that order, symbolized by the Greco-Roman world, to recover what is most essential: the intuitive, the spontaneous, the beauty of the inner self, unmediated by canon or rational order. Looking to the artistic productions of prehistory, the art of early civilizations, non-Eurocentric art, and the art of so-called primitive peoples, contributed to the revaluation of textiles as a form of artistic expression and transformed them into a medium for compelling contemporary works of art. Thus, twentieth-century art, and contemporary art in particular, incorporated spinning, weaving, and the creation of a second skin through body painting into forms of artistic expression that remain highly relevant. In reality, it is important to highlight the parallel between the progressive historical development of textile technology and current debates and strategies, with the inherent implications of planned obsolescence in textile products, the pollution generated by this production model, and the sustainability of a business model based exclusively on consumption. It is in this sense that we can say that the privileged position of artists looks to the past to envision the future.

Conclusion

Textile technology and its evolution are another part of the hominization process and the set of survival strategies that humanity has generated to build

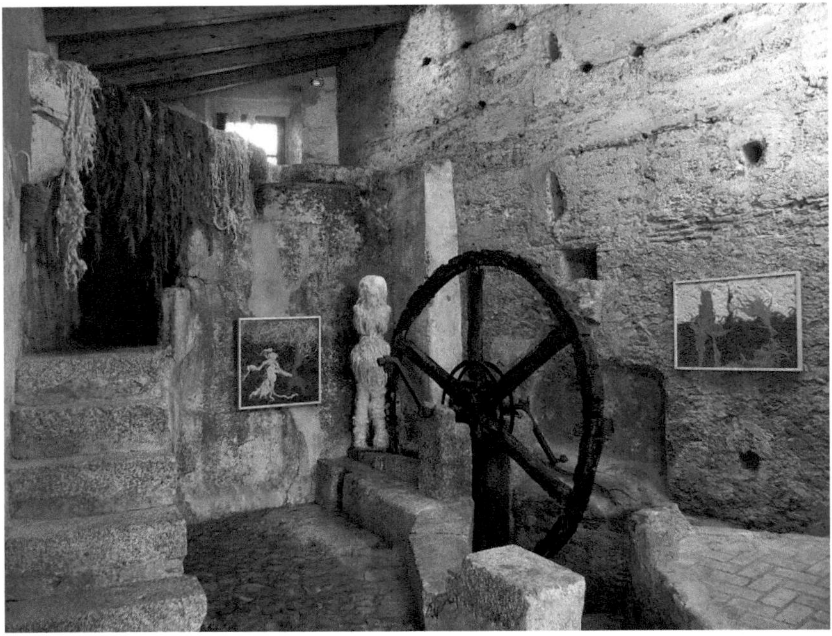

Figure 28. María Jesús Manzanares, *The denatured body*, 2004. Vostell *Museum, Malpartida.*

a protective second skin due to its ability to provide warmth and prevent dehydration of the body, from which a nonverbal language has been constructed. Any study that addresses fashion, clothing or textiles must always be based on knowledge of the underlying technology involved in the three essential activities: sewing, spinning, and weaving, whether with needles, spindle, spinning wheel, frame, vertical or horizontal loom in any of their formal variations. These are technological achievements that have made man the complex human being he is today.

References

Alfaro Giner, C. (1984). *Tejido y cestería en la Península Ibérica: Historia de su técnica e industrias desde la Prehistoria hasta la romanización* [Weaving and basketry in the Iberian Peninsula: History of their technique and industries from prehistory to Romanization]. CSIC.

Anderson, J. A. (1988). *Pedro de Mena, seventeenth century Spanish sculptor*. Edwin Mellen Press.
Barba, M. Á. (2008). *Arte y mito: Manual de iconografía clásica* [Art and myth: Handbook of classical iconography]. Sílex.
Barber, E. W. (1991). *Prehistoric textiles*. Princeton University Press.
Baró Zorrilla, F. (1923). *El esparto y su explotación* [Esparto grass and its exploitation]. Calpe.
Boyd, R., & Silk, J. B. (2021). *How humans evolved*. Norton & Co.
Broudy, E. (1979). *The book of the looms: A history of the handloom from ancient times to the present*. University Press of New England.
Burnett Tylor, E. (1871). *Primitive Culture*. Cambridge University Press.
Cameron, D. W. (2004). *Hominid adaptations and extinctions*. University of New South Wales Press.
Caplan, J. (2000). *Written on the body: The tattoo in European and American history*. Princeton University Press.
Carroll, D. L. (1983). Warping the Greek loom: A second method. *American Journal of Archaeology, 87*(1), 96–9.
Corbishley, M. (1994). *What we know about prehistoric people?* Peter Bedrick.
Darwin, C. (1859). *The origin of species*. John Murray.
Demoule, J. P. (2009). *La révolution néolithique dans le monde* [The Neolithic revolution in the world]. CNRS.
Derry, T. K., & Williams, I. (1977). *Historia de la tecnología desde la Antigüedad hasta 1750* [A history of technology from antiquity to 1750]. Siglo XXI.
Deter-Wolf, A., Robitaille, B., Krutak, L., & Galliot, S. (2016). The world's oldest tattoos. *Journal of Archaeological Science: Reports, 5*, 19–24. https://doi.org/10.1016/j.jasrep.2015.11.019
Endrei, W. (1968). *L'évolution des techniques du filage et du tissage, du Moyen Âge à la Révolution industrielle* [The evolution of spinning and weaving techniques from the Middle Ages to the Industrial Revolution]. Mouton & Co.
Fleckinger, A. (2009). *Ötzi, el hombre del hielo* [Ötzi, the iceman]. Museo Arqueológico Regional.
Flügel, J. C. (1964). *Psicología del vestido* [The psychology of clothes]. Paidós.
Forbes, R. J. (1987). *Studies in ancient technology*. Brill.
Franquemont, A. (2009). *Respect the spindle*. Krause Craft.
Gilbert, S. (2000). *Tattoo history: A source book*. Juno Books.
González Zymla, H., & Prieto López, D. (2020). Testimonials of the textile material culture through the Arachne myth in the Middle and Ancient

Ages. In *Textiles, identity, and innovation: In touch* (pp. 560–6). Taylor & Francis.
Harris, J. (2020). *A companion to textile culture*. Wiley Blackwell.
Hoffmann, M. (1974). *The warp-weighted loom*. Robin and Russ Handweavers.
Jaiswal, A. (2007). *The hominization process of Homo sapiens*. University of Delhi.
Leakey, R. (1994). *The origin of humankind*. Science Masters Series.
López Álvarez, A. (1996). *Ideología, control social y conflicto en el Antiguo Régimen: El derecho de patronato de la Casa ducal sobre la procesión del Corpus Christi de Béjar* [Ideology, social control, and conflict in the Ancien Régime: The ducal house's right of patronage over the Corpus Christi procession in Béjar]. Centro de Estudios Bejaranos.
López-Cordón Cortezo, M. V. (1996). La rueca y el huso, o el trabajo como metáfora [The spinning wheel and the spindle, or work as metaphor]. In *El trabajo en la historia* [Work in history] (pp. 175–98). Universidad de Salamanca.
Mallett, M. (1990). A weaver's view of the Çatal Hüyük controversy. *Oriental Rug Review, 10*(6), 1–27.
Martín i Ros, R. M. (1999). Tejidos [Fabrics]. In *Las artes decorativas en España II* [Decorative arts in Spain II]. Epasa Calpe, Summa Artis.
Martínez Fernández, G. (1998). El vestido en la prehistoria: De la piel desnuda al símbolo de estatus [Dress in prehistory: From naked skin to status symbol]. In *Moda y sociedad: Estudios sobre educación, lenguaje e historia del vestido* [Fashion and society: Studies on education, language, and the history of dress] (pp. 381–408). Universidad de Granada.
Odar, B. (2008). A Dufour bladelet from Potocka zijalka (Slovenia). *Archeoloski Vesnik, 59*, 13.
Reau, L. (1995). *Iconografía del arte cristiano. Iconografía de la Biblia. Antiguo Testamento* [Iconography of Christian art. Iconography of the Bible. Old Testament] (Vol. 1, Pt. 1, pp. 111–8). Serbal.
Reau, L. (1996). *Iconografía del arte cristiano. Iconografía de la Biblia. Nuevo Testamento* [Iconography of Christian art. Iconography of the Bible. New Testament] (Vol. 1, Pt. 2, pp. 182–202). Serbal.
Rudenko, S. I. (1970). *Frozen tombs of Siberia: The Pazyryk burials of Iron Age horsemen*. University of California Press.
Ruíz Álvarez, R. (2023). Hilar la lana: Una actividad femenina en la Edad Moderna [Spinning wool: A feminine activity in the Early Modern

Period]. In *Los trabajos de las mujeres en la Edad Moderna* [Women's work in the Early Modern Age] (pp. 1–12). Universidad de Granada.
Stoichita, V. I. (2021). La rueca de Velázquez [Velázquez's spinning wheel]. In *Velázquez: El arte nuevo* [Velázquez: The new art] (pp. 257–74). Fundación Amigos del Museo del Prado.
Tournay, S. (2009). Du corps humain comme marchandise, mythe primitiviste et harcèlement photographique dans la vallée de l'Omo, Éthiopie [The human body as merchandise, primitivist myth, and photographic harassment in the Omo Valley, Ethiopia]. *Afrique & Histoire, 7*, 331–42.
Tylor, E. B. (1871). *Primitive culture*. Cambridge University Press.
Wilkinson, P., & Merriman, N. (2000). *Early humans*. Dorling Kindersley.

CHAPTER 13

Classical Authors as a Source for the Study of Textile Production and Trade in Roman Times in the *Municipium Augusta Bilbilis* (Calatayud, Spain)

*Diego Prieto López**

ABSTRACT
The Roman city of *Bilbilis* has been a part of a comprehensive study conducted for my doctoral thesis on textile production and trade in that geographical area. This paper, a small extract from my doctoral thesis, aims to analyze the textile production and trade of the inhabitants of the Roman municipality through the study of texts by classical authors who refer to the city and its immediate surroundings.

Keywords: *Bilbilis*, production, trade, textile, Antiquity, Calatayud

Introduction

The city of Calatayud, located in the middle Jalón valley, owes some of its prosperity to its privileged geostrategic position. It was one of the central points of the region we call Celtiberia, within the Roman province of Tarraconensis. From ancient times, it developed as a strategic crossroads, controlling the natural passage formed by the Jalón-Henares corridor and the confluence of the Jiloca River. The corridor appears as Via 24 of the Antonine Itinerary (Alejandre Alcalde, 2016, pp. 265–84; 2017; 2018a, pp. 53–75; 2018b; 2022, pp. 133–62), which provides access from the Ebro Valley to the Plateau, connecting the ancient cities of Zaragoza (Caesaraugusta) and Mérida (Emerita Augusta). As for the confluence of the Jiloca River with the Jalón, it facilitates communication between the Plateau and the Ebro Valley with the Mediterranean Coast. It also connects with Navarra and the upper Ebro via the Manubles river valley (Jiménez Carrera & Chordá Pérez, 2023, pp. 71–95). This advantageous position would foster and stimulate the development of urban settlements throughout history in the entire area surrounding the current city of Calatayud.

* Universidad Politécnica de Madrid.
(ORCID: https://orcid.org/0000-0002-7813-0097)

The strategic location of the middle Jalón valley led to continuous occupation over time, with highly significant settlements periodically structuring and hierarchizing this region. Prominent among these settlements are Segeda, Valdeherrera, the *oppidum* of Calatayud during the Celtiberian period, Valdeherrera in the Republican era, Bilbilis Italica and the Municipium Augusta Bilbilis during the late Republican and Roman Imperial periods, and Qal'at Ayyub (Calatayud) from the Andalusian Emiral period to the present (Sáenz Preciado, 2014, p. 432).

Methodology

The study of textile production and dress through classical sources employs various research methods drawn from the humanities, history, and art history, adopting a pluralistic approach. These methods include the historiographical method, the documentary method, the semiotic method, and the comparative method. Each of these methods has been used in an interrelated way to present the results and conclusions.

The integration of all these methods has been materialized through the qualitative method, which has allowed us to study primary and secondary sources with the aim of formulating hypotheses through our work. Classical authors have served as the primary source for our investigation, while secondary sources consist of works published by other researchers who have studied Calatayud's Roman past and are continually subject to revision. We must also consider that textile production and dress have not, until now, been of interest to researchers in this region. Therefore, we are the first to systematically organize what classical texts say in this regard.

Results

The Roman province of Tarraconensis, where the city of Bilbilis is located, has historically boasted a significant abundance of livestock. Written sources consistently highlight the importance of sheep farming. This is likely because the region's arid conditions were conducive to producing large wool cloaks to combat the cold. Additionally, the physical terrain, with its pastures, was suitable for sheep and goat farming, as the poor, mountainous soil may not have been ideal for agriculture. This suggests that livestock, along with metals, provided a foundational source of wealth for this Roman province (Blázquez Martínez, 1968, p. 213). While coastal areas of Tarraconensis also had wool manufacturing workshops, livestock farming throughout history was primarily associated with inland regions, not coastal ones.

Several classical authors, including Diodorus (*Bib. Hist. V*, 33, 2), Martial (*Ep. I*, 96, 8), and Pliny (*Hist. Nat*, VIII, 191), tell us about the production of thick, black wool cloaks in Celtiberia. The quality of wool in the Ebro Valley and other regions of Celtiberia was so high that it even served as a form of tribute payment to the Romans after their regions were subdued, particularly when silver coinage was unavailable. For instance, the Numantines had to yield 9,000 wool sagi to Pompey (Diodorus, *Bib. Hist. XXXIII*, 16, 1). The information gathered from classical texts points to significant production since such high tribute payments suggest a large number of wool-bearing animals and a structured production system, not necessarily limited to domestic use. The most characteristic sheep was very likely black, yielding a coarse black fabric similar to goat hair, as described by Diodorus Siculus (*Bib. Hist. V*, 33, 2). This aligns with Pliny's description of an animal whose fleece resembled that of a goat more than a lamb (Pliny, *Hist. Nat. VIII*, 199), indicating an animal adapted to water scarcity and sparse fresh pastures. Nonius Marcellus corroborates this observation, connecting the term *Spanum* with the black wools generally produced in the peninsula (549). We find similar references in Martial's epigrams, who mostly praises the golden wools of Baetica, although he occasionally mentions Celtiberian wool cloaks. When describing Maternus, Martial clearly states that a characteristic feature of his friend was wearing dark and somber lacernae (Martial, *Ep. I*, 96).

In the region relevant to our study, sheep were shorn twice a year (Varro, RR. II, 11, 7). This indicates the presence of a well-maintained sheep flock dating back to the third century BCE, a practice that continued through the Roman occupation of the Ebro Valley and throughout history. The primary tool used for shearing sheep was shears, which have been employed across the European continent since the Iron Age. Carmen Alfaro distinguishes between different sizes of shears: those of 15 to 17 cm likely used for domestic tasks; the ones of 25 to 30 cm considered appropriate for shearing, as well as for other harvesting and pruning tasks and large shears (around 1 m in length), used for finishing fabrics, as seen in a relief from the Museum of Sens in France (Alfaro Giner, 1984, p. 60). The medium-sized shears that Carmen Alfaro deems ideal for sheep shearing were used until recently in many regions of Spain for the same purpose they served since their appearance in Iron Age contexts. Numerous examples of these types of shears are preserved in the Iberian Peninsula, including those published from the Celtiberian area in Soria and Guadalajara. We also have documented examples, such as those by Shüle, found in tomb D at Arcóbriga (Monreal de Ariza, Zaragoza), currently of unknown whereabouts, with only a description available. The approximate average size of these shears is around 17 cm, perhaps slightly small for cutting wool, but still capable of the task when compared to those found today and preserved in ethnographic museums in Aragon and Castile.

Classical literary sources describe the types of wool found in antiquity. Those from the Iberian Peninsula are what Cato (*De agri cultura*, 212) calls *oves pascales* or *pasculaes*. These were sheep with less well-maintained fleeces that grazed freely and formed the most numerous group. Pliny the Elder, in his Natural History, mentions the existence of a *non absimilis* ovine breed, typical of Corsica and Spain, whose fleece resembled that of a goat more than a lamb (Pliny, *Hist. Nat*, 199). He also refers to the ovine breed of the peninsula as *genus colonicum* (Pliny, *Hist. Nat*, 189). Wool received numerous names depending on its shades, and these tones directly correlated with its consumption (Alfaro Giner, 1984, p. 19). White wool, which was bright, was considered of better quality due to its luster, and the silky, smooth nature of its fiber. Romans knew it as *lana alba*. However, classical sources don't indicate its production was linked to the Iberian Peninsula (Varro, RR. II, 2, 18; Columella, *De re rustica*, VII, 2, 4; Virgil, *Georgics*, 2, 465; Petronius, *Satyricon*, 54; Pliny, *Hist. Nat.*, 190). This doesn't mean white or similar wool wasn't present in the Iberian Peninsula, though. Therefore, we also cannot forget Martial, who dedicates an entire epigram to this type of wool (Martial, *Ep. XIV*, 155).

The most famous Peninsular wool was the reddish kind, which Martial consistently mentioned in his epigrams as one of the products of greatest interest in Baetica, which is why he often referred to it as *baeticatus* (Martial, *Ep. I*, 96; V, 37, 7; IX, 61, 3; *XII*, 63, 3–5; 65, 5; 18, 2; XIV, 133). Brown and black colors, like those from Pollentia or Corduba, had a reasonable price, according to Columella (*De re rustica*, VII, 2, 4). He mentions them as *pullus ataque fuscus*. The grayish-brown wool was called *impluviata*, later transformed into *mutinensis*, due to being the shade of wool that came from Mutina, the current city of Modena (*Nonius Marcellus*, 548). Dark gray or ash-colored wool had the highest production on the Iberian Peninsula. It was known as *pulla*, and later as *nativa* or *Spana* (Martial, *Ep. I*, 96; 8, Pliny, *Hist. Nat. VIII*, 191), although Marcus Valerius Martial also mentions it as *leucophaeta*, in reference to people who wore clothes made from wool of this color, which today we would call ash-colored (Martial, *Ep. I*, 96, 5).

In the Iberian Peninsula, only a few textile fragments made from wool have been preserved. These were documented in a study by Morgado-Roncal (2021, pp. 193–4) after being discovered in Oiasso (Irún), likely due to their location within a mining and port context. Currently, there is no further record of material remains of this animal fiber in the Iberian Peninsula. The disappearance of wool fibers is attributed to the acidic composition of the soils found on the peninsula, which has prevented the necessary conditions for the preservation of these textile fibers from sheep (Alfaro Giner, 1984, p. 23).

The most commonly used plant fiber for textile production in antiquity was linen. In the Iberian Peninsula, we have evidence of its use, including surviving fiber fragments, the seeds documented in archaeological sites, and written records (Alfaro Giner, 1984, p. 53). Most of the fiber remains are found in funerary contexts. The textiles accompanying cremation rituals were exposed to high temperatures; some, like linen, can resist heat by fusing with metal objects, but wool fabrics have no heat resistance whatsoever (Morgado-Roncal, 2021, p. 198).

Linen seeds documented in archaeological excavations can't definitively be identified as materials used solely for the textile industry. They could have also been used for both human and animal consumption due to their high caloric and vitamin content, thus demonstrating that they were cultivated. The earliest discoveries of linen seeds, from the Neolithic, were found in Southwest Iran and the Middle Tigris region, as well as in Çatalhöyük on the Anatolian peninsula (Eiroa García, 1994, p. 48). In Europe, the oldest remains have been documented in Italy, in the Po Valley, and in the Swiss valleys. The Iberian Peninsula boasts some of the oldest remains, thanks to the findings of the Siret brothers at the El Argar (Siret & Siret, 1980, Lam. 23, 72 and 75) and La Zapata (Siret & Siret, 1980, Lam. 84–6) sites, as well as other sites discovered by the same researchers in the Almizaraque region of Almería (Buxó y Camdevilla & Piqué i Huerta, 2008). These remains are highly carbonized, which makes their study challenging. However, despite the challenges, the use of linen in the textile industry in the Iberian Peninsula is thoroughly proven by discoveries in tombs of the Argaric culture in the Southeast (Jover Maestre & López Padilla, 2013, pp. 151–7). At El Argar culture sites, a series of extremely fine linen fragments have been documented, adhered to metal objects such as earrings, diadems, daggers, etc. These fragments have been preserved due to mineral salts, which slowed their decomposition. In Castro de Vila Nova de San Pedro, Portugal, linen seeds were also collected, demonstrating that linen was already known in the western part of the Iberian Peninsula before the Iron Age (Paço & Costa, 1953, pp. 151–8). All these findings confirm that linen was being cultivated in the Iberian Peninsula since the 2nd millennium BCE, for oil extraction, food, and as a vegetable fiber for textiles.

The study of linen production and cultivation areas in the Iberian Peninsula during the Classical period is documented through literary sources, which complement our vision of a global world stressed by the appearance of material remains found at some Roman sites. We know that this plant was produced in regions such as: Ampurias (Strabo, *Geog. III*, 4, 6), Tarraco (Pliny, *Hist. Nat. XIX*, 10), Saetabis (Catullus, *Poems*, XII, 14; XXV, 5–7), Cadiz (Silius Italicus, *Punica*, III, 24), Lusitania (without a specific location indicated) (Strabo, *Geog. III*, 3, 6), and the northwestern Peninsular region (Pliny, *Hist. Nat. XIX*, 10). The importance of Hispanic linen even appears in Martial, who, complaining about the daytime and nighttime noise of Rome, describes a flax beater whose polished rod strikes Hispanic linen against a stone (Martial, *Ep. XII*, 57).

The Calatayud area completely lacks remains of linen cultivation. While no linen crop remains have been preserved, future archaeological interventions and archaeobotanical analyses might potentially uncover these seeds in some areas. As previously mentioned, classical authors do not refer to Celtiberia as a place of production, and it's possible that even these analyses may not yield any remains of this type of seed.

Linen fabric accounts for the largest number of material remains preserved in museums across the Iberian Peninsula. Thanks to this fiber's suitability for preservation, we have been able to document a high number of fragments (Alfaro Giner, 1984, p. 113). However, none of these fragments are from our specific study area. The only fragments documented in Aragón come from the sites of Azaila (Teruel), La Bovina (Vinaceite, Teruel), and Castillejo de la

Romana (La Puebla de Híjar, Teruel). These remains appear to be twill weave fabric, indicating their use in sites whose occupation was contemporary with that of Bilbilis. At Azaila, the documented remains were found adhered to large, flat plaster lids (35 to 40 cm). It was the imprints on these lids that allowed for the determination that it was likely twill weave fabric. In the site of Castillejo de la Romana, on a lid, clear remains of a 2x2 twill weave canvas are visible, with a thread thickness of 1 mm. The preserved thread remains at the Azaila site have a similar thickness to those from Castillejo (Beltrán Lloris, 1976, p. 252; 1979, p. 78 and p. 92). According to Beltrán, following J. P. Wild, wool would be an ideal fiber for producing twill weave fabric, although we also know that linen was used for this type of weave (Wild, 1972, pp. 3–18).

Alfaro highlights that the only textile fibers woven in the Iberian Peninsula were linen and wool, not esparto grass, which many researchers refer to as the sole significant textile fiber in a territory as vast as that occupied by Roman civilization (Alfaro Giner, 1984, p. 28). This assertion, accepted by the rest of the scientific community studying Roman-era clothing and textile production in the Iberian Peninsula, leads us to believe that due to the lack of material evidence for linen cultivation in the Calatayud region (though we don't rule out future positive archaeobotanical analysis results, as mentioned), the only textile fiber used for garment production in Bilbilis was wool. If linen was used, which we are confident it was, it must have been imported.

Our hypothesis is supported by the wealth of sheep livestock that always existed in Aragon, especially during the Roman imperial period. It's also backed by the material remains found at the site related to the presence of looms, as already discussed, and other spinning and manufacturing tools, all connected to the use of animal textile fiber (Prieto López, 2024, pp. 17–41).

The remaining fibers, both plant-based and animal-based, must have reached Bilbilis through trade. Similar to other goods, textile products and fabrics would have arrived as secondary cargo at local markets. We must consider that the city of Bilbilis is located inland, therefore all merchandise would have arrived via redistribution from the city of Tarragona, the ancient Tarraco, which, as a provincial capital, would redistribute and regulate products based on market demand from its port, especially in the case of imports from outside the province. This way inland products could arrive directly and more quickly. To achieve it, the Romans took advantage of existing communication routes and waterways, which would complement each other to form stable lines of commerce and communication (Chic García, 1990, p. 13). The Ebro River would have been the natural and fastest communication route between the plateau and the Mediterranean coast (Parodi Álvares, 2001, pp. 67–94), where the main seaports for imported products were located. Pliny (*Hist. Nat. III*, 21) tells us about the navigability of the Ebro River, whose shallow-draft boats reached Vareia. The Ebro's tributaries with significant flow played a role in redistributing products to cities with inland ports, likely distributed from the river port of Zaragoza (Aguarod Otal & Erice, 2003, pp. 143–56). Thus, considering the discovery in Bilbilis of Dressel 2–4 amphorae carrying wine from Campania, Etruria, and Latium, Rhodian amphorae from Rhodes (with examples also found in Colonia Celsa), and possible Galloise amphorae from Gaul, as well as one of the *tituli picti* on an amphora from Bilbilis (Padilla Roy, 2005–2006), we can establish trade routes from different parts of the Empire and the products that reached this city. Threads, manufactured fabrics, jewelry, and other personal care items could have been another product, arriving as secondary cargo to be sold in the local markets of major cities, probably as prestige items.

The Ebro River and all its tributaries would significantly contribute to the early Romanization of areas under their influence through these fluvial trade routes. Parodi states concerning the Ebro that

> The river's navigability conditions are confirmed by the archaeological findings demonstrating not only the habitual use of the Ebro and its tributaries as navigable waterways, but also the influence of the main channel and its affluents even beyond their navigable limits. It's not an axiom that every navigable river developed significant activity in this regard (nor vice versa: that rivers in suitable conditions were not used at all, or only secondarily, for and by navigation), but the Ebro River demonstrates that this must indeed have been the case for it. (Parodi, 2001, p. 88)

Similarly, Parodi (2001, p. 89) also raises the question of whether the Jalón River was navigable as far inland as Calatayud. He considers this possibility due to the substantial water input from its tributary, the Jiloca. However, the water deficit and variable flow only allowed for seasonal use by small barges.

Bilbilis has always held a strategic position overlooking a pass between various routes. That is why we can't overlook that goods would have arrived relatively quickly, thanks to the combination of inland waterways, which significantly lowered transportation costs, and land routes. In fact, during the conquest wars of the peninsular interior and the Civil Wars, the city of Bilbilis acted as a bridgehead, not only for the entry of armies but also for the arrival of products and provisions for them, with logistics being one of the keys to any conquest process.

The geographical location of Bilbilis as well as the arrival of imported commercial products from neighboring areas via communication routes demonstrate the city's involvement in trade networks and the early assimilation of its inhabitants into Roman customs.

Contemporary fashion shows clear echoes of the Celtiberian wool tradition, stemming from platforms such as *Made in Slow*, which seek to recover and preserve the rich traditional heritage of different regions of Spain. This platform has collaborated on projects with María Lafuente, notably in her *Âme* Autumn–Winter 2016–2017 collection, which aimed to use *Nómada* wool—sustainable and sourced from native sheep breeds—similar to the wool used by ancient peoples. *Made in Slow* has also collaborated with other designers such as Ulises Mérida and Ángel Schlesser in collections where Hispano Merino wool played a central role. Other designers, such as Oteyza, have consistently turned to the native roots of the Hispano Merino sheep as a source of traditional wealth, with the aim of preserving wool production traditions from antiquity to the present day.

Conclusion

The studies of classical authors like Martial (who was from Bilbilis), Columella, Pliny the Elder, and Cato, among others, mention wool as the only fabric we can confidently say was produced and manufactured in Bilbilis. This shows that using these primary sources to analyze textile production is quite limited, though it does allow us to understand the type of wool found in the region, its purpose, and its quality.

All other textile products, at least the fibers themselves, must have been imported. This is because, so far, we lack any material or literary evidence to suggest their local production. So, the production of linen or other fibers in the Roman city cannot be confirmed but given the importance of trade in the Roman era and Bilbilis's location, we are sure these types of products arrived as secondary cargo to meet the consumption needs of its population. The sources clearly indicate an extensive communication network reaching from various points on the peninsula. We also cannot forget that wearing Roman clothing was part of the Celtiberian population's assimilation of Roman customs. This leads us to believe that both production and trade were more extensive than what the material and literary evidence currently suggests.

Bibliography

Aguarod Otal, C., & Erice Lacabe, R. (2003). El puerto de Caesaragusta [The port of Caesaragusta]. In G. Pascual Berlanga & J. Pérez Ballester (Eds.), *Puertos fluviales antiguos: ciudad, desarrollo e infraestructuras* (pp. 143–56). Universidad de Valencia.

Alejandre Alcalde, V. (2016). Los caminos reales en Madrid a Zaragoza entre los siglos XVI y XIX según las guías de la época y su incidencia en la comarca de Calatayud [The royal roads from Madrid to Zaragoza between the sixteenth and nineteenth centuries according to contemporary guides and their impact on the Calatayud region]. In *IX Encuentro de Estudios Bilbilitanos* (Vol. 1, pp. 265–84). Institución Fernando el Católico. Centro de Estudios Bilbilitanos.

Alejandre Alcalde, V. (2018a). Caminería histórica de la Comarca de Calatayud: Caminos de Ateca a Soria y Almazán [Historic roads of the Calatayud region: Routes from Ateca to Soria and Almazán]. *Cuarta Provincia*, 53–75.

Alejandre Alcalde, V. (2018b). *La N-II y sus precedentes camineros* [The N-II and its road predecessors]. Institución Fernando el Católico. Centro de Estudios Bilbilitanos.

Alejandre Alcalde, V. (2022). La provincia de Calatayud: territorio, comunicaciones, demografía y economía [The province of Calatayud: Territory, communications, demography, and economy]. En J. Urzay Barrios (Ed.), *La provincia de Calatayud durante el Trienio Liberal* (pp. 133–62). Centro de Estudios Bilbilitanos.

Alfaro Giner, C. (1984). *Tejido y cestería en la Península Ibérica. Historia de su técnica e industria desde la prehistoria hasta la romanización* [Textiles and basketry in the Iberian Peninsula: History of their technique and industry from prehistory to Romanization]. Centro Superior de Investigaciones Científicas.

Beltrán Lloris, M. (1976). *Arqueología e Historia de las ciudades del Cabezo de Alcalá, de Azaila (Teruel)* [Archaeology and history of the cities of Cabezo de Alcalá in Azaila (Teruel)]. Monografías Arqueológicas.

Beltrán Lloris, M. (1979). *El poblado íbero de Castillejo de la Romana (La Puebla de Híjar, Teruel)* [The Iberian settlement of Castillejo de la Romana (La Puebla de Híjar, Teruel)], Vol. 103. Colección Excavaciones Arqueológicas de España.

Blázquez Martínez, J. M. (1968). Economía de los pueblos prerromanos en el área NO ibérica hasta la época de Augusto [Economy of the pre-Roman peoples in the northwestern Iberian area up to the time of Augustus]. In M. Tarradel (Ed.), *Estudios de Economía Antigua en la Península Ibérica. Ponencias presentadas en la 1ª Reunión de Historia Antigua de la economía antigua de la Península Ibérica. Valencia* (pp. 191–269). Barcelona.

Buxó y Capdevilla, M., & Piqué i Huerta, R. (2008). *Arqueobotánica. Los usos de las plantas en la Península Ibérica* [Archaeobotany: The uses of plants in the Iberian Peninsula]. Ariel Historia.

Chic García, G. (1990). *La navegación por el Guadalquivir entre Córdoba y Sevilla en época romana* [Navigation on the Guadalquivir between Córdoba and Seville in Roman times]. Gráficas Sol.

Diodorus Siculus (2004). *Biblioteca histórica. Libros IV–VII* [Library of History] (J. Torres Esbarranch, Trans.). Gredos.

Eiroa García, J. J. (1994). *La prehistoria I* [The prehistory]. Madrid.

Gaius Petronius Arbiter (1998). *El Satiricón* [The Satyricon]. Gredos.

Gaius Plinius Secundus (1624). *Historia Natural* [Natural History] (G. Huerta, Trans.).

Gaius Valerius Catullus & Albius Tibullus (1993). *Poemas; Elegías* [Poems; Elegies]. Gredos.

Jiménez Carrera, A., & Chordá Pérez, M. (2023). Una nueva propuesta para la vía Bilbilis–Numancia como empalme estratégico entre los itinerarios XXV y XXVII [A new proposal for the Bilbilis–Numantia route as a strategic junction between itineraries XXV and XXVII]. (2023). *Salduie, 23*(1), 71–95. https://doi.org/10.26754/ojs_salduie/sald.202318817

Jover Maestre, F. J., & López Padilla, J. A. (2013). La producción textil durante la Edad del Bronce en el cuadrante suroriental de la Península Ibérica: Materias primas, productos, instrumentos y procesos de trabajo [Textile production during the Bronze Age in the southeastern quadrant of the Iberian Peninsula: Raw materials, products, tools, and work processes]. *Zephyrus, 71*(1), 140–71.

Lucius Junius Moderatus Columella (2004). *La labranza* (*De re rustica*) [The agriculture]. Gredos.

Marcus Porcius Cato (1985). *De agri cultura* (A Castresana Herrero, Trans.) [On agriculture]. Clásicos del Pensamiento.

Marcus Terentius Varro (1992). *De las cosas del campo (De re rustica)* [On rural matters] (D. Tirado Benedí. Trans.). México.
Marcus Valerius Martialis (2007). *Epigramas* [Epigrams] (J. Guillén Trans.). Institución Fernando el Católico.
Morgado-Roncal, L. (2021). Vestes Hispaniae: Análisis histórico-arqueológico de los restos textiles localizados en la Península Ibérica [Vestes Hispaniae: Historical and archaeological analysis of textile remains found in the Iberian Peninsula]. *Onoba. Revista de Arqueología y Antigüedad, 9*, 187–201.
Paço, A., & Costa Arthur, M. L. (1953). Castro de Vila Nova de S. Pedro IV. Sementres pre-históricas de linho. *Archivo de prehistoria levantina, 44*, 151–8.
Padilla Roy, F. B. (2005–2006). *Aproximación al estudio de las ánforas del Mucipium Agusta Bilbilis* [An approach to the study of amphorae from the Municipium Augusta Bilbilis]. Universidad de Zaragoza.
Parodi Álvares, M. J. (2001). *Ríos y lagunas de Hispania como vías de comunicación. La navegación interior en la Hispania Romana* [Rivers and lakes of Hispania as communication routes: Inland navigation in Roman Hispania]. Écija.
Prieto López, D. (2024). La industria textil del Imperio Romano. El caso del Municipum Agusta Bilbilis [The textile industry of the Roman Empire: The case of the Municipium Augusta Bilbilis], In *XI Encuentro de Estudios Bilbilitanos* (pp. 17–46). Institución Fernando El Católico.
Publius Vergilius Maro (1990). *Bucólicas, Geórgicas, Apéndice Virgiliano* [Eclogues, Georgics, Virgilian Appendix]. Gredos.
Sáenz Preciado, J. C. (2014). De indigenismo a la municipalización en el valle del Jalón [From indigenism to municipalization in the Jalón Valley]. In *XVIII CIAC: Centro y periferia en el mundo clásico* (pp. 431–4). Mérida.
Silius Italicus (2005). *La guerra púnica* [The Punic War] (J. Villalba García, Trans.). Akal.
Siret Cels, E., & Siret Cels, L. (1890). *Las primeras edades del metal en el sudeste de España* [The early metal ages in southeastern Spain]. Barcelona.
Strabo (1998). *Geografía. Libros III*–IV [Geography]. Gredos.
Wild, J. P. (1972). Prehistoric and Roman textiles. In J. G. Jenkins (Ed.), *The Wollo Textile Industry in Great Britain* (pp. 7–18). London.

CHAPTER 14

The Hand of the Artisan

Crafting fashion in eighteenth-century Spain

*Mónica Bueno Ortega**

ABSTRACT
The arrival of the French-born monarch Philip V in Spain in 1700 marked a shift in the Spanish artisanal production system based on guilds. The change was characterized by the establishment and promotion of factories. The fundamental difference between these factories and guilds lay in their labor systems. While guilds were composed of artisans specialized in specific tasks who worked independently, factories concentrated the entire production process in one place. Guild artisans thus lost control over their production and, consequently, over innovations.

Shift in taste and fashion also drove changes in the demand for products that aligned with new trends. All of these factors contributed to the need for Spanish artisans in the eighteenth century to adapt to changes in the production system and the creation of new products, leading to a renewal throughout the century through the introduction of technique and production system innovations.

Keywords: fashion, Spain, artisans, textile industry

Introduction

The 1700 death of King Charles II of Spain, the last Habsburg monarch, and the subsequent accession of the French Bourbon Philip V, ushered in a period of significant change in Spain. This shift in power notably impacted fashion and thus, artisanal work.

Firstly, in the realm of fashion, it signaled the definitive ascendancy of French style and abandonment of Spanish style, affecting everything from colors and fabrics to patterns and trims. This profound influence reshaped consumer tastes and, consequently, demanded significant adaptations within the artisanal textile production sector. Artisans were compelled to align their creations with the prevailing French fashions, which emphasized new garments, vibrant color palettes, and intricate embellishments. This marked the beginning of the Rococo era, both in fashion and art, extending to all

* Universidad Politécnica de Madrid.
(ORCID: https://orcid.org/0009-0006-2816-6274)

aesthetic aspects of the highest social groups. There was a shift from an austere fashion, which in the case of men was characterized by the tightness of the garments, to a new more relaxed style that allowed for greater freedom of movement. In the case of women's clothing, although colors were already used and ornamented, the latter became more elaborated, with an increase in the use of lace, ribbons, and other embellishments. Regarding the shapes, the change was less compared to men's fashion. While the general stiffness was maintained, especially in the upper part of the body, which remained very tight, the volume of the skirts increased, both due to the use of the panier, an interior structure with which this volume was achieved, and due to the profusion of ruffles.

Secondly, the traditional guild-based production system underwent a transformative shift toward a more industrialized model. This transition fundamentally altered the organization of artisanal work. The rise of factories and the increasing demand for standardized, mass-produced goods challenged the autonomy and self-sufficiency of the traditional artisan.

These transformative forces compelled artisans to innovate, necessitating the refinement of their techniques, the development of new products, and the adoption of more efficient production methods to remain competitive in a market increasingly driven by fashionable demands.

Two distinct trends emerged within this evolving fashion landscape: new garments and ornamentation. The introduction of new garments in men's fashion such as the jacket and the waistcoat was accompanied by a palette of vibrant colors, such as blue, red, green … incorporating new colors such as "rat skin," "thorn," and "blush."[1]

Regarding decoration, it gained prominence. This was enriched by the use of gold and silver elements in buttons, tapes, ribbons, etc. Luxurious fabrics like damasks, floral-printed textiles with Oriental influences, and delicate laces epitomized the era's penchant for opulent aesthetics. Fashion itself became a powerful language of social and economic status. Consequently, everyone aspired to dress accordingly to the new fashion and project an image of better status than they really had. This was especially reflected in the use of fabrics, such as silk, reserved for the most privileged groups.

---

1 Archivo General de Palacio (AGP). 335. 1701–1746.

Beyond its specific historical context, the transformation of artisanal production in eighteenth-century Spain offers a valuable framework for reflecting on broader processes of technological change. The tensions between innovation and tradition, autonomy and regulation, skill and mechanization that shaped the experiences of artisans during this period resonate with contemporary debates on technological disruption, labor transformation, and the redefinition of craftsmanship. In this sense, current discussions surrounding technological accessibility, the cost of production, and the availability of technological tools echo many of the challenges faced by eighteenth-century artisans. Questions regarding the recognition of artisanal labor, the valuation of skill and expertise, and the pressures exerted by industry to impose lower costs, faster production rhythms, and compulsory adaptation to new technologies find clear historical precedents in the conflicts between guilds, factories, and merchants examined in this chapter. By analyzing these historical dynamics, this study seeks not only to reconstruct a past process, but also to contribute to a deeper understanding of how societies negotiate technological change and its social consequences across time.

The evolution of artisans and their relationship to changing tastes

These changes in fashion and taste translated into a surge in demand for new products, like fabrics and trimmings that reflected the new fashion and aesthetic, placing significant pressure on artisans and merchants within the textile sector to meet the evolving needs of their customers.

The success that a guild was having thanks to the interest in these fashionable items could encourage new artisans to join them. This trend is depicted in Table 3, which presents the evolution of the number of textile artisans who underwent guild entrance examinations in the city of Seville between 1710 and 1726, as recorded in documents preserved in the Seville Municipal Archive.[2]

Two dates stand out in particular: 1718 and 1724. In the first case, 1718 was the year after the transfer for Seville to Cádiz of the Casa de Contratación and

2 Archivo Histórico Municipal de Sevilla (AHMS). Sección V, tomo 114, 2.

Table 3. Number of guild examinations in Seville, 1710 and 1726

Year	Hat maker	Shoe maker	Passa-manetier	Cord maker	Silk maker
1710	2	6		2	1
1711	1		4	3	2
1712	1	2		2	2
1713		4		1	
1714		1	7		1
1715		1			3
1716		3		1	
1717		6	7		
1718			1	2	2
1719	4		2	1	
1720	8		4		1
1721	5		7	3	2
1722	1				2
1723	5		6		3
1724	1		10	1	3
1725			2		3
1726			2		

Source: Archivo Histórico Municipal de Sevilla (AHMS). Sección V, tomo 114, 2.

the Maritime Consulate, whose role was in regards of all overseas matters, like commerce. This transfer particularly affected luxury goods (Hernández Núñez, 1994) and therefore, their producers. Thus, compared to the eighteen examinees in the year 1717, in 1718 the number dropped to ten, highlighting the significant reduction in the number of *passementiers*: from seven to just one person.

In 1724 a significant increase in the number of *passementiers* taking guild exams is observed, with eleven individuals examined compared to the low number of other craftsmen. This surge likely coincided with the accession to the throne and subsequent death of King Louis I. Royal coronations and other court events traditionally stimulated the demand for new fashionable garments among the nobility, consequently increasing the demand for the services of artisans, particularly those specializing in decorative trims and embellishments, since it was cheaper to change the ornaments of the clothing rather than buying new garments.

It becomes clear that the artisans' situation was precarious and unstable, always depending on external events that they could not control, such as changes in fashion, political changes, economic changes, etc.

The artisans of the eighteenth century in Spain had to face also the arrival of an industrial system, coexisting with and gradually replacing the guild system under which they had worked and organized.

At the beginning of the eighteenth century, the Spanish textile industry was still organized under the guild system that had developed since the Middle Ages. Within this system, each artisan played a specific role in the fashion production system. Each guild possessed its own ordinances that established its running, including work practices, organizational structures, artisans training, the type of products that each guild was allowed to produce and sell.

Guilds were established at the local level, resulting in variations in guild structures and ordinances across different towns. For instance, artisans who specialized in tape-making in Madrid might have counterparts specializing in ribbon making in Seville.[3] Consequently, Spain witnessed a diverse array of guilds, including *passementiers*, *rubaniers*, *frangiers*, and others, often with overlapping or vaguely defined areas of expertise. This inherent ambiguity sometimes led to conflicts between guilds with similar or overlapping activities, while simultaneously facilitating the exchange of knowledge and best practices among guilds in different localities.

Guild ordinances were therefore the fundamental regulations for artisans. They established minimum quality standards that artisans were obliged to adhere to. However, these very ordinances were detrimental to the artisans themselves, who saw their work restricted by the ordinances themselves. This was because most of them had been approved decades, even centuries earlier, without being able to introduce the innovations demanded by customers.

The products that were not explicitly mentioned in the guild ordinances lacked legal protection, leaving them vulnerable to the exploitation of merchants or not guilded craftsmen seeking to capitalize on these unregulated,

3 AHMS. Sección V, Tomo 283, Escribanía 1ª, 41. 1681.

but demanded products. This led to multiple disputes between the guilds and merchants for the control of these unregulated articles. For instance, documentation dated in 1726 preserved in the National Historical Archive reveals a petition by the Five Guilds of Merchants of Puerta de Guadalajara, in Madrid. This guild, founded in 1667, was composed of the guilds of Jewelers, Mercerers, Silk Weavers, Clothiers, and Druggists.[4] They demanded that only those who belonged to the guild could sell the articles specified in their 1688 ordinances. This persistent gap between the rigid and often outdated ordinances and the realities of artisanal production ultimately led to various rulings being issued in 1726, culminating in the promulgation of new ordinances in the year 1741.

Further evidence of the challenges posed by unregulated markets can be found in numerous lawsuits against individuals selling products without guild membership. These individuals often produced goods of inferior quality, undermining the standards upheld by the guilds.

A prime example is the 1701 investigation conducted by the Silk Guild of Seville.[5] Inspectors, upon examining the wares of several merchants, discovered "different batches of tapes and half-tapes of colors, all of them of poor workmanship, harmful to the public because they were mostly poorly manufactured." These substandard goods fell short of the guild's established quality standards. For instance, the guild's ordinances stipulated that tapes and half-tapes should possess ten threads per pick, whereas the inspected goods contained only five. Similarly, the cloth should have been made with four threads on fine cloth, but these samples had only three. Moreover, the edges of these fabrics were deficient, exhibiting only 12 threads instead of the required 23.

This incident underscores the guilds' unwavering commitment to quality. They vehemently argued against the sale of these substandard goods, emphasizing the harm they inflicted upon both consumers and the reputation of legitimate guild members.

---

4 Archivo Histórico Nacional (AHN). CONSEJOS, 26692, Exp.3. 1726.

5 AHMS. Sección V, Tomo 13, 27. 1701.

The role of women in artisanal production

Regarding the women's participation within the guild system, it was severely limited. They were rarely recognized as masters, being typically relegated to the roles of wives or daughters of the master artisans, thus remaining dependent on male figures. An examination of the notarial protocols preserved in the Historical Archive of Protocols in Madrid reveals this disparity (Agulló y Cobo, 2012). For instance, in guilds such as the one of the *passementiers*, only one woman appears, Josefa María Jesús, compared to the almost 50 men recorded over two centuries. Notably other guilds, such as the *rubaniers*, or embroiderers, exhibit a complete absence of female members, despite historical evidence that in the mid-seventeenth century there were several female master embroiderers in Madrid, such as Sebastiana Palacios, who was the royal embroiderer to King Philip IV (Barreno Sevillano, 1974).

However, the fact that they were not female masters registered does not imply that there were no female workers in the textile sector. This is evident in the preserved documentation such as the dispute between the guild of lacemakers against the guild of merchants of Puerta de Guadalajara regarding the sale of buttons.[6] The lacemakers claimed that these types of articles were specific to their guild, to which the merchants responded:

> The lacemakers do not make or manufacture the buttons they sell, since some buy them from different people who support themselves by dedicating themselves to this work, and for the most part they are honest women who by this means supply their need without indecency, which is considerable for the inconvenience that would result from closing the door to this form of help.

Furthermore, the production of lace, a predominantly female-dominated craft, provides further evidence of women's significant contributions to the textile industry. The Royal Monastery of Santa Isabel in Madrid, for example, operated a school for orphan girls where lace-making was taught as a vocational skill, with the younger girls being specialized in the most delicate lace-making, since their hands were small enough to do the most intricate work. The sale of the lace produced by these young girls provided them with

---

6 AHN. CONSEJOS, 26692, Exp.3. 1726.

a means of livelihood within the confines of the monastery, being the work considered as a good deed.[7]

In both the case of the independent button makers and the lace-making school, the argument was that employment in the textile industry offered a crucial form of economic support and social protection for women, preventing them from falling into poverty or engaging in the considered immoral occupations, such as prostitution.

This same idea persisted throughout the century, as evidenced by the emergence of academies and the rise of formal art and artisanal education by the end of the century. Thus, in 1776, the embroiderer Francisco Tolosa presented a project to the Council for the creation of an Embroidery School in Madrid, where all kinds of embroidery would be taught. This project failed and was relegated (Barreno Sevillano, 1974).

In 1779, following complaints that the guild of cord makers, passementerie makers, and button makers of Valencia was preventing the teaching of activities specific to their guild to women, the publication of the Royal Decree of January 12, 1779, brought about significant changes in the presence of women in the artisanal sphere.

This Decree therefore ordered that the teaching of women and girls could not be prevented:

> From all those works and trades that may be suitable for their strength, as well as that they may sell the fruit of their labor freely in order to form their dowries or assist in the maintenance of their families, with male labor being applied to agriculture, heavier work, the Army or the Navy.[8]

The figure of the working woman was thus recognized, but always with the aim of being a family support, and not being the main provider of sustenance for families.

Finally, the Embroidery School was created in 1780 at the behest of the master embroiderer Josefa Careaga, in which her students would be women and girls, marking an important milestone in the presence of women artisans beyond the dependent figure of their father, husband or charity (Barreno Sevillano, 1974).

---

7 AGP. 7484. 1692–1701.

8 AHN. CONSEJOS. 6009. N.4. 1779.

From guilds to factories: the king's impact on industrialization

The accession of King Philip V marked also the beginning of a period of significant transformation in the organization of work within the Spanish textile industry. Faced with the pressing need to enhance Spain's competitiveness in both domestic and international markets, the new monarch recognized the need to modernize the existing artisanal system, which was perceived as outdated and insufficient to meet the demands of the evolving marketplace.

The previous King, Charles II, had already initiated this process by encouraging the establishment of privately owned factories, such as a cloth factory in Novés, Toledo, founded by Melchor Lorenzo in 1682. Royal patronage played a crucial role in supporting these early ventures. For example, to demonstrate the King's support for the Novés factory, the cloth produced there was frequently used to dress the monarch's wife and mother, as evidenced by accounts preserved in the General Archive of the Palace in Madrid.[9] Thanks to the 1749 Catastro of Ensenada, a census conducted by the Spanish Crown, we know that by the mid-eighteenth century, descendants of Lorenzo were still employed in the factory, although its significance may have diminished from its earlier peak.[10]

King Philip V continued this policy of promoting industrial development since the beginning of his reign, a policy that his successors continued throughout the century. In 1708, Francisco García de Navas established a textile factory in Madrid, marking the beginning of a trend that would continue throughout the century.[11] Factory owners often played a pivotal role in introducing innovative production techniques and technologies from abroad. A prime example is the silk factory founded in Vinalesa in the mid-eighteenth century (Lapayese, 1779). This factory incorporated the innovative spinning, reeling, folding, and twisting methods developed by Mr. Vaucanson in France, significantly improving the silk production efficiency. The establishment of this factory was facilitated by the support of the Royal Economic Society of Friends of the Country of Valencia, and its founder,

---

9 AGP. 38. 1700–1703.

10 Archivo General de Simancas (AGS). Novés, fol. 444.

11 Archivo Histórico de la Villa de Madrid (AHVM). 2-369-7. 1708.

José Lapayese, successfully mechanized the reeling and twisting processes, thereby reducing labor requirements.

To incentivize the establishment of such factories, the Crown granted various privileges to factory owners, such as exemptions from customs duties on imported raw materials. In 1715, for example, when granting privileges to Francisco Vazquez de León, the royal decree outlined the specific procedures that craftsmen needed to follow to establish a factory.[12] This typically involved demonstrating their ability to produce high-quality fabrics that could successfully compete with, and even surpass, foreign imports.

King Philip V, following the French example that he experienced while still living in his home country, established factories. These factories were based on the ones founded by Jean-Baptiste Colbert, like the Gobelins Manufactory. Their objective was to promote the Spanish industry, while providing to the royalty luxury goods. In this sense, it was founded in 1719 the Royal Cloth Factory, in Guadalajara (Calle, 2010). This factory served as an example for the artisans that wanted to copy the production model. This is evident in the 1716 lawsuit between the inspectors of the weavers' guild in Ágreda, Soria, and José López and Miguel Cabello, masters of the same guild, regarding the method of cloth manufacturing. López and Cabello were accused of dyeing, fulling, and weaving cloth in the same dwelling, using looms smaller than those recognized by the guild's ordinances.[13] Two important aspects emerge from this lawsuit, shedding light on the situation at the time:

Firstly, artisans were compelled to produce goods according to the rules of their guild's ordinances. This limited their natural evolution as manufacturers and hindered the introduction of innovations.

Secondly, in relation to the organization of the production system, the defendants defended themselves against the accusations by arguing that this system was "observed in all factories, both in Castile, Aragon, and Navarre. What is mentioned is not fraud, but rather utility and convenience to avoid mixing and exchanging wools." In other words, it was both for their own convenience as artisans and to guarantee the quality demanded by their guild.

12 Archivo del Reino de Valencia (ARV) Escribanías de Cámara, año 1715, Exp. 30. 1715.

13 Archivo de la Real Chancillería de Valladolid (ARCHV) PL CIVILES, ALONSO RODRÍGUEZ (D), CAJA 489,4. 1716–1731.

The guild responded that López and Cabello could not be compared to "the Guadalajara factory, because it is royal and the Prince can dispose of it at will. The main thing is that the law mandates how the said cloth should be made and the law be imposed."

Again, two important aspects emerge: firstly, the guilds knew they could not impose their way of working on the Royal Factories, thus limiting their power in this new production system and losing control over the products manufactured there. Secondly, the law ultimately imposed changes on the production system.

Finally, the judgment decreed that López and Cabello must respect the ordinances, working with the looms specified therein, and each in their own workshop. Thus, tradition prevailed over innovation.

The relationship between artisans, guilds, and merchants

The imperative to produce articles of comparable quality to those manufactured abroad, and therefore boost the national economy and being not so dependent on imported goods, fostered the emergence of a new figure: the merchant-craftsman, or simply the merchant. This figure assumed control over the production process, dictating aesthetic preferences, quality standards, and production techniques, effectively transforming the traditional artisan into a mere manufacturer. A notable example of this transition is Juan de Bedoya of the city Valladolid.[14] He began his career as a craftsman, and evolved into a prominent merchant by the early eighteenth century. He established a vast network of merchants throughout northern Spain to distribute his products, becoming then an important fashion figure in the area.

Despite the rise of this merchant-craftsman system, the traditional guild system did not entirely disappear. Guild-affiliated artisans continued to cater to segments of the population who could not afford the often-exorbitant prices of factory-produced goods. While factory products could and needed to offer the last trends to their customers, artisans could offer cheaper articles to not so wealthy customers. This coexistence of guilds and factories created

[14] ARCHV. SALA DE HIJOSDALGO, CAJA 1763,6. 1716.

a distinct social hierarchy, where the source of a product—whether from a guild or a factory—became a significant marker of social status, often transcending considerations of quality.

In the case of factory artisans, this new work system allowed for the accelerated introduction of innovations, even promoting the arrival of foreign artisans, as happened in the Royal Factories. Such was the case of Jacob Vandergoten, from Flanders, who arrived in Madrid in 1720 to work in the Royal Tapestry Factory of Santa Bárbara, or shortly after, the Frenchman Gabriel Bouquet, who introduced the high-warp loom to Spain, having worked at the Manufacture Royale des Gobelins.

Conclusion

The eighteenth century witnessed a profound and interconnected evolution of artisans, industry, and fashion. Artisans were at the forefront of this transformation, facing significant and different pressures to adapt to the new market demands. This transformation raises the question of how the changes in fashion and the subsequent demand for new materials, products and technology actually affected artisans. Likewise, how did it impact their skills and whether there was a loss of knowledge related to the traditional production processes that were transformed in the eighteenth century with the arrival of new technology.

This adaptation therefore often involved embracing new production methods and shifting their roles, sometimes leading to the loss of the artisans traditional identity as they transitioned into merchants or incorporated new imported technologies and organizational structures within the evolving factory system.

Regardless of the chosen path, these transformations inevitably diminished the artisan's autonomy, creativity, and traditional role as a master craftsman within their community. The overarching societal and economic shifts of the era compelled artisans to navigate a new order that significantly curtailed their independence and creative freedom.

Viewed from a contemporary perspective, the experiences of eighteenth-century Spanish artisans provide a historical lens through which to reconsider current responses to technological innovation. Much like today's debates surrounding digital fabrication, or artificial intelligence, the introduction of new production systems in the eighteenth century generated fears of loss of creative control, and erosion of professional identity. The historical case demonstrates that technological change is not solely a matter of efficiency or progress, but also one of power, social organization, and cultural values. Understanding how past societies navigated these transformations allows us to critically assess present-day technological shifts and to question who benefits from innovation, who bears its costs, and how traditional knowledge can be preserved or reimagined rather than simply displaced.

References

Agulló y Cobo, M. (2012). *De bordadores, tapiceros y tejedores* [Of embroiderers, upholsterers, and weavers] (Vol. 1). Joseph P. Healey Library, University of Massachusetts. https://openarchives.umb.edu/digital/collection/p15774coll2/id/10654

Barreno Sevillano, M. L. (1974). Bordadores de cámara y situación del arte de bordar en Madrid durante la segunda mitad del siglo XVIII [Court embroiderers and the state of the art of embroidery in Madrid during the second half of the eighteenth century]. *Archivo Español de Arte, 47*(187), 273–300.

Calle, L. de la (2010). La Real Fábrica de Tapices de Madrid: Muerte y resurrección de un arte [The Royal Tapestry Factory of Madrid: Death and resurrection of an art]. *Anales de Historia del Arte, 20*(20), 243–70. https://doi.org/10.5209/rev_anha.2010.v20.36409

EDU4Fashion-Tech (2018). *Fashion-Tech, Education and Research Benchmarching Report*. European Commission.

Hernández Núñez, J. C. (1994). Noticias sobre la Alcaicería de la Seda de Sevilla y su transformación en el siglo XVIII [Notes on the Silk Market of Seville and its transformation in the eighteenth century]. *Laboratorio de Arte, 7*(7), 115–30. https://doi.org/10.12795/la.1994.i07.07

Lapayese, J. (1779). *Tratado del arte de hilar, devanar, doblar y torcer las sedas según el método de Mr. Vaucanson, con algunas adiciones y correcciones a él* [Treatise on the art of spinning, winding, doubling, and twisting silks according to the method of Mr. Vaucanson, with some additions and corrections to it]. Impresor Blas Román.

Vishali and Singh, B. (2024). The resurgence of traditional textiles in 21st century fashion design. *International Journal of Home Science*, 10(3), 32–36.

CHAPTER 15

Knitting Beyond the Needles

*Gianni Montagna**

ABSTRACT
This article explores the evolution of knitting design as a transformative material, social, and technical culture capable of evolving from simple handicraft to a universal and democratic form of expression. An expressive element for thousands of years, knitting is a multidimensional element that has easily adapted to social dynamics over time. Whether a manual or industrial creative technique, knitting has always exposed the bridge between cultural heritage and technological innovation, between personal expression and community identity.

Through ongoing ethnographic studies of historical textile artifacts recovered over time in different geographies, it is possible to draw a parallel between knitting and technological advances, through a cultural adaptation that continues today, a journey that intersects design and know-how, inspired by the needs of the user. This research aims to contextualize the historical social analysis through case studies of knitting, exploring its cultural, social, and technological impact. The results highlight the transformation of knitting from a traditional, handcrafted craft to the use of innovation platforms—including AI-enhanced design, smart textiles, and 3D manufacturing. We aim to demonstrate and discuss how these advances maintain meaningful connections with cultural roots, while proposing new possibilities for sustainability, accessibility, and creativity.

Keywords: fashion design, fashion cultural capital, knitting culture, knitting identity, digital fashion

Introduction

When I ask people to describe the knitwear they're wearing in a single word, terms like "comfort," "warmth," and "home" consistently come up. Whether it's a warm, cozy sweater or a scarf, these pieces carry memories of the maker, establishing emotional connections that aren't accidental, but reflect knitting's unique and symbolic place at the intersection of utility, visual expression, and human connection.

Knitting involves different forms of language and communication—between maker and material, between designer and wearer, and between

* CIAUD, Research Centre for Architecture, Urbanism and Design, Lisbon School of Architecture, Universidade de Lisboa.
(ORCID: https://orcid.org/0000-0002-5843-2047)

generations sharing techniques and patterns. As Turney (2009) notes, knitting brings together surface, material, structure, texture, form, and color in its own expressive language, allowing makers to communicate through more than just words, fostering a multi-sensory understanding through the tactile and visual qualities of their work. This multi-sense approach reveals its enormous potential in its ability to engage the user in a deeply interactive, highly personalized, multi-layered experience, providing not only a strong personal experience but also an emotional connection to the various elements that make up the object. In this sense, Margetts (2013) already mentioned that objects created by a designer or maker are the result of a blend of different elements, options, and visions. The final object is not the previously conceived result, but the result of the possibilities offered by the author's imagination, says Margetts, which connect and confront the contingencies of the material and, above all, the manual ability to produce the envisioned object. This combination of elements that relate to all human senses, and especially the visual and tactile aspects, converges with the designer's need to communicate and represent their own creative and cultural discourse, placing them at the center of building material and immaterial bridges to the user's understanding of the value of knitting. These possibilities of thinking and producing, which blend objective and subjective elements, are present in all objects, whether analog or digital, precisely because they transcend the intimate and personal dimension and compete with cultural and market issues. In this sense, and assuming that designers express and communicate through their objects, whether material or not, their engagement with cultural, environmental, and economic issues is inevitable, influencing and shaping their career path and practice.

Knitting, as an expressive form of creation and communication, presents enormous possibilities for revising and prioritizing elements and values in creative projects, in a continuous shift in position and appreciation throughout the design process. Here, subjective experience, combined with an understanding of the current world, provides a thoughtful response and a renewed vision of a society in constant change and renewal.

From ancient Nordic socks to today's 3D-printed smart textiles, knitting has traveled an extraordinary journey through time and culture (Rutt, 2003; Turnau, 1991). This article aims to delve deeper into this narrative, examining not only the techniques used, but also the motivations and emotions that underpin this activity, without forgetting to project its future, in an era of rapid technological and social change, on a planet in need of rapid renewal.

Data collection methods

The methodology used to prepare this paper is non-interventionist and qualitative. Primary and secondary sources are the core of this information collection, sourced from international peers and evaluated through double-blind peer review. Therefore, internationally published articles were used, and international case studies were researched, tailored to the paper's objectives. This article uses the main concepts of the idea of cultural capital developed by Pierre Bourdieu in the 1980s as a starting point for framing the designer's creative work.

Stitch by stitch, the story is knitted

Knitting has a historical trajectory spanning millennia, and long before it was recognized as an art or craft, it was already part of human history. Archaeology offers us fascinating glimpses into its beginnings with artifacts that can surprise even experts. Through an investigation conducted by Moor et al. (2016), using radiocarbon dating technology applied to both the material and the traces of its manufacture, it was possible to confirm that the oldest sock, found in Saqqara (sock T 564), in Egypt, dates back to the historical period between the third and fourth centuries AD.

The earliest ancient pieces found were not produced using knitting techniques as we know them today, but through a related process called Nålbinding. This is a technique that uses circles of thread formed around the tip of the index finger and interconnected with the help of a single needle. Passing the thread between them, the different circles are fixed, and a three-dimensional fibrous structure is created, capable of assuming different shapes (Andersson, 2023; Montagna et al., 2021; St. Clair, 2019). Despite the fragility of historical textiles and the rarity with which they survive, the Coppergate sock, discovered in York, England, and dated before the end of the first millennium, highlights how these ancient techniques were already widespread, crossing geographic and cultural boundaries (Wild, 1989; Rogers, 1989; Walton, 1989). In the thirteenth century, European royalty highly valued knitted items and took them to their tombs, as evidenced by the exquisite silk pillows found in Spanish royal tombs, belonging to Fernando de la Cerda, dating from 1275, as described by Barrigón (2022).

What we currently recognize as knitting—the use of two or more needles to create interlocking loops—appears to have emerged in the Middle East between the third and fifth centuries AD (Barber, 1991). The use of more than one needle is also ancient, and iconographic representations of this practice appear as early as the mid-fourteenth century. Two well-known paintings, such as the knitting Madonna, painted by Ambrogio Lorenzetti in 1345 in his work *The Holy Family*, and another by master Bertram of Minden, entitled *Visit of the Angel*, created between 1400 and 1410, clearly represent the importance of this technique. It is essential to note that, in the work of Ambrogio Lorenzetti, the Virgin Mary is depicted knitting a piece of knit with two needles. About 60 years later, master Bertram depicts her knitting a sweater with four needles, demonstrating the significant advancement in the understanding of this craft and its technique (Hohti, 2023; Rodríguez Peinado, 2023).

The design culture

The concept of culture is by nature very broad, dynamic, and multifaceted. The Mexico City Declaration, held in 1982 within the context of the UNESCO World Conference on Cultural Policies, presented a definition of culture that encompasses human experience with its "distinctive spiritual, material, intellectual, and emotional characteristics that characterize a society or social group. This includes not only the arts and letters, but also ways of life, fundamental human rights, value systems, traditions, and beliefs" (UNESCO, 1982). In this sense, considering the vast cultural wealth that culture itself aggregates, organizes, adapts, influences, relates, and makes available, among many other characteristics, the concept of "cultural capital" has gained strength and space within a renewed vision, which understands culture as a type of "capital," allowing it to achieve "transactionable" possibilities typical of other types of capital. Cultural capital is specifically related to "cultural" activities such as experiences and know-how connected to art, design, music, and theater. This concept fully applies to the production of knitwear, whether handcrafted or industrially produced, where cultural capital permeates the product and the process of collective and personal identity references. Within the realms of art and design education, cultural capital is considered highly valuable (Strickfaden & Heylighen, 2010; Ritzer, 2005).

Cultural capital derives from the credentials accumulated throughout the formal educational system, as well as from the intellectual and cultural dispositions, skills, and tastes incorporated through socialization within the family, community, or social class to which the individual belongs (Bourdieu, 2002).

In the vision of culture developed by Bourdieu (1986; 2002), three types of information sources are identified that contribute to the foundation, perception, and construction of this new understanding of culture: Cultural capital and social capital, which coexist with economic capital and facilitate the acquisition of the elements that give rise to a cultural and social capital that is complex and dynamic. Strickfaden and Heylighen (2010) emphasize that Pierre Bourdieu was the first to introduce the notion of cultural capital by examining the depth of holistic environments, and views it through an integrative theory of capital, field and habitus. Different authors, such as Bennett & Silva (2011), Huang (2019), Xu & Xu (2016), Reich (2018), based their investigations and theoretical developments on the concept of cultural capital, although they have pointed out the need for renewal or revision of Bourdieu's original vision.

The aim here is not to discuss how a given concept should be classified or elaborated within the set of elements that make up cultural capital, but rather to use the analysis already produced on this topic to relate it to design in general, and fashion in particular. As stated by Strickfaden & Heylighen (2007), cultural capital is "an individual's accumulation of knowledge through education and life experiences but also involves the overriding culture of the field of design and of handicrafts."

When we refer to design and its specificities, we unconsciously allude to its ability to create bridges between different concepts, in a dynamic and unifying way. The designer, in turn, as a transformative and communicative element, aims to mediate, discern, evaluate, and prioritize the specific cultural and identity elements of a dynamic human geography, as reported by Foley (1987) and Knapp (2017).

Taking as a starting point Pierre Bourdieu's initial formulation of cultural capital theory (1986), and considering the diverse debates and opinions produced by countless other authors and thinkers in recent decades, this work adopts the general lines of his thinking for the epistemological framework of design, which is still often understood as something casual, superficial, or dissociated from the dynamics of the contemporary world. The unconscious way of acting and operating within the social sphere, in order to be part of it and be recognized as such, is defined by Bourdieu with the term "Habitus," which encompasses the unconsciously acquired ways of being and behaving, which he defines as "embodied cultural capital." These cultural elements can also be considered the subjective elements that make up the cultural universe. This article aims to argue that knit textiles are far from exhausted in their technique. The personal contribution of the designer or maker, with their layered and unique experience, is an inexhaustible source that has always fueled a creative process that has constantly shaped the form of expression in knit and consequently its technique and technology, continuing to do so today, moving from paper and pencil to infinite technological possibilities.

Cultural capital is defined by Bourdieu (1986) as the set of elements inherent to the individual, which, through their experience, they may have a greater or lesser capacity to understand and utilize in their lives. We speak of the acquisition of one's own cultural wealth in relationships with oneself and others, and in the ability to analyze events. This can include personal knowledge, the ability to understand past and present events, the ability to interact with others, personal skills (soft skills), or personal tastes acquired through experiences lived in a specific social reality. Bourdieu (1986) also states that the way an individual behaves in society reflects their social belonging, unconsciously, as they have acquired these behaviors naturally through being part of their ecosystem. These cultural elements can also be considered the subjective elements that make up the cultural universe.

Bourdieu defines social capital (1986) as the set of cultural elements external to the individual that are typically introduced into the social environment by the set of norms recognized by their group and geography. This is what can be defined as the most objective aspect of the cultural universe, and where so-called hard skills could be included. This type of capital is governed by the possibilities offered by the social fabric in which the individual is inserted, which defines specific ways of being, thinking, and acting. Thus, each social group builds its "capital" by defining the essential elements for adequate social recognition, the readings to be valued, the educational references, the most representative works of art, and the symbolic criteria that define it as a stratified society. In turn, social capital derives from the set of relationships and social networks accumulated throughout an individual's life trajectory, as well as the social status and prestige that derive from them (Bourdieu, 2002). This cultural ecosystem, where individuals live and belong, influences and is influenced by the territory in which they are located, giving rise to reciprocal adaptation and contamination, which shapes and adapts to local and cultural needs, both physical space and of society. If in the past ladies gathered around candles to knit and share personal experiences, improving their knitting techniques and building a social culture that associated them with a specific identity group, nowadays knitting clubs, virtual groups like Ravelry or Addicted to Knitting, or weekly meetings in knitting shops, continue, in a modern way, to bring people together and share social and technical aspects, just like in the old days.

Bourdieu's (1986) economic capital assumes that any capital, due to its concentration and accumulated value through time and experience, has a commercial and/or social value that can be traded and that allows for advantages, social, and economic recognition. Economic capital refers to income, wages, and any source of financial resources (Bourdieu, 2002). Based on the concepts presented so far and in direct connection with the fashion sector in general, identifying and structuring its cultural capital facilitates the understanding of knitting culture. Martina Motta (2018), citing the renowned Italian knitwear designer Giugliano Marelli, an internationally recognized expert who asserts that knitting and the act of knitting is culture, refers to the different elements and levels of knitwear fashion as a set of elements that not only allow materials, shapes, and techniques to remain alive, but also evolve with society and its perspective on the spirit of the future. The knitwear designer values this dynamic capital, evolves with society and perpetuates intergenerational symbolism, enriching it over time and increasing its economic value.

Just as promoters and artisans relate to the plasticity and formal aspects of textile materials, such as softness, determining which techniques reveal their characteristics, designers and others relate to the communicative elements of clothing, such as its symbolism and social meaning and the visual aspect achieved by the material used to make it (Helgadottir, 2011). Thus, the collective construction of valued cultural capital with tradable values is revealed to be communal and multidisciplinary, expanding the benefits of each area involved and enhancing their identity value. Knitting is and continues to be one of the forms of cultural and social expression that most clearly expresses and communicates an objective (identity) culture, while also encompassing a creative (subjective) development capable of transforming and renewing its spirit for future generations.

A personal and shared complexity

The individual and their personality, shaped by the time and spaces they share, have always been the subject of discussion, comparison, union, and separation, when experiences and behaviors mark different ways of being and existing.

This concept of adaptation and recognition of the individual and their social environment was already widely discussed by the ancient Romans, who designated it as a form of reciprocal belonging, the *genius loci* or "spirit of the place." This form of reciprocal contagion manifests itself concretely in the production of objects created by humans throughout history, which reflect the traditions and territorial and cultural contexts specific to their place of origin (Lokas et al., 2023; Vecco, 2020; Norberg-Schulz, 1980), including knitting. Anderson (2021) presents a sketchy history of cultural geography, before and beyond representation, as well as the methods and techniques of cultural geography. It investigates the places and traces of corporate capitalism, nationalism, ethnicity, youth culture, and the place of the body. This notion of *genius loci* is highly relevant in the field of design and creativity because, as a practice that combines function, aesthetics, and meaning, it cannot be dissociated from the context in which it is embedded, establishing the conditions for culturally sensitive and socially significant production.

Regarding knitting, for example, the development of finely patterned, colorful work in Northern European traditions is directly related to both the availability of wool and the need to produce insulating garments in cold climates (Turney, 2009; Rutt, 2003). Knitting transcends its utilitarian foundations to become a powerful symbolic and cultural asset, markers of identity and personalization of clothing. In communities around the world, distinctive knitting patterns still serve as visual signatures of their cultural heritage. "Textiles occupy the space between the personal and the cultural, often linking specific individual expressions to established and hierarchical social structures" says Jane Burns (2002). For example, Norwegian and

Icelandic sweaters illustrate how knitting intertwines with national identity. Referring to a fabric or knitted item as a national symbol, argues Helgadottir (2011), leads the reader to a sense of originality, purity, and authenticity. This often-falsified notion of an authentic heritage that has not undergone acculturation and is free from cultural hybridization is very present in these types of representations, even if the origin of this symbolism, which has already adapted to underlying cultural evolution, is not fully understood.

By wearing these garments, people not only protect themselves from the cold weather but also engage in cultural narratives. One of the most striking examples from the Iberian Peninsula comes from Portuguese fishing communities, where knitted sweaters took on different functional definitions, personal protection, belonging and identity, through the use of traditional *Poveira* initials. The traditional *Póvoa do Varzim* sweater, also called the *poveira* sweater, is a natural white wool garment embroidered with family symbols, with distinctive black and red patterns that, in addition to their primary function, reinforced the sense of geographic and cultural belonging. They also allowed for the quick identification of fishermen lost at sea, as they were designed to prevent them from being removed in the event of drowning. Thus, these sweaters, with their embroidered symbols, helped identify each fisherman, transforming them into an element of both remembrance and personal and community resilience. These knitted garments, like so many others, act as mediators between individuals and their community, conveying values, needs, and cultural identities, and reflecting artisanal traditions. Design here assumes an increased responsibility in communicating its identity and culture, which has been constructed over time and through time, a direct result of personal and communal, subjective and objective cultural and social evolution. Thus, knitwear production becomes a process that embodies the spirit of the place, respecting and valuing the unique techniques, patterns, and materials of each territory, while contributing to its cultural transformation and dynamism (Lokas et al., 2023; Vecco, 2020).

Tradition, therefore, stands for a successful cultural principle of transforming, expanding upon, and transmitting knowledge and skills in a sustainable form across multiple generations (Sandgruber et al., 2019). Knitting embodies what anthropologists call "material culture"—physical objects that carry social meanings and cultural values. Through the transmission of knitting techniques from parent to child, from teacher to student, these practices create what sociologist Pierre Bourdieu termed *cultural capital*—knowledge and skills that confer social status and maintain community ties (Bourdieu, 1986; Turney, 2009).

Community building in the knit design

Knitting groups represent one of humanity's oldest forms of social networking. Long before digital platforms connected people vastly apart, knitting groups brought individuals together in a shared creative practice. Mayne's (2016) research demonstrates that these gatherings foster significant psychological and social benefits, including reduced stress, improved cognitive function, and a heightened sense of belonging. In the study by Lamont and Ranaweera (2020), hundreds of participants were involved in analyzing the happiness and well-being levels of non-professional knitters (835 participants) and musicians (122 participants), also non-professional. After the study ended, say Lamont and Ranaweera (2020; p. 1), surveys were administered to each participant, and the result left no doubt: "Knitters scored significantly higher on happiness than musicians." Contemporary knitting communities have expanded beyond local gatherings to global networks through digital platforms. Websites like Ravelry, with over 9 million registered users, function as massive repositories of knowledge and social spaces (Orton-Johnson, 2014). These platforms democratize access to techniques and patterns while facilitating connections across geographic and generational boundaries.

The social dimension of knitting has increasingly taken on activist dimensions. The Pussy Hat Project, which produced thousands of pink knitted hats for the 2017 Women's March, demonstrated knitting's potential as a means of political expression (Black, 2017). Similarly, yarn bombing—the practice of covering public spaces with colorful knitted or crocheted pieces—represents a form of tactical urbanism that uses traditional crafts to comment on contemporary issues (O'Neill, 2022).

Technology support

The industrial knitting process began with the invention of the power loom by William Lee in 1589 (Spencer, 2001). This technological innovation generated great controversy in English society—the creation of a machine that could produce in minutes what took a person hours to do manually provoked fear and resistance, foreshadowing profound transformations in work methods and economic dynamics. Although it marked the beginning of the mechanization of knitting, traditional hand knitting continued to exist alongside these new technologies, each with distinct roles and values in society. It is important to emphasize that the possibility of producing in greater quantities and at lower costs obviously led to a different perspective on clothing production at that time, opening a range of possibilities for the future.

The digital tools that support the creative process in fashion design, which are currently indispensable for the creation and production of textiles and clothing in knit and other materials, are varied and meet the multiple output needs of the fashion industry. Digital tools for digital fashion design and virtual try-ons, such as Clo3D, DesignaKnit, Kaledo, etc., are extremely important as they save significant time compared to physical and analog prototyping of products, allowing for quick visualization of the product proposal. These tools offer high integration capabilities with existing industrial production technologies, enabling leading knitwear companies, such as Japan's Shima Seiki and Germany's Stoll, to create, visualize, modify, and 3D print designed objects and produce them in various formats, such as the production of Wholegarment® pieces, seamless and with virtually zero raw material waste. Modern industrial knitting machines, such as Shima Seiki's Wholegarment® technology, are said (Shima Seiki, 2017), to represent quantum leaps in capabilities, that is, a profound shift toward a complex paradigm that involves different forms and levels of change. These machines create seamless, three-dimensional garments without stitching and minimum waste, significantly improving sustainability indicators while enabling new aesthetic and functional possibilities (Shima Seiki, 2017; Santos, 2024). The minimum-waste production model aligns with growing consumer demand for environmentally responsible manufacturing processes.

More transformative recent innovations integrate digital technologies with traditional knitting processes. Shima Seiki's Wholegarment® technology represents a paradigm shift in production methods, creating seamless, three-dimensional garments that eliminate post-production assembly and reduce material waste by up to 30 % compared to traditional cut-and-sew manufacturing (Shima Seiki, 2017). Compared to the knit process produced with patternmaking, the lack of the need to join the different components creates production advantages, competitive gains, and improves comfort. As previously mentioned by Margetts (2013), the objects created today are complex and are the result of the designer's own vision, their methodological capabilities, and the challenges posed by the materials used. In addition to the inclusion of objective and subjective elements, the contribution of social and identity values further complicates the knit design project, hindering critical and informed decision-making.

The integration of digital technologies extends beyond creative and productive design, encompassing the entire product design cycle. Computer-Aided Design (CAD) software, also specific to knitting, allows designers to visualize complex structures and simulate physical properties before production (Yang & Love, 2008). These virtual prototyping capabilities reduce development time and material waste, while expanding creative horizons (Santos, 2024).

The example of some projects realized through knitting attests to the ability of this technique to create strong community bonds. The "KnitAid" project exemplifies how knitting communities mobilize these functions for humanitarian purposes. By coordinating global networks of knitters to produce warm clothing for refugees, this initiative transforms individual craft practice into collective social action (https://knitaid.com/). Digital platforms have dramatically expanded the reach and impact of knitting communities. Ravelry.com, with over 9 million registered users, functions both as an extensive pattern database and as a vibrant social network (Orton-Johnson, 2014). The activist dimension of contemporary knitting represents a significant evolution in how textile practices engage with social issues. Spinning bomb interventions in public spaces challenge conventional distinctions between craft and art, private and public, while making political statements through traditionally "feminine" means (O'Neill, 2022).

The recent introduction of AI into civil society and its dissemination and application across a wide range of knowledge fields has significantly expanded its application to fashion design and most design-related disciplines. Currently, the importance of this technology is widely recognized, and its support across various areas of knowledge and life is highly relevant, as it helps humans establish a closer relationship with the unknown, bridging the gap between advanced technology and human beings, greatly facilitating the integration of knowledge and the operationalization of complex or data-intensive tasks. For design to develop in a structured and systemic way and to leverage technology effectively, designers must understand the underlying technology of the equipment they use. According to Motta (2018), knitting, due to its complexity, requires designers to possess not only creativity but also technical knowledge that allows them to constantly monitor the condition of the used material and the process they use to create something new. Integrating this knowledge with the help of AI facilitates understanding and blurs the gap between designer and machine. Wholegarment® technology, as Yang and Love (2008) point out, exemplifies and facilitates this transformation phase, ensuring AI has a close approximation of the human to the complex problems of technical programming, while AI-generated knitting patterns currently occupy the refinement phase, automating aspects of design while still relying on human creativity for context and meaning.

While AI's capabilities in assisting designers in a more technical approach to their work are significant, its ability to assist in improving the creative direction of a design project can be even greater, expanding objectives, meanings, and processes, allowing designers to direct and focus on the values of their work.

One of the most revolutionary developments in recent years is the emergence of "smart textiles"—knitted fabrics enhanced with electronic functionality. MIT research on pressure-sensitive knitted textiles demonstrates how traditional textile structures can be transformed into sophisticated sensing platforms capable of detecting body movements with remarkable accuracy (Wicaksono et al., 2022). These advances point to a future where our clothing actively interacts with our bodies and the environment. The application of intelligence to textile materials and knit products is another major possibility, allowing the integration of electronic functionality with knitted structures, and represents perhaps the most revolutionary development in the long history of knitting. From textiles with sensors to collect physiological signals, environmental conditions, or body movement, new textile materials can be responsive, reacting to an external input with a physical change, such as a change in shape, color, and/or structure. They can also be super-active when, following a specific input, they are able to react to the inputs, acting directly with a response, whether it be data or image communication. The knit substrate for this type of material proves to be very suitable, given its ability to adapt to the body.

MIT's pressure-sensitive knitted rug, capable of detecting yoga poses with 99 % accuracy, demonstrates the sophisticated sensory capabilities possible within knitted structures (Wicaksono et al., 2022). This technology uses thermoforming to precisely calibrate pressure sensors within multilayer knitted textiles, creating a responsive surface that accurately tracks body position and movement. Another project called "NeuroKnitting" represents other fascinating frontier, translating brainwave patterns recorded during musical experiences into knitted patterns (Vega et al., 2018). This project literally materializes internal emotional states into textile structures, suggesting new possibilities for expressing subjective experience through objective form.

Conclusion

Knitting's journey from simple handcraft to technological platform illustrates the potential of traditional practices to remain culturally relevant while embracing innovation. In this sense, knitting offers a model for how other traditional crafts can navigate the complex relationship between heritage and future possibilities.

Knitting functions as form of nonverbal material communication, encoding cultural knowledge, personal expression, and social values within its structures and patterns. The symbolic language of knitting remains relevant even as technological capabilities transform production methods. At times, this technological dimension allows for a deeper exploration of its identity articulation, allowing the cultural object to transform and adapt to the ever-changing needs of new users.

Technological innovation, beyond mere efficiency improvements, opens up entirely new functional and creative possibilities through a more facilitated designer presence throughout the design and production cycle. Currently, new platforms such as Clo3D or Apex software, among many others, allow for 3D creations and visualizations that are very faithful to the physical objects, enabling real-time creation and multifaceted control over the product. Smart textiles represent a frontier in this technological evolution applied to fibrous materials, transforming passive fabrics into interactive interfaces between bodies, environments, and information systems, where knit, due to its characteristics, is a privileged element for adaptation to the human body.

Knitting communities demonstrate remarkable adaptability, embracing new technologies while maintaining connections with cultural heritage. New designers and manufacturers have turned the tension between tradition and innovation into a source of creative energy rather than conflict, with practitioners finding value in both ancestral techniques and cutting-edge applications.

Through design, future designers propose a continuous alternation between material and immaterial issues, integrating traditional and technological knowledge, but also the need for innovation throughout the design process. Through acquired knowledge and experimentation with materials, they can think, adapt, create, and propose continuous new approaches and adaptations to their products or services.

References

Anderson, J. (2021). *Understanding cultural geography: Places and traces* (3rd ed.). Routledge.

Andersson Lindberg, I. (2023). Nålbinding connections: Making, mapping and describing connections. *FormAkademisk, 16*(4). https://doi.org/10.7577/formakademisk.5419

Barber, E. J. W. (1991). *Prehistoric textiles: The development of cloth in the Neolithic and Bronze Ages with special reference to the Aegean*. Princeton University Press.

Barrigón, M. (2022). Textile techniques in the Iberian Peninsula (thirteenth to fourteenth centuries). In *Textiles of medieval Iberia: Cloth and clothing in a multi-cultural context* (pp. 41–68). The Boydell Press.

Bennett, T., & Silva, E. (2011). Introduction: Cultural capital—Histories, limits, prospects. *Poetics, 39*(6), 427–43. https://doi.org/10.1016/j.poetic.2011.09.008

Black, S. (2017). KNIT + RESIST: Placing the Pussyhat Project in the context of craft activism. *Gender, Place & Culture, 24*(5), 696–710. https://doi.org/10.1080/0966369x.2017.1335292

Bourdieu, P. (1986). The forms of capital. In J. Richardson (Ed.), *Handbook of theory and research for the sociology of education* (pp. 241–58). Greenwood.

Bourdieu, P. (2002). *Distinction: A social critique of the judgement of taste* (11th print). Harvard University Press.

Burns, E. J. (2002). *Courtly love undressed: Reading through clothes in medieval French culture*. University of Pennsylvania Press.

Foley, R. (1987). *Another unique species: Patterns in human evolutionary ecology*. Longman Scientific & Technical.

Helgadóttir, G. (2011). Nation in a sheep's coat: The Icelandic sweater. *FormAkademisk: Forskningstidsskrift for design og designdidaktikk, 4*(2). https://doi.org/10.7577/formakademisk.201
Hohti, P. (2023). Knitting history through reconstruction: The making and meaning of early modern stockings. *Textile History, 54*(1), 100–31. https://doi.org/10.1080/00404969.2024.2393229
Huang, X. (2019). Understanding Bourdieu—Cultural capital and habitus. *Review of European Studies, 11*(3), 45. https://doi.org/10.5539/res.v11n3p45
Klimczuk, A. (2015). *The Wiley Blackwell encyclopedia of consumption and consumer studies*. Wiley-Blackwell.
Knapp, G. (2017). Human ecology. In *International encyclopedia of geography* (pp. 1–9). John Wiley & Sons. https://doi.org/10.1002/9781118786352.wbieg0477
Lamont, A., & Ranaweera, N. A. (2020). Knit one, play one: Comparing the effects of amateur knitting and amateur music participation on happiness and wellbeing. *Applied Research in Quality of Life, 15*(5), 1353–74. https://doi.org/10.1007/s11482-019-09734-z
Lokas, I., Petrović, R., & Rakonjac, I. (2023, December). *The essence of place: Understanding genius loci through phenomenology*.
Margetts, M. (2013). Action not words. In D. Charny (Ed.), *Power of making: The importance of being skilled*. V&A.
Mayne, A. (2016). Feeling lonely, feeling connected: Amateur knit and crochet makers online. *Craft Research, 7*(1), 11–29. https://doi.org/10.1386/crre.7.1.11_1
Montagna, G., Delgado, M. J., & Morais, C. (2021). The knitting of an (im)material presence. In C. S. Shin, G. Di Bucchianico, S. Fukuda, Y.-G. Ghim, G. Montagna, & C. Carvalho (Eds.), *Advances in industrial design* (Vol. 260, pp. 665–72). Springer International Publishing. https://doi.org/10.1007/978-3-030-80829-7_82
Moor, A. de, Fluck, C., & Linscheid, P. (2016). *Textiles, tools and techniques of the 1st millennium AD from Egypt and neighbouring countries: Proceedings of the 8th conference of the research group "Textiles from the Nile Valley", Antwerp, 4–6 October 2013*. Study Group Textiles from the Nile Valley / Uitg. Lannoo N.V.
Motta, M. (2019). *Designing knit designers*. FrancoAngeli.
Munk, M. D., & Krarup, T. M. (2011). Cultural capital theory revisited: Explanations of educational reproduction and beyond.
Norberg-Schulz, C. (1980). *Genius loci: Towards a phenomenology of architecture*. Rizzoli.

O'Neill, E. (2022). Knitting: The destructive yarn-bomb. TEXTILE, 1–10. https://doi.org/10.1080/14759756.2022.2138062

Orton-Johnson, K. (2014). Knit, purl and upload: New technologies, digital mediations and the experience of leisure. *Leisure Studies, 33*(3), 305–21. https://doi.org/10.1080/02614367.2012.723730

Reich, K. (2018). *Surplus values – A new theory of forms of capital in the twenty first century*. University of Cologne. http://konstruktivismus.uni-koeln.de/english/surplus_value/reich_surplus_values_2018.pdf

Ritzer, G. (Ed.). (2005). *Encyclopedia of social theory*. Sage Publications.

Rodríguez Peinado, L. (2023). Trabajo textil femenino en la Edad Media: Ocupación señorial y oficio profesional [Female textile work in the Middle Ages: Seigniorial occupation and professional craft]. *Asparkía. Investigación Feminista, 42*, 103–25. https://doi.org/10.6035/asparkia.6901

Rogers, P. W. (Ed.). (1989). *The archaeology of York* (Vol. 17, Fasc. 5). York Archaeological Trust.

Rutt, R. (2003). *A history of hand knitting*. Interweave Press.

Sandgruber, R., Bichler-Ripfel, H., & Walcher, M. (2019). *Traditional craftsmanship as intangible cultural heritage and an economic factor in Austria: Study of the Austrian Commission for UNESCO; commissioned by the Austrian Federal Chancellery and the Austrian Federal Ministry for Digital and Economic Affairs* (C. Roth, Trans.). Austrian Federal Chancellery.

Santos, L. (2024). *Hiper-imagem: A imagética hipermoderna em design de moda* [Hyper-image: Hypermodern imagery in fashion design] (Doctoral thesis, Universidade de Lisboa, Faculdade de Arquitetura). Repositório da Universidade de Lisboa.

Shima Seiki. (n.d.). *Ever onward: Annual report 2017* (p. 54). https://www.shimaseiki.com/ire/library/pdf/ar1703.pdf

Spencer, D. J. (2001). *Knitting technology: A comprehensive handbook and practical guide*. Woodhead.

St. Clair, K. (2019). *La trama del mondo: I tessuti che hanno fatto la storia* [The fabric of the world: The textiles that made history]. UTET.

Strickfaden, M., & Heylighen, A. (2007). Exploring the "cultural capital" of design educators. In *International Conference on Engineering Design, ICED'07* (28–31 August), Cité des Sciences et de l'Industrie, Paris. The Design Society.

Strickfaden, M., & Heylighen, A. (2010). Cultural capital: A thesaurus for teaching design. *International Journal of Art & Design Education, 29*(2), 121–33. https://doi.org/10.1111/j.1476-8070.2010.01653.x

Turnau, I. (1991). *History of knitting before mass production*. Institute of the History of Material Culture, Polish Academy of Sciences.
Turney, J. (2009). *The culture of knitting* (English ed.). Berg.
UNESCO. (1982). *World Conference on Cultural Policies: Final report* (Programme and Meeting Document [214648] 2; p. 236). UNESCO.
Vecco, M. (2020). Genius loci as a meta-concept. *Journal of Cultural Heritage, 41*, 225–31. https://doi.org/10.1016/j.culher.2019.07.001
Walton, P. (1989). *Textiles, cordage and raw fibre from 16–22 Coppergate*. York Archaeological Trust.
Wicaksono, I., Haddad, D. D., & Paradiso, J. (2022). Tapis magique: Machine-knitted electronic textile carpet for interactive choreomusical performance and immersive environments. *Creativity and Cognition, 2022*, 262–274. https://doi.org/10.1145/3527927.3531451
Wild, J. P. (1989). The archaeology of York. Vol. 17, Fasc. 5. *Textiles, cordage and raw fibre from 16–22 Coppergate*. By Penelope Walton. *The Antiquaries Journal, 69*(2), 367–8. https://doi.org/10.1017/S0003581500085826
Xu, Y., & Xu, L. (2016). Enlightenment of Bourdieu cultural capital theory. In *Proceedings of the 2016 International Conference on Arts, Design and Contemporary Education*. 2nd International Conference on Arts, Design and Contemporary Education, Moscow, Russia. https://doi.org/10.2991/icadce-16.2016.91
Yang, S., & Love, T. (2008). Integrated system for fashion design using computerised WholeGarment knitwear production. In D. Cook (Ed.), *Proceedings of ANZSYS'08: 14th International Conference*. Perth, Western Australia: SECAU Security Research Centre, Edith Cowan University.

CHAPTER 16

The Birth of Lunéville's Bead Embroidery and Its Introduction Into Spanish Haute Couture

*José Antonio Fernández Fernández**

ABSTRACT
In the mid-eighteenth century, tambour embroidery gained popularity in France due to the influence of Madame de Pompadour, who practiced this art with great precision and skill. A century later, the entrepreneur Louis Ferry, owner of the Ferry-Bonnechaux embroidery house in Lunéville, devised a method for sewing beads and sequins based on tambour embroidery. This new method would posthumously award him the Gold Medal for innovation at the 1889 Universal Exposition in Paris. Since then, Ferry's process has been adopted by fashion houses across the globe, including that of the renowned designer Pedro Rodriguez, consolidating itself as one of the main decorative formulas of Spanish haute couture.

Keywords: tambour embroidery, Madame de Pompadour, Lunéville embroidery, Louis Ferry, Pedro Rodríguez

Introduction

Lunéville bead embroidery (in French, *broderie perlée de Lunéville*), or simply Lunéville crochet, is a French technique of textile ornamentation associated with haute couture. Its name refers to the town of the same name, where it was invented by Louis Ferry in 1867. The technique involves threading glass beads, pearls, or sequins onto a spool of thread and affixing them to the fabric via a chain stitch. It is achieved using a specialized tool comprising a wooden handle and a fine crochet needle joined together by a brass clamp. Consequently, the artisans who dedicate themselves to this craft—traditionally women—are known as *crocheteuses* [crocheters] or *lunévilleuses* [Lunéville embroidery artisans].

The decorative method itself is not particularly old. Still, it is heir to the delicate hook embroidery developed in India during the Mughal Empire, from where it was introduced to France in the mid-eighteenth century. Today, because of its richness and uniqueness, Lunéville crochet is recognized

* Universidad Rey Juan Carlos.
(ORCID: https://orcid.org/0000-0002-8152-5284)

as an independent artistic expression in its own right and is present in collections from top fashion houses. The present work attempts to offer a documented synthesis of the origins of this technique and its introduction into Spanish haute couture in recognition of the outstanding role that expert crocheters played—and continue to play—in decorating high-end dresses and accessories.

Tambour embroidery, the precursor of Lunéville crochet

Tambour embroidery is a visually appealing type of embroidery in which the up-and-down motion of a fine crochet needle creates a chain stitch on a base fabric. The needle utilized in this technique is unique and specifically designed for this purpose. It features a sharp point, which facilitates its insertion into the material, and a hook-shaped notch, which enables the thread to be picked up from the underside of the fabric and brought to the upper part, where the interlacing of the loops is performed. The French term *tambour* embroidery, which literally means "drum embroidery," is derived from the technique's resemblance to the stretching of a drumhead on a drum frame, as observed by Lefébure (1887, p. 14). Despite its apparent simplicity, the technique demands meticulous and continuous practice to attain proficiency, with the process often spanning several months or even years.

Historians have long believed this technique was developed in the Hindu regions of Uttar Pradesh and Gujarat, specifically by the Mochi caste, a traditional community of shoemakers and saddlers. The Mochi used this technique to make and decorate leather goods such as shoes, sandals, gloves, belts, saddles, and even sleeping mats. It is commonly accepted that this hook-shaped shoemaker's awl was adapted to textiles in the seventeenth century to meet the Mughal court's demand for embroidery, whether in clothing or tapestries to decorate their palaces. It resulted in the emergence of a craft called *mochi-bharat*, which is still regarded as one of the most exquisite examples of Hindustani civilization.

However, Rosemary Crill (2022, p. 10), a researcher specializing in Indian textiles and curator at the Victoria and Albert Museum until 2016, questions this narrative. She notes that the earliest hook-needle work firmly linked to the Mochi community dates to the early eighteenth century. Early embroidery, although done with chain stitch and intended for the Mughal court, was executed with a straight needle, evident in several pieces held at the Victoria and Albert Museum.[1]

Similarly, Shilpa Shah (2022, p. 35), a scholar and co-founder of the TAPI Collection—an acronym for the Textiles and Art of the People of India—, noted that although the Mochi may have introduced chain-stitch embroidery to their leather goods in the seventeenth century, reliable records of the use of the hook needle in textiles are not found until the dawn of the eighteenth century. At this time, the caste became a community of artisans, including wall painters, ivory carvers, woodworkers, and embroiderers; in short, artisans dedicated to the different decorative trades.

It is thought that the Mochi may have originated in the Pakistani region of Sind, from where it is believed they arrived in India sometime in the fourteenth century; however, there is no definitive evidence to support this claim. Other sources propose that the Mochi originated in Gujarat and that it was the Sufis of Sind who first introduced them to the practice of embroidering on leather (Crill, 2022, p. 9; Naik, 1996, p. 21). In any case, it is certain that in 1664, with the founding of the French East India Company—planned by Jean-Baptiste Colbert, Louis XIV's finance minister—France obtained a fifty-year monopoly on the trade of all the territories located east of the Cape of Good Hope, the eastern seas, and almost all of India. Thus, the French began a process of colonization of the Hindustani peninsula that persisted throughout the following century. It was accompanied by a profitable trade in exotic goods, including porcelain, spices, ivory, wallpaper, high-quality fabrics, and an array of colorful chain-stitch embroideries from Gujarat. These designs encompassed various motifs, from arabesques and floral patterns to human figures, fruits, and animals.

This evidence, in addition to the research of the scholars Crill and Shah, indicates that the technique of tambour embroidery could not have been introduced in France before the eighteenth century. Moreover, we know almost the exact date thanks to Charles Germain de Saint-Aubin (1721–1786). In his celebrated *L'art du Brodeur* (1770), Saint-Aubin, who, together with his

1 For example, a splendid coat that was made around 1610–1630 for a man of the Mughal court. (Inventory number: IS.18-1947; URL: https://collections.vam.ac.uk/item/O16066/hunting-coat/). This garment was embroidered with Gujarati silk thread using the chain-stitch technique with a straight needle.

father, Gabriel Germain de Saint-Aubin (1696–1756), designed embroidery for the court of Louis XV, writes:

> The embroidery in chain stitch, with which many ladies occupy their leisure, has for a long time been either made by hand or on an ordinary frame with a sewing needle. The town of Vendôme was famous for this type of work. About ten years ago [ca. 1758], a method [executed with a hook] was imported from China that is just as accurate and six times more expeditious. Now, the other method of working has been abandoned. (Saint-Aubin, 1770, p. 27)

Saint-Aubin's account of the introduction of this new technique may be accurate; however, he was mistaken regarding its origin. This study, along with the observations of textile historian Edward Maeder (1983, p. 54, note 33), has demonstrated that this technique was not imported from China, as previously thought, but rather from India. It is also interesting to note that the swiftness with which the chain stitch could be carried out led to its rapid adoption by French women, including Madame de Pompadour, who demonstrated remarkable precision and skill in its execution. This is perfectly illustrated in a satirical drawing by Saint-Aubin himself from 1758, in which we see a smiling Cupid handing Louis XV a frame while the king's official mistress is busy with her embroidery (Figure 29). The epigram below them reads: "In 1758, the men of high society embroidered in the company of ladies, [and] in compensation, it was a woman who governed the State."[2] Saint-Aubin's sarcastic criticism of the political role of the influential marquise is evident. It is even more telling when we consider that, as Rousseau pointed out in his *Emile* (1892, p. 171), embroidery should be reserved for the female gender, thus accentuating the effeminate, dissolute, and lazy profile of the so-called Beloved King. In the words of Lee Hyde (2013, p. 117), this caricature reflects "the overbearing influence of women, and the attendant effeminacy of men, of which Pompadour was the most visible symbol in the eyes of many critics during this period."

In addition to Saint-Aubin's caricature, the marquise's affinity for tambour embroidery is also evident in the renowned painting of *Madame de Pompadour at her tambour frame*, painted by the Versailles court portraitist

2 "En 1758, les hommes de la haute société brodaient en compagnie des dames, [et] en compensation, c'était une femme qui gouvernait l'État."

François Hubert Drouais between April 1763 and May 1764 (Figure 30). The intelligent and powerful *maîtresse-en-titre* was not only a great patron of the arts and letters, contributing to the establishment of Paris as one of the most prominent artistic centers of the eighteenth century, but she was also an ardent supporter of the decorative arts. A portrait of her carrying out her embroidery exercises may have served to disguise a strategic maneuver designed to promote the craft industry and stimulate the production of luxury goods in France, thereby reinvigorating the country's economy (Callan, 2017, p. 7).

Moreover, as a patron of the arts and literature, Madame de Pompadour sponsored sculptors and painters of the galant style, such as François Boucher. She was also instrumental in promoting one of the most significant cultural works of the Age of Enlightenment: Diderot's *Encyclopédie*. It is not surprising, therefore, that its 1763 edition included an engraving by Prévost that illustrated both the tools and the process of executing tambour embroidery, thereby demonstrating that, at this date, its use was fully established in France.[3]

The practice of tambour embroidery reached its apogee during the reign of Louis XVI and the Napoleonic Empire. During this period, the practice was introduced as a form of education for talented young women, and it subsequently gained popularity as an elegant leisure pursuit among other European courts. It is important to note that the immense prestige of Versailles meant that the entire continent observed the fashions proposed by the French and, by extension, the activities related to textile craftsmanship. Nor should we overlook that, at this time, needlework was proof of the good breeding of ladies, being associated with a relaxed lifestyle and genteel ideals of feminine behavior; ideals that were energetically promoted by many Enlightenment thinkers, among others Rousseau (Lee Hyde, 2013, p. 108). This was evidenced by Joshua Reynolds, who, in his 1780 group portrait of Charlotte, Elisabeth, and Anna Waldegrave, stepdaughters of Prince William Henry of Gloucester, immortalized the sisters engaged in their customary embroidery work (Figure 31).

Moreover, given the nomenclature of this craft, it is fitting to explain that in 1843, the 27-year-old Marguerite Boulard founded a tambour embroidery

---

3 See Prévost's engraving on the Cooper-Hewitt Museum website, at the link: https://collection.cooperhewitt.org/objects/18613523.

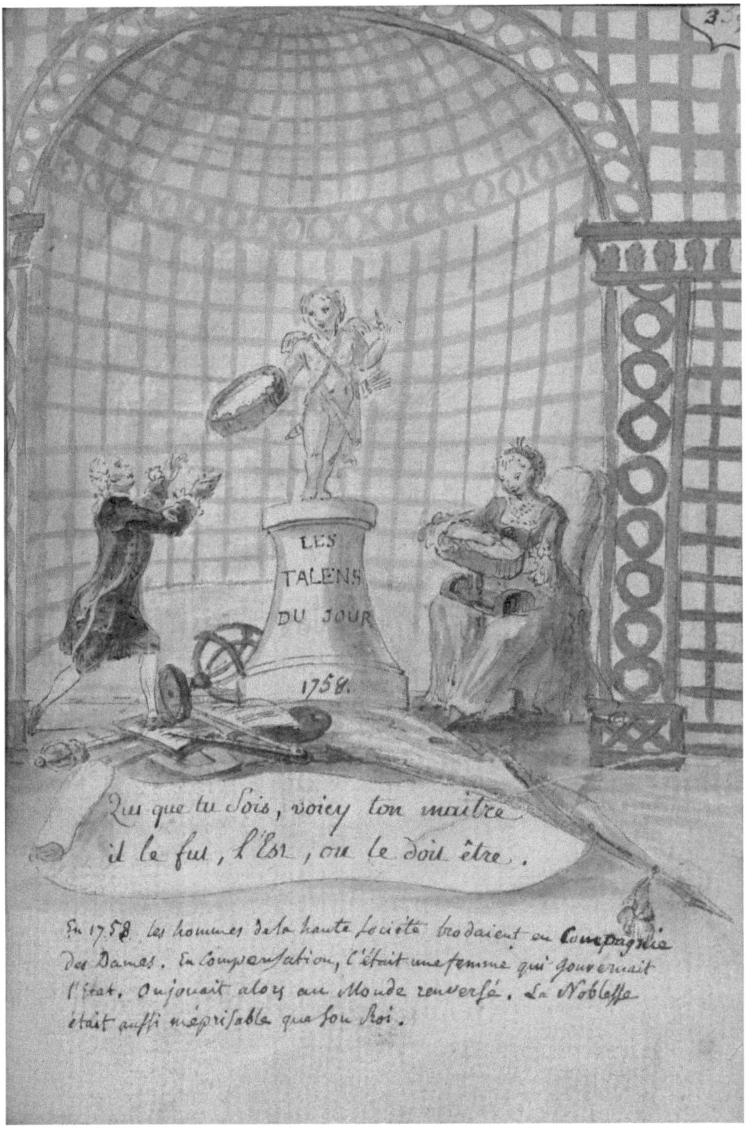

Figure 29. Charles Germain de Saint-Aubin, Livre de caricatures tant bonnes que mauvaises, "Les talens du jour," 1758. Watercolor, ink, and graphite on paper, 18,7 × 13,2 cm.

Waddesdon, Waddesdon Manor, The Rothschild Collection, The National Trust.

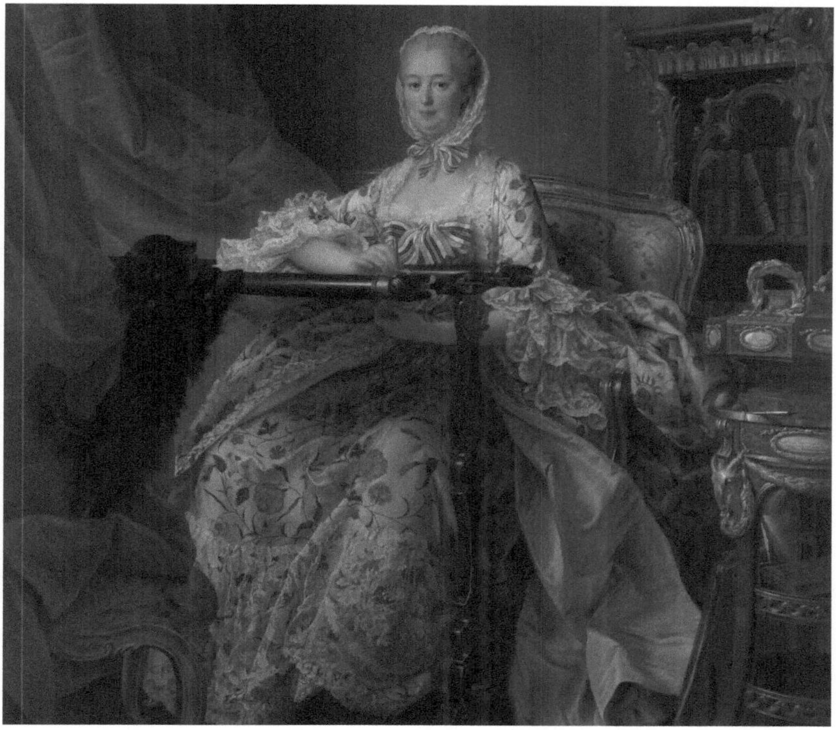

Figure 30. François Hubert Drouais, Madame de Pompadour at her tambour frame, 1763–1764. Oil on canvas, 217 × 156.8 cm.
London, National Gallery.

workshop in the French town of Bourg-le-Roi, thus contributing to the prosperity of the region (Boulard, 1917, p. 218). At that time, the colorful tapestries of Beauvais were held in high regard for their excellence. So much so that, in order to enhance the appeal of their merchandise and impress their clientele, Parisian merchants began to refer to the ornamental textiles produced in Bourg-le-Roi as *Beauvais* (Boulard, 1917, p. 232). This explains why tambour embroidery is also known today as *Beauvais stitch* or, alternatively, *Pompadour stitch*, after the mistress of Louis XV, who has the honor, if not the merit, of giving her name to this technique.

In Spain, the nineteenth-century women's press, which was always on the lookout for French fashion trends, included several embroidery works made

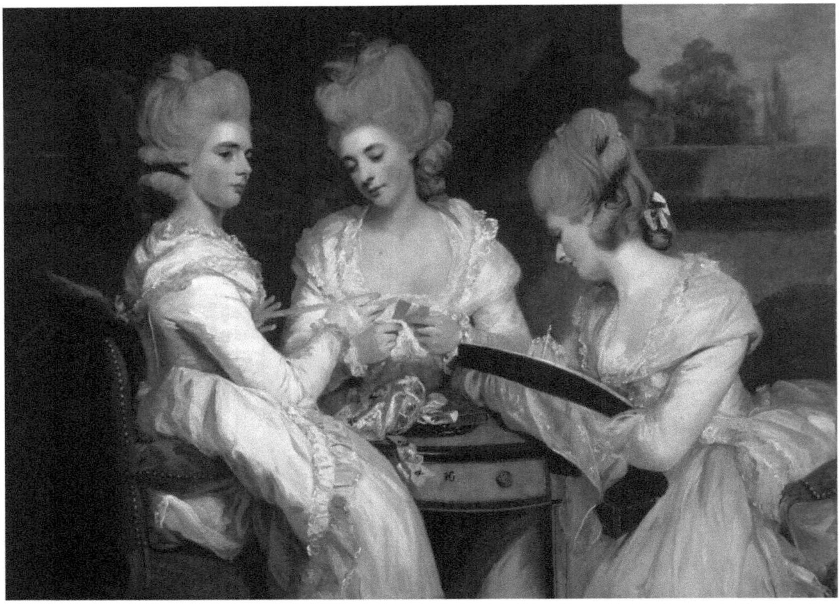

Figure 31. Joshua Reynolds, The Ladies Waldegrave, 1780. Oil on canvas, 143 × 168,3 cm.
Edinburgh, Scottish National Gallery.

with the hook needle. For instance, on November 1, 1851, *El Correo de la Moda* described how to make a "hat veil embroidered with a hook on tulle" (p. 16), revealing that this technique was also practiced in Spain during the nineteenth century. Such was the case that, at the Great Exhibition held in London in 1851, in addition to the handicrafts from other countries,

> There were also crocheted embroideries of a fineness surpassing anything made in France and Switzerland, as well as a Spanish coat of arms and tablecloths embroidered with soutache, velvet, and gold of great opulence. These various objects showcased by Spain, all exceedingly beautiful and rich, constituted works of art rather than commercial products. (Commission française sur l'industrie des nations, 1854, p. 106)

We even know that in the early years of the nineteenth century, the city of Nancy boasted 30 embroidery workshops employing over 4,000 workers, of which approximately 80 were Spaniards who had immigrated to France (Vrignaud-Masson, 1982, p. 11).

The invention of Lunéville crochet: a new technique for sewing rhinestones and sequins

In 1867, Louis Ferry (1835–1888), head of the Ferry-Bonnechaux embroidery house in Lunéville, devised a method for sewing rhinestones from tambour embroidery (Vrignaud-Masson, 1982, p. 5). Until then, rhinestones had been sewn with a straight needle, yet Ferry envisioned a process in which the beads or sequins would be threaded onto a spool of thread beforehand and then affixed to the fabric with a chain stitch. This method would allow the process to be exponentially faster and result in a superior finish. Ferry's ingenious contribution consisted of varying the fabric's arrangement, specifically by working with the reverse side facing upwards. This way, when the chain stitch was made with the hook, the beads were contained between two stitches on the right side of the fabric.

However, as with any innovation, its development was gradual. Initially, the journeymen in Ferry's workshop began working with diaphanous fabrics, such as tulle or silk organza. As they became more skilled, they introduced more elaborate stitches and less transparent fabrics. The opacity of the fabrics was a significant concern, as it presented a considerable challenge for the embroiderers, who were required to identify the tiny beads with their fingertips. It required a degree of manipulative skill comparable only to that of the visually impaired.

Ferry opened his embroidery workshop at *rue de Viller* 30 in Lunéville after marrying Anne Rosalie Bonnechaux (1842–1906) on June 23, 1863 (Benoît, 1870, p. 154; Almanach-annuaire de l'arrondissement de Lunéville, 1903, p. 12). From this union, six children were born: Eugène (1864), Anne (1865), Jeanne (1870), Mansuy Louis (1872), Andrée (1881), and Jean (ca. 1883). Throughout his life, Ferry was committed to politics and social action, as attested by his nomination as a candidate for the Vigilance Commission against child exploitation by the General Council of the Meurthe-et-Moselle department on April 10, 1878. This appointment was in accordance with the law passed on May 19, 1874, by the French State, which prohibited children under the age of 12 from working in the manufacturing industry, in factories, or workshops. The nomination was reported on in the political newspaper *L'Ami du peuple* (No. 15, April 14, 1878, p. 59), and in the report on the deliberations of the local authority (Conseil Général du département de la Meurthe-et-Moselle, 1878, p. 51). Moreover, Ferry's patriotism was reflected in his participation in the Franco-Prussian War, where he was appointed captain of the Fifteenth Company. Following an injury sustained during the Battle of Cresancey on December 31, 1870, he was honored with the distinction of Knight of the Legion of Honor (Lepage, 1871, p. 42; Seinguerlet, 1883, p. 413). Louis Ferry passed away on December 8, 1888, at the age of 53. He served as mayor of Lunéville during the final four years of his life.

Following Ferry's death, his wife, whose attention was more oriented toward embroidery than on its commercialization, formed a partnership with Monsieur Millet; the company was renamed *Maison Millet et veuve Ferry* [Maison Millet and Ferry's widow] to expand its products and increase its sales. In preparation for the 1889 Paris Universal Exposition, which was intended to celebrate the centenary of the French Revolution and boost the country's economy, the company presented several samples of embroidery made with jet beads on black tulle, which had been very popular in women's fashion since 1875. The exhibition provided an unprecedented opportunity for Madame de Ferry's atelier to gain international recognition. As it was the largest showcase of design, art, and technology ever organized, it also served to project the image of Paris as the world's cultural capital. Ferry's method gained its due notoriety, to the point that it was awarded the Gold Medal for Innovation in recognition of the evident technical advance it represented for the embroidery craft process. Alfred Picard, curator of the Paris Universal Exposition of 1889, commented as follows in his general report on the event:

> More modest in appearance is the production of *Maison Millet et veuve Ferry*, from Lunéville, which embroiders in different ways. In the past, they embroidered with braided and crochet stitches on white tulle garments, which were once very popular in this country [...]. Today, jet embroidery on black tulle has become very popular in the [Lorraine] region, where the articles displayed in these exhibits are made. It was Monsieur Louis Ferry who conceived the idea, a few years ago, of threading the beads in advance and fixing said thread by making a chain stitch. This process makes sewing the beads easier and faster. The jury [of this exposition] awards the Gold Medal to Monsieur Millet and Ferry's widow. (Picard, 1891, pp. 208–9)

The decision made by this international jury to award such an honorary prize to Madame de Ferry was certainly not without reason. The technique was so novel that after the Franco-Prussian War of 1870–1871, it was introduced in other cities, such as Saarburg, which had been annexed to Germany because of the conflict (Vrignaud-Masson, 1982, p. 13). The technique was later adopted by the embroidery house of Albert Michonet in Paris, revealing its rapid circulation among the commercial suppliers of haute couture (Mauriès, 2020, p. 19). Likewise, around 1890, at the height of the Belle Époque, the embroidery house of Madame de Ferry opened a branch in Paris. This establishment employed highly skilled female workers, such as Madeleine Forey, who, as published in the *Journal Officiel de la République Française*, was awarded the Medal of Honor for Work by the French Ministry of Commerce and Industry in 1897. The award was in accordance with the implementation of the decree of July 16, 1886, which created this professional distinction. As noted in the press release:

> Paris, November 14, 1897. Under the decree of July 16, 1886, the Minister of Commerce, Industry, Post, and Telegraphs awarded in Paris, on the occasion of special ceremonies during the months of September and October, medals of honor to the workers and employees whose names follow: [...] Madame Widow de Forey (Madeleine), embroiderer at *Maison Millet et veuve Ferry*. (*Journal Officiel de la République Française*, No. 310, November 15, 1897, pp. 6387–8)

In that same year of 1897, the distinction was also awarded to several seamstresses, namely Julie Guyon, Julie Martin, and Joséphine Lagneau, employed by the House of Worth, which, by then, was already run by Jean-Philippe Worth, son of Charles Frederick Worth. Following the death of its founder in 1895, this fashion house's generational succession coincided with the use of Lunéville crochet in haute couture. The clothing of the so-called *femme ornée* advocated evening gowns enriched with luminous three-dimensional embroidery of crystals and sequins. It was, therefore, the most sophisticated version of fashion, which served as the driving force behind this artisanal technique, elevating the prestige of the great couture houses and becoming an integral part of the very definition of Parisian luxury.

The joyous 1920s was a period marked by the desire for luxury in the aftermath of the First World War. It represented an important period of prosperity for Lunéville embroidery, resulting from a fashion in which shiny elements and rhinestones were the leitmotifs of evening dresses. To meet this rise in demand, the French press carried advertisements offering employment to craftswomen specializing in bead embroidery. It also led to the establishment of the *École d'Apprentissage de la Broderie* [Lunéville School of Embroidery Apprenticeship], which included an elementary and an advanced course (Delorme, 1927, p. 95). The school was inaugurated on April 3, 1924, thanks to the financial contributions of lamp manufacturer Edmond Dannhausser,[4] with additional support from surgeon Edmond Delorme[5] and Paul Léon, the director of the National School of Fine Arts in Paris, who had the honor of presiding over the inauguration (Vrignaud-Masson, 1982, p. 16).

It is important to note that while Lunéville embroidery uses a chain stitch as its basic stitch, the hook needle allowed for other, more complex, stitches to be made. To fully understand the decorative possibilities offered by Ferry's technique, it is necessary to briefly describe these additional stitches.

Firstly, one of the stitches that requires mastery of the change of direction with the hook needle is the so-called *point crénelé* [crenelated stitch], which consists of arranging the beads in a broken line, simulating the battlements of a castle. In contrast to the above, the *point tiré* [draw-back stitch] involves arranging beads in parallel and successive rows, each row consisting of multiple beads fixed to the fabric by a single stitch.

On the other hand, the *point de vermicelle* [vermicelli stitch] covers the fabric's surface with beads or sequins, avoids angles and intersections, and uses only curved lines. The difficulty of this stitch lies in the fact that these lines are not previously traced but are random. This peculiarity implies that no two designs can be identical, since their execution depends on the embroiderer's improvisation. A variation of this stitch is the *vermicelle égrené* [vermicelli with empty stitches], which only differs from the previous one in that a bead is placed every two or three stitches, leaving several empty

---

4 Edmond Dannhausser was a businessman who produced nickel-plated bronze and wrought iron lamps during the interwar period. It had a factory at 16 Pierre Levée Street in Paris, and several stores in Lunéville, Brussels, and Paris.

5 Edmond Delorme (Lunéville, 1847–Paris, 1929) was a distinguished doctor and surgeon who practiced his profession in the French army. He served as president of the Academy of Medicine and founded the Association of Friends of the Fine and Industrial Arts of Lunéville. In 1927 he explained the history of his hometown in the book *Lunéville et son arrondissement* [Lunéville and its district].

stitches between each bead. It is also usually made with gold or silver lamé thread to make it more striking.

The *point à plat* or *passé plat* [flat stitch] consists of leaving an empty stitch between beads, while the *point riche* [rich stitch] consists of two superimposed elements. The first of these two elements, which can be a chain of beads, a cord, or a strand of wool, acts as the base, while a second, always a zigzag chain of beads, is placed on top.

Finally, it should be noted that Ferry's technique also allows for the application of beads by placing the right side of the fabric facing up on the frame, although it is less frequent because the process is slower. In this case, the beads or sequins are not previously inserted on a spool of thread, but are placed directly by penetrating the hole of the beads with the hook. In French, it is called *pose à la puce,* which literally means "applying to the shaving," as it is common for the beads to jump when the hole is pierced, reminiscent of the shavings that come off when puncturing metal or wood. This process is precisely the same as that of Aari embroidery.

The introduction of Lunéville's beaded embroidery in Spanish haute couture

The Paris Universal Exposition of 1889 played a pivotal role in elevating Ferry's technique to a prominent international standing, promoting it worldwide. This was partly because the exhibition received nearly 30 million visitors from all over the world, but also because the jury that awarded the prize was composed of 15 renowned lace and embroidery manufacturers from France, Italy, Switzerland, Belgium, Ecuador, and Spain. Among them were Jaime Nos, a Spanish lace merchant, and Ernest Lefébure (1835–1913), a textile entrepreneur who was also the administrator of the Museum of Decorative Arts in Paris and author of the monograph *Broderie et dentelles* (1887) (Picard, 1891, p. 181). Therefore, it seems logical to think that one of the means by which Lunéville's embroidery technique was introduced in Spain could have been through Nos, or at least he must have spoken of its existence in Spain.

However, there is no doubt that Lunéville's beading embroidery took its first triumphal steps in Spanish haute couture through the figure of Pedro Rodríguez (Valencia, 1895–Barcelona, 1990). In 1920, following the guidelines set by the *Paris Chamber of Haute Couture*, Rodríguez began to present complete collections using live mannequins in his Barcelona salon. While this innovation may have been the first of its kind in Spain, it had been pioneered by Charles Frederick Worth in Paris during the mid-nineteenth century (Rosés Castellsaguer, 2020, p. 124).

From the very beginning, Pedro Rodríguez had been a staunch advocate of handcrafted fashion; he was among the first Spanish couturiers to incorporate Lunéville crochet in his designs, all of which were meticulously crafted in his own workshops.[6] One of the embroiderers who worked under Pedro Rodríguez was Cándida Romero—born in Madrid in 1908—, who was responsible for ornamenting the designer's exclusive outfits since the opening of his branch house in Madrid in 1939. Cándida's direct contact with Rodriguez's exquisite designs inspired her to create her own embroidery house in Madrid in 1948, specifically at 202 Bravo Murillo Street. The atelier was named Bordados Carlos in honor of Cándida's firstborn son, Carlos Fernández Romero—born in Madrid in 1928—, who managed the workshop and designed the embroideries (José María Fernández Romero [brother of Carlos Fernández Romero], personal communiqué, March 27, 2023).

Since its inception, Bordados Carlos sought to position its products in direct competition with Parisian fashion. To do so, it used the Lunéville technique regularly, to the point that it became a hallmark of the company's identity. With it, Cándida Romero and Carlos Fernández responded to the orders of the most prominent haute couture designers of the period of Franco's dictatorship, such as Manuel Pertegaz, Rafael Herrera and Enrique Ollero, Lino Martínez, and Elio Berhanyer. Spanish fashion lived its maximum splendor at this time, establishing itself as an international reference of elegance.

6 The Costume Museum in Madrid houses two dresses by Pedro Rodríguez that were embroidered in the 1950s using the Lunéville technique. One of them is a cocktail dress embroidered with horizontal sequin borders on organza (inventory number MTFCE126488). The other is a beige satin evening gown embroidered with floral motifs in jet beads, white sequins, and black velvet cord (inventory number MT088898). I would like to take this opportunity to thank Juan González, head of the contemporary clothing collection at the Costume Museum in Madrid, for the information provided.

In the mid-1980s, Carlos Fernández transitioned his business away from haute couture and toward industrial embroidery, thus adapting to fast fashion. The continuation of handmade embroidery came from the hand of a talented disciple of François Lesage, Johan Luc Katt, born in Casablanca in 1954. Following the establishment of his workshop in Madrid in 1987, Katt began to work for several of the most renowned Spanish designers of the time, including Pedro del Hierro, Elio Berhanyer, and María Teresa de Vega, among others. Years later, other prominent Spanish couturiers, such as Lorenzo Caprile and Felipe Varela, would join Katt's list of clients.

The continuity of Lunéville bead embroidery in contemporary Spanish fashion: a dialogue between past and present

Lunéville bead embroidery, whose cultural value was recognized by UNESCO in 2020, has transcended its original nineteenth-century application to become an integral part of contemporary design proposals. All the major French haute couture houses draw upon it as a symbol of historical identity and savoir-faire. Yet it has also established itself within Spanish fashion as a means of expression and refinement. It features prominently in the creations of both established and emerging designers, such as Petro Valverde, Felipe Varela, Basalda, Navascués, Santiago Bandrés, and Kerstin Krause, among others.

This is evident, for example, in the emblematic dress designed by Nacho Aguayo for Pedro del Hierro, which Cristina Pedroche wore in 2020 during Antena 3's *Las Campanadas* New Year broadcast in Spain. It can likewise be observed in Basaldúa's refined bridal ensembles embroidered by María Luisa Castellanos,[7] and in Queen Letizia's official wardrobe (designed by Felipe Varela), where Lunéville crochet appears consistently. Given its institutional significance, mention should be made of the abdication of Juan Carlos I, on which occasion Doña Letizia wore a skirt embroidered with jet butterflies. Likewise, at the proclamation of Felipe VI as King of Spain, she opted for

---

7 See the embroideries by María Luisa Castellanos in: Basaldúa, Blanco, and Herranz's *Basaldúa, el traje de novia* (2011) [Basaldúa, the bride's dress].

an elegant white crepe coat, whose neckline was embroidered by Katt with beads of varying sizes, colors, and textures, thus creating a harmonious *ombré* effect.[8] This *dégradé* technique, employed within Lunéville bead embroidery, began to be used in the 1920s by the Maison Lesage, where Katt was taught it in the late 1960s by his mentor, François Lesage (Mauriès, 2020, p. 57). By incorporating it into Queen Letizia's coat in 2014, Katt established a clear dialogue between artisanal heritage and contemporary design, or, more explicitly, between tradition and modernity.

Lunéville bead embroidery has therefore found a space within Spanish fashion in which to persist and reinvent itself. Far from being a static vestige of the past, it represents a living form of knowledge that has progressively adapted over time to respond to the aesthetic transformations of the present.

In keeping with the Parisian model, Spain's founding haute couture houses, such as Pedro Rodríguez's, established a work ethic grounded in the excellence of their craftsmanship and the intergenerational transmission of their knowledge. This is reflected in the case of Cándida Romero, whose grandchildren, José María and Rebeca, remain involved with the tradition of Lunéville bead embroidery.

Beyond its profound and lasting influence on Spanish haute couture, Lunéville crochet has also helped sustain a form of fashion that values history and defends hand craftsmanship in the face of industrialized production.

In this way, haute couture reaffirms its singularity through artisanal work, a form of work that cannot be reproduced industrially with the same quality. It is precisely in this exclusivity that its fundamental value resides, a value which, together with artisanal excellence, continues, and will continue, to shape the course of luxury fashion.

Nevertheless, despite the continuing relevance of Lunéville crochet within Spanish fashion, it also faces a major challenge: addressing the shortage of artisans capable of ensuring its continuity. In order to address this serious threat, the training initiatives undertaken by certain embroiderers have proved indispensable, such as those of José María Fernández and his daughter

---

8 The *ombré* effect (from the French, "shaded") is a technique employed within Lunéville crochet. It consists in producing a gradual transition (*dégradé*) through the harmonious combination of beads of different sizes, colors, and textures.

Rebeca, and especially those of Johan Luc Katt. Between 2017 and 2021, Katt delivered several embroidery courses at the Jalón Academy in Málaga and at Javier Barroeta's School of Haute Couture. However, as in any artistic discipline, training takes time; to achieve technical mastery in Lunéville bead embroidery requires years of experience and a profound understanding of materials if harmonious results are to be achieved.

Conclusion

Since its introduction in France in the mid-eighteenth century, tambour embroidery has enjoyed great success due to its eye-catching and delicate nature. The interest shown by the Marquise de Pompadour led to its emergence as a popular pastime among the ladies and girls of the European aristocracy. It also became an outstanding decorative formula that, mixed with other embroidery techniques, offered delightful effects on both men's and women's clothing, where garlands of flowers ran along the front of vests and jackets.

At the dawn of the nineteenth century, the discovery of mechanical tulle prompted the embroiderers of Lunéville to contribute to the growth of the technique by developing an important manufacturing center for chain-stitch embroidery. This embroidery, when executed on tulle, sought to imitate the refined lace of Flanders and Alenzon. In this same location, in 1867, Louis Ferry was the first to add beads and sequins to tambour embroidery. These innovations were quickly incorporated into haute couture collections, thereby elevating the prestige and distinction of a newly emergent sector that was here to stay.

The 1889 Paris Universal Exposition played a pivotal role in the dissemination of Ferry's technique on a global scale, and particularly in Spain, it was widely used from the beginning of the twentieth century in the fashion house of Pedro Rodríguez, from which an independent atelier was established under the embroiderer Cándida Romero and her son Carlos Fernández. Today, Ferry's technique has garnered profound universal acclaim, finding expression in the dresses and accessories of all haute couture firms. In 2020, its artistic value was recognized by UNESCO, which included it in its list of Intangible Cultural Heritage.

References

Almanach-annuaire de l'arrondissement de Lunéville. (1903). *Imprimerie Nouvelle*. https://gallica.bnf.fr/ark:/12148/bpt6k11916416/f1.item

Basaldúa, C., Blanco Carpintero, M., and Herranz Rodríguez, C. (2011). *Basaldúa, el traje de novia* [Basaldúa, the wedding dress]. Museo del Traje de Madrid.

Benoît, J. (1870). *Indicateur universel du commerce des tissus en général, soie, coton, fil, laine, dorure, etc., et des industries qui s'y rattachent* [Universal directory of the trade in fabrics in general—silk, cotton, thread, wool, gilding, etc.—and the related industries] (Vol. 1). Moniteur des soies. https://gallica.bnf.fr/ark:/12148/bpt6k62430971/f389.item

Boulard, F. (1917). Une industrie d'art au village [An art industry in the village]. *Bulletin de la Société Historique et Archéologique de l'Orne, 36*, 210–34. Imprimerie Alençonnaise. https://gallica.bnf.fr/ark:/12148/bpt6k55126643/f244.item

Callan, R. (2017). Hooked together: The shared history of aari and tambour embroidery. *Costume Commission Poster of the United States Institute for Theatre Technology (USITT)*, 1–11. http://costumearchive.usitt.org/files/Costume%20Poster%20Sessions/2017/Callan-Hooked%20Together.pdf

Commission Française sur l'Industrie des Nations. (1854). *Exposition Universelle de 1851: Travaux de la Commission Française sur l'Industrie des Nations* [Universal Exhibition of 1851: Works of the French Commission on the industry of nations] (Vol. 5). Imprimerie Impériale. https://cnum.cnam.fr/pgi/fpage.php?8XAE35.13/380/100/628/0/0

Conseil Général du département de la Meurthe-et-Moselle. (1878). *Rapport de monsieur le Préfet et délibérations du Conseil (Session d'avril 1878)* [Report of the Prefect and deliberations of the Council (April 1878 session)]. Imprimerie Départementale. https://gallica.bnf.fr/ark:/12148/bpt6k5746673m/f1.item

Crill, R. (2022). Chain-stitch embroidery of Kutch. In S. Shah & R. Crill (Eds.), *The shoemaker's stitch: Mochi embroideries of Gujarat in the TAPI Collection* (pp. 9–33). Niyogi Books.

Delorme, E. (1927). *Lunéville et son arrondissement* [Lunéville and its district] (Vol. 1). Imprimerie du Journal de Lunéville. https://gallica.bnf.fr/ark:/12148/bd6t54067769/f124.image

El Correo de la Moda. (1851, November 1). *No. 1*. https://hemerotecadigital.bne.es/hd/es/viewer?id=f790c05c-dfd7-4945-812b-56dc094caa4a&page=16

Journal Officiel de la République Française. (1897, November 15). *No. 310*. https://gallica.bnf.fr/ark:/12148/bpt6k62571596/f1.item

L'Ami du peuple. (1878, April 14). *No. 15*. https://gallica.bnf.fr/ark:/12148/bpt6k2379585n/f1.item

Lee Hyde, M. (2013). Needling: Embroidery and satire in the hands of Charles Germain de Saint-Aubin. In E. Mansfield and K. Malone (eds.), *Seeing satire in the eighteenth century* (pp. 107–30). Voltaire Foundation.

Lefébure, E. (1887). *Broderie et dentelles* [Embroidery and lace]. Maison Quantin. https://bibliotecadigital.jcyl.es/es/consulta/registro.do?id=24234

Lepage, H. (1871). *Le tableau d'honneur de la Meurthe* [The roll of honor of Meurthe]. N. Collin. https://gallica.bnf.fr/ark:/12148/bpt6k96194882/f9.item.r=maison%20Ferry%20Bonnechaux%20%20a%20Lun%C3%A9ville

Maeder, E. (1983). *Art of the embroiderer.* [Fascimile copy of *L'art du brodeur* by Charles Germain de Saint-Aubin, with additional notes and commentaries by Edward Maeder]. Los Angeles Country Museum of Art.

Mauriès, P. (2020). *Maison Lesage: Haute couture embroidery*. Thames & Hudson.

Naik, S. (1996). *Traditional embroideries of India*. APH Publishing.

Picard, A. (1891), *Exposition Universelle Internationale de 1889 à Paris: Rapports du jury international* [Groupe IV: Tissus, vêtements et accessoires. Classe 34: Dentelles, tulles, broderies et passementeries]. Ministère du Commerce, de l'Industrie el des Colonies. Imprimerie Impériale.

Rosés Castellsaguer, S. (2020). La muerte de la alta costura española: Crónica de un final [The death of Spanish haute couture: Chronicle of an ending]. *Anuario del Departamento de Historia y Teoría del Arte*, Volume 32, pp. 123–35. https://revistas.uam.es/anuario/issue/view/anuario2020_32/628

Rousseau, J. J. (1892). *Oeuvres complétes de J.J. Rousseau: Emile* [Complete Works of J. J. Rousseau: Emile] (Vol. 2). Libraire Hachette et cie.

Saint-Aubin, C. G. (1770). *L'art du brodeur* [The art of embroidery]. L.F. Delatour Publishers. https://gallica.bnf.fr/ark:/12148/bpt6k1065586m/f21.item

Shah, S. (2022). Who are the Mochis?. In S. Shah y R. Crill, *The shoemaker's stitch: Mochi embroideries of Gujarat in the TAPI Collection* (pp. 35–43). Niyogi Books.

Seinguerlet, E. (1883). *Revue alsacienne: littérature, histoire, sciences, poésie, beaux-arts*. Berger-Levrault et cie. https://gallica.bnf.fr/ark:/12148/bpt6k9637866s/f7.item.r=maison%20de%20broderie%20Ferry%20Bonnechaux

Vrignaud-Masson, G. (1982). *Le point de Lunéville, hier et aujourd'hui* [Lunéville lace, yesterday and today]. Vrignaud-Masson–Mut'imprim.

CHAPTER 17

The Value of What Was Lost

Spanish haute couture

*Elena Díaz Martín**

ABSTRACT

Spanish haute couture, particularly between the 1940s and 1960s, stood out as one of the highest expressions of artisanal design and craftsmanship. Figures such as Pedro Rodríguez and Flora Villareal led this movement, supported by a system of workshops where manual labor was the core of creation. These fashion houses, located mainly in Barcelona, Madrid, and San Sebastián, gained international recognition for their elegance and quality, attracting prestigious clients. However, factors such as luxury taxes and the rise of *prêt-à-porter* led to their decline in the 1970s.

The role of seamstresses, essential yet historically undervalued, deserves special recognition. These women, known as *modistillas*, started as apprentices at a young age and perfected their work through orally transmitted techniques. Their entirely artisanal work ensured the durability, aesthetics, and functionality of each garment. Without these workers, haute couture garments would not have existed.

Today, industrial fashion has largely replaced these techniques, but rescuing this artisanal legacy is key to preserving sustainability, quality, and tradition in fashion—values that Spanish haute couture embodied during its golden age.

Keywords: fashion, haute couture, dressmaking, Spain, sustainability

Introduction

When fashion is discussed in most academic and social settings, it is often associated with "frivolity." The garments we wear daily are perceived merely as tools to embellish our bodies and feed our egos. However, fashion transcends these superficial notions. Fashion is identity, social change, architecture, construction, differentiation, and much more. Since the beginning of time, humans have used fashion as a tool to protect themselves from the cold, cover their modesty, express magic, and, above all, differentiate themselves. Everything we place on our bodies—hairstyles, makeup, tattoos, piercings,

* Escuela Superior de Diseño de Madrid.

and clothing—forms our identity. Fashion is not just aesthetics; it is a visual language that communicates who we are and how we interact with the world.

Fashion cannot exist without the human body, which is its canvas and ultimate goal. Garments do not merely cover the body; they associate with it, dialogue with its shapes, and create a unified whole. Each piece of clothing results from a complex engineering process, which unfortunately few appreciate today. The average consumer visits a store like Zara and buys the trendy garment they believe suits them, without considering the history and evolution behind that object. Each garment carries a narrative—not only its memory as a product but also its place in the history of clothing.

The importance of dressmaking

The invention of the eyed needle about 40,000 years ago marked a technological milestone in human history. According to James Laver: "this invention made it possible to sew pieces of hide together to make them fit the body." (Laver, 2019). Since then, garment-making has evolved into a precise science. The construction of a garment begins with a morphological analysis essential for adapting to the organic characteristics of the human body: curves, straight lines, soft areas, rigid zones, heights, and proportions. Every garment must be functional and aesthetic, capable of transforming the perception of the body.

If we deconstructed a garment, we would find a pattern that acts as a guide to cut fabric pieces into specific shapes. These pieces, when assembled like a puzzle, define the final structure of the garment. The pattern is cut onto fabric that, when sewn, gives the design a three-dimensional shape. Any error in this process compromises the final product.

There are numerous studies on pattern-making methods and materials but sewing techniques have received less academic attention. Historically, sewing has been seen as secondary work, mainly carried out by women. Yet without these techniques, garments would not exist—there would be no connection between their parts or three-dimensionality.

Dressmaking, in addition to assembling, plays a crucial role in details such as the garment's drape, aesthetic finishes, and durability. Careful dressmaking ensures a longer lifespan for the garment, contributing to sustainability.

As Mariu Emilas notes in her book *Balenciaga: Mi Jefe*, referring to her father's work as a tailor at Balenciaga:

> El trabajo de una prenda es todo un mundo. Entretelas, organzas, galones, sostenidos, frunces, estiramientos, embebidos, picados, pinzas, cortes ... que ayudan a que esta se sustente y caiga perfecta. Y a que su fisonomía exterior resulte de gran simplicidad, cuando lo cierto es que dentro de sí encierra un mundo muy complejo. [The work of a garment is a whole world. Interlinings, organza, ribbons, gathers, stretching, easing, stitches, darts, cuts ... all these help sustain it and make it fall perfectly. Its outer appearance may seem simple, but inside, it hides a very complex world.] (Emilas, 2017)[1]

Spanish haute couture

Haute couture represents the highest expression of garment craftsmanship. According to Vaquero Argüelles, "la alta costura es la creación firmada y, por tanto, de diseño original, de moda de la más alta calidad y de confección totalmente artesana" [haute couture is the signed creation and, therefore, an original fashion design of the highest quality and entirely handcrafted] (Vaquero Argüelles, 2007). When discussing haute couture, we often think of English designer Frederick Worth, founder of the Chambre Syndicale de la Confection et de la Mode, the predecessor of the Chambre Syndicale de la Couture, which was led by his sons Gaston and Jean-Philippe in 1910, marking the beginning of the modern luxury fashion system. This institution established "las diferencias entre alta costura, media costura—casas que no hacían desfiles, pero recibían clientes privados y compradores profesionales—y pequeña costura, o confección, de los modistos tradicionales que hacían ropa a medida" [the distinctions between haute couture, moyenne couture—houses that did not hold runway shows but catered to private clients and professional buyers—and petite couture, or traditional tailoring by designers who made custom clothing] (Vaquero Argüelles, 2007). However, Spain also experienced a golden era of haute couture between the 1940s and 1960s, during the Franco regime.

1 All translations are my own unless otherwise noted.

Pedro Rodríguez, considered the father of Spanish haute couture, "fue el primero en realizar desfiles en pasarelas con maniquíes en España, y, con ello y gracias a él, nació la alta costura española" [was the first to hold runway shows with models in Spain, and thanks to him, Spanish haute couture was born] (Calzadilla, 2012). Rodríguez, born in Valencia in 1895, presided over the Cooperativa de la Alta Costura Española from its founding in 1941 until its closure in the 1970s. This cooperative, inspired by the Chambre Syndicale de la Couture, initially had 20 members, including the so-called Big Five of Spanish haute couture: Pedro Rodríguez, Asunción Bastida, Santa Eulalia, El Dique Flotante, and Manuel Pertegaz. In 1960, Pertegaz left, and designers Pedro Rovira and Carmen Mir joined; in the cooperative's final years, Elio Berhanyer was also a member. These designers presented their collections twice a year at the Hotel Ritz in Barcelona in an event known as the Salón de la Moda.

In addition to the aforementioned designers, other fashion houses stood out during this period, such as Marbel, Flora Villareal, Natalio, Lino Fernández, and Herrera y Ollera in Madrid—a city that was already competing with Barcelona to claim the title of Spain's fashion capital. Of course, we must not forget Cristóbal Balenciaga and his EISA fashion house in Spain. Barcelona, Madrid, and San Sebastián formed a golden triangle of haute couture, attracting clients from Spain's aristocracy and high society. The Franco regime supported this industry as an international propaganda tool, facilitating its presence at events like the 1958 Brussels World's Fair, where the following fashion houses were given an exhibition pavilion: Asunción Bastida, Marbel, Pertegaz, El Dique Flotante, Pedro Rodríguez, Vargas-Ochagavía, and Santa Eulalia, which presented collections inspired by Francisco de Goya. Another example was the 1964 New York World's Fair, where Asunción Bastida and Pedro Rodríguez showcased their designs.

Spanish haute couture offered elegant, high-quality designs at a lower cost than French fashion, thanks to cheaper labor, attracting international clients, particularly Americans. However, this golden age began to decline in the 1960s due to luxury taxes: in 1959, all haute couture houses were required to pay one million pesetas proportionally, and this amount increased each year until they could no longer afford it. This tax raised production costs, forcing fashion houses to stop holding runway shows to avoid being classified as haute couture and, consequently, being subjected to the tax. As Castellsaguer explains, "si una casa no hacía desfiles, no podría ser catalogada como alta costura ni vinculada al sector del lujo y, en consecuencia, no se le podría aplicar dicho impuesto" [if a fashion house did not hold runway shows, it could not be classified as haute couture or linked to the luxury sector, and thus, the tax would not apply] (Castellsaguer, 2020). This situation led to the so-called Mannequin War: models lost their jobs, and although many adapted to other roles within major haute couture houses, sales declined due to the lack of runway shows. While they were no longer taxed, clients lost interest in their fashion. Additionally, without runway shows, there was no media coverage in national or international press. This abandonment of the national haute couture industry by the regime, combined with the social changes brought by the rise of *prêt-à-porter* in Spain, led to the downfall of most major fashion houses in the 1970s. As a result, the radiant years of Spanish haute couture were forgotten.

The hidden role of female workers

None of these fashion houses could have survived without their workers. Flora Villareal had over one hundred employees, including the tailoring workshop for suits and coats, the fantasy workshop for cocktail and evening wear, and the boutique workshop for shirts, skirts, and other garments. Manuel Pertegaz had up to 750 workers, all of whom were true fashion artisans.

In these workshops, the *modistillas* (female seamstresses) were responsible for crafting haute couture garments. As their very name suggests, they were often overlooked and undervalued. However, without these women, these garments would not have existed. These workers played a fundamental role in garment construction, yet their contributions have been underestimated compared to those of cutters or pattern makers, who were traditionally men.

These women started working in fashion houses at a very young age, sometimes as young as 11 or 12. They began as apprentices, then became assistants, and later reached the rank of *oficialas* (journeymen). Some specialized in tailoring techniques (*sastras*), while others focused on dressmaking techniques (*modistas*). However, it was rare for them to attain the title of *maestra* (master dressmaker), the highest rank in the workshop. This was partly because such positions were limited and only became available when a previous master retired or left the house. Additionally, most girls left the workshop upon getting married; very few continued working after marriage. Only unmarried women could aspire to the rank of master, and even then, very few achieved it—most of these positions went to men, who had greater social advantages.

These women worked long hours and in an entirely artisanal manner. "Las obreras, como también eran denominadas las modistas y sastras, trabajan en los talleres como aplicadas abejas: con gran precisión, esmero y maestría en el oficio." [The workers, also known as seamstresses and tailors, worked in the workshops like diligent bees: with great precision, care, and mastery of the craft.] (Emilas, 2017).

The transmission of knowledge among them was based on observing their superiors, oral explanations, and, above all, the repetition of learned techniques until they mastered them. This knowledge was passed down from one worker to another and was rarely documented in publications, unlike many pattern-making methods. This lack of documentation was likely because many of the girls working in the workshops came from humble backgrounds and were nearly illiterate.

Artisanal dressmaking in Spanish haute couture

These women employed artisanal dressmaking techniques through which garments were constructed by the meticulous joining of their constituent pieces, previously created by master patternmakers and cutters. A fundamental question thus arises: what differences exist between those techniques and those used today? Can they truly be considered artisanal in the present day?

Today, a distinction must be made between industrial garment production and made-to-measure dressmaking, the latter being closer to the sewing practices used by the women discussed in this article. Industrial garment production, characteristic of the fast-fashion market, prioritizes quantity over quality. It is a highly automated process in which a specific machine exists for each phase of a garment's construction. Care is not the objective; rather, speed and productivity are emphasized through an assembly-line system in which each worker specializes in a single part of the process. For example, the technician responsible for attaching the collar of a shirt does not necessarily know how to set in the sleeve; in other words, a single person is not capable of constructing an entire garment from start to finish.

Furthermore, industrial production employs rapid construction techniques, even if they are less aesthetic, without considering the durability of the product, as is the case with the use of overlocking to finish interior seams. In contrast, in artisanal dressmaking, detail and quality are paramount. Every part of a garment is carefully assembled and conceived with precision. Each look is created and constructed for a specific body, with particular morphological characteristics, and the garment is designed for a specific client. Today, a comparable form of this type of production can be found in made-to-measure dressmaking, which still exists in Spain and in other neighboring countries.

To understand the construction techniques of Spanish haute couture during the 1940s, 1950s, and 1960s, it is first necessary to distinguish between those used in tailoring workshops and those employed in the fantasy workshop. In tailoring workshops, where women's suits and outer garments were produced, pieces were constructed using techniques close to those of men's tailoring, incorporating various reinforcements and interlinings joined by *puntadas de picar* (pad stitch). Many designers of this period, such as Cristóbal Balenciaga, had been trained in traditional men's tailoring and adapted these techniques to women's clothing in a softer manner. One example of this adaptation is the use of silk organza as an interlining reinforcement in various seams.

In contrast, fantasy ateliers produced garments intended for social and ceremonial events, generally luxurious and highly elaborate dresses made from high-quality fabrics, most of them composed of natural fibers such as silk. In these cases, construction techniques were adapted to the specific characteristics of each garment and, although machine stitching was used, it was not generalized; it was applied only in specific instances, such as joining side seams or along long seam lines.

Among the most common hand-sewn stitches were initial *hilvanes* (basting stitches), temporary stitches made with cotton or silk thread to hold pieces together, which were removed once the final seams had been completed. *Sobrehilado* (overcasting) was also common and was used to finish fabric edges and prevent fraying. This was carried out with great precision, using stitches measuring between 3 and 5 millimeters: "trabajadas de derecha a izquierda y con un solo hilo, dando puntadas en diagonal sobre el canto del tejido" [it was worked from right to left, with a single thread, making diagonal stitches over the edge] (Smith, 2025). During the 1940s and 1950s, this technique was widely used on the interiors of garments. In the 1960s, the use of inner linings that covered the interior of garments became more widespread, preventing their internal construction from being visible and leading to the decline of visible sobrehilado.

Hand topstitching was also frequent, especially on fine fabrics such as silk chiffon or certain types of lace, achieving an exceptional level of fineness, with stitches measuring as little as 2 millimeters. Other common techniques included the *puntada de escapulario* (catch stitch), worked in a crisscross pattern, typically used to secure overlapping inner facings at necklines, as well as the use of tiny hand-worked *corchetes* (hooks) that engaged with minute *presillas* (eyes). These examples illustrate only a portion of the wide range of artisanal hand-sewing techniques used in garments from the decades in question.

Seamstresses were responsible for executing these techniques and transmitting them manually and orally from one generation to another, achieving a level of refinement that could only be attained after many years of experience. This savoir-faire, based on repetition, observation, and manual skill, constitutes one of the most valuable—and at the same time most fragile—forms of heritage within Spanish haute couture.

Conclusion

With the closure of haute couture houses in the 1970s and the passing of their workers, many artisanal dressmaking techniques were lost. Today, garment production is predominantly industrial, relying on mechanized and assembly-line processes that are far more economical but of much lower quality. Only small groups of designers attempt to revive artisanal fashion, creating unique and sustainable pieces. However, the complexity of haute couture techniques and the lack of documentation make teaching and preserving them challenging.

Artisanal fashion is not only a cultural legacy but also a solution to today's sustainability problems. A well-made garment lasts longer, reducing textile waste. Recovering these techniques would allow for a more environmentally respectful future. As a society, we must look to the past to appreciate and learn from these practices, integrating them into the present and ensuring their continuity. Only by doing so can we achieve a balance between tradition, innovation, and sustainability in fashion.

References

Calzadilla, P. (2012). *Pedro Rodriguez. Alta Costura sobre el papel. Figurines 1940–1976. Catálogo de la exposición* [Pedro Rodríguez: Haute couture on paper. Fashion sketches 1940–1976. Exhibition catalog]. CIPE, Museo del Traje. Ministerio de Educación, Cultura y Deporte. https://www.cultura.gob.es/mtraje/dam/jcr:2d88242a-c0db-42aa-a3e0-7b346a7a6b8b/catalogo-acpapel.pdf

Castellsaguer, S. R. (2020). La muerte de la alta costura española: Crónica de un final [The death of Spanish haute couture: Chronicle of an ending]. *Anuario del Departamento de Historia y Teoría del Arte, 32,* 123–35. https://doi.org/10.15366/anuario2020.32.006

Emilas, M. (2017). *Balenciaga: mi jefe* [Balenciaga, my boss]. Editorial Círculo Rojo.

Gennaioli, D. (2023). La Oficina y la Comisión Interministerial para la Promoción de la Moda: La proyección internacional de la alta costura durante el Franquismo desarrollista [The Office and the Interministerial Commission for the Promotion of Fashion: The international projection of haute couture during developmental Francoism]. *Historia Contemporánea, 72*. https://doi.org/10.1387/hc.22934

Laver, J. (2019). *Breve historia del traje y la moda* [A brief history of dress and fashion]. Cátedra.

Smith, A. (2025). *Corte y confección. Prendas de vestir a medida* [The Tailoring Book]. DK.

Vaquero Argüelles, I. (2007). El reinado de la alta costura: la moda de la primera mitad del siglo XX [The reign of haute couture: Fashion in the first half of the twentieth century]. *Indumenta, 0,* 155. https://www.cultura.gob.es/mtraje-indumenta/dam/jcr:0cd96564-482f-4d6c-9db8-8fd441f869b4/indumenta00-13-iva.pdf

Costume Studies and Fashion Studies as Diverging Fields for the Same Object of Study

The clothed body

*Caterina Cucinotta**

ABSTRACT
This chapter examines film analysis through the lens of clothing, exploring the theoretical differences between two closely related fields of study: Costume Studies and Fashion Studies. These two disciplines are compared to understand how, over the past 50 years, their respective methodologies have highlighted or overlooked the social and artistic dimensions of cinematic costumes.

On the one hand, the concept of fashion has often overshadowed the meticulous work of costume designers, who focus on shapes, fabrics, and details that are integral to visual storytelling and spatial composition. On the other hand, to grasp the differences between costume designers and fashion designers, it is essential to analyze and deconstruct their creative processes, emphasizing the distinctive nature of costume work in cinema.

The aim of this chapter is to direct the study of cinematic costumes toward an approach more deeply rooted in filmic components, moving beyond issues that have historically risked isolating it from the broader context of film analysis.

Keywords: cinematic costume, costume studies, fashion studies, creative processes, film analysis

Introduction to *fashion studies* and *costume studies*

The clothing we wear in our daily lives has been established as a crucial cultural mediation between the individual and the society they inhabit (Simmel, 1998, p. 12). From its origins, clothing has represented far more than mere practical functionality. The aesthetic significance inherent in each garment has become inextricably intertwined with a critical perspective on social dynamics, creating divisions, hierarchies, and groupings within communities (Bogatyrëv, 1986, p. 105). In this way, the textile surface acts as a second skin, imbued with meaning.

* Universidad Rey Juan Carlos.
(ORCID: https://orcid.org/0000-0002-0572-6930)

Throughout history, social classes, distinctions of origin and cultural traditions have found in clothing a medium through which they can be expressed, perpetuated, and transformed. The three-dimensionality of garments not only ensures essential responses to practical needs, such as climate or comfort, but also plays a vital role in the construction of identities and contexts. Clothing, when displayed, communicates messages about who we are, what we belong to, or what we aspire to project.

In this sense, it is not overemphasis to state that the clothes we choose to wear are a complex reflection of our needs, aspirations, and realities. Beyond physical protection, they connect us to a social world where the dynamics of inclusion, exclusion, and belonging are evident in every stitch, choice of color, fabric, or design. Fashion, therefore, is not merely an act of aesthetic creation but also a space where meanings, values, and ways of inhabiting the world are negotiated.

Fashion studies are the field that understand clothing as a communicative system, acting as a symbolic language to construct identities and as a means to understand the complex dynamics of contemporary society. The term originated in the first issue, in 1997, of the journal *Fashion Theory*, of which Valerie Steel is the principal editor,[1] integrating the aesthetic dimension with the sociological one, focusing on the process rather than the product. Before Valerie Steel fixed the name of the study area, fashion theory found important antecedents in George Simmel, Walter Benjamin, Edward Sapir, Peter Bogatyrëv, Roland Barthes, and Patrizia Calefato, among others.

From Georg Simmel's 1895 essay (1998) on fashion to Roland Barthes' writings (2009), the theories put both fashion and dress at the center of research, trying not to fall into purely textual or historical analyses. Simmel placed fashion within the individual/society binomial. From this binomial, others were born, such as man/woman, rich/poor, imitation/differentiation, binomials with which, first Simmel and later Veblen (1969), deduced how fashion, before being understood in general terms, needed to be framed in society in order to better understand its function. It is necessary to go through Structuralism to better understand the distinction between fashion and costume. It was Saussure (2009) who brought fashion closer to language and,

1 *Fashion Theory. The journal of dress, body, and culture* is active from 1997, published by Taylor and Francis.

from then on, other semioticians and cultural historians became interested in clothing. In 1937, Petr Bogatyrëv (1986) published an essay on folk costumes in which he applied the functionalist method to clothing, identifying within it a tier of five main functions. With Roland Barthes and Patrizia Calefato (1986), the concept of fashion finally became a social discourse. While the former analyzes fashion through the didascalies of specialized magazines, the latter focuses on the analysis of fashion and the mass media, including cinema. Barthes develops the concept of the spectacle body, Calefato, that of the clothed body.

Costume studies, in turn, studies the role of clothing in the creation of meanings in different cultural and media contexts. In some specific cases, these theoretical assumptions from Fashion Studies fields are applied to analyze how clothing communicates and reproduces meanings and identities, as well as its means of production, consumption, and dissemination in areas such as film, theater, television, and the press. In the specific case of this chapter, the area of film and television, the audiovisual medium, is the one we are most interested in analyzing because of certain issues we consider fundamental.

> The firsts texts on film costume theory appear in the 1990s. Jane Gaines, Charlotte Herzog, Sue Harper, Pam Cook, Stella Bruzzi, and Pamela Church Gibson were influenced by feminist film studies, cultural and fashion studies, semiotics, and psychoanalysis. These writers accepted that costume design can be an area of scholarly study. (Yance-Martin, in Nadoolman Landis, in press, p. 3)

The last decade (2010–2020) has been significant for costume studies and its development as an independent field of research (Pantouvaki & Prihodová, 2021), although the history of costume and textiles in its broader aesthetic, and cultural sense is still being developed, especially in Spain but also in Portugal (Cucinotta, 2021). Often the denomination of *Fashion in Cinema* (Arranz, 2015), precisely in the Iberian context, hinders costume studies as it privileges the economic aspects over the creative aspects of cinema. In both countries, Spain and Portugal, some attention has been paid to theatrical costumes (Castro, 2010; Fernández & Jacome, 2018), as well as short biographies (Benard da Costa, 1996).

In general, if fashion studies already has an advanced path, a systematic approach that began with Simmel's 1898 text, for costume studies field, the theory structure has been gaining ground in recent years, especially with the work of Deborah Nadoolman Landis, a costume designer and theorist of film costumes and Giuliana Bruno, an art theorist. Also interesting is the theory advancement handled by journals such as *Costume and Performance studies*, where interesting articles on new and innovative theorizations of film costumes are often received. Authors such as Pam Cook (1996), Sarah Street (2001), Prisca Morrissey (2014; 2021), among others, have included and include film costumes in in-depth studies ranging from contemporary history, gender studies, art history, and textiles to their own cinema history.

It is very important to establish cohesions and differences in the audiovisual representations of the clothed body, taking into account the two-dimensional environment of the screen and the three-dimensional environment of real life, where both spheres are at work.

In particular, cinematic and fashion codes include a new point of view on the different profession of fashion designer and the craft of costume designer (Landis, 2012), which explain a lot about the differences in work that are to be emphasized. In the field of costume studies, the centrality given to the body has often had a fundamental deviation that has led to some confusion between two concepts: costume as a representation of the social individual and costume as an artistic representation of the character.

In particular, in the study of film costume design, fashion studies has often been treated as the only concept linking film and costume. It is important nowadays, and with all the advances in the study of the body and its coverings, to make a distinction between the types of studies that can be carried out, taking into account the fields of action. Moreover, with the introduction of the use of artificial intelligence in design and in fashion design, many of the techniques related to the two professions are becoming obsolete, not helping to resolve the underlying disorder that has been created between the two fields of activity.

This chapter seeks to critically examine the role of fashion as the predominant lens through which costume has traditionally been understood in cinematic analysis. Over the years, fashion has emerged as the primary framework for interpreting a character's manner of dressing, often overshadowing deeper explorations of how costume contributes to the narrative, cultural, and psychological dimensions of film.

The methodology in three points

The centrality of this chapter lies in understanding how it is possible to extrapolate concepts from the historical and theological path of fashion studies that can be applied to costume studies in audiovisuals. These concepts, intrinsically linked to the meaning of the body's performance, bring back the representation and interpretation of clothing on the screen as a much more complex element than contemporary analyses dedicated to fashion studies alone. In particular, for this reflection, the concept of the "clothed body," taken up and abundantly explored by Calefato, makes the methodology used in this chapter clearer and more distinct with respect to the object of study.

From a theoretical perspective, the concept of the *clothed body* was first discussed in 1986 in a text of the same title by the Italian sociologist Patrizia Calefato. There, the theory of the clothed body was developed for the first time, linked to the studies on *Fashion Theory*, in the context of the so-called Mass-fashion and bodily performance.

> Clothes clothe, cover, cover, cover, clothe: they insistently teach us the meaning of successive and infinite surfaces, as if it were a principle of indeterminacy that governs the laws of clothing. This means that the limit point of the clothed body is not the naked body, but the repetition of the covering. The body is thus structured in the succession of its appearances, never just a mask, never skinned nakedness: rather metamorphosis. The perpetual mutability that clothing confers on the body is on the side of carnivalization and imprecision of character, contaminated by the typification and individualization of fashion. (Calefato, 1986, p. 8)

According to Calefato, talking about typification and masks accompanied us to think about the differences between fashion and costume, fashion and the stage costume, the three-dimensional fashion of the reality we live in, and the clothes constructed for the two-dimensional screen of cinema and audiovisual. The overarching premise is that an in-depth exploration of the creative process, along with its fictional context, can uncover critical insights that underscore the greater significance of costume studies over fashion studies in analyzing the clothed body within audiovisual media. This perspective emphasizes the unique contributions of costume to narrative construction, character development, and visual storytelling, which extend beyond the more surface-level concerns typically associated with fashion.

> The costume, as seen in the filmic context, is not only made of fabric, to be clear, but, as a filmed dress, of lights, of angles, of amplified details that, because of the way they are framed and put in relation to the rest, sometimes assume a more important position than the dress as a whole, they become its center. (Giannone in Calefato, 1999, p. 23)

The fundamental aspect of the *detail*, understood here also as filmic terminology, is able to explain how film technologies have amplified textual narration from handcrafted visual elements.

In order to be able to explore the aspects of this construction and begin a methodological systematization, the element that will be analyzed is the creative process of the costume designer. In particular, with a specific focus on costume studies, the issues to be addressed are divided into three main points that highlight some of the many differences between the two fields, emphasizing the material work of the costume designer as opposed to that of the fashion designer:

- The distinctive creative process in film costume design;
- The environment of a typology of collective work with a specific element that is not found in the fashion designer creative process, which is the collective work for a project that does not belong to the costume designer;
- The fashion cut only as a sociological and psychological method in the creation of a character.

Results as a contextualization of the *costume studies* on film

The creative process of film costume design differs significantly from other forms of design, particularly fashion design, in that it is closely linked to the narrative, emotional, and psychological dimensions of a character. Unlike fashion, which often favors current trends, aesthetics, and commercial viability, film costume design begins with an in-depth analysis of the script, character arcs, and the director's vision. The costume designer must work closely with the director, production designer, and actors to ensure that the costumes not only reflect the personality, social status, and cultural context of the character, but also align perfectly with the visual language and narrative objectives of the film.

This process often involves extensive research into historical periods, cultural settings, or speculative futuristic worlds, depending on the needs of the film. Each costume becomes a world-building tool, providing subtle clues to the setting of the narrative and contributing to the spectator's immersion. In addition, the designer must envisage how the costumes will function within the dynamic framework of the cinematography, including considerations of movement, lighting, and camera angles, ensuring that the costumes maintain the intended visual impact on screen.

In fact, the creative processes are completely different if we take into account that only after a first reading of the script, the costume designer can start a materialization of the director's ideas. This is the central point in fashion and costume: whoever designs or assembles the pieces to create a character, does so taking into account several meetings with the director, taking into account the production budget and how often the piece will be used: will it be central to the narrative? How many times will it be used? How many of the same pieces will he have to produce?

Deborah Nadoolman Landis affirmed:

> Costume design is an intellectual pursuit, and a pursuit of the imagination costume designers have to be really smart. It's not really about designing a dress, it's not really about designing a gown. It's really about are you a good reader of the literature and then after you read that screenplay can you have a conversation with David Fincher, Wes Anderson, Guillermo del Toro, Stanley Kubrick, or Steven Spielberg, or John Landis, or whoever can you have that kind of a level of conversation. I think you kind of have to be Vanessa Williams in the center court at Wimbledon you're having that level of a conversation with the director about what matters the most those people in that screenplay because a costume designer's single purpose is to bring those people in the story to life period so if costume designers talk about clothes my feeling is that we diminish our work because our work is not about the clothes, our work about does the audience care about those people in the story and if we can create those personalities every single time we're doing our job. (*Le giornate del cinema muto*, 2022, 7m 41s)

In practice and taking into account these elements, fashion is an industry and has economic achievements directly related to the design of the pieces, so it needs an environment of professionals who study the trends of society, the economic outlets dedicated to the purchase of clothing, the whole media environment deeply growing in recent years, influencers and social networks in the first place. What we have on the costume design side is not half of all these implications.

Costume designers are paid weekly until their last day in production. They have no share in the profits of the clothes they design. Nor do they share in the financial success of the film. Modern film marketing has just found in the costume designer an asset to promote its product.

This issue is something that has sparked recent debates. Yance-Martin says:

> However, the relationship between fashion designers and the film industry has not always been a good one, as fashion designers have sometimes been criticized for being more concerned to record their authorship than to subordinate their creations to character and narrative. (Yance-Martin, 2024, p. 66)

In recent times, increased press coverage of costume design and designers has raised the profile and prestige of the field, but, disappointingly, salaries have been deflated. In fact, costume designers own nothing about the film.

Costume designers work to materialize other people's ideas, they do not dress a mannequin but the recognizable body of an actor, which has to performatize the clothes, the fabrics, the colors, the movements, as Giannone (1999, p. 23) stated.

Above all, this question is not only important in order to differentiate between the two fields, but also to strengthen costume studies where the costume techniques of the craft connected to the film set raise other issues, also taking into account tradition in craftsmanship and innovation in technology.

A new theoretical perspective takes into account the relevance of the formation of a field of studies that brings film and costume closer in a more artisanal way for an innovation that is urgent in this emerging field of study.

Thus, one arrives at the predominant thought that this chapter seeks to augment: fashion and costume in cinema as distinct methodologies of analysis.

Actually, one of the most commonly used methodologies is the assimilation of costume design with fashion design. Having analyzed the present literature on film costume design, in fact, this way of talking about costume design has always been the most widely used. It has, in a certain way, isolated the clothed body present in the cinematographic frame in order to analyze it as a part, as a component that does not belong to cinema and film studies. It generates an assimilation between fashion and costume and fashion as costume.

Giuliana Bruno (2014) proposed a different reading of costume design, based on the filmic space, the colors present in the frame, the gestures practiced by actors, imagining an incorporation of costume into other filmic elements such as light, art direction, and, in general, creative processes. Fashion has been able to isolate the costume element from the others by focusing on semiotic and sociological analyses, imagining the character as an extension of the real society. On the other hand, analyzing the costume as one of the plastic elements of the frame, would bring it back into a study more oriented to the history of art, architecture, and cinema. If Bruno referred to this specific area of costume studies as "Sartorial Philosophy," the interpretation of this concept highlights how the sartorial element of tailoring goes beyond mere garment construction to actively shape cinematic forms and visual lines. Tailoring, in this context, becomes a dynamic tool for creating shapes and silhouettes that interact with the spatial and narrative dimensions of film. The interplay between fabric, structure, and movement not only defines the physicality of characters but also contributes to the film's visual language, creating a dialogue between the clothed body and the cinematic frame. This approach underscores the philosophical depth of costume design, where each sartorial and crafting choice serves as a deliberate act of storytelling and visual articulation.

Discussion as an open conclusion

What is the importance of fashion in the study of film costumes? Can film costumes be assimilated purely and exclusively to a sociological and mass-media analysis?

Analyses of film costumes abound with these perspectives that make the binomials proposed by Simmel the central point: gender studies, society studies, and social class studies.

The importance that semiotics gives to Fashion Studies is relevant especially in recent years when the binomial Fashion and Mass-media is one of the most analyzed. The semiotic codes present in the costumes make it an interesting object of study if we want to study it, once again, by isolating it from the rest of the filmic material construction.

Barthes and Calefato come very close to what fashion studies could become if applied to costume studies, considering the concept of *performance* and the more cinematographic concept of *second skin*. Once again, however, we remain anchored to the body of the actor who, in both cases, will have to deal with a camera and stylistic choices that reduce the tridimensionality of reality, but also of theater for example, to a two-dimensionality typical of audiovisuals.

Turning to recent studies, Deborah Nadoolman Landis and Giuliana Bruno agree that fashion and its sociological analysis has always downgraded the costume object as a separate area of analysis, as if it were not part of typically cinematic itineraries and categories.

> It is a process that calls into question what fashion usually means in the language of cinema, and the restrictive way in which the term is generally used. It asks us to revise a common understanding that fashion in film is simply costume design. Here fashion goes beyond costume and becomes an altogether different object for the circulation of meaning. (Bruno, 2014, p. 39)

It's not a question of continuing to think of the fashion element as a separate component within the film, but of beginning to reformulate its presence as essential to the language of the film, "contributing to the shaping of its aesthetic texture," according to Bruno.

> In thinking of fashion in this new way, we need to move beyond issues of spectacle and commodity and elaborate a playful form of sartorial theorization, concerned less with sociology or the semiotics of clothing and connected more closely to the history of art and the design of space, and to their theorization. (Bruno, 2014, p. 40)

When the object of study results from the intersection of several disciplines, its initial path can take different directions depending on the main starting point. In fact, so far very few approaches, apart from inserting, comparing and analyzing the two disciplines separately, have attempted to create a visual union that is more linked to artistic and aesthetic results in terms of theoretical consequences.

This chapter proposes that one effective way to explore the coexistence of fashion and costume—while acknowledging the diversity and limitations of each—is through the framework suggested by Deborah Nadoolman Landis. Specifically, this involves studying and understanding the distinct creative processes a costume designer undertakes to craft a costume, rather than merely designing a dress.

Discussing about these theoretical issues is to watch at *Fashion Theory* as one of the tools to analyze cinematographic costumes. This is not only important in order to differentiate the two fields, but also to strengthen costume studies where the "costume" techniques of the profession connected to the film set raise other questions, also taking into account tradition in craftsmanship and innovation in technology.

Bruno (2014, p. 51) proposes moving away from the widespread opinion that fashion in cinema consists simply of costume designs and sketches. These working materials can be important in another way when, as with architecture, they are witnesses to a "fabrication of the material surface of things."

References

Arranz, F. (Ed.). (2010). *Cine y género en España. Una investigación científica.* Cátedra.

Benard da Costa, J. (Ed.). (1996). *Jasmim*. Cinemateca Portuguesa.

Bogatyrev, P. (1986). Le funzioni del costume popolare nella Slovacchia morava [The functions of folk costume in Moravian Slovakia]. *La ricerca folclórica, contributi allo studio della cultura delle classi popolari, 14*, 93–120.

Bruno, G. (2014). *Surface. Matters of esthetics, materiality, and media.* The University of Chicago Press.

Calefato, P. (1986). *Il corpo rivestito* [The clothed body]. Edizioni Dalsud.

Castro, V. (2010). *O papel da segunda pele* [The role of the second skin]. Athena.

Cook, P. (1996). *Fashioning the nation. Costume and identity in British cinema.* BFI Publishing.

Cucinotta, C. (2021). Para una genealogía del oficio de "figurinista" en Portugal. Una lucha de género en curso [For a genealogy of the profession of "fashion illustrator" in Portugal: An ongoing gender struggle]. RIHC. *Revista Internacional De Historia De La Comunicación, 16*, 153–78. https://doi.org/10.12795/RiCH.2021.i16.08

Fashion Theory: The Journal of Dress, Body & Culture. (1997–present). Taylor & Francis

Fernández, D., & Jácome, D. (2018). *Vestir al personaje. Vestuario escénico: de la historia a la ficción dramática* [Dressing the character: Stage costume from history to dramatic fiction]. Ediciones Cumbre.

Giannone, A. (1999). La costruzione del senso fílmico tra abbigliamento e costume [The construction of filmic meaning between clothing and costume]. In P. Calefato, P. (Ed.), *Moda e cinema. Macchine di senso. Scritture del corpo.* Costa & Nolan.

Landis, D. N. (2012). *Film craft: Costume design.* Routledge.

Le giornate del cinema muto. (2022, October 6). *Deborah Landis / Giovedì 6 ottobre / Le giornate del cinema muto 2022.* [Video]. *YouTube.* https://www.youtube.com/watch?v=0OPuWOejLxc

Morrissey, P. (2014). La Garde-Robe de Georges Méliès: origines et usages des costumes dans les vues cinématographiques [The wardrobe of Georges Méliès: Origins and uses of costumes in cinematic views]. In A. Gaudreault, L. Le Forestier (Ed.), *Méliès: carrefour des attractions. Suivi de la correspondance de Georges Méliès (1904–1937).* PUR.

Morrissey, P. (2021). Where Did the Costumes in Early Cinema Come From? In J. Bernardi (Ed.), *Provenance and early cinema.* Indiana University Press.

Pantouvaki, S., & Příhodová, B. (Eds.). (2021). Studies in Costume and Performance, Special issue 6.2 on "Costume Agency." *Studies in Costume and Performance,* 6(2). https://www.intellectbooks.com/studies-in-costume-performance

Saussure, F. de. (2009). *Corso di linguistica generale* [Course in general linguistics]. Laterza.

Simmel, G. (1998). *La moda* [Fashion]. Oscar Mondadori.

Veblen, T. (1969). *The theory of the leisure class.* Modern Library.

Yance-Martín, E. (2024). Influences and connections between fashion and cinema. In C. M. Valverde, R. H. Cisnal, & L. Villanueva (Eds.), *Reflections on fashion and art today.* Icono 14.

Yance-Martín, E. (in press). History of the study of film costume (books and methodologies). In D. Nadoolman Landis (Ed.), *Encyclopedia of film and television costume design.* Bloomsbury.

CHAPTER 19

Reflections on the History of Spanish Fashion

A look into the twentieth century

*Maialen Salcedo Berrueta**

ABSTRACT
In recent years, the history of twentieth century Spanish fashion has received greater academic and curatorial attention. Despite the notable contributions made by many scholars, the study of this topic remains highly unstructured. This literature review chapter seeks to establish a solid historiographical framework that will serve as a starting point for future research and thus contribute to the development of the history of fashion in Spain. To this end, a critical review of the existing literature on the history of twentieth century Spanish fashion will be conducted in order to identify the methodological gaps that persist in the field. Finally, a series of improvements will be put forward with the aim of constructing a more comprehensive approach to the history of Spanish fashion.

Keywords: Spanish fashion history, twentieth century fashion, fashion research, historiography

Introduction

Over the last 15 years, there has been a growing academic and curatorial interest in the recent history of Spanish fashion. Researchers such as Laura Casal-Valls (Casal-Valls, 2013), Josep Casamartina i Parassols (Casamartina i Parassols, 2021), Daniele Gennaioli (Gennaioli, 2023), Juan Gutiérrez Fernández-Barja (Gutiérrez Fernández-Barja & Alvarado, 2022), Laura Jiménez-Izquierdo (Jiménez-Izquierdo, 2024), Uxía Otero González (Otero González, 2023), and Victoria Vásquez Pecile (Vásquez Pecile, 2024a; 2024b; 2024c; 2023)—among others—have approached this topic from diverse perspectives. Their work has examined the production of fashion over the years, addressing a wide array of themes and providing a deeper understanding of the subject.

However, their contributions, although contemporary, are often unrelated. They all provide a piece of the puzzle in the construction of the history of Spanish fashion, but they lack the glue that would make a cohesive narrative possible. Therefore, the objective of this chapter devoted to the

* Université Paris 1 Panthéon-Sorbonne, ED441, HiCSA.
(ORCID: https://orcid.org/0009-0005-9279-8359)

literature review is to establish a solid historiographical framework that will serve as a starting point for future research and thus contribute to the development of the history of fashion in Spain. To achieve this, a critical review of the existing literature on the history of twentieth century Spanish fashion will be conducted. Next, we will identify the methodological gaps that persist in the field, while putting forward a series of improvements with the aim of constructing a more comprehensive approach to the history of Spanish fashion.

Revisiting the history of Spanish fashion

A survey of publications on the history of twentieth century Spanish fashion reveals a wide array of resources, ranging from encyclopedias and books to exhibition catalogs, scientific publications, doctoral dissertations, press coverage, documentaries, and blogs.

To begin, particular attention will be given to a selection of encyclopedias and dictionaries, specifically the following six titles: *Diccionario textil y del vestir* (Estany Segalás, 1987), *Diccionario de la moda: los estilos del siglo XX* (Rivière & Mirò, 1996), *El vestido y la moda XX* (Bandrés Oto, 1998), *Desvistiendo el siglo XX* (Urrea Gómez, 1999), *Geografía de la moda española* (ACME, 2009), and the entry of *Spain* in the eighth volume of the *Berg Encyclopedia* (Ventosa, 2010, pp. 264–78).

The first of these, *Diccionario textil y del vestir* (Estany Segalás, 1987) by Manuel Estany Segalás, was published in 1987. This volume builds upon his earlier works, including the *Diccionario terminológico textile* (Estany Segalás & Hirshc, 1980), co-edited with Pierre Hirsch in 1980, and the *Diccionario profesional textil y de la confección* (Estany Segalás, 1968) from 1968. Written by a member of the Consejo Intertextil Español (Spanish Intertextile Council), these works are considered essential for the study of cutting and sewing techniques. As such, they are regarded as valuable resources by "fashion researchers" for the analysis and description of garments and items of clothing.

The next three works—*Diccionario de la moda: los estilos del siglo XX* (Rivière, 1996) by Margarita Rivière, *El vestido y la moda* (Bandrés Oto, 1998) by Maribel Bandrés Oto, and *Desvistiendo el siglo XX* (Urrea Gómez,

1999) by Inmaculada-Irene Urrea Gómez—are notable for their compilation of terminology and their inclusion of a repertoire of key figures in the history of Spanish fashion. Taken together, these publications provide a valuable point of departure from which to explore the Spanish fashion scene. However, the format imposes certain limitations, such as the information limited in detail.

The last two titles fall within the realm of systematic encyclopedias, in this case divided and classified by geographic regions. In this context, it is worth highlighting the publication of *Geografía de la moda española* (ACME, 2009), edited by the Asociación de Creadores de Moda de España (Association of Fashion Creators of Spain), as well as the entry dedicated to Spain in volume 8 of the Berg Encyclopedia, written by Silvia Ventosa (Ventosa, 2010).

When delving into publications on the history of twentieth century Spanish fashion, it is important to distinguish between general studies and monographs dedicated to prominent figures.

Among the general studies, two authors stand out for the breadth of their work and the impact of their contributions to the historiography of fashion: Margarita Rivière (Rivière, 2013a; 2013b; 1998; 1996; 1995; 1992; 1984; 1977) and Josefina Figueras (Figueras, 2014; 2009; 2005; 2003; 1997). Over a span of 35 years, they have published at least 12 books on the subject of Spanish fashion. Also noteworthy is a more recent author, Ana Velasco Molpeceres, who has maintained an impressive publishing pace, with nearly one publication per year (2024; 2023; 2021; 2016; 2015), establishing herself as a rising figure in the field. However, it is important to note that quantity does not necessarily equate to quality, a point that will be addressed in the following section.

Monographs on the *alta costura* houses or the *modistas*, on the other hand, are less numerous. Most of these publications are the result of cultural and museum initiatives. Examples include the collective work on Loewe (Argullol et al., 1995), the biography of Manuel Pertegaz by Isabel de Villalonga (2000), the self-published book by the curious Navarrese José María Sanz Suescun about his fellow countryman Emilio Ochagavía García (Sanz Suescun, 2009), and the monograph by Lola Gavarrón dedicated to María Rosa Salvador and her store and sewing workshop *Dafnis* (Gavarrón, 2010).

Building on this discussion, it is also important to mention exhibitions. The number of such exhibitions has increased considerably in recent years,[1] especially those dedicated to Spanish *alta costura* and fashion during the Transition. In this context, the contributions of two key figures deserve special mention: Josep Casamartina i Parassols,[2] director of the Col-lecció Tèxtil Antoni de Montpalau, and Juan M. Gutiérrez Fernández-Barja,[3] head of the twentieth century clothing collections at the Museo del Traje. They stand out for their exhaustive documentary work, resulting in major exhibitions and significant advances in the understanding of Spanish fashion.

In the academic realm, there has been a recent surge of interest in the history of Spanish fashion, as evidenced by an increase in conference—and

1 To give an example: Cortés, I. (2024). *L'ull de l'agulla* [Exhibition held at Museu Tèxtil de Terrassa, Terrassa, March 17–July 28, 2024]. Centre de Documentació i Museu Tèxtil; *España, 50 años de moda* [Exhibition held at Palau de la Virreina, Barcelona, October 27, 1987–January 10, 1988], Ajuntament de Barcelona, 1987; Suárez, G. (Com.). (2003). *Tras el espejo: moda española* [Exhibition held at Museo Nacional Centro de Arte Reina Sofía, Madrid, June 17–September 29, 2003]. Ministerio de Ciencia y Tecnología, Sociedad Estatal DDI, Ministerio de Economía; Outumuro Conde, M. (Com.). (2007). *Genio y figura: la influencia de la cultura española en la moda* [Exhibition held at Museo del Traje-CIPE, Madrid, from November 30, 2006–February 5, 2007] Ministerio de Educación, Cultura y Deporte. Área de Cultura.

2 Casamartina i Parassols, J. (Com.), & Núñez Muñoz, I. (Com.). (2024). *Andreu, el modisto de la gauche divine* [Exhibition held at the Fundación Rocamora, Barcelona, from October 27–December 1, 2024]; (2024) *Sabadell Teixteix* [Exhibition held at Espai Cultura Fundació 1859 Caixa Sabadell, Sabadell, from September 6–March 17, 2024]; (2023). *Joan Antoni Fàbregas: costura y glamour* [Exhibition held at Museu de Badalona, Badalona, from October 26, 2023–Mars 31, 2024]; (2023). *Jeans. De la calle al Ritz* [Exhibition held at Museo del Traje. CIPE, Madrid, from November 24, 2023–December 1, 2024]; and many more.

3 Gutiérrez Fernández-Barja J. (Com.) (2022). *Antonio Alvarado. Baja costura* [Exhibition held at Museo del Traje-CIPE, Madrid, from December 1, 2022–March 26, 2023]. Ministerio de Cultura; (2019). *El poder de la imagen. Agatha Ruiz de la Prada* [Exhibition held at Museo del Traje-CIPE, Madrid, from February 6, 2022–March 31, 2019]; (2014) E*spaña de moda* [Exhibition held at Museo del Traje-CIPE, Madrid, from May 13, 2014–September 7, 2014]; (2013) *La moda imposible. Moda de vanguardia en el museo del Traje, 1960–2010* [Exhibition held at Museo del Traje-CIE, Madrid, February 27, 2022–June 16, 2013].

their proceedings[4]—, scientific articles,[5] and doctoral dissertations[6] dedicated to this subject.

Among these contributions, special mention should be made of the work of the Fundación Historia del Diseño [Design History Foundation], a non-profit organization founded in 2006 that promotes and supports the study of design history, both in Catalonia and Spain as well as at the international level. The organization has facilitated four notable colloquia: the *I Coloquio de Investigadores en Textil y Moda* [1st Symposium of Textile and Fashion Researchers] (Carbonell, 2017), *Nombres en la sombra* [Names in the Shadows] (Campi & Ventosa, 2019), *Enseñar y aprender* [Teaching and Learning] (Campi, 2021), and *Tejidos, moda y cuerpos* [Fabrics, Fashion and Bodies]

---

4 See also: CSDMM. (2024). *Tech & Crafts 2024. Artesanía, Tecnología e Innovación en Moda* [II Congreso internacional en Historia, Arte y Diseño de moda, organized by the ETSAM of the Universidad Politécnica de Madrid, the Art History Department of the Universidad Complutense of Madrid, and the Museo del Traje-CIPE, November 12–14, 2024]; *Id.* (2021). *Mujeres al poder. Vestir el poder en femenino* [I Congreso internacional en Historia, Arte y Diseño de moda, organized by the CSDMM, the ETSAM of the Universidad Politécnica de Madrid, the Art History Department of the Universidad Complutense of Madrid, and the Museo del Traje-CIPE, April 13–15, 2021].

5 Here is a small sample: Sala, M. L. (2022). *Vestir es soñar: Breve historia de la moda española: de Fortuny a Palomo*. Turner; Santacana, J., & Llonch Molina, N. (2019). *El gusto en España: Indumentaria y gastronomía en el crisol de la historia*. Ediciones Trea; Pinilla García, A. (2006). La mujer en la posguerra franquista a través de la Revista Medina (1940–1945). *Arenal. Revista de Historia de las Mujeres*, 13(1), 153–79; Pena González, P. (2008). Óbito y transfiguración de la alta costura. *Indumenta: Revista del Museo del Traje*, 1, 9–22.

6 See, for example: Azcona, M. (2021). *Madrid, Hollywood capital of Franco's 1950s: Construction of a cinematographic imaginary of modernity* [Doctoral dissertation, Sorbonne Université, Paris]; Garcés, M. T. (2010). *(Re)membering the Madrid Movida: Life, death, and legacy in the contemporary corpus* [Doctoral dissertation, University of Minesota, Minneapoli]; Gennaioli, D. (2021). *Aline Romanones y el oficio de Madrid editor para Harper's Bazaar y Vogue. Estrategias y modelos utilizados en el proceso de construcción de una identidad internacional para la moda española (1952–1975)* [Doctoral dissertation, Universidad Politécnica de Madrid, Madrid]; Muñoz Ruiz, M. del C. (2002). *Mujer mítica, mujeres reales. Las revistas femeninas en España, 1955–1970* [Doctoral dissertation, Universidad Complutense, Madrid]; Otero González, U. (2021). *Domesticando cuerpos femeninos en el franquismo (1939–1975): La (re)modelación de la feminidad normativa y su encarnación sartorial en la transición de los cincuenta* [Doctoral dissertation, Universidade de Santiago de Compostela, Santiago de Compostela].

(Campi & Ventosa, 2023).[7] These events have served to validate the existence of a community of historians and researchers in the field of textile and fashion studies within the Spanish-speaking world, as well as to underscore the academic excellence of this community, as articulated by Isabel Campi (Campi & Ventosa, 2023, p. 14).

Finally, the role of press articles and documentaries[8] must be acknowledged. While the subject of Spanish fashion has been extensively covered in both national and international media,[9] a particular emphasis is placed on the contributions of one journalist: María Pilar Comín Ros (Zaragoza, 1921–Barcelona, 2004). Comín, who is likely well known within the field, began working at *La Vanguardia Española* (now *La Vanguardia*) in 1960. There, she was responsible for the *Retablo Femenino* section as well as fashion and style columns.[10] She soon established herself as one of the most prestigious

---

7 They also organized (2024), *Comida, memoria y sociedad. La configuración del quehacer gastronómico* [V Simposio de la FDH, November 28–9, 2024]; (2022). *Turismo y diseño: Materialidad y relato del viaje de placer* [IV Simposio de la FDH, Museo del Diseño de Barcelona, Barcelona, November 24–5, 2022]; (2020). *To be or not to be. El papel del diseño en la construcción de identidades* [III Simposio de la FDH, Museo del Diseño de Barcelona, Barcelona, March 12–13, 2020]; (2018). *Diseño y franquismo* [II Simposio de la FDH, Museo del Diseño de Barcelona, Barcelona, February 22–3, 2018]; (2015) *Modernos a pesar de todo. Historia del diseño en España: teorías, métodos y retos* [I Simposio de la FDH, Museo del Diseño de Barcelona, Barcelona, February 12–13, 2015].

8 For example: Galán, D. (2013). *Elio Berhanyer, maestro del diseño* [Documentary]. Altube Filmeak S. L., Corleone Films & Dosdecatorce Producciones; Hernández, M. (2018). Manuel *Pertegaz, el hombre que vestía a los cisnes* [Documentary]. Coorporación de Radio y Televisión Española; Mata, J. (Director). (2023). *Mi última condena. La verdadera historia de una mujer inventada* [Documentary]. Juan Mata, Yolaperdono & Sala46 Films.

9 To mention just a few: (April, 1976). Los de la cuerda floja, *Anta. Revista de Alta Costura, 362*, 7; (1968). La Alta Costura Española apoyada estatalmente, *Boletín de la NUEVA Moda*, 153, Año XVI, Época II, 76; (1944). Costume jewelry: Spanish influence continues, *Women's Wear Daily*, *69*(14), 20; Ashley, I. (1953, January 23).

10 The following is a concise illustration: Comín, M. P. (1969, January 25). Presentación de la alta costura española a la prensa y compradores extranjeros. *La Vanguardia Española*, 6.; *Id.* (1971, June 3). Retablo de él y ella: Sin límites … *La Vanguardia Española*, 49; *Id.* (1973, June 6). III Semana de la Moda Adlib, *La Vanguardia Española*, 7; *Id.* (1975, July 17). Un capítulo de la exportación española, *La Vanguardia Española*, 45; *Id.* (1978, July 29). Sangre joven en las colecciones, *La Vanguardia Española*, 3; *Id.* (1978, October 21). Moda del Mediterráneo, un certamen con vitalidad, *La Vanguardia*, 21;

and influential journalists in this domain. Her articles constitute a valuable collection of firsthand accounts that shed light on the evolution of fashion in Spain. It is noteworthy that no publishing house has yet compiled and published her writings in a single volume—an omission that represents a significant gap in the field.

A brief overview of the various publications that have contributed to the history of twentieth century Spanish fashion reveals a progressive historiographical development, albeit one that is still fragmented: although the first studies emerged in the late 1980s, the field experienced a resurgence from 2009 to 2010 and has grown steadily since 2017. However, there are still significant gaps in terms of thematic diversification. Advancing in this field requires greater reliance on primary sources, a strong commitment to interdisciplinary approaches, deeper integration of regional perspectives, and closer collaboration between scholars and curators.

Silencing the history of Spanish fashion

The title of this section may seem bold—intentionally so. Following a thorough review of the extant literature, this section will examine the construction and narration of the history of twentieth century Spanish fashion. To this end, a meticulous analysis will be conducted to identify and highlight the prevailing gaps and inaccuracies within the historiography of the subject. Ultimately, the aim is to illuminate the obstacles hindering a deeper understanding of this field.

First, we will look at the pioneering authors who wrote about twentieth century Spanish fashion. The earliest publications on this subject were largely produced by journalists. As previously mentioned, the most prolific figures in this regard were Margarita Rivière (Barcelona, 1944–2015) and Josefina Figueras (?–Madrid, 2023). While their contributions are invaluable, the absence of a formal research methodology in their work occasionally resulted in inaccuracies.

One illustrative example is the founding date of the *Cooperativa de Alta Costura de Barcelona* [Barcelona Haute Couture Cooperative]. Figueras situates

Id. (1979, February 14). El Salón de la Moda Española y sus nuevos rumbos, *La Vanguardia*, 25.

this event in 1942 and attributes its organization to Pedro Rodríguez (Figueras, 2003, pp. 57–76). This claim has not only been widely disseminated in various publications[11] but has also been uncritically accepted by scholars who date the event between 1940 and 1942.[12] However, subsequent research has uncovered official documentation housed in the *Archivo General de la Administración*, specifically in Section 14, dedicated to labor affairs. These records confirm that the cooperative was officially established on February 10, 1941, providing a more precise account of the event.[13] This underscores the pivotal distinction between quantity and quality in the context of scholarly research, as highlighted above. Consequently, it is imperative to categorize these works as popular science books rather than as reliable sources for academic research.

The issue, therefore, does not stem from the work of Rivière or Figueras—far from it. Rather, the problem lies within us, the researchers, who often fail to apply a critical approach to sources and lack rigorous fact-checking practices. As a result, we—myself included—tend to perpetuate unverified

---

11 For example, Palmer, A. (Ed.). (2001). *Couture & commerce: The transatlantic fashion trade in the 1950s*, 18. UBC Press [u.a.]; Pelka, A. (2014). Mujer e ideología en la posguerra española: Feminidad, cuerpo y vestido. *Historia Social*, *79*, 40; Sterlacci, F. (2009). *The A to Z of the fashion industry*, xxvii. Scarecrow Press; Steele, V. & Gale (Firm) (Eds.). (2005). *Encyclopedia of clothing and fashion*, vol. 2, 188. Charles Scribner's Sons.

12 For example, Ávila López, E. (2015). *Modern Spain*, 360. ABC-Clio; Calzadilla, P. (2012), *Pedro Rodriguez. Alta Costura sobre papel. Figurines 1940–1976*, Secretaría General Técnica. Subdirección General de Documentación y Publicaciones, 19; Fernández de Alba, F., Garcés, M. T., & Smith, P. J. (Eds.). (2021). *Fashioning Spain: From mantillas to Rosalía*, 11. Bloomsbury Visual Arts; Gennaioli, D. (2022). La alta costura española y su reproductibilidad en el mercado estadounidense (1952–1975). *i+Diseño. Revista Científico-Académica Internacional De Innovación, Investigación Y Desarrollo En Diseño*, 17, 10. doi: https://doi.org/10.24310/Idiseno.2022.v17i.14738; Horcajo, J. (ed.) (2003). *España de moda*, 24. Artec impersiones; Rivière, M. (2015). *Diccionario de la moda* ("Pedro Rodríguez"). Penguin Random House: Grupo Editorial España; Rosés Castellsaguer, S. (2020). La muerte de la alta costura española: crónica de un final, *Anuario del Departamento de Historia y Teoría del Arte*, vol. 32, 123–35; Sousa Congosto, F. de. (2007). *Introducción a la historia de la indumentaria en España*, 222. Istmo.

13 Rodríguez, P., Beleta Quer, F., Sans, L., Bastida, A., Arnau, J., Batle, J., Naccari, E., Morell, M., Solsona, Pertegaz, M., Ferrer Artigas, J., Volart y Cia., Beleta, F., Rocafort, Tapbioles y Pirretas, & Maese, R. (1944, December 5). *Estatutos de la Cooperativa de Alta Costura de Barcelona* ((14)001.005, 74/1946, nº 2889). Archivo General de la Administración.

claims, reinforcing narratives that blur the distinction between empirical data and unsubstantiated information.

Furthermore, it is imperative to acknowledge that fashion history does not constitute an independent discipline—at least in Spain. There is no such thing as a "fashion historian" *per se*. Fashion serves as the object of study, but the methodological approach varies depending on the researcher's field—whether history, art history, anthropology, sociology, philosophy, or other disciplines (Warschaw, 2017, pp. 2–6).

In Spain, the network of "fashion researchers" remains largely fragmented and disconnected. At the national level, two main centers for the study of fashion history can be identified: the Centro Superior de Diseño de Moda de Madrid (CSDMM-UPM) and the GRAMOC research group at the Universitat de Barcelona. However, none of these institutions offer a doctoral training program that would allow students to explore the latest advances in the state of the art, the different approaches and methodologies being used, etc.[14] In addition, there is also a significant number of researchers working from institutions abroad, further exacerbating this sense of disconnection. It is akin to working in isolation within a crowded room—surrounded by others yet without a true sense of community or shared purpose.

A salient illustration of this disconnection is evident through a comparative analysis of two articles: *Mujer e ideología en la posguerra española: feminidad, cuerpo y vestido* [Women and Ideology in Post-War Spain: Femininity, Body, and Dress] by Anna Pelka (Pelka, 2014) and *L'élégance de la Femme Bleue. De la mode nationale à la couture internationale en Espagne, 1939–1952* [L'élégance de la Femme Bleue. From national fashion to international couture in Spain, 1939–1952] by Miquel Martínez Albero (Martínez Albero, 2022).

In this article, historian Anna Pelka examines the female body as a site of political and ideological intervention. Applying a gender perspective to the study of Franco's regime, she explores the policies designed to shape women's bodies, to mold them to an idealized standard, and to equip them to spread the regime's values (Pelka, 2014, pp. 23–4). Similarly, art historian

14 In Madrid, the Ph.D. program is not exclusively dedicated to fashion research, but includes students from various disciplines, including architecture, design, fashion and social studies. Similarly, the Ph.D. program associated with the GRAMOC research group is housed within the Department of Art History.

Martínez Albero investigates the model of woman conceptualized by the *Falange Española* and the search for a fashion that would embody the values of the nation (Martínez Albero, 2022).

A comparative reading of these articles reveals that much of the information they present is quite similar. This observation is corroborated by the subsequent findings. Firstly, both authors rely their analysis on the same sources: women's press from the period of Franco's dictatorship, such as *Medina*, *Ya*, *La Moda en España*, and *Vértice*. Secondly, despite presenting their ideas differently, the same issues are raised: the archetypal woman promoted in post-war Spain and the possibility of a genuinely Spanish fashion. Finally, they reach comparable conclusions: the assertion that the archetypal woman was confined to the roles of spouse, mother, and housewife; that the influence of Christian modesty in dress was limited; and, as for patriotic or national fashion, both conclude that Spanish fashion remained influenced by international trends.

In summary, both are valuable texts. While Pelka focuses on biopolitics and its consequences for women in the post-war period, Martínez Albero introduces a novel perspective to the analysis by exploring the nationalist efforts of Ana de Pombo and Laffitte. However, the influence of Pelka's work is evident in the latter's (Martínez Albero, 2022, p. 67) and deserves greater recognition. This practice highlights a crucial problem within the academic community dedicated to studying Spanish fashion: the lack of academic attributions and insufficient acknowledgment of others' contributions.

A similar phenomenon can be extrapolated to primary sources. A pervasive lack of trust among colleagues frequently compels researchers to exercise caution when citing their sources. This hesitancy can result in the selective or complete exclusion of references in academic articles and communications. This issue is illustrated in the doctoral thesis of Luis Casablanca Migueles, in which the author examines the Cámara de la Moda Española [Spanish Fashion Chamber] and makes the following statement:

> La Cámara de la Moda Española, nace en 1971 y entre sus objetivos, está impulsar y organizar la creación de una moda de estilo español, basada en artículos manufacturados en España. [...] La Cámara se financiará por subvenciones estatales y por las cuotas de sus socios.

> [The Spanish Fashion Chamber, founded in 1971, has among its objectives to promote and organize the creation of Spanish-style fashion based on items manufactured in Spain. [...] The Chamber is financed by state subsidies and membership fees. (All translations are my own unless otherwise noted)]. (Casablanca Migueles, 2009, p. 51)

Notwithstanding the persuasive nature of the aforementioned content, Casablanca does not disclose the sources from which this information is derived. To advance our understanding, it is imperative to ensure transparency in source citation and, most crucially, to exercise caution when referencing unverified information, as this could compromise scholarly integrity.

It can be posited that this practice is associated with the prevailing aspiration of being recognized as pioneers in the field of fashion studies in Spain.[15] This impetus has often resulted in a single researcher endeavoring to encompass a wide range of chronologies and diverse methodologies, often without due acknowledgment of their colleagues. As Dr. Uxía Otero González accurately asserts, "una perspectiva más transdisciplinar, transnacional y de largo recorrido nos ayuda a tener una visión más completa" [a more transdisciplinary, transnational, and long-term perspective facilitates a more comprehensive understanding] (Otero González, 2023b). In essence, extensive coverage is not inherently detrimental; however, mutual recognition and collaboration are indispensable for progress.

Subsequently, we will direct our attention to the manner in which this narrative is constructed. On multiple occasions, efforts have been made to equate fashion with the status of art. As a result, the discourse surrounding fashion often emphasizes the technical expertise of designers, focusing on their craftsmanship and proficiency. A clear illustration of this approach can be found in statements such as the following: "Con la depuración de las

---

15 *Fashion studies* is an interdisciplinary field that emerged in the late 1980s in Anglo-Saxon countries, particularly driven by the work of authors such as Elizabeth Wilson and Valerie Steele. It is an academic field that approaches fashion from multiple angles—including history, sociology, cultural theory, and gender studies—with the aim of examining fashion not only as an aesthetic phenomenon, but also as a key element in the cultural and individual construction of identities. Although recent years have seen an increase in research that treats fashion as an object of study, I would hesitate to say that it has been fully integrated into Spanish university curricula.

líneas, el culto al detalle y la pasión por los acabados, la imagen final de sus piezas, que combinan la más refinada estructura con acabados artesanales, es sencilla, pura, esencial." [With the refinement of lines, the cult of detail, and a passion for finishes, the final image of their pieces—combining the most refined structure with artisanal finishes—is simple, pure, and essential.] (Casablanca Migueles, 2009, p. 51).

In order to make such observations and carry out material analyses, it is essential to have a thorough knowledge of cutting and sewing techniques. In this regard, studies such as those conducted by Victoria Vásquez Pecile (Vásquez Pecile V. 2024a; 2024b; 2024c; 2023) serve as a valuable point of reference. Vásquez Pecile's research on the history of patternmaking in Spain, alongside her work on the digitization of patterns, toiles, and garments in a state of deterioration, has significantly enhanced our understanding of the techniques and skills employed by dressmakers. Without this technical foundation, judgments often become subjective evaluations, which, in many instances, appear to serve the sole purpose of elevating the figure of the designer and perpetuating a constructed narrative. In the end, all we achieve by doing this is to fictionalize the account.

Finally, within the context of Spanish fashion historiography, it is crucial to dedicate a portion of our discussion to the examination of primary sources. The challenges associated with locating textile and documentary archives can be attributed to several factors. Firstly, it is possible that the main actors were not aware of the importance of keeping records and documenting their activities. Secondly, the period under study is relatively recent, which means that these archives have not yet been properly cataloged or, with any luck, are still in the hands of their descendants. In some cases, these records remain inaccessible, not because they have been lost but due to the reluctance of their owners to share them. It is therefore the responsibility of the academic community to use this platform to convey our sincere request for greater trust and to gain access to the invaluable materials held by private collectors and families.[16] Consequently, fashion researchers find themselves entrapped

16 In recent years, there has been a notable increase in the number of private collectors dedicated to the preservation of twentieth century Spanish fashion. Prominent examples include the López Trabado Collection, which centers on Spanish luxury fashion through both textiles and documentary archives; the Carlos Milla Collection, which

within a vicious cycle: they are systematically denied access to the personal archives, yet they demonstrate no initiative in attempting to gain entry.

Moreover, the challenges associated with accessing primary sources, coupled with the limited availability of in-depth studies on the subject, have often led to a disproportionate emphasis on haute couture within fashion historiography. This tendency arises from the reliance on readily accessible archives, while documentation of "the dress of the people" (Styles, 2008) from the last century remains comparatively scarce. Therefore, it is essential to reinforce the efforts in the preservation and critical study of all expressions of fashion—whether folkloric, popular or haute couture—, regardless of their geographical origin within Spain, in order to achieve a rounded and inclusive vision of the history of dress.

Thus, by conducting a historiographical study of the history of twentieth century Spanish fashion, it has been possible to identify the main deficiencies that must be addressed to foster a deeper understanding of the subject.

Conclusion

To summarize, the history of twentieth century Spanish fashion remains an evolving field, akin to an incomplete jigsaw puzzle, with many pieces yet to be assembled. While significant advancements in research have been made, much work is still to be done to integrate the various approaches and attain a more unified and complete understanding.

This endeavor necessitates a critical examination of extant sources, the cultivation of mutual support among colleagues, and the promotion of

---

comprises traditional clothing and Spanish haute couture; and the R. R. Colagrossi Collection. The Pedro Usabiaga Collection is distinguished by its strong interest in twentieth century Spanish haute couture, while the Ozcaraiz Collection, dedicated to Balenciaga and EISA, is housed at the Balenciaga Foundation in Getaria. Other noteworthy collections include the Alventosa Talamantes Collection, which encompasses a comprehensive array of twentieth century Spanish fashion, and the Enrique Lafuente Muñoz Collection, which centers on garments by Cristóbal Balenciaga and Ramón Esparza. The Javier Martín Galán Collection also boasts a noteworthy selection of Cristóbal Balenciaga and EISA garments. Beyond private collections, several historic fashion houses have maintained their own archives, including Santa Eulalia, Pertegaz, and Elio Berhanyer. Access to the latter two is quite complex, and therefore the volume of the archive they keep cannot be determined.

interdisciplinary collaboration, as well as between the academic community and institutions.[17] To make progress in this area, it is imperative to nurture a research culture that not only emphasizes methodological precision but also adopts an interdisciplinary approach. Addressing these elements will be key in overcoming the historiographical silences that have long hindered the study of twentieth century Spanish fashion.

References

Argullol, R., Hernández, F., Luján, N., Marí, A., Puértolas, S., Racionero, L., Regàs, R., & Rodríguez, J. (1995). *Loewe, 1846–1996*. Loewe.

Asociación Creadores de Moda de España (Ed.). (2009). *Geografía de la moda española*. ACME.

Bandrés Oto, M. (1998). *El vestido y la moda* [Dress and fashion]. Larousse Planeta.

Campi, I. (Coord.). (2021). *Enseñar y aprender: La transmisión del conocimiento en la moda y el textil* [Teaching and learning: The transmission of knowledge in fashion and textiles] [III Coloquio de Investigadores en Textil y Moda, Centre de Documentació i Museu Tèxtil de Terrassa, Terrassa, November 18–19, 2021]. https://historiadeldisseny.org/web/wp-content/uploads/Llibre-Actes_III-COLOQUIO-TEXTIL_complet_bx.pdf

Campi, I., & Ventosa, I. (Coords.). (2019). *Nombres en la sombra: Hacia la deconstrucción del canon en la historia de la moda y el textil* [Names in the shadows: Toward the deconstruction of the canon in fashion and textile history] [II Coloquio de Investigadores en Textil y Moda, Museu del Disseny de Barcelona, November 21–2, 2019]. https://historiadeldisseny.org/web/wp-content/uploads/NOMBRES-EN-LA-SOMBRA-online_.pdf

Campi, I., & Ventosa, I. (Coords.). (2023). *Los coloquios textiles y la emergencia de los investigadores: Tejidos, moda y cuerpos* [The textile colloquiums and the emergence of researchers: Fabrics,

17 In an ideal scenario, institutions and scholarly researchers should engage in active collaboration. A notable example is the MET Costume Institute's initiative this year to invite Monica L. Miller, professor at Barnard College, as a guest curator to contribute to the scholarly dimension of its exhibitions. After all, these cultural events serve not only as platforms for showcasing material culture but also as tangible expressions of academic research, thereby reinforcing the significance and value of knowledge.

fashion, and bodies] [IV Coloquio de Investigadores en Textil y Moda, MEV, Museu d'Art Medieval, Vic, November 23–4, 2023]. https://historiadeldisseny.org/web/wp-content/uploads/IV-COLOQUIO-TEXTIL-LibroActas_LD.pdf
Carbonell, S. (2017). *I Coloquio de Investigadores en Textil y Moda* [First Colloquium of Researchers in Textiles and Fashion] [Centre de Documentació i Museu Tèxtil de Terrassa, Terrassa, November 17–18, 2017]. https://cdmt.cat/wp-content/uploads/2018/01/publicacions/COLOQUIO%20TEXTIL_final_bx.pdf
Casablanca Migueles, L. (2007). *La moda como disciplina artística en España: Jesús del Pozo y la generación de los nuevos creadores* [La moda como disciplina artística en España: Jesús del Pozo y la generación de los nuevos creadores] [Doctoral dissertation, Universidad de Granada, España].
Casal-Valls, L. (2013). *La figura de la modista i els inicis de l'alta costura a Barcelona: Trajectòria professional i producció d'indumentària femenina (1880–1915)* [The figure of the dressmaker and the beginnings of haute couture in Barcelona: Professional career and production of women's clothing (1880–1915)] [Doctoral dissertation, Universitat de Barcelona, Art History Department]. https://www.tdx.cat/handle/10803/129559#page=1
Casamartina i Parassols, J. (2021). *Pedro Rovira, 1921–1978*. Museo de Badalona.
Estany Segalás, M. (1968). *Diccionario profesional textil y de la confección* [Professional dictionary of textiles and garment making]. Estany.
Estany Segalás, M. (1987). *Diccionario textil y del vestir* [Textile and clothing dictionary]. Estany.
Estany Segalás, M., & Hirsch, P. (1980). *Diccionario terminológico textil: Inglés-Francés-Español = Textile glossary: English-French-Spanish = Lexique textile: anglais-français-espagnol*. Estany.
Figueras, J. (Ed.). (1997). *La moda, sus secretos y su poder* [Fashion, its secrets and its power]. Albacore.
Figueras, J. (Ed.). (2003). *Moda española: Una historia de sueños y realidades* [Spanish fashion: A history of dreams and realities]. Ediciones Internacionales Universitarias.
Figueras, J. (Ed.). (2005). *Protagonistas de la moda* [Protagonists of fashion]. Ediciones Internacionales Universitarias.
Figueras, J. (Ed.). (2009). *Moda y valores: El desafío de lo nuevo* [Fashion and values: The challenge of the new] (Yumelia sociedad). EUNSA.

Figueras, J. (Ed.). (2014). *Moda y estilos de vida: El poder de la novedad* [Fashion and lifestyles: The power of novelty]. Ediciones Internacionales Universitarias.

Gavarrón, L. (2010). *La gran dama de la moda: María Rosa Salvador y el tiempo de Dafnis* [The grand lady of fashion: María Rosa Salvador and the time of Dafnis]. Esfera de los Libros.

Gennaioli, D. (2023). La Oficina y la Comisión Interministerial para la Promoción de la Moda: La proyección internacional de la alta costura durante el Franquismo desarrollista [The Office and the Interministerial Commission for the Promotion of Fashion: The international projection of haute couture during developmental Francoism]. *Historia Contemporánea*, 72, 595–629. https://doi.org/10.1387/hc.22934

Gutiérrez Fernández-Barja, J., & Alvarado, A. (Eds.). (2022). *Antonio Alvarado. Baja costura* [Antonio Alvarado: Low couture]. Ministerio de Cultura y Deporte, Ediciones Palacio & Museos.

Jiménez-Izquierdo, L. (2024). *Título y cuaderno con método de corte y confección. Elisa Sacristán Utrilla 1942–1943. Modelo del mes* [Title and notebook with cutting and sewing method. Elisa Sacristán Utrilla 1942–1943. Model of the month]. https://www.cultura.gob.es/dam/jcr:286f3fc1-f674-4a5b-a896-a71fe2fb6923/mdm10-2024-tituloymetodo-digital.pdf

Martínez Albero, M. (2022). L'élégance de la Femme Bleue. De la mode nationale à la couture internationale en Espagne, 1939–1952 [The elegance of the Blue Woman: From national fashion to international couture in Spain, 1939–1952]. *Histoire, Europe et relations internationales*, 1(1), 65–73. https://doi.org/10.3917/heri.001.0065

Otero González, U. (2023a). "Ser mujer" en el franquismo (1939–1950): La construcción discursiva de la feminidad normativa ["Being a woman" under Francoism (1939–1950): The discursive construction of normative femininity]. In *Galicia, un golpe sin cuartel, una guerra sin trincheras. La construcción sociopolítica de la dictadura franquista (1936–1960)* (pp. 331–56). Publicacions de la Universitat de València.

Otero González, U. (2023b). Catholic dressing in the Spanish Franco dictatorship (1939–1975): Normative femininity and its sartorial embodiment. [Conference presentation]. *Sartoria*, Paris, France.

Pelka, A. (2014). Mujer e ideología en la posguerra española: Feminidad, cuerpo y vestido [Woman and ideology in postwar Spain: Femininity, body, and dress]. *Historia Social*, (78), 23–42.

Rivière, M. (1977). *La moda ¿comunicación o incomunicación?* [Fashion: Communication or miscommunication?]. Gustavo Gili.

Rivière, M. (1984). *La generación del cambio* [The generation of change]. Planeta.
Rivière, M. (1992). *Lo cursi y el poder de la moda* [Kitsch and the power of fashion]. Espasa-Calpe.
Rivière, M. (1995). *La década de la decencia: Intolerancias "prêt-à-porter", moralina mediática y otras indecencias de los años noventa* [The decade of decency: "Prêt-à-porter" intolerances, media moralizing, and other indecencies of the nineties]. Anagrama.
Rivière, M. (1998). *Crónicas virtuales: La muerte de la moda en la era de los mutantes* [Virtual chronicles: The death of fashion in the age of mutants]. Anagrama.
Rivière, M. (2013a). *Entrevistas: Diálogos con la política, la cultura y el poder* [Interviews: Dialogs with politics, culture, and power]. Publicacions i Edicions de la Universitat de Barcelona.
Rivière, M. (2013b). *Historia informal de la moda* [Informal history of fashion]. Plaza & Janés.
Rivière, M., & Mirò, A. (1996). *Diccionario de la moda: Los estilos del siglo 20* [Dictionary of fashion: The styles of the twentieth century]. Grijalbo.
Sanz Suescun, J. M. (2009). *Emilio Ochagavía García (1922–1996), Vargas & Ochagavía: Alta Costura* [Emilio Ochagavía García (1922–1996), Vargas & Ochagavía: Haute couture]. Sanz Suescun.
Styles, J. (2008). *The dress of the people: Everyday fashion in eighteenth century England*. Yale University Press.
Urrea Gómez, I.-I. (1999). *Desvistiendo el siglo XX* [Undressing the twentieth century]. Ediciones Internacionales Universitarias.
Vásquez Pecile, V. (2023, November 22). *Patterns and toiles heritage 3D reconstruction* [Conference presentation]. *Digital craft: savoir-faire et outils numériques*. Institut Français de la Mode, Paris, France.
Vásquez Pecile, V. (2024a, December 19). *Facing the twins: Methodologies for the digitalization of clothing. The Vionnet of the Alaïa Foundation* [Conference presentation]. *Conservation et restauration: des savoirs oubliés ?*, Institut Français de la Mode, Paris, France.
Vásquez Pecile, V. (2024b). *Los patrones de las memorias de la ESM. La importancia de las fuentes técnicas en la indumentaria tradicional* [The patterns of the ESM memoirs: The importance of technical sources in traditional clothing] [Conference presentation]. *IV Seminario La Palabra Vestida*, Museo Provincial del Traje Popular, Morón de Almazán, Soria, España.

Vásquez Pecile, V. (2024c). *Abrigo (y toile), ca. 1964, Cristóbal Balenciaga. El modelo del mes, abril* [Coat (and toile), ca. 1964, Cristóbal Balenciaga: Model of the month, April], Museo del Traje CIPE. https://sciencevalue.udit.es/cgi/viewcontent.cgi?article=1112&context=articulos_cientificos
Velasco Molpeceres, A. M. (2015). *Moda y prensa femenina en España (siglo XIX)* [Fashion and women's press in Spain (nineteenth century)]. Ediciones 19.
Velasco Molpeceres, A. M. (2021). *Historia de la moda en España: De la mantilla al bikini* [History of fashion in Spain: From the mantilla to the bikini]. Los Libros de la Catarata.
Velasco Molpeceres, A. M. (2023). *Ropa vieja: Historia de las prendas que vestimos* [Old clothes: History of the garments we wear]. Los Libros de la Catarata.
Velasco Molpeceres, A. M. (2024). *La moda en el franquismo: Tul, ilusión y arriba* [Fashion under Francoism: Tulle, illusion, and "arriba"]. Los Libros de la Catarata.
Velasco Molpeceres, A. M., & Reguero Sanz, I. (Dirs.). (2016). *La historia a través de los mass media: Prensa, cine y moda (siglos XX y XXI)* [History through the mass media: Press, cinema, and fashion (twentieth and twenty-first centuries)]. Creaciones Vincent Gabrielle.
Ventosa, S. (2010). Spain. En *Berg encyclopedia of world dress and fashion* (Vol. 8, pp. 264–78). Berg.
Villalonga, I. de. (2000). *Pertegaz*. Ediciones Polígrafa.
Warschaw, O. (2017). Researching fashion studies: A brief historiography. *Art Libraries Journal*, 42(1), 2–6. https://doi.org/10.1017/alj.2016.39

PART 4

From craft traditions to the final product in contemporary fashion

CHAPTER 20

Methodological Approaches for Fashion Design Practice

From inspiration to project

*Gisela Beatriz Fortuna Mantellini**

ABSTRACT
The purpose of this research is to present a documental repertoire of methodological approaches applied to fashion design that are in use in current research in the field, in order to identify and characterize how fashion creators progress from inspiration to an orderly and systematic project. A review and summary of theoretical and empirical research that address the subject proposed in this work was conducted, by way of literature review research in Spanish, Portuguese, and English language, obtained through different databases that are currently used in the research field. The main conclusions of this work show that project methodologies formulated for product design remain valid in current research on fashion design and are also the basis for developing specific methodologies for this field. However, new methodological proposals for fashion design that incorporate other perspectives are currently emerging, in tune with paradigm shifts in the current context.

Keywords: Project methodologies, fashion design, creative process, design thinking

Introduction

Fashion design is a creative act, where the designer's inspiration and subjectivity have always been valued above all else. In this regard, Bruno Munari warns that "creativity does not mean improvisation without method" (1981, p. 21). Thus, a design method supports creativity, facilitating its development, as it allows the project to be carried out with greater precision and confidence. However, it is often overlooked that fashion design, in addition to being creative, is also projective, in the sense that it projects ideas, first, onto a flat surface—paper, fabric, or a mannequin (Amoroso Peralta, 2018)—and then combines observation, analysis, and reflection in the development of the clothing/fashion project (San Martín, 2009).

* Universidad Politécnica de Madrid.
(ORCID: https://orcid.org/0000-0002-6291-7979)

Design is a projective activity oriented toward problem-solving (Vilchis, 2016) that requires a process that supports the development and generation of ideas, and for this, it requires methodological applications. According to Zizumbo Alamilla, "design methods are strategies that allow for more effective and efficient solutions" (2019, p. 32); in other words, they optimize the creative process. This notion of a project appears in almost all design-related disciplines (industrial, interior, graphic, etc.), but in the fashion industry, there seems to be a certain skepticism toward scientific methodologies and research. In fact, most fashion manuals consider inspiration as the foundation and support of collections; however, in many cases, this inspiration becomes an obstacle for designers, since it consists of external, "guided" inspirations that do not provide solutions or coherence to the problems the designer must solve in a specific project (Fortuna, 2014). As a result, a tension arises between creative thinking and market demands (Dieffenbacher, 2013). This is partly because fashion design, associated with the development of products with a relatively short life cycle and conditioned by often seasonal trends, is understood as a projective practice that does not require extensive theories or allow for prolonged development (Broega, 2018). However, reality shows that we live in an era of unprecedented paradigm shifts, where aesthetic novelty and ingenuity are not enough to guarantee the success of a fashion collection. This radical change requires the incorporation and application of creative process methodologies in the field of fashion design, both in education and professional practice (Fortuna, 2014).

In the current fashion landscape, market segmentation and specific audience niches are becoming increasingly important for fashion companies. Regarding the satisfaction expectations (desires and needs) of these consumers, fashion companies and designers need to apply methodological tools for project management and product development (Bona et al., 2019). Based on this, the purpose of this literature review is to present a documentary repertoire of methodological proposals specific to the fashion sector, in order to investigate which ones are considered in current research in this field and how fashion designers progress from inspiration to an organized and systematic project. The hypothesis underlying this work is that the use of project design methodologies optimizes creative processes and makes the work of the fashion designer more efficient.

Theoretical/concept framework

The creative process

In fashion design, creativity plays a central role; however, the creative process is not completely free and independent, but is conditioned by different factors (cultural, social, economic, production, technological, among others) that influence the creation. Therefore, creativity must be oriented to the realization of a "creative product" (in this case, a garment, an accessory, a collection, etc.), which arises "from the balance between fantasy and logic, desire and goal, or by the approach given by the definition of creativity that relates novelty with utility" (López-Forniés, 2020, p. 31).

Löbach (1981) believes that the design process is creative, but also rational and systemic in its search for solutions; being a process of adapting products to the physical and psychological needs of the users, the designer must have the competence to elaborate aesthetic and symbolic functions of the products, to satisfy these needs.

López-Forniés (2020) defines three actions that are essential for the creative process development, referred to as the PIS Model:

- Problem: implies sensitivity, recognition, definition, preparation and/or collection of data and experiences.
- Ideation: involves the application of techniques, individual and group work, intuition, imagination, abstraction, copy-transformation-combination, inspiration, and illusion.
- Solution: involves the integration and evaluation of ideas, the generation of new concepts, validation, and verification that the solution meets the needs of the problem, as well as a conceptual analysis of what has been done from which learning emerges.

Project design methods

The representation of the creative process proposed by López-Forniés (2020) is the foundation of design methodologies, which according to Cano Redondo et al. are based on the resolution of the problem-solution binomial, where "from the understanding and analysis, or even discovery, of a problem (what we understand as a design need) we follow a path that allows us to reach the solution (what we understand as a designed object)" (2020, p. 106).

Several authors have approached the analysis of the different phases that make up design methodologies from a theoretical standpoint. These are called project methodologies because they are based on a planned work process consisting of a series of stages that are implemented in a logical order, prior to obtaining the final product. Table 4 presents some of the main project methodologies theorists and the stages they propose to develop a design project.

Table 4. Project design methodologies. Main theoretical contributions

Authors		Phases of the design process
Archer (1968)	1.	Analytical: problem definition, preparation of the detailed program, collection of relevant data, and preparation of specifications that will later be used for process feedback.
	2.	Creative: analysis and data synthesis in order to prepare design proposals. Development of prototypes.
	3.	Executive: involves critical assessment and adjustment of the idea.
Asimow (1970)	1.	Planning and morphology: feasibility study, preliminary design, detailed design, production process planning, distribution planning, consumption planning, product recall planning.
	2.	Detailed design: design preparation, total subsystem design, total component design, detailed part design, assembly drawing preparation, experimental construction, product test program, analysis, and redesign.
Bonsiepe (1990)	1.	Structure of the design problem: discovery and assessment of a need, general and particularized formulation of the problem, problem fragmentation, hierarchization of the partial problems, and analysis of the existing solutions.
	2.	Design: development of basic ideas, evaluation of alternatives, selection of the best alternatives, detailing of the selected alternative, construction and evaluation of the prototype, testing of the prototype, modification of the prototype according to the results of the test, preparation of definitive technical drawings for manufacturing.
	3.	Realization: cost studies, production, evaluation of the product after a certain time of use, introduction of eventual modifications of use, introduction of eventual modifications.
Jones (1966)	1.	*Black box*: the designer is able to produce results that they trust and are often successful, but is unable to explain how they arrived at such results.
	2.	*Transparent box* or *glass box*: problem, divergence, transformation, convergence and evaluation.

Authors		Phases of the design process
Löbach (1981)	1.	Preparation: Problem analysis: needs analysis, social relationship, relationship with the environment, historical development, market, structural function, materials and manufacturing processes, risks, etc. manufacturing processes, risks, etc.
	2.	Incubation: Possible solutions to the problem: sketches or test models for the solution of the problem.
	3.	Illumination: Evaluation of problem solutions: the best possible solutions to the problem are chosen.
	4.	Verification: Realization of problem solution: details are refined with necessary drawings and graphical explanations and the solution is realized in a product/object.
Munari (1981)	1.	Define the problem to establish the limits within which the designer must operate.
	2.	Define the type of solution in order to decide between the different possible alternatives.
	3.	Decompose the problem into its various elements to discover the particular problems or subproblems.
	4.	Collect the necessary data to study the elements of the problem.
	5.	Analyze the data collected to see how some subproblems have been solved in each case.
	6.	Creativity, which is not synonymous with intuitive idea or "magic" solution; while the idea is linked to fantasy and may propose unrealizable solutions, creativity remains within the limits of the problem, considering all the necessary operations that arise from the data analysis.
	7.	Collection of data relating to the materials and technologies that the designer has at his disposal to carry out the project.
	8.	Partial scale or life-size models of two or more solutions.
	9.	Verification of the models to check their validity, as well as an economic control of the production cost.
	10.	Constructive drawing, to communicate to people who do not understand the information necessary to make a prototype. They must be clear, legible, and sufficiently detailed.

Source: Compiled by the author

Another design method that is widely used in the field of design in general and fashion design in particular is Design Thinking, which can be defined as a methodology "that uses the designer's sensibility and methods to match people's needs with what is technologically feasible and what a viable business strategy can convert into customer value and market opportunity." (Brown, 2009, p. 86). According to this definition, Design Thinking is based on people-centered design and its main objective is to solve problems through a creative strategy to gain a competitive advantage in the market.

In turn, Brown and Wyatt point out that Design Thinking is in fact a "system of overlapping spaces rather than a sequence of orderly steps" (2010, p. 33). Based on this they identify three "spaces":

1. Inspiration. The market problem or opportunity that motivates the search for solutions. It is initiated by a briefing that provides the design team with a framework for ideas to flow to discover the needs of the target audience. Brown and Wyatt (2010) warn that conventional research methods (such as surveys or focus groups) can be useful, but generally do not usually lead to innovative ideas; therefore, they propose that in a Design Thinking system the starting point should be the observation of people's actual experiences.
2. Ideation. In this second space the designer synthesizes ideas that can lead to solutions or opportunities, with an approach that helps multiply creative options. Its objective is to generate multiple alternatives, based on expansive or divergent thinking that suppresses value judgments. For divergent thinking to emerge, the authors recommend using the brainstorming technique based on provocative questions. Each idea is written down and shared with the team. Visual representations are useful here, because they facilitate the understanding of more complex ideas.
3. Implementation. The third space of the Design Thinking process appears when the best ideas generated during ideation are turned into something concrete. The focus of this space is prototyping because it enables ideas to be converted into tangible products and services, which helps to visualize possible solutions by highlighting elements that need to be improved or refined before reaching the final result. Testing can also be performed to try out prototypes with a sample of users who may be involved in the solution being developed. This makes it possible to identify failures and introduce significant improvements. In other words, in this space the idea evolves until it becomes a real solution.

Project design methods for fashion

Based on these methods, several authors in the field of fashion design have proposed a series of steps that guide the design process until achieving the final product. For Sánches (2017), projective practices in fashion design should be carried out and refined throughout the project process, based on the integrated experimentation of constructive, productive, and physical and psychological interaction aspects.

However, this implementation is subject to the delimitation of orientation criteria to promote the generation of these formal solutions. In this sense, it is important to emphasize that in the industrial reality the development of fashion products is carried out in a complex and accelerated path, in which the designer is not always the one who commercializes, and production decisions depend on the diversified chain of manufacturers of fibers, pigments, fabrics.

Faced with this scenario, authors such as Jones (2008), Renfrew and Renfrew (2010), San Martín (2009), Sánches (2017), Sorger and Udale (2009), and Treptow (2013), among others, highlight planning as an indispensable process to adapt the creative process to the production systems and marketing strategies in the field of fashion design. Table 5 presents some references of this specific field and the stages they propose to develop a fashion design project.

Table 5. Stages in the fashion design process

Authors	Stages in the fashion design process	
Jones (2008)	1.	Briefing: time management, customer profile, target market, design constraints, choice of fabrics and materials, costing.
	2.	Inspiration: trend and behavioral research.
	3.	Presentation: storyboards, moodboards, sketches.
	4.	Evaluation.
Renfrew y Renfrew (2010)	1.	Briefing: customer profile, competition study, trend analysis, timeline, collection cost planning, research of fabrics, colors, silhouettes, and details, and accessories.
	2.	Creation: development of fashion designs.
	3.	Production: modeling, production of toiles—moulage, pilot pieces, technical sheets.

(Continued)

Table 5. (*Continued*)

Authors	Stages in the fashion design process
San Martín (2009)	1. Research: trends, styles, images, materials, market, and target audience data, etc., to serve as inspiration and conceptualization of the designer's proposed project. 2. Elaboration of a sketchbook: including all the notes, sketches of the first ideas, development, and experimental and creative approaches. 3. Experimentation of the proposals: with different materials, lines, silhouettes, chromatic palette. 4. Elaboration of a concept book: specific and clear ideas that emerge from the graphic section (illustration, sketching) are expressed in specification sheets and patterns. 5. Cutting and sewing of garments and prototypes.
Sánches (2017)	1. Delimit / Investigate: socio-cultural and aesthetic codes (fashion context and content), user environment (needs/desires/ availabilities), corporate/productive environment (expectations/ strategies/resources), contextualize (identify demands and specify guidelines to formulate identify/express/understand/evaluate problems). 2. Generate / Create: interface parameters (usability / adaptation / perception / communication), user experience possibilities (tangible and intangible), concepts, experience configuration, connection / representation possibilities (externalize ideas), connect ideas. 3. Evaluate/Configure: configuration details, experimentation, integration of technical communications, debugging and evaluating the effectiveness of interactions, consolidating, testing, refining and implementing the proposed solution, reflecting on the process.
Sorger and Udale (2009)	1. Research market segment, analyze trends, look for references. 2. Create a concept moodboard analyzing and synthesizing information, including photos and images; color palettes, fabrics, prints, and textures, sketches, patterns, inspirational phrases, images of possible users of that particular garment or collection, accessories that can accompany the garment or collection, among others. 3. Sketch the proposals that are directly related to the inspiration and concept of the collection or garment, considering that what is designed in drawings must show clearly and concretely how the garment will look on the designed body.

Authors	Stages in the fashion design process
Sorger and Udale (2009)	4. Experiment with different fabrics and materials. 5. Prepare technical data sheets with all the necessary specifications: color palette, supplies, materials, technologies, drawings in plans of the garment and detailing its seams, the more details are present, the better the results of the product will be. 6. Manufacture the garment or garments that will make up a collection. 7. Evaluation of the process.
Treptow (2013)	1. Identify the consumer and the brand: identifying the brand's target market and how it is perceived by its consumers. 2. Design management: assess production capacity, analyze past sales and define the sales calendar. 3. Fashion research: listing variables that will influence the collection design, differentiating it from previous collections and making it suitable for its target market. 4. Planning: determine what to manufacture, in what quantities, when and according to which trends. 5. Design: translate inspiration into identifiable aspects in the products of a collection. 6. Fashion product development: includes modeling, prototyping, grading, cost studies, and adjustment for mass production. 7. Promotion and marketing: strategies to promote the diffusion and sale of a collection.

Source: Compiled by the author

Materials and methods

A literature review methodology with a qualitative approach is used to determine a relevant problem through a systematized four-phase process proposed by Gómez-Luna et al. (2014):

1. Problem definition: the subject defined as the research problem is investigating what methodological proposals are being considered in current research in fashion design, in order to identify and characterize how creators progress from inspiration to an orderly and systematic project.

2. Research: first, a general search for literature related to the topic was carried out in Google Scholar, since it hosts scientific content from different databases. Then, the search was extended to other databases, such as Researchgate, Dialnet, Scielo, and Redalyc, in Spanish, English, and Portuguese.
3. Information selection: once the information was obtained, the publications were analyzed, with a total of 18 papers to be reviewed. Publications selection process
4. Information organization: once the publications with the closest relationship to the research study object were selected, they were classified and grouped by topic, in order to expedite the information analysis procedure. Table 5 shows the record of selected works and the topic they address.

Results and discussion

Most of the analyzed works are based on traditional design methodologies. For Babinski Júnior et al. (2020) methods used for fashion development originate from product or industrial design development process, such as the models proposed by Löbach (1981), Bonsiepe (1990), Jones (1966) or Munari (1981), widely used in Brazil for apparel design.

Babinski Júnior et al. (2020) consider that project thinking starts from a state of disorder—understood as the absence of harmony or organization—which is identified as a design problem; to solve this situation, design methodologies are chosen and activated to lead the process from creative inspiration to problem resolution. This appreciation coincides with Munari (1981, p. 21) when he states that "Creativity does not mean improvisation without method." However, in the case of fashion design, "when the project is completed or the product is finished, a new disorder arises from the entropy generated in the process, which allows us to affirm that disorder tends to method and method tends to disorder" (Babinski Júnior et al., 2020, p. 22).

Bona (2019) analyzes Löbach's (1981) proposals for industrial design and Brown's (2009) proposals on Design Thinking, among others, on the basis that design methodologies applied to product design are also useful tools for fashion designers as they facilitate the advancement of processes and decision-making. The author bases the usefulness of Löbach's proposals

(1981) and other theorists on design methodologies (such as Baxter or Burdek, cited by Bona, 2019) on the fact that fashion design is a creative, inventive, and innovative activity, but each design is the result of a process whose development is also determined by conditions and decisions and not only by inspiration. It also incorporates the Design Thinking approach as significant and innovative in design in general and fashion design in particular.

Valentine et al. (2017) also address Design Thinking as an applicable methodology to fashion design processes. These authors' argument is that textile design has unique ways of thinking and, therefore, designing. These unique and sometimes complex ways of thinking demand different approaches to design, especially in the current context where fashion market trends are oriented toward sustainability and collaborative practices (co-creation/co-design) implying the need to develop innovation-oriented design thinking to respond to market demands. These perspectives agree with Brown (2009) when he states that currently there is a need for an approach to innovation that is powerful, effective, and widely accessible, while integrating all aspects of business and society.

Ortiz Bolaños (2020) draws from Brown's (2009) contributions on Design Thinking—understood as a non-linear process that goes from inspiration to implementation—to apply it to the business redesign of a textile apparel company in order to optimize operational and creative performance. This work demonstrates, empirically, that the application of Design Thinking simplifies the design process and improves operational performance, since it allows innovative ideas to emerge from creativity, which increase productivity. Specifically in the inspiration phase, designers try to streamline their processes during data collection, seeking to obtain lower response times. On the other hand, in the ideation phase, prototyping and evaluation of previous proposals lead to the emergence of new proposals that can drastically change the processes in the way they are being carried out.

Bona et al. (2019) also rely on the contributions of product design methodologies applicable to fashion design, because they consider the project as a "bridge" from the intangible (the ideas, the inspiration) to the tangible (the product). In this sense, Löbach states that "design is an idea that is embodied in a project or a plan to solve a particular problem" (1981, p. 16). Along the same lines, Sánches (2016) explores the idea of project as a tool that enables shaping the intangible and conceptual. This author states that, due to the importance of social use and the production of meanings conferred to fashion design products, the design process cannot be reduced to the isolated appreciation of the product, without considering the multiple contextual assimilations or the relevance of research to understand them. Sánches (2016) argues that the expression "intangible project" synthesizes this conception that the form provides the sensory medium (tangible) for the construction of meanings, articulating subjective links (intangible) with the design product.

Broega (2018) argues that project methodologies support creativity, both in academic contexts as well as in the fashion designer's professional practice. According to Munari (1981), creativity emerges from an association between fantasy and invention. Thus, in the field of fashion design, creativity represents "the free way of thinking" to address the most varied aspects of a problem: image, function, psychological, social, human, and economic aspects. However, to help fashion designers in the process of developing collections, the methodology used must question all the factors involved in the problem of fashion creation, whether environmental, cultural, functional, or symbolic, as well as visual aspects such as colors and materials.

In the same analysis trend, Vázquez Álvarez (2017) mentions that in order to develop a creative process it is necessary to take into account the design methodology to be worked with, given that methods, more than a path to reach a goal, are the foundations of the proposed solution. In this sense, the author explores the contributions of Archer (1968), Asimow (1970), Jones (1966), and Munari (1981) as a theoretical basis and of the practical activities of the subject Fashion Design Projects II in a Higher School of Design specializing in Fashion, in the community of Castilla y León, Spain. The empirical evidence showed that these methodologies promoted the development of basic, specific, and transversal competencies to achieve a professional profile adapted to the professional demands of the sector, as well as to enhance the autonomy, creative, reflective, and critical thinking and professional skills of the students. Likewise, the author points out that the use of project methodologies in the training of future fashion designers allowed the social and professional interaction of students with their environment through the development of the phases of the design process, the proposals for solving problems in collaborative work and the development of the technical and communication process of the project. These methodologies greatly facilitated the possibility of keeping control over the design and learning process.

However, Orozco and Urueña (2022) observed a disarticulation between theory and practice, considering that the current Fashion Design education must train professionals who understand the socio-cultural complexity of the context in which they develop, since design is not dissociated from social, cultural, industrial, and economic processes of the context. But Fashion Design curricula in different countries, in general terms, includes theoretical subjects related to the history of fashion and textiles, practical subjects associated with the construction of garments (pattern making and tailoring), supported by subjects related to disciplines such as digital design, illustration, fashion marketing, entrepreneurship, textile design, among others.

According to these authors, globalization-imposed changes in the Fashion Design profession have not been accompanied by the curricula; and one of the main obstacles they identified is that career curricular designs prioritize theory and individualized teaching methodologies far from the new trends of collaborative design such as co-creation and co-design, which seek to include the consumer in the design process to meet their needs efficiently. Orozco and Urueña (2022) also found that Fashion Design curricula do not train future designers to adapt their creative proposals to the emerging needs of the context in which they find themselves and that they must now also contemplate problems of environmental impact, sustainable production, and access to new technologies now available to the fashion industry, generating the loss of employment opportunities for designers by not being able to respond adequately to the demands of the target market. Similar observations are made by Fortuna (2014).

Fiorini (2020), on the other hand, raises the need to introduce changes in the methodological models developed in the field of fashion design education, due to the impact of socio-cultural transformations in consumption models and the emergence of other production logics, which force to review the disciplinary conceptions in design education and in the professional field. The author proposes Design Thinking as a model of project thinking that allows developing innovation in the field of fashion, covering issues related to the relationship between design and technologies, or between design and sustainability. "This means understanding the complexity of the meaning of the objects we design and their relationship with the experiences, emotions, ideas, and discourses that clothing traverses, both in projectuality and in the professional field" (Fiorini, 2018, p. 59).

Paz y Miño Ferri and Véliz Matute (2015) highlight the value of project methodologies for developing the creative process in fashion design, because they allow "not to waste time on mistakes that can be made by not following an already experienced project method" (p. 53). In this sense, Munari (1981, p. 19) points out that "the series of operations of the design method obey objective values that become operative instruments in the hands of creative designers." From this perspective, by reclaiming the idea of fashion design as a project activity, it becomes necessary to apply a design methodology in order to enhance and improve creativity, which becomes essential in each of the phases of a design process. Paz y Miño Ferri and Véliz Matute point out that:

> The solution of a problem established through creativity during a design process is the fundamental work of the designer, since they face productive and technological challenges, in addition to giving coherent answers to the circumstances found in the human-object relationship. (2015, p. 65)

Thus, project methodologies as support for the creative process in fashion design allow for the development of a functional and efficient response that relays creativity with technique, in other words, between the inspiration and knowledge that drive the designer to think differently. In this regard, Cajilima Malan and Matute Genovez (2020) state that the creative process is born from inspiration, but for the development of this process, selected and classified information is required to make the final product.

Despite the overall consensus, there are also some critical voices. Thus, Burgos (2018) questions the linear methodological schemes in the design disciplines (Archer, 1968; Asimow, 1970; Bonsiepe, 1990; Jones, 1966; Löbach, 1981; Munari, 1981; among others), taking graphic, architectural, and clothing design as particular case studies. For this author, the project models retain their rigid, systematic, and deterministic structures, which do not agree with the actual practice of current design. However, these schemes persist both in teaching and in professional practice, due to factors such as: resistance to the abandonment of classical categories derived from positions such as problem-solving; the restriction of professional practices to logical decision-making mechanisms, centered in the sphere of the individual and subjective; the primordial function of the methodology centered on sequential step-by-step mechanisms, which are not consistent with the complex plots of the concrete action of current design. This leads to generating prescriptions for procedures to achieve a proposal "adequate" to the requirements and intentions.

Burgos (2018) recommends changing the log of problem-solving methodological approaches as the dominant conception for the activity, to move to a more open relational-reticular vision that allows recovering all the complexity and transcendence that design has in the current construction of culture. This author proposes that the design process does not respond to the prescriptive or pre-established fulfillment of stages, but to a configuration of actions and decisions that are organized from the recognition of a plot of relationships that becomes explicit in the project procedure. According to Burgos:

> Problems and methods do not pre-exist the process, but are constituted at the very moment when the activity is carried out. It is the network of interactions that gives entity to the problems, to the subjects involved, to the response processes and to the objects that define the proposal. (2018, p. 125)

Sánches (2016) also raises a critical view of design project methodologies considered as "linear," arguing that in the field of fashion design the project must link multiple variables, which are articulated in organized and interdependent actions to constitute an integrated whole; therefore, the project must be faced as a systemic design process that expands the project approach in the search for networked solutions.

Within the scope of specific methodologies applied to fashion design, Carrión Vidal (2018) bases her research on the methodologies developed by referents in this field (such as San Martín, 2009; Sorger & Udale, 2009; among others) and compares these processes with the systematized method taught in the Fashion Design degree program. In her conclusions, the author suggests that students should be motivated to solve their design problems effectively and efficiently on the basis of a methodology for developing a project, stimulating creativity, critical thinking, reflection, research, and constant analysis. For this, the educational proposal should be oriented to analyze the context in which the garment or collection is being developed in order to generate fashion products that "work" and satisfy the user's needs, without copying existing models but taking these references as a basis for innovation and not imitation.

Additionally, in the field of fashion design education, Steffenello Ghisleni et al. (2021) describe a practice proposal they call *educommunicative* for the recreation of project methodologies in the teaching and development of fashion collections, using Renfrew and Renfrew (2010), Sorger and Udale (2009), and Treptow (2013) as their framework. The authors conclude that the use of project methodologies to develop a collaborative fashion collection exercises the ability to solve problems collectively. From an operational point of view, it becomes clear that the project process arises from the context's demands and therefore, each project must have a flexible methodology that can be adapted to the complexity of the scenario. In summary, project methodologies for the development of fashion collections can use *educommunicative* practices to enhance and facilitate the teaching process in the development of collections, articulating the collaborative process among students. Steffenello Ghisleni et al. conclude that:

> With *educommunication*, an education for communication is built for fashion that thinks of the human being as a whole and respects the identity, meaning, and purpose of life through connections between the individual and the social. (2021, p. 78)

Carvajal-Villaplana (2017) revisits the idea that fashion design can be systematized through the linear model proposed by design methodologies. The author states that, in general terms, a fashion design methodology is composed of six stages that define a linear process: 1) determination of the problem to be solved or the need to be satisfied; 2) research; 3) fashion design theory; 4) design; 5) graphic representation and prototyping; and 6) solution or concretion of the product. However, this theoretical model which follows strict stages often cannot be applied in practice because "reality is more complex, since designers do not work with a consensus model, but with design practices with variants and procedural modes" (Carvajal-Villaplana 2017, p. 9), which often differ from the designer's intentionality and are faced with the challenge of responding to industrial processes involved in the mass production of garments. Facing the changes in the fashion market, where new conceptions such as *sustainable fashion*, *slow fashion*, or fashion based on the Life Cycle of the Garment appear, the author proposes to incorporate ethics and the idea of harm as components that have to be part of the values of designers, as well as of the fashion industry.

Amoroso Peralta (2018) presents an alternative aesthetic proposal for fashion design referred to as Alterotopia, based on Sorger and Udale's (2009) methodology. The alterotopic methodology proposed by this author is based on inspiration as one of the essential steps to project clothing. Such inspiration can be conceived from two perspectives: concrete or literal inspiration and abstract inspiration. The "literal" inspiration (a concept that this author takes from Sorger & Udale, 2009), refers to a concrete inspiration whose managing motifs are of a material and perceptible type, while the abstract inspiration is based on ideas or concepts and events. For Amoroso Peralta (2018) the latter form of inspiration has greater possibilities for creation, although both are closely related; abstract inspiration becomes a concrete form when it materializes, and concrete or literal inspiration can trigger a series of meanings that will lead to abstract inspiration. What's important is to reflect on both practice and conceptualization.

However, Amoroso Peralta (2018) doesn't dismiss project methodologies because "the designer must consider what is requested in the brief [...], understand that it has limits and deadlines, so a research planning strategy comes into play" (p. 107). She also emphasizes the traditional visual methods of fashion design (such as sketchbook or moodboard) as tools not only for inspiration, but also to help thinking. Thus, in the altertopic methodology proposed by this author, theory is not separated from practice, given that theorization is an essential part of the creative process where the real challenge lies in maintaining a balance between the object, the concept, and how it's received.

This methodology sets out to rethink the professional practice of fashion designers by reflecting on the communication between the designer, who they design for, and context. In this way, the gap between designer and "user" is shortened, to establish a connection of the sender/author and receiver/audience type, in which "the intention is not to obtain a client who wears the garments according to fashion, but a receiver who engages in a dialog; the aim is a shared aesthetic experience" (Amoroso Peralta, 2018, p. 129).

Conclusions

The literature review performed revealed that the project methodologies formulated for product design are still in force in current research on fashion design, being also the basis for the development of specific methods for this field. But new methodological proposals are also emerging for fashion design that incorporate other perspectives, in tune with the changes of paradigms in the current context, such as Design Thinking (with overlapping spaces), reticular schemes (search for networked solutions), or systemic models. These new proposals, while criticizing the linear-sequential models of traditional project methodologies, recognize the importance of a method in the creative process, arguing that in the field of fashion design the project must link multiple variables that are articulated in organized and interdependent actions to constitute an integrated whole.

It also confirmed that inspiration is always the starting point that initiates a design process, considering that creative activity is a free and spontaneous act; however, it becomes necessary to further develop the creative process, which in the field of fashion takes place not only in the inspiration and transcendence of the designer's thoughts and ideas, but also in the conscious construction of a new knowledge, of a new proposal.

The literature review confirmed the hypothesis proposed in this study, verifying that the use of project design methodologies allows for the optimization of the creative processes and makes the fashion designer's work more efficient. Indeed, introducing a work methodology during the development of the design process makes it easier to determine the problem's purpose, to analyze it from different perspectives, to assign adequate procedures for its development and to stipulate timing and the different stages. These factors contribute to the logical and systematic organization of the process developed by the designer, as well as to the creation of innovative and original ideas.

In the process of searching and selecting publications, it was possible to determine that there are few scientific studies focused on project methodologies for fashion design and their importance in the academic and professional use, especially considering that some of the analyzed research showed that there is a gap between the academic environment and the professionalization of fashion design. It is important that design theory and practice remain intertwined for the construction of knowledge in a useful and meaningful way. Therefore, the development of more research in this field is recommended because it would provide a greater understanding of the subject.

Finally, a breakthrough in this field of knowledge, specifically with regard to fashion designers and as an agenda for future research, are research studies carried out by large organizations, which include more than one professional fashion designer, and are aimed at understanding collective creative processes.

References

Amoroso Peralta, S. M. (2018). *Alterotopías: propuesta estética para la generación de formas periféricas de vestir en Cuenca-Ecuador 2015* [Alterotopias: an aesthetic proposal for generating peripheral ways of dressing in Cuenca-Ecuador 2015] [Master's thesis, Universidad de Cuenca, Ecuador].

Archer, B. (1968). *The structure of design processes* [Doctoral dissertation, Royal College of Art].

Asimow, M. (1970). *Introducción al proyecto* [Introduction to design]. Herrero Hermanos.

Babinski Júnior, V., Holanda Maciel, D. M., da Rosa, L., & Silveira, I. (2020). *O pensamento projetual no design de vestuário: da desordem ao método* [Project thinking in fashion design: From disorder to method]. DAPesquisa, 15, 1–25.

Bona, S., Silveira, I., Rech, S. R., & dos Santos, C. T. (2019). O desenho no design de moda: as diferentes linguagens de representação aplicadas no processo projetual [Design in fashion design: Different representation languages applied in the projectual process]. *Revista Projetica, Londrina, 10*(2), 63–80.

Bona, S. F. (2019). *Método de projeto de coleção em design de moda: uma configuração para micro e pequenas empresas* [Collection design method in fashion design: A configuration for micro and small companies] [Master's thesis, Universidade do Estado de Santa Catarina UDESC].

Bonsiepe, G. (1990). *Teoría y práctica del diseño industrial* [Theory and practice of industrial design]. Gustavo Gili.

Broega, A. C. L. (2018). A criatividade no ensino do Design de Vestuário de Moda: uma experiência acadêmica [Creativity in fashion apparel design education: An academic experience]. *Revista de Ensino em Artes, Moda e Design, 2*(2), 92–119.

Brown, T. (2009). *Change by design: How design thinking transforms organizations and inspires innovation.* Harper Business.

Brown, T., & Wyatt, J. (2010). *Design thinking for social innovation.* Stanford Social Innovation Review (winter 2010).

Burgos, C. E. (2018). Modelos reticulares como superación de los esquemas metodológicos lineales en las disciplinas proyectuales [Reticular models as a way to overcome linear methodological schemes in design disciplines]. *ADNea, 6*(6), 119–27.

Cajilima Malan, K. I., & Matute Genovez, K. V. (2020). *Diseño de indumentaria a partir del registro de los procesos creativos y uso de elementos identitarios en el etno-diseño de indumentaria ecuatoriano* [Fashion design based on identification of creative processes and use of identity elements in Ecuadorian ethno-designed clothing] [Bachelor's thesis Universidad del Azuay, Cuenca, Ecuador].
Cano Redondo, A., Gómez Carruthers, M., Mercader Inglés, J., & Salvador del Pozo, P. (2020). *Proyectos de diseño. Teoría y metodología del proyecto* [Design projects. Project theory and methodology]. Consejería de Educación y Cultura de la Región de Murcia.
Carrión Vidal, M. C. (2018). *Habitar el cuerpo. Propuesta sistematizada para el diseño de vestuario para obras de teatro* [Habitating the body. A systematized proposal for theater costume design] [Bachelor's thesis, Universidad del Azuay, Cuenca, Ecuador].
Carvajal-Villaplana, Á. (2017). Diseño, innovación y moda: entre la tecnología y el arte [Design, innovation, and fashion: Between technology and art]. *Revista Legado de Arquitectura y Diseño, 1*(22), 1–17.
Dieffenbacher, F. (2013). *Fashion thinking: Creative approaches to the design process.* Bloomsbury Publishing.
Fiorini, V. (2020). Diseño de indumentaria: Nuevas estrategias de enseñanza y modelos de innovación en el marco del consumo de moda [Fashion design: New education strategies and innovation models in the context of fashion consumption]. *Centro de Estudios en Diseño y Comunicación. Cuaderno 78*, 51–60.
Fortuna, G. (2014). *Dinamización del proceso creativo en las empresas de moda* [Creative process dynamization in fashion companies]. Hijos de Muley Rubio (HMR).
Gómez-Luna, E., Fernando-Navas, D., Aponte-Mayor, G., & Betancourt-Buitrago, L. A. (2014). Metodología para la revisión bibliográfica y la gestión de información de temas científicos, a través de su estructuración y sistematización [Literature review methodology and information management of scientific topics, through its structuring and systematization]. *Dyna, 81*(184), 158–63.
Jones, J. C. (1966). Design methods reviewed. In S. A. Gregory (Ed.), *The design method* (pp. 295–309). Springer Science+Business Media.
Jones, S. J. (2008). *Diseño de moda* [Fashion design]. Blume.
Löbach, B. (1981). *Diseño industrial. Bases para la configuración de los productos industriales* [Industrial design: Basis for industrial products configuration]. Ed. Gustavo Gili.

López-Forniés, I. (2020). *Taller de diseño, creatividad y proceso creativo* [Design, creativity, and creative process workshop]. Prensas de la Universidad de Zaragoza.
Munari, B. (1981). *¿Cómo nacen los objetos?* [How are objects born?] (2ª ed.). Gustavo Gili.
Orozco, C., & Urueña, W. (2022). Ejes problemáticos del diseño de modas: importancia y repercusión en el ejercicio de la profesión en la provincia de Imbabura, Ecuador [Problem areas in fashion design: Their importance and repercussion in professional practice in the Imbabura province, Ecuador]. *Sabios 2*(1), 5–22.
Ortiz Bolaños, E. F. (2020). *Aplicación del design thinking al rediseño de procesos productivos. Estudio de caso: Empresa del sector de confección textil en Ecuador* [Design thinking application towards the redesign of productive processes. Case study: Textile manufacturing company in Ecuador] [master's thesis, Universidad Nacional de Colombia].
Paz y Miño Ferri, M. B., & Véliz Matute, C. R. (2015). *El proceso creativo en la resolución de problemáticas relacionadas al diseño de modas* [The creative process in the resolution of problems related to fashion design] [bachelor's thesis, Universidad del Azuay, Cuenca, Ecuador].
Renfrew, E., & Renfrew, C. (2010). *Creación de una colección de moda* [Developing a collection (Basics fashion design)]. Gustavo Gilli.
San Martín, M. (2009). *El todo-en-uno del diseñador de moda: secretos y directrices para una buena práctica profesional* [All-in-one fashion designer: Secrets and guidelines for good professional practice]. Promopress.
Sanches, M. C. de F. (2016). *O projeto do intangível na formação de designers de moda: Repensando as estratégias metodológicas para a sintaxe da forma na prática projetual* [The design of the intangible in training fashion designers: Rethinking methodological strategies for form syntax in design practice] [Doctoral dissertation, Universidade de São Paulo e à Universitat Politècnica de València].
Sanches, M. C. de F. (2017). *Moda e projeto-estratégias metodológicas em design* [Fashion and project methodological strategies in design]. Estação das Letras e Cores.
Sanches, M. C. de F. (2018). A educação projetual no design de moda: diretrizes pedagógicas [Project education in fashion design: Pedagogical guidelines]. *ENSINARMODE Magazine*, 2(1), 9–28.
Sorger, R., & Udale, J. (2009). *Principios básicos de diseño de moda* [The fundamentals of fashion design]. Ed. Gustavo Gilli.

Steffenello Ghisleni, T., de Quadros Sandri, R., & Spode Becker, E. L. (2021). Metodologia projetual para educomunicar o desenvolvimento de coleções de moda [Project methodology to educommunicate the development of fashion collections]. *Comunicação & Educação, 26*(1), 65–79.

Treptow, D. (2013). *Inventando moda: planejamento de coleção* [Inventing fashion: Planning collections] (4ª ed.). Doris Treptow.

Valentine, L., Ballie, J., Bletcher, J., Robertson, S., & Stevenson, F. (2017). Design thinking for textiles: Let's make it meaningful. *The Design Journal, 20*(1), S964–S976.

Vázquez Álvarez, N. P. (2017). *Proyectos de diseño en moda. Análisis de sus fases, procesos, coreografía didáctica y resultados* [Fashion design projects: Phases, processes, didactic choreography, and results analysis] [Doctoral dissertation, Universidad de Burgos].

Vilchis, L. del C. (2016). *Diseño: universo de conocimiento* [Design: Universe of knowledge] (4th ed.). Quartuppi.

Zizumbo Alamilla, A. (2019). Innovación orientada por la creatividad. Desarrollo de alternativas de productos de diseño. Experiencias en México, Uruguay y Cuba [Creativity-driven innovation. Development of product design alternatives. Experiences in Mexico, Uruguay, and Cuba]. In M. V. Ferruzca Navarro (Ed.), *Exploraciones, intercambios y relaciones entre el diseño y la tecnología* (pp. 29–45). Universidad Autónoma Metropolitana.

CHAPTER 21

Documenting Fashion

Trend reports as a tool for heritage analysis. A century of innovation, from sample books to digital reports

*María Arcas Ruiz**

ABSTRACT
Fashion trend documentation constitutes a valuable legacy for the study of both tangible and intangible heritage. It is an excellent source for contextualizing the use of clothing, yet it is often overlooked by scholars. This article aims to highlight and reassess the significance of these valuable documentary materials.

It explores how trend forecasting, its methods, and its documentary formats have evolved over the past one hundred years—from the emergence of the first reports after World War I, produced by national color committees, or the trend books that included fabric and fiber samples, to today's trend observatories that sell digital reports.

Keywords: fashion research, fashion documentary sources, trends, coolhunting

Introduction

The trend forecasting industry has been producing reports for over a century. These materials are a valuable and diverse source for the study of fashion in each historical period and have been created by experts from both public institutions and private companies.

This article aims to reaffirm the analytical value of trend studies, as these documents offer significant insights for historians, researchers, and students alike, contributing to a greater understanding of textile heritage through the analysis of reports that capture innovations from major designers as well as street fashion since the 1960s.

Methodology

Through a concise review of the history of trend reports, key moments at the international, European, and Spanish levels have been gathered into

* Universidad Politécnica de Madrid.
(ORCID: https://orcid.org/0000-0003-3773-5329)

a timeline. Additionally, the perspectives of writers, sociologists, and prominent designers—such as Christian Dior—regarding these materials and trend research methods have been included. The aim is to demonstrate that these materials are crucial for a deeper understanding of fashion and the way of life in each era.

The article also describes the activity of the trend hunter from the perspectives of anthropology, ethnography, ethnology, and marketing, in order to validate these reports and materials.

Results

The commercialization of trends always serves an economic purpose: to anticipate consumer desires. These reports reveal how people think, act, and interact within society. They offer highly valuable information for analyzing fashion, reflecting on the success of certain colors or garments, and, most importantly, serve as a crucial source for studying and understanding fashion in each historical period.

It has been documented that fashion trend reports have existed since the end of World War I. These early reports consisted of physical samples of fabrics and threads. Today, similar practices continue, albeit with digital materials. This reinforces the importance of these documents as direct reflections of society.

Coolhunting is, therefore, a form of participant observation whose goal is to discover, identify, forecast, and supply trends originating from "cool" individuals, in exchange for compensation. It may be defined as the collection of information from cool individuals to guide the production and planning of future products likely to succeed with the public, used for commercial and/or branding purposes. This practice helps companies enrich their brand experience and tailor content for stakeholders and target audiences. The added value provided by the coolhunter lies in offering insights that cannot be extracted through traditional marketing research or data-driven consumer statistics.

An analogy can be drawn with anthropology, specifically with Malinowski's concept of participant observation. Through inductive methods, the researcher provides an insider's perspective on the society being observed (Malinowski, 1985). This supports the idea that coolhunting contrasts with deductive research, which offers an outsider's perspective lacking prior knowledge of what is being studied—akin to an anthropologist studying a tribe without understanding its language or cultural codes. The resulting information would lack the depth and accuracy that a member of the same group—one who understands and can decode those elements—could offer.

Moreover, Giddens defines ethnography as participation and cohabitation with the group being studied, which includes customs, beliefs, language, stories, and many other elements (Giddens, 1985). This aligns with the Real Academia Española's definition of *ethnography* as the "descriptive study of popular culture" (Real Academia Española, 2021a).

In this way, coolhunting is also linked to ethnology, which is the comparative study of shared traits among different societies or ethnic groups. The word *ethnology* comes from the Greek *ethnos* (people) and *logia* (study), and the *Diccionario de la lengua española* defines it as the "science that comparatively studies the origins and cultural expressions of peoples based on data provided by ethnography" (Real Academia Española, 2021b).

When a coolhunter visits multiple communities, they make comparisons based on prior observations. Through repetition, they can identify which innovations are emerging in both contexts. This demonstrates the use of both scientific methodologies: ethnography, to detect new behaviors or styles within cool spheres, and ethnology, to verify that these trends are also emerging in other neighborhoods or communities.

What is particularly interesting is when the coolhunter is a member of the community being observed. This provides firsthand, direct information grounded in knowledge of the group's roles and symbols. The trend hunter is a validated insider, not an outsider, implying a form of participant observation *inter pares*, or in other words, among equals.

Judith Dell refines the concept of participant observation by stating: "The immersion of an individual in an imaginative and emotional experience in which the fieldworker learns to live in, and to understand, the new world" (Dell, 2005, p. 173).

This highlights how the type of understanding described by Dell is essential for extracting compelling and useful information for the industry.

Trend observatories and the adaptation of products to future demand

Seivewright underscores the importance of trend reports for corporate production planning. He notes, "As we have said, keeping up with street cultures, new trends, new technologies, and global interests is crucial at the research stage when preparing a new collection or developing a new brand" (Seivewright, 2013, p. 65).

He clarifies that the work of these companies extends beyond anticipating developments in the textile industry. Instead, they monitor a variety of factors that significantly influence consumer desires. He explains,

> Tracking trends is not just about watching fashion, but also about observing demographics, behaviors, technologies, and lifestyles. Consumption analysis can often help designers create the right garments and accessories that consumers will want in the future. (Seivewright, 2013, p. 65)

The history of trend hunting and the early color forecasting associations created after World War I

To provide some background, it is essential to recall the significance of William Henry Perkin's discovery of aniline in 1856 for the textile industry. This was the first synthetic dye to be commercially produced on an industrial scale, creating a vivid and long-lasting violet color. That moment revolutionized the textile sector. Natural dyes used until then posed several problems: they were not safe, healthy, or affordable. Synthetic dyes solved these issues, progressively allowing for the industrial production of more durable, less toxic colors with better overall results. Moreover, these dyes and their mordants were more resistant to time and washing, representing a major improvement in performance.

By the early twentieth century, Germany had the most advanced laboratories in Europe for producing textile dyes. However, World War I and its economic and political aftermath diminished this dominance. Trend forecasting experts Scully and Johnston explain,

> At that time, 90 percent of the dyes used by the U.S.A. textile industry were produced by major German chemical companies like BASF or Bayer. When World War I broke out, the U.S.A. industry became isolated from Parisian influence and from German dyes. (Scully & Johnston, 2012, p. 44)

It was during this period that color forecasting associations began to develop in the United States. The authors recounts:

> Due to this isolation, textile companies, clothing manufacturers, and related industries formed a committee to develop a palette of fashionable colors for the upcoming season using domestic dyes. They also published their own color card. In 1915, this group became the Textile Color Association, the first organization to attempt to forecast and coordinate color trends across the industry. This marked a new and different approach compared to color cards provided by textile mills to showcase available products or those chosen by Parisian couturiers. After the war, American chemical companies acquired German patents and developed a broad range of dyes, pigments, and paints. (Scully & Johnston, 2012, p. 44)

These national associations helped companies align their production with upcoming trends, ensuring that manufactured garments would meet consumer demand. In the United States, the association changed its name but continued to perform the same function for decades.

> The Textile Color Card Association was chaired by Margaret Hayden Rorke, a former actress and suffragette, who became the first professional color forecaster in the United States. Rorke traveled with Bettina Bedwell, a fashion journalist from the Chicago Tribune based in Paris. Bedwell observed color trends and reported to Rorke, who compared the reports to her forecasts. New York's fashion industry and its suppliers welcomed this work, and the Textile Color Card Association gained a strong reputation. In 1955, it became the Color Association of the United States. Rorke and the association had launched a process of color forecasting in the U.S. based on research conducted at the top of the fashion pyramid: Paris and haute couture. (Scully & Johnston, 2012, p. 44)

As demand for color forecasting services increased among manufacturers, the private agency Tobe Associated was founded in 1927. Its regular reports were referred to as the *fashion industry's bible*, offering predictions based on consumer behavior and retail insights (Scully & Johnston, 2012, p. 44).

The analysis of purchasing behavior introduced a new sociological dimension to commercial research, giving these reports added value as resources for studying fashion in specific periods or for contextualizing fashion-related objects.

This information is often compiled into trend books, which are sold each season to fashion companies. These books provide extensive technical details on future garments, including tones, materials, silhouettes, and manufacturing processes expected to be in demand in upcoming seasons.

Brazilian researcher Nathalie Cristina Bonome also analyzes trend books:

> They are produced by national or international trend research agencies and take various forms, such as physical and digital catalogs, which provide general and/or specific information for different stages of fashion product design. Some books present information on the entire trend chain—from design concepts and themes to raw materials, colors, patterns, silhouettes, and details. Others only offer suggestions for final products. (Bonome, 2011, p. 23)

The traditional way to share these emerging trends is through what are commonly known as trend books or magazines, although some agencies refer to them as trend books. These documents contain vast collections of images from runways, trade fairs, presentations, and street scenes; clippings from the press; fabric swatches; types of buttons or zippers; drawings; patterns; and moodboards (also referred to as inspiration boards or collages). Trend books also include in-depth analyses of colors, silhouettes, graphic details, materials, techniques, and patterns. Some contain vector images ready for direct application to any product. They address highly specific topics: some focus on footwear, accessories, lingerie, swimwear, sportswear, or menswear, while others are dedicated to children's and baby fashion and accessories.

These reports can also be organized by city, allowing users to gain insight into market developments in any of the world's fashion capitals. The companies provide visual documentation of major storefronts, displays, and brand websites. These tools make it possible to stay updated on sector-specific news without traveling, attending hundreds of runway shows, reading dozens of magazines, or walking through the busiest shopping streets. They offer a window into current events directly from the office. Additionally, the digitalization of content has made it easier and faster to access and use these materials, with updates occurring weekly or even daily, including images and future trend forecasts. Companies can subscribe to online trend services or purchase physical copies of these trend books.

In their educational book *Color Forecasting for Fashion*, Scully and Johnston emphasize the value of the information provided by color forecasting associations. They note:

> Color forecasting is in the hands of skilled individuals with extensive experience, aptitude for color, and insatiable curiosity. Most have backgrounds in art and design related to textiles or fashion, although knowledge and experience in psychology, sociology, anthropology, marketing, art, design history, and critical analysis are also required. There are also professional organizations, trend agencies, trade fair consortiums, and product development teams from commercial retailers involved in color forecasting. Many independent professionals in the field gained experience while working for trend consultancy firms. (Scully & Johnston, 2012, p. 13)

This confirms that color forecasting extends beyond the textile industry, impacting consumer goods, the automotive sector, interior design, and even beverages—sectors that can use such documentation to study the past.

Trend agencies in Europe

The development of early forecasting associations in Europe is also discussed by fashion experts:

> From 1931 to the 1960s, the British Colour Council was responsible for predicting and establishing color standards for textile manufacturers and suppliers. In 1934, the BCC published its *Dictionary of Colour Standards*, which defined color by hue, tone, and intensity, and was intended for fabric manufacturers and the dyeing industry. (Scully & Johnston, 2012, p. 44)

In France, a private trend forecasting service, *Carlin International,* was founded to provide a French perspective. Various countries began to recognize the importance of anticipating trends in order to align production and increase profits.

The birth of France's first trend observatory: Fred Carlin, 1937

Maillet has studied in depth how France's first fashion forecasting company, *Fred Carlin*, was established. Its success stemmed from Carlin's deep understanding of textile manufacturing and awareness of industry needs. Born in 1902 in the industrial city of Lyon, Carlin grew up surrounded by silk and weaving workshops. At that time, sample books were commonly used by fabric companies to showcase their innovations. Some firms even sold these books at competitive prices to both domestic and international clients (Maillet, 2009).

Maillet confirms another early example. In 1928, the sample company *J. Claude Frères et Compagnie* added, for the first time, a trend forecasting page with seasonal commentary to its sample albums. In 1937, Carlin opened his fashion consultancy and trading office on the busy *Rue du Faubourg Saint-Honoré* in Paris, where he advised numerous international companies. His sample books provided information on fabric types, threads, qualities, and weights, along with guidance on future collections. This served as a valuable reference for producers about what would soon be in demand.

Extensive information on the bureaux de style can be found in Thierry Maillet's work, Histoire de la médiation entre textile et mode en France: des échantillonneurs aux bureaux de style (1825–1975). He states, "In the late 1950s, the first bureau de style opened, and three more followed in the 1960s. These trend offices gained increasing influence, confirming the role of mediation in fashion development" (Maillet, 2013, p. 1).

Maillet also emphasizes their strong relationship with American department stores, which were their main clients. In line with this idea, he states, "They were created within the buying departments of New York department stores based in Paris" (Maillet, 2013, p. 1).

This confirms the high demand for trend information in the United States to support the industrial production of garments.

The commercialization of trend information as analyzed by Christian Dior

Sharing fashion news is not a recent practice. Since the 1940s, various—sometimes fraudulent or borderline criminal—methods have emerged to report to clients about fashion: the latest fabrics, the most in-demand silhouettes, and trending prints, colors, and accessories seen on runways. Historically, designers have feared the copying of their designs, counterfeiting, and above all, the reproduction of their new models by international competitors.

Hiring third parties to report on seasonal collections is not new, as Christian Dior explained in his memoir *Christian Dior et moi*, published in 1956:

> Despite strict union regulations and surveillance by each couture house, it is impossible to completely eliminate freeloaders and cheats. There are five classic ways to copy; but the most demoralizing is the betrayal of a staff member. For those who understand what goes into the creation of a collection—this teamwork that unites the owner, head seamstresses, apprentices, workers, and models, all of whom tie their future to the success or failure of the house—such conduct is odious. (Dior, 2007, p. 147)

Dior also acknowledged:

> The second form of copying occurs later, when the collection is presented to the press. In most cases, this is a regrettable abuse—not so much because of direct copying but because of the information shared with the public. All French journalists must sign an agreement with the *Chambre Syndicale de la Couture* before receiving a special press card granting them access to the shows. They know the limits of their rights, but some foreign colleagues, less informed, unintentionally violate these rules. Fortunately, we have three or four people in each salon whose sole mission is to detect indiscretions. Violators are discovered immediately and politely asked to return any sketches made. The law of couture is implacable: write, but never draw. More serious—though thankfully rare—are deliberate acts of espionage. We unmasked one person using a tiny camera no bigger than a button to take microscopic photographs. He was simply expelled from the salon. (Dior, 2007, p. 147)

These statements reveal the intense effort made by designers and institutions to protect their creations. The creator of the New Look was keenly aware of the economic power of design and the commercial potential of fashion in France, across Europe, and in the United States—where he secured agreements with department stores for the production and marketing of his designs. Together with Courrèges, Dior was a pioneer in the licensing model and clearly understood the economic potential of well-managed innovation.

He continued, explaining:

> The third form of copying—and perhaps the most common—is used by clients who do not respect the rules of the profession. These individuals try to sketch the models during shows. Sometimes they claim to do it only to remember the general line of a dress whose name they missed. When caught, we force them to buy the model in question, keeping the deposit. Related to this are agreements among provincial or foreign dressmakers. Each one buys a model, and then they combine their purchases to create a small collection at very low cost. This is more of an extension of their buyer's rights than outright fraud. (Dior, 2007, p. 148)

Dior described another illegal practice:

> Model renters were particularly active in the years following the war, and it was not until 1948 that the main culprit—a remarkably clever woman—was discovered. She arranged for various intermediaries—typically private clients—to buy the best models from major French designers. Back in New York, she organized semi-official 'digest shows' at the Plaza Hotel by invitation. Each guest paid between $350 and $500 for entry. For that price, they could take the selected model and return it three days later after carefully copying it. If they wanted more dresses, they paid accordingly. If another client wanted the same model, they would be scheduled to copy it later. (Dior, 2007, p. 150)

These ethically dubious strategies were rigorously prosecuted in Europe. However, in the United States, protections for intellectual property were more relaxed. This allowed for the rise of *figurine publishers*. Dior observed:

> Immediately after designers presented their collections, a group of subscribers would receive, cash on delivery for $1,000, a figurine booklet with every model from each major fashion house. Buyers could order additional booklets at a decreasing rate. This gave them abundant and comprehensive documentation without having to travel. (Dior, 2007, p. 151)

He emphasized the scope of this shadow industry:

> In August 1955 alone, over one thousand subscribers received around three hundred models from leading Paris designers. I alone accounted for about 140 models, 57 of which were exact copies. The main promoter of this incredible business earned more than all the authorized exports combined. He recruited subscribers orally, both legally and illegally, and even reached countries like Switzerland, Germany, and Belgium. (Dior, 2007, p. 151)

Dior concluded: "These smugglers must be exceptionally talented people. The level of accuracy is remarkable and indicates the work of professional observers" (Dior, 2007, p. 153).

Even at that time, Dior recognized the essential qualities of a good trend hunter: sharp observational skills and excellent memory. During shows, about 150 to 200 models might be presented—only trained eyes could memorize that many details. Photographic memory remains one of the most valuable assets for any trend hunter.

Parisian trends: Nelly Rodi, from public to private

Nelly Rodi's son recounts the company's history and explains:

> In the 1950s, *prêt-à-porter* was an American phenomenon, and the French offering was perceived as disorganized and outdated. After a trade mission to the United States to see how the sector was structured there, the French government created the Comité [Committee], which essentially functioned as a state-sponsored trend coordination agency funded by the textile industry. What was the purpose of coordinating trends? Simply to minimize uncertainty: if the same information is provided to those who market garments, design them, purchase the fabrics, and manufacture them, the economic benefits for textile producers are enormous, because they know in advance what kind of fabric will be in demand and where to focus their efforts. Similarly, if all retailers stock violet-colored items this year, demand for violet is inevitably generated, and retailers end up selling all their stock. The committee's idea was to reduce the margin of error in the risky fashion sector. (Tungate, 2008, p. 120)

The ultimate goal of international trend forecasting agencies that advise companies across various sectors is what Tungate calls "minimizing uncertainty" (Tungate, 2008, p. 119)—that is, getting materials, designs, and colors right to align with future consumer demand.

In 1973, Madame Rodi was in charge of communications for the designer Courrèges, just before being appointed director of an organization known as the *Comité International de la Mode*, which had been established by the French government two decades earlier (Tungate, 2008, p. 119). After leaving the public committee, Rodi founded her own trend forecasting company in 1985. In 1991, she acquired the recently privatized *Comité International de la Mode*, thus ensuring her appointment as a fashion consultant for numerous companies.

Today, the company operates with a team of trend hunters who travel the world observing social phenomena, youth subcultures, and emerging movements. In addition to providing clients with this insight, the agency offers brand strategy consulting, produces marketing materials, designs collections, organizes events, and provides stylists and photographers.

Tungate notes:

> Nelly Rodi's most well-known products are the trend books: these hefty volumes, filled with photos, illustrations, fabric swatches, and explanatory texts, resemble

> luxurious scrapbooks. They summarize the agency's trend forecasts and serve as inspiration tools (or more precisely, as prompters in a theater) for designers seeking the next big idea. Each season, the agency produces about a dozen independent trend books covering categories such as *prêt-à-porter*, knitwear, lingerie, colors, prints, textiles, lifestyle, and beauty. The agency even creates a fragrance trend box containing vials of notes, blends, and scents. Each book sells for around €1,400, with only 200 printed per category. Their primary clients are retailers and the beauty sector. Le Louet observes that 'luxury brands typically don't buy these books because they see themselves as trendsetters. However, photocopies of the books can often be found in many designers' studios. (Tungate, 2008, p. 121)

In 1997, Malcolm Gladwell wrote an article in *The New Yorker* profiling DeeDee Gordon (Gladwell, 1997), a trend hunter working for the sportswear brand Converse. Gordon explained how she connects street culture with corporate boardrooms, helping companies understand consumers' desires and concerns so they can incorporate them into their products, services, or communications strategies.

Tungate also refers to the major global trend forecasting company, WGSN, founded in London in 1998 by brothers Julian and Marc Worth. Cited by several authors as the most influential trend agency internationally, WGSN provides sector-specific reports, including babywear, lingerie, sleepwear, and detailed analyses of international runway shows and collections across segments such as denim and footwear.

In this regard, Tungate clarifies:

> Other trend trackers do not operate so much as consultants to the fashion industry but rather as observers of cultural changes that might influence product development. One such agency is Style-Vision, founded in 2001 (www.style-vision.com). In addition to its bimonthly megatrend reports, it produces sector-specific publications—not just on fashion but also food, personal care, and technology—and regularly organizes roundtables on consumer trend evolution. (Tungate, 2008, p. 123)

He continues:

> The agency is less concerned with predicting trends than with penetrating consumers' minds. We are interested in individuals within a social context. Through research involving consumers and opinion leaders, we imagine future scenarios, consumer reactions to them, and what types of products and services they will require. (Tungate, 2008, p. 123)

In addition to offering insights into design, these trend consultancies observe social shifts, emerging ideas, political developments, and the evolving needs of consumers. In sum, Tungate views their role as monitoring and forecasting consumption habits.

In Italy, agencies such as Future Concept Lab stand out, operating well beyond the textile industry. In Spain, trend research companies such as TPR (Tomorrow People Research) have emerged, originating from Advira, a market research and public opinion firm.

Below is a timeline outlining key milestones in the international history of coolhunting and the foundation of major trend agencies:

Table 6. Milestones in the international history of coolhunting and the foundation of major trend agencies

Year	Event
1915	Textile Card Association founded, United States
1927	Tobe Associated, the first private fashion consultancy (The Tobe Report), United States
1931	British Colour Council, United Kingdom
1947	Carlin International, trend agency, France
1955	Color Association of the United States, United States
1955	Comité des Industries de la Mode, linked to the Marshall Plan, France
1956	Christian Dior denounces industrial espionage: 1) internal staff leaks, 2) drawings and photos taken by attendees, 3) designer-to-designer borrowing, 4) model renters, and 5) figurine publishing, France
1959	*Centre d'Information de la Couleur*, initiated by Fred Carlin; precursor to Carlin International, France
1962	Color Marketing Group, nonprofit color forecasting organization, United States
1973	*Comité International de la Mode*, chaired by Nelly Rodi, France
1985	Nelly Rodi trend agency founded, France
1989	Future Concept Lab, trend and market research firm, Milan, Italy
1991	Privatization and acquisition of the *Comité International de la Mode* by Nelly Rodi, France
1994–1996	"All major cool-style consulting firms—Sputnik, The L Report, Bureau de Style—were founded between 1994 and 1996" (Klein, 2005, p. 103), United States

(Continued)

Table 6. (*Continued*)

Year	Event
1997	Brand Futures Group established at Young & Rubicam (Matathia, 1997, p. 15), United States
1997	First edition of trend research book in Dutch mentions long-distance collaboration since 1994 (Matathia & Salzman, 2001, p. 25), Netherlands
1997	First use of the term *coolhunting* by Malcolm Gladwell in the March issue of *The New Yorker*, United States
1997	First trend book discussing coolhunting, Netherlands
1998	WGSN trend agency founded in London, United Kingdom
2001	Style-Vision trend agency founded, France
2003	TPR (Tomorrow People Research) founded within Advira, Madrid, Spain
2009	First Spanish-language book on coolhunting published, Spain

Source: Compiled by the author

Conclusion

Over the past 100 years, outstanding materials on fashion trends have been produced, offering valuable resources for fashion studies. Public institutions, private agencies, individuals, and even hired trend scouts have created and commercialized trend information in the form of drawings, patterns, photographs, fabric swatches, threads, buttons, and other elements that are particularly useful for the analysis of fashion and heritage. These sources are well-documented and temporally defined, allowing us to understand the spirit of an era through the garments worn by people at that time. This makes them highly applicable to heritage analysis.

Ultimately, the coolhunter conducts market research through participant observation inter pares, reflecting strong parallels with both ethnology and ethnography.

From fabric swatch books and skeins of thread to digital trend reports, a vast body of documentation exists that captures and analyzes the tastes of each season. This archive constitutes a valuable resource for historical, technical, scientific, and sociological research on fashion. These materials, crafted by professionals, may indeed succeed in capturing what Lipovetsky (2000) once referred to as "the invisible."

References

Bonome, N. C. (2011). *Cominicação e coolhunting: Os caçadores de tendências* [Communication and coolhunting: The trend hunters] [Master's thesis, Universidade Estadual Paulista Júlio de Mesquita Filho]. Carlin International.

Dell, J. (2005). *Cómo hacer tu primer trabajo de investigación* [How to do your first research paper]. Gedisa.

Dior, C. (2007). *Dior by Dior: The autobiography of Christian Dior* (A. Fraser, Trans.). V&A Publishing. (Original work published 1957).

Giddens, A. (1985). *The nation-state and violence* (Vol. 2). University of California Press.

Gladwell, M. (1997, March). The coolhunt. *The New Yorker.*

Lipovetsky, G. (2000). *El imperio de lo efímero: La moda y su destino en las sociedades modernas* [The empire of the ephemeral: Fashion and its destiny in modern societies] (F. Hernández & C. López, Trans., 7th ed.). Anagrama.

Maillet, T. (2009). *Histoire de la médiation entre textile et mode en France: Des échantillonneurs aux bureaux de style (1825–1975)* [History of mediation between textiles and fashion in France: From sample makers to style offices (1825–1975)] [Doctoral dissertation, École des Hautes Études en Sciences Sociales]. *L'Atelier du Centre de Recherches Historiques, 11*. https://doi.org/10.4000/acrh.5610

Maillet, T. (2013). *Histoire de la médiation entre textile et mode en France: Des échantillonneurs aux bureaux de style (1825–1975)* [History of mediation between textiles and fashion in France: From sample makers to style offices (1825–1975)] [Doctoral dissertation, École des Hautes Études en Sciences Sociales]. *L'Atelier du Centre de Recherches Historiques.*

Malinowski, B. (1985). *Magic, science and religion and other essays*. Waveland Press.

Matathia, I., & Salzman, M. (2001). *Tendencias: Claves del futuro próximo* [Trends: Keys to the near future]. Planeta.

Real Academia Española. (2021a). *Etnografía* [Ethnography]. https://dle.rae.es/etnografía?m=form

Real Academia Española. (2021b). *Etnología* [Ethnology]. https://dle.rae.es/etnología

Scully, K., & Johnston Cobb, D. (2012). *Colour forecasting for fashion*. Laurence King Publishing.

Seivewright, S. (2013). *Diseño e investigación* [Design and research]. Gustavo Gili.

Tungate, M. (2008). *Fashion brands: Branding style from Armani to Zara* (3rd ed.). Kogan Page.

CHAPTER 22

Samplers

Pedagogical tools for cultural rooting in the discipline of fashion design

*Adriana Cagigas Gil**

ABSTRACT
This proposal examines samplers and their productive rituality as a learning model for transmitting and preserving intangible heritage in academia and the textile industry. Analyzing and categorizing the learning methods and the knowledge encapsulated in samplers allows the development of tools to make ancestral knowledge accessible in industrial and educational spaces. This contributes to the creation of sustainable imaginaries within the textile sector by promoting the connection and revaluation of heritage.

Keywords: embroidery sustainability, samplers, cultural heritage

Introduction

This text explores the potential of samplers if their learning methodology and heritage transmission role were reintroduced as a pedagogical tool to foster cultural rootedness in professional training within the fashion design discipline. The gap between heritage knowledge—both material and intangible—and students and industry professionals is becoming increasingly evident. Encounters with popular culture should symbolize belonging, rootedness, and balance across previous, current, and future generations. However, interest in folk art and crafts is no longer fostered during childhood within the family context, as these traditions are often forgotten, undervalued, or replaced.

The academic context, particularly in creative disciplines such as textiles when understood holistically, could provide a space to relearn and reconnect with our traditions and popular cultures (Barbosa, 2009, cited in Revista Digital do LAV, 2019). We must bring the worldview and popular knowledge back into the university context (and, by extension, into the industry), promoting not only their study but also their application from contemporary perspectives. Studying, analyzing, and categorizing the learning methods

* Universidad de Diseño, Innovación y Tecnología.
(ORCID: https://orcid.org/0009-0005-2700-337X)

and the knowledge encapsulated in samplers can provide the tools needed to make ancestral knowledge accessible to the fashion sector on a global scale.

Uprooting: gaps between heritage, academia, fashion, and industry

One of the greatest shortcomings of today's textile industry is its disconnection from the material and intangible heritage that constitutes it. The acceleration of our world and the consequent speed at which we experience reality is a result of detachment from a specific time and place. Never has the world been so fast paced, where temporality and place, self and others, nature and culture have ceased to be coherent links, instead transforming into paradoxes and risks of uncertainty (Santamarina, 2005).

This detachment causes all aspects of human existence to increasingly define themselves through immaterial and insubstantial relationships, which only lead to existential emptiness due to their limiting nature, preventing any sense of rootedness. These relational dimensions have gradually been lost, particularly those that connect humans to one another and those that embed individuals within their spatial and temporal contexts (Aguirre, 2024–2025).

As Aguirre states, "we have untied the shared bonds with our cultural landscape and our history, as well as those that connect us to our fellow human beings with whom we share the world" (Aguirre, 2024–2025, p. 17).

It is therefore not surprising that we find ourselves in such a clear state of uprooting: uprooting from time, matter, the social fabric, and, of course, from everything inherited from our ancestors—everything that shaped us and gave us the form we have today. Living in immediacy frees us from local influences and the continuity of time; that organic time of waiting, questioning, and remembering; the ebb and flow that allow for the creation of a space for individual and collective construction (Choay, 2007); that temporality which enables the development and legitimization of common identities with shared values and similar objectives.

The continuous increase in uprooting prevents us from respecting our cultural, social, and environmental context, generating dynamics that are harmful to any environment in which we find ourselves. This destabilization is particularly evident in the fashion and design sector. Following Simone Weil's words, any society that seeks to subordinate human relationships to the act of buying and selling is an absolutely uprooted society that, therefore, cannot fulfill its most fundamental and basic obligation: respect. Human beings possess a universal destiny and, therefore, an obligation: to respect one another (Weil, 2014). Since human collectives root themselves in the past while reaching into the future, feeding the souls of the living and those yet to be born, the preservation of the spiritual treasures of our ancestors is crucial. It serves as the only channel of communication with those who came before us (Weil, 2014).

Craftsmanship, its productive rituals, and its practices of transmission and use are, therefore, key pillars that provide the discipline of fashion design with an inescapable capacity for connection. Since this discipline (and the entire infrastructure that supports it, including academia and industry) is currently experiencing an undeniable debt to its heritage—as a genuine cultural expression—craftsmanship and the tacit knowledge held in human hands have great potential to act as a lever for healing uprooting. Its experiential and ideological nature (Aguirre, 2024–2025) makes this possible.

Returning to take root in a land that was once fertile, as Weil aptly points out, may be the most important need of the human soul that has been ignored. A human being, Weil says, has roots by virtue of their real, active, and natural participation in the existence of a collective that keeps certain treasures of the past alive while harboring premonitions of the future (Weil, 2014). Within this context, the ritual of textile craftsmanship constitutes an original substratum for generating the multiple connections we currently need to develop coherently in any sphere that goes beyond the productive realm—whether it be spiritual, moral, intellectual, or critical, particularly in the textile sector.

To connect with the heritage issues that define the world of design and fashion through a real understanding of its potential for social transformation, it is essential to comprehend that heritage, as a phenomenon of modernity, is rooted in and entails the legitimization of collective identities. Consequently, it is possible to observe how every identity-building process involves an interpretation and selection of the past to establish and give meaning to its identification.

The conceptualization of heritage leads to a multitude of images, with particular characteristics in different cultural contexts, reflecting a map of complex attributes and values upon which certain resources—considered encapsulators of a presumed cultural essence—are selected, legitimized, and idealized to be preserved and passed on (Santamarina, 2005). Heritage is, therefore, a subjective and symbolic selection of elements from the past that are revitalized, adopted, or reinvented from and for our present. In the specific case of the fashion design field, this selection would have a determining future potential if consciously and critically integrated during formative processes.

Since heritage is a socio-cultural construct, we quickly realize that it depends not so much on the cultural assets transmitted but rather on their recognition as such by the collective (González-Varas, 2015). What is common plays a unique role in the construction of the identity of communities; it generates belonging and, therefore, has the capacity to promote shared goals, symbols, and visions. Moreover, it allows a society to move in a determined direction, supported by the assurance that the process is embraced by other members of the group: life feels more profound when it is shared, communicated, and expressed; satisfaction is often greater when it is collective; a living community begins, and in a sense, never ends (Esquirol, 2018). There is nothing more eternal or more shared than the legacy of inherited assets, for which we take responsibility when we embrace them, and which, as a heritage, we can recognize, preserve, or even enhance (González-Varas, 2015).

In the act of sharing, of learning the common through oral, gestural, and symbolic transmission, samplers are proposed as a pertinent study example to create learning spaces conducive to the reception and integration of cultural heritage. Samplers embody ways of doing and experiencing learning. They are narratives articulated in gestures that, weaving beauty, can transmit the worldview and cultural universe of a community. Sepúlveda (2003, cited in Cattan Lavín, 2019) describes how craftsmanship has the capacity to "generate cognitive maps that illustrate the dialogue between humans and their environment, highlighting the relationship between technical knowledge and the natural world" (p. 1).

Understanding both the material and immaterial reality that surrounds textile techniques allows us to establish more coherent relationships with the space around us and with those who inhabit it. It also enables us to discern the conditional links between the object dimension and the individual (Munari, 2016), recognizing that all materiality that shapes artifacts inevitably affects and configures us. Craftsmanship in general, and the making of samplers in particular, are cultural practices that reflect a unique, holistic, and complex universe where multiple dimensions coexist—from the territory to the world of objects, which are more than mere objects. They are meaningful artifacts and material representations of a singular reality (Walker, 2018; Mier y Terán, 2013, cited in Cattan Lavín, 2019, p. 2), experienced through the intimacy generated in the space between the creator, the material, and the piece (Metcalf, 2007; Shiner, 2007, cited in Cattan Lavín, 2019, p. 2).

The richness and diversity of a community can be observed in its crafts and the resulting objects, as both reflect the interaction between materials provided by the physical environment, the technological processes developed by individuals, the organization of production (Turok, 1988, cited in Cattan Lavín, 2019, p. 2), their use, and their care. Recovering this communal richness and vitality is essential today, given the gaps that exist between academia, industry, and craftsmanship.

Current context: challenges and limitations of education in creating a sustainable fashion industry rooted in its intangible cultural heritage

The current state in the academic context: student difficulties as a synonym for uprooting

In my role as an educator, both in sustainability and in theoretical content related to textile raw materials, I have encountered certain limitations that prevent the content taught from being accepted or understood in ways that allow its practical application in the professional field by students. These difficulties, generally present across various student profiles, include:

- Lack of knowledge about both material and intangible cultural heritage.
- Disconnection from the codes and symbols that define cultural heritage.
- Disinterest in the potential study of textile heritage.
- Lack of interest due to the abstract, distant, and minimally relatable nature of the content to the students' everyday environments.
- Lack of engagement caused by theoretical contexts disconnected from real-world practice.

- Lack of motivation in the face of future paradigms framed by negativity, presented within the conceptual framework that defines current sustainability strategies.
- Hierarchical individualism is reinforced by practices that promote competition rather than cooperation among actors within the same system.
- Lack of knowledge about the processes involved in creating raw materials (and their implications).
- Inability to connect and draw conclusions that allow for strategies with a lower impact in the production of materials and garments, as students acquire knowledge exclusively through theory and intellectualization rather than a global and experiential perspective.
- Incomplete understanding of the concepts of heritage and craftsmanship, leading to insufficient application and development of these concepts within the industry.

The current state of the industry: challenges to foster rootedness in heritage and sustainability

The current deficiencies are not limited to the educational field. The industry also faces a series of shortcomings that contribute to the sector's negative impact, making it difficult to transform the value chain in the search for circular strategies that are increasingly disconnected from heritage. The issues that future professionals must address as challenges to overcome in the textile industry—and which become a key focus for developing the skills and competencies required by new profiles within the fashion design discipline—include:

- Lack of systems that cooperate logically, respectfully, and regeneratively, promoting connections with local territories, their customs, and traditions.
- Absence of actions that break away from the hegemonic and individualistic practices of design, which are entirely disconnected from traditional patterns of connection through artisanal practices rooted in popular heritage.
- Inability to generate regenerative value chains that truly have circularity as the core of their natural functioning.
- Absence of collective awareness to promote new approaches to fashion, design, and the use of products and services related to the textile sector.

- Lack of multicultural, multidisciplinary, and intergenerational dialogues and collaborations that foster diverse codes, beliefs, and local rituals.
- Shortage of new narratives and languages that enhance diversity.
- Absence of traceability and transparency due to absolute delocalization and uprooting.
- Limitations in defining craftsmanship as a strategy to reduce impacts within the value chain.
- Disconnection from the material realities of everyday life.
- Diverse understandings of the role that clothing plays in daily spaces, aiming to propose alternative solutions to overconsumption.
- Scarcity of multiple decision-making centers.

The sampler: its pedagogical dimension and potential for cultural rootedness in fashion design

Samplers are living books, didactic materials. Undoubtedly, they are the quintessential books of popular embroidery, where the most important patterns are gathered (González Mena, 1994), transmitted orally within a shared, inherited, received, and experienced learning context. "In the twentieth century, studies in Hispanic philology revisited the analysis of the analogy between the textual and the textile, reiterating in the case of the sampler its origin from the Latin *dictatum*—a text dictated by a teacher to their students—derived from *dictare*, to dictate, and from *dicere*, to say" (Ávila et al., 2023, p. 10). Art historians have also emphasized this connection by conducting a more specific analysis of school environments, explaining that the sampler refers to a kind of dictated text transmitted orally by teachers to their students, who, at a slower pace, record what is dictated (Ávila et al., 2023).

However, the sampler should not be understood merely as a static model showcasing patterns to replicate without any soul driving the action. On the contrary, Ávila et al. (2023) states: "Samplers are symbols of knowledge, cognitive correlates that go beyond the mere imposition of an ideal. They carry local memory and have represented not individual skill and prowess but collective design memory" (p. 11).

The sampler is, therefore, an instrument that impeccably exemplifies the process of learning from a local context, as its purpose was precisely that: to practice by observing in order to perfectly imitate the technical and aesthetic norm dictated. Its nature as an embroidered book can teach us the value of learning and studying through interaction with bodily actions and engagement with textile materials, aimed at acquiring the knowledge that shapes an individual's cognition. These pieces show us how weaving, thread, and the act of engaging with textile practices have always been tied to our development while narrating the stories we live and the myths we believe in. They speak of the person, the environment, and the material, and they are examples of commitment, mastery, and serenity of spirit (Sennett, 2009)—the kind of serenity required to engage in meticulous study based on perfecting a dictated norm or pattern.

Samplers are texts, testimonies with their own identity, crafted by individuals who, through the technique and mastery of thread, weave the collective history they were living in their immediate surroundings. Developed across all spheres of society—in professional environments, rural areas, farming regions, schools, and courts—samplers are contemporary models that exemplify and expose different ways of living in the same time and place. They reflect diverse ways of experiencing routines and the stages of personal development, from the earliest phases of growth in school to the leisure activities of courtly women. Samplers are writings of the worldview of different profiles which, when united, provide a comprehensive understanding of how life was perceived in a specific territorial and historical context. Additionally, in the realm of leisure, it is fascinating how samplers were seen as open books—constantly under construction, as long as the space on the fabric allowed for it (González Mena, 1994).

This preliminary description of these textile pieces, it is worth remembering that samplers have been the foundation of the book, which, in turn, has failed to surpass the plastic, educational, ornamental, or symbolic qualities that these textiles have exercised through their various functions. Books, in the format we know today within the context of learning textile techniques, have been nothing more than inert copies, confined by pages that must be opened to reveal their content.

In contrast, the sampler presents all its information at a single glance, allowing for a global and integrative perspective of the subject being observed. It also clearly and intelligibly conveys the technique, color, material, and meaning of all its elements, making it more accessible to the student. The ability to engage and relate the learner's bodily space with the object of study makes the act of learning more integrative, as it occurs through the relationship between the student, the material, the tools, the teacher, the symbolism, and the history (see Figure 32).

This integrative aspect, when considering the deficiencies currently observed both in the classroom and in the industry, is one of the fundamental reasons why this heritage object is being revalued as a potential solution to the challenges facing the sector.

Textile practices embody a vast methodological richness. They are highly valuable due to their procedural and material nature in various fields, such as pedagogy, research, and therapeutic support (Cattan Lavín, 2019). Embroidery reveals specific forms of knowledge that emerge from the continuous relationship between transmission shaped by orality and physicality, learning through adaptability, limitation, and repetition, as well as a set of elements

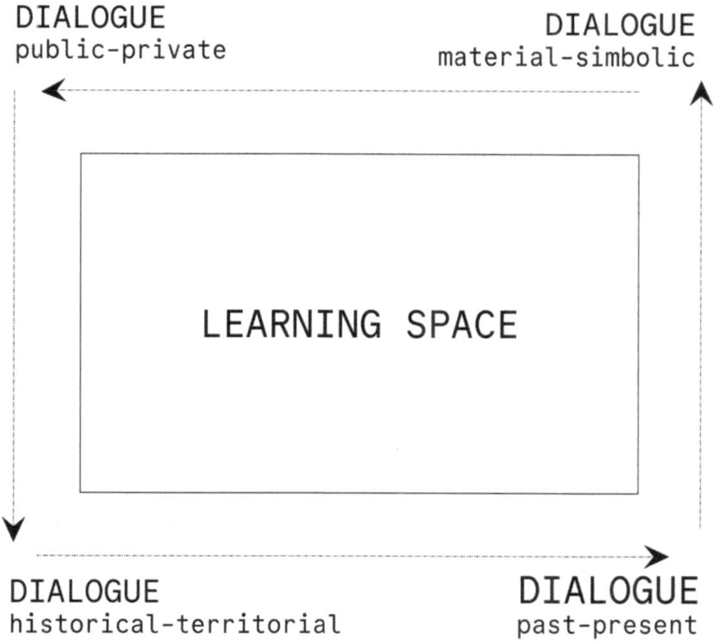

Figure 32. Table in which the main dialogues established within the space of study and practice of samplers are described.

Image by the author.

that generate decorative systematizations in spaces of coexistence and study (see Figure 33).

Given that, today, the everyday space dedicated to studying and learning various aspects of textiles and fashion design demonstrates a widespread disconnection among the agents involved in the skills acquisition process, the practice space of samplers is taken as a symbolic model for developing new forms of intangible heritage preservation in contemporary academia. The disunity among the main agents involved in the textile industry (teacher, student, artisan, environment, cultural heritage, textile transformation processes, and industry) fosters ways of living disconnected from their cultural

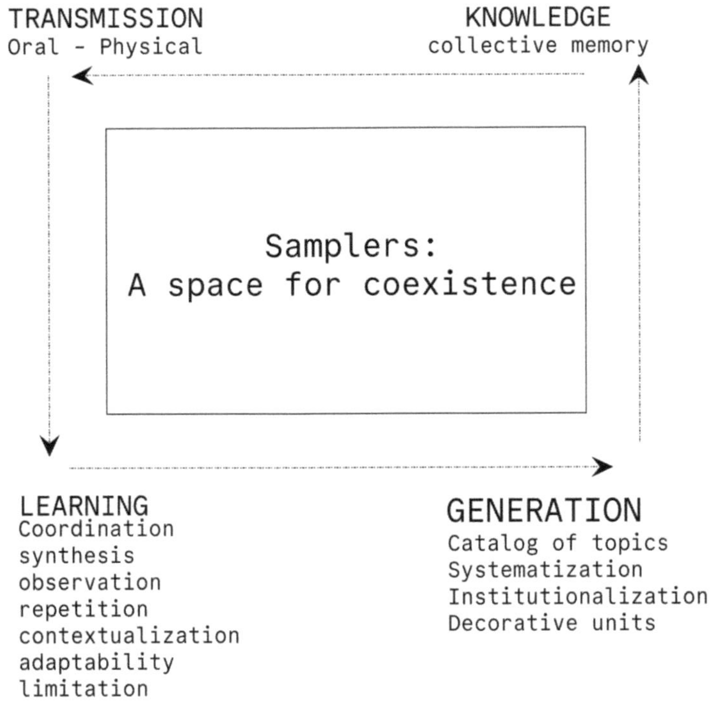

Figure 33. Table in which the potential of the spaces of coexistence created by samplers is described, highlighting four key forces for the acquisition of heritage wisdom: transmission, learning, creation, and knowledge.

Image by the author.

heritage, given the inability to establish rootedness caused by widespread ignorance.

This uprooting is one of the greatest modern tragedies, leading to alienation, a lack of purpose, and the loss of identity (Weil, 2014). Rooting oneself is key to achieving social and personal stability; it is fundamental for fostering individual and collective well-being, and it occurs through the connection with cultural heritage, which serves as a shared framework of values, history, and traditions.

In this need to take root, the space where embroidery practice takes place is a key reference for study. This space is characterized by establishing a continuous dialogue between multiple dualities that, through their simultaneous experience, manage to generate more robust learning strategies, primarily due to its holistic and experiential perspective.

Samplers, moreover, always have a distinct morphology and structural character (generally rectangular pieces divided into bands embroidered on homemade linen). However, their content reflects the multiplicity of contexts and territories in which they are developed. They embody diversity through the rigor of a transmitted and inherited learning process that continually evolves according to the embroiderer's criteria within their era. This practice has always served to define the structural boundaries of women: either their own limits through introspection while embroidering in solitude, or collective margins that help them understand their specific place within a community. In doing so, it becomes possible to determine an individual's position through communion with others (see Figure 34).

The cultural treasure inherited and experienced during the creation of a sampler is a collective wealth, both in its formation and transmission, in its material and intangible aspects. This allows us to understand that our individual and social existence is inscribed in a long-term temporal process, one that involves a precise awareness of temporality and enables the maintenance of our historical identity as a human community.

Around the sampler, various flows emerge from the connection between coexistence and transmission, giving rise to knowledge through repetition. This continuous flow generates a system of interconnected dualities that are, at the same time, synergistically united with one another. This continuous synergy enhances an optimal learning dynamic due to its capacity for logical and contextual comprehension.

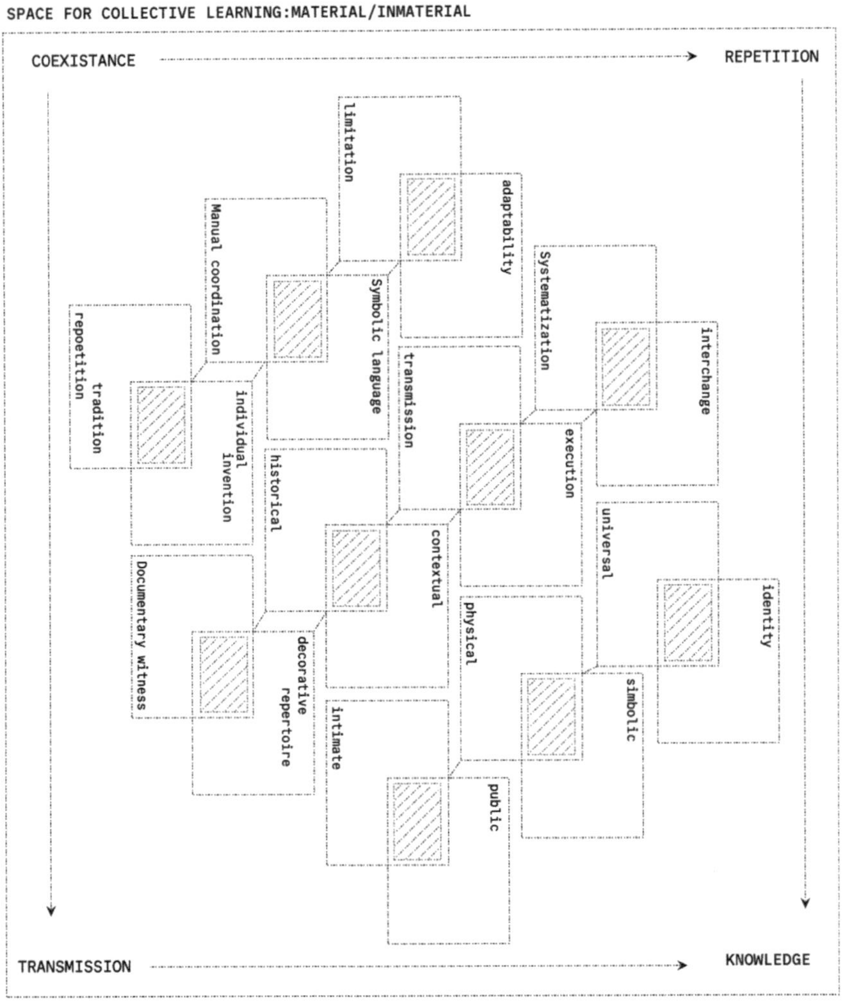

Figure 34. Figure that describes the dualities established within the collective learning space of samplers.
Image by the author.

The space of coexistence and learning defined by the sampler is shaped by the union of dual realities, which serve as a connection not only to textile heritage but also to the cultural heritage of any community. The connections we can observe include, on one hand, the link between the repetition of tradition and individual invention, where the anonymous criteria of a community converge with the personal discernment of the embroiderer. This fosters critical thinking through community integration. Additionally, there is the union between manual coordination and symbolic language, which feeds narratives and connects us with the history of a place. The implicit movements reinforce this constitutive narrative thread, fostering a creative environment where artifacts are produced through collective symbolic abstraction. Another key characteristic of the space of coexistence created by samplers is the constant limitation, particularly the size of the fabric, which enhances the adaptability of the learner. Among the most important dualities is the relationship between transmission and execution, with the latter being the process that materializes the accumulated knowledge of the community.

Samplers also strengthen cultural diversity through the systematization of codes that enable exchange. They are constructed within the universal context of the act of embroidering, allowing them to narrate the identity roots of each community through the continuous union between the physical and the symbolic, the intimate and the political, depending on the space and intention of the embroiderer. Finally, samplers act as historical documents situated within a specific context, reflecting decorative movements that tell the story of the community through their narrative capacity.

Conclusion

This article does not aim to be utopian by proposing a literal return to the productive context of the sampler. On the contrary, it suggests revisiting the intangible aspects surrounding this moment of learning and transmitting popular knowledge, with the goal of strengthening the deteriorated links that are currently evident between academia, industry, and artisanal practice.

The misinterpretation and misunderstanding of the latter in particular, often exploited in false advertising slogans and stripped of the complete patrimonial makeup that defines it (both material and immaterial), undoubtedly serve as a source of production for textile pieces that fail to embody rootedness or responsible industrial practices. As a result, the market—and therefore society—continues to be flooded with empty objects that do not foster any kind of collective connection, other than the one that unifies us in haste, detachment, and irresponsibility.

Creating new spaces that reinforce collective textile knowledge and transmit it—not only among industry professionals but also among the users of products and artifacts—is undoubtedly a way to rebuild societies rooted in their traditions. This can be achieved through the connection with fabric: the material that composes it, the technique used, and the symbolic codes from which the final piece is designed and produced.

References

Aguirre, J. M. (2024–2025). Artesanía, industria y una deuda pertinaz [Craftsmanship, industry, and a persistent debt]. *Cuaderno 237 / Centro de Estudios en Diseño y Comunicación* (237), 17–26.

Ávila, A., Flores, M., & Gámez, A. P. (2023). *In octacatl, in machiyotl: Dechados de virtud y entereza* [In octacatl, in machiyotl: Exemplars of virtue and fortitude]. Fundación Alfredo Harp Helú Oaxaca.

Cattan Lavin, M. (2019). Artesanía. Repensando "lo tradicional" y la relación Artesanía/Diseño [Craftsmanship: Rethinking "the traditional" and the craftsmanship/design relationship]. *RChD: Creación Y Pensamiento, 4*(7). https://doi.org/10.5354/0719-837X.2019.55285

Choay, F. (2007). *Alegoría del patrimonio* [Allegory of heritage]. Gustavo Gili.

González Mena, M. A. (1994). *Manual de la colección pedagógica textil* [Handbook of the textile pedagogical collection]. Editorial Complutense.

González-Varas, I. (2015). *Patrimonio cultural: Conceptos, debates y problemas* [Cultural heritage: Concepts, debates, and issues]. Cátedra.

Munari, B. (2016). *¿Cómo nacen los objetos?: Apuntes para una metodología proyectual* [How are objects born?: Notes for a design methodology]. Gustavo Gili.

Revista Digital do LAV. (2019). Arte y cultura: Un análisis desde la diversidad cultural [Art and culture: An analysis from the perspective of cultural diversity]. *Revista Digital do LAV, 12*(1), 38–54. https://doi.org/10.5902/1983734837114

Santamarina, B. (2005). *La memoria construida: Patrimonio cultural y modernidad* [Constructed memory: Cultural heritage and modernity]. Tirant lo Blanch.

Weil, S. (2014). *Echar raíces* [Putting down roots] (2nd ed.). Editorial Trotta.

CHAPTER 23

Handweaving Fashion

*Lala de Dios**

ABSTRACT
This paper aims to highlight the importance of the choice of *materials* and *weaves* in fabrics intended for the production of clothing, or fashion accessories. As Anni Albers already observed, it is the interrelation between these two elements, highlighting, canceling, or modifying each other which constitutes the essence of any fabric. Examples will be presented based on the interaction of the properties inherent to the fibers themselves, the structure of the yarns created from these fibers, and that of the weaves used to construct the fabrics

However, the different finishes applied to the constructed textile are another important factor capable of modifying not only the appearance and aesthetics of the textile but also its performance. Wet finishing for example can create very powerful textures on the surface of the fabric depending on the fibers shrinkage/felting coefficient, the amount of twist in the yarns, the spacing of the warp and/or weft ... The final result will allow the garment to act as a container for the body, like an external shell, or to mold and stick to it like a second skin. Main game changing designers and weavers in the field will be recognized.

Keywords: finishes, handweaving, material, twist, structure, yarn

The forerunners: highlighting the importance of woven fabrics in fashion

In 1984, Junichi Arai (Japan, 1932–2017) and Reiko Sudo (Japan, 1953) founded *Nuno Corporation*, a company that, with a deep knowledge and respect for artisanal textile techniques as their starting point, quickly became a leader in technological innovation in textiles by experimenting with materials, techniques, and finishes and collaborating with industry. Their collaborations with Miyake and other Japanese fashion designers had the effect of having their fabrics exhibited in modern art museums such as the MoMA in New York. Their example contributed to changing the approach and aesthetics of fabric production, which in the following years focused on obtaining reliefs and textures by mixing traditional fibers with the new materials resulting from technological innovation. The contrast with the impeccably flat fabrics made with the classic noble fibers that dominated the market until that time was astounding.

* Independent researcher.

While Arai and Sudo can rightly be described as game changers in the field of textile and fashion design at large, the importance that the research carried out by figures such as Ann Richards (UK, 1949) and Lotte Dalgaard (Denmark, 1944) has had for handweavers cannot be overlooked. Both are weavers, teachers, and authors that study, from the point of view of handweaving practice, what can be gained from designing with a deep understanding of the properties of fibers, yarns, and textile structures and their different reactions to different finishes, most especially of the effects of wet finishing on high-twist yarns. In 2012 they both published their first books. Dalgaard's book *Magical Materials to Weave. Blending Traditional & Innovative Yarns* (Dalgaard, 2012) was based primarily on the use of innovative industrial yarns, especially high-twist yarns which were traditionally not available to artisan weavers but which she could easily obtain through an association that she and other Danish weavers had founded precisely for that purpose (with the help of the Danish government). Her collaborations with fashion designers such as Elisabeth Hagen and Ann Schmidt-Christensen allow her to react quickly, adapting materials and techniques to obtain the effects desired by the designers.

Ann Richards' first book had the revealing title *Weaving Textiles that Shape Themselves* (Richards, 2012). Trained and worked as a biologist before going on to study woven textiles, this earlier background in biology remains an important influence on her work, since she often draws upon form and function in nature as a source of ideas. The history of textiles and techniques used in antiquity has also been a source of inspiration and has guided her research on, for example, the methods used in ancient Egypt to weave finely pleated linen fabrics.

Both experts will coincide again in 2021 with the publication of their second works *Weaving. Structure and Substance* (Richards, 2021) and *Thread Magic. Weaving for Shape and Texture* cowritten by Lotte Dalgaard and Pauline Adam (Dalgaard & Adam, 2021) and translated into English by Richards herself.

Fabric shaping for garments

The idea of loom-to-body garments can be approached in a variety of ways and is not new. The Romans wove semicircular togas on their warp-weighted looms and a technique that required weaving overlapping layers of fabric has been used from the seventeenth to the twentieth century to produce seamless shirts that came off the loom fully finished and ready to wear. However, the construction of shaped pieces of cloth is well known in knitting but not so much in woven textiles in spite of its usefulness to reduce waste.

Many of the methods I will discuss in this paper will alter the location of threads inside the piece of fabric while this will still retain their rectangular shape. However shaping the piece of fabric itself is possible by a combination of materials, structures, and finishings. According to Ann Richards in *Weaving. Structure and Substance*:

> Such shaping on the loom relies on the ability of some yarns, structures, or combinations of the two to shrink more than other parts of the cloth. Varying the shrinkage in only one direction, either warp or weft, will give simple flared, waisted or bulging shapes, while varying the shrinkage in both warp and weft allows for greater complexity of form. (Richards, 2021, p. 139)

This paper will describe a series of factors relating to materials, structure, and finishes that break up the grid, the orderly interlacing of warp and weft inherent to loom weaving, creating an appearance of movement and chaos that can ultimately affect the shape of the piece of fabric itself. This fabric shaping can be achieved by combining the amount and direction of twist applied to the fibers in the spinning process, playing with the different shrinkage coefficients of the materials used, using weave structures such as double weave, or the combination of opposite weaves. An example could be the creation of pleated fabrics by alternating narrow vertical stripes of 1/3 and 3/1 twills. By playing with the thickness of the weft, changes are produced in the width of the piece of fabric. The finer the weft, the narrower the piece of fabric, and the thicker the weft, the wider the piece. Obviously, all these techniques can be combined with each other.

Material and structure

All the designers and experts mentioned above share the approach of *designing through making, already* championed by Anni Albers when in 1946 she wrote in her article *Constructed Textiles:* "A design on paper cannot take into account the fine surprises of a material and make imaginative use of them." (Albers, 2000, p. 31)

Color and pattern are probably what most attracts attention in a fabric at first glance. But beneath these obvious features, a fabric needs to have textures and tactile properties that go beyond mere texture and hold everything together... fabrics need to have substance. These are aspects that are often not given much attention, although all weavers know that they are essential for the fabric to fulfill the function for which it has been designed and made. The weave structure, that is the way the warp and weft interlace, has great importance and effects in the design of a fabric, but it is only a plan that specifies how the threads will move, be it drawn on paper, or on a computer screen. Just by itself it does not define nor show what the weave will look like nor how the real fabric will behave because the selection of fiber, yarn structure, warp density, scale, and finishes can create many different results. Peter Collingwood (UK, 1922–2008) stated in his work *Textile and Weaving Structures* that structure and material are equally important and the interaction between them is a fascinating study as sometimes the material is the dominant factor and other times it is the structure (Collingwood, 1987).

In this interaction between the chosen materials and fabric structure the main factors that must be taken into account are:

- The properties of the *textile fibers*, especially their tensile and abrasion resistance, their elasticity, shrinkage coefficient, and their capacity to felt.
- The structure of the *yarns*, both the direction of the twist and, above all, the amount of twist applied to the fibers to form the thread. If the twist is too high, the threads will be unstable and if wet will tend to shrink and move on the surface of the fabric, causing texture effects to appear (crepe fabrics).
- The *structure* of the fabric, fundamentally the weave used, the sett of the warp (number of threads per centimeter), and that of the weft (number of picks per centimeter).
- *Finishes*, especially hot washing and fulling.

Fibers and yarns

When it comes to materials, most weavers tend to equate the basic properties of fibers and the yarns made from those fibers, but while this is generally true, it is worth considering the effect that different spinning production methods and possible fabric finishes can have on the basic characteristics of textile fibers that are three: strength, flexibility, and toughness. Toughness being the ability of a material to absorb, or accumulate, deformation energy without breaking.

If we compare the four most commonly used natural fibers in industry, we see that linen is strong, stiff, and has low toughness; wool is not strong, but very flexible and has moderate toughness; cotton is moderately strong and flexible as is silk, but this fiber is extremely tough while cotton is not.

There are two categories of fibers: long, continuous filaments that do not need to be spun, and *staples,* short fibers that need to be spun together to give them strength and resistance by twisting. Silk is the only natural fiber in filament form and does not need to be spun, although it is common to add a little twist to increase its strength. The rest of natural fibers are short and must be spun, although there are some exceptions. Bast fibers are long enough that they do not need to be spun, and can be made into thread by tying or splicing fibers together, although this method (which the ancient Egyptians used for linen) is rarely used today and most bast fibers are spun.

All regenerated and synthetic fibers can be made into filaments, which is a cheaper process, although when the aim is to obtain yarn with properties similar to natural fibers, long fibers are cut and spun as short fibers.

There are two methods to prepare the fibers prior to spinning. Both have to do with the way the fibers are organized in parallel before spinning and result in combed yarns (smooth, strong, and shiny), or carded yarns (textured, soft, not very strong, and matte).

The structure of the yarn is a result of the method used in its manufacture and can modify the original properties of the fibers but there are two aspects of yarn construction that are common to all fibers and manufacturing methods: thickness and the amount and direction of twist.

The amount of twist produces by far the most interesting effects because it directly affects the physical properties of the yarn itself. Yarns with a very high twist are called crepe yarns and are very unstable, which makes them active yarns that produce wrinkles and deformations on the surface of the fabric. This begins to become evident as soon as the fabric is cut from the loom, but much more so when it gets wet because natural fibers swell when wet and this causes an even stronger reaction of the threads. The most used natural fibers are the softest: wool, cotton, and silk. Among the artificial fibers, the only suitable one is viscose; synthetic fibers barely swell when wet. The use of high-twist yarns will also result in a rougher feel to the fabric.

There are of course other types of yarns, such as elastic yarns to a greater or lesser degree, luminescent yarns, fluorescent yarns, soluble yarns... Also, metal yarns that have a long historical tradition of use in the manufacture of fabrics. In addition to wire yarns in different thicknesses and colors, we now have a wide variety of yarns made by plying together a textile yarn and a very fine metal wire, and there are also 100 % metal threads. These materials produce a crisp texture and, most interesting, they have *memory* for shapes keeping in place any textural effects such as folds and pleats.

The direction of the twist, represented by the letters S and Z, has no effect on the physical properties of yarns, but it does affect the resulting cloth because light is reflected differently depending on the direction of the yarns and this creates subtle shadow reflections on the fabric, a feature that can be used in its design.

The combination of high-twist yarns with the two directions—S and Z—in which yarns can be spun is very interesting: if warp and weft have the same direction an effect called *tracking* is produced, if they have opposite directions a wavy effect is produced.

Fabric structure

One of the aspects directly related to the structure of the fabric is the calculation of the density of the warp and weft, which, as all weavers know, is crucial to the appearance and performance of the fabric. In addition, this allows us to play with and create variations in warp density, for example, in combinations that create vertical stripes of different densities (cramming and spacing), which will affect our perception of colors and texture. An extreme case would be to leave vertical gaps in the fabric, which, if combined with the use of a high-twist weft, can produce spectacular textures.

Another resource is the alternation of warps and/or wefts of different thicknesses, well known by artisan weavers who usually reserve them for strong and rigid fabrics such as carpets or table mats woven in warp rep (much used in Scandinavia from old times) but which can also be used with thinner and lighter materials with interesting results.

Generally, varying the density of the warp, or using thicker and thinner threads in the weft, does not require a second warp beam on the loom. This is absolutely necessary when the warp is made of two yarns with different fiber composition that in turn will have different degrees of elasticity, or when we wish to combine different tensions in the same warp. The classic example of this is the weave called *seersucker*, in which a number of threads are wound alternately on different warp beams with different tensions. This produces a fabric with completely flat vertical stripes on those parts of the warp wound at higher tension, alternating with vertical stripes showing a crinkled texture formed where the warp is wound.

As regards the influence of the weave selected, that is, the way in which the warp and weft are interwoven, even the most common structures like plain, twill, or satin can be altered beyond recognition by introducing variations in the materials, density, or finishes applied to the cloth. There are also weaves whose very structure favors the obtaining of textures that increase the elasticity of the fabrics and therefore their capacity to adapt to the body. Gauzes, spot and lace weaves, float weaves, waffle, Brighton honeycombs. deflected double weave, and double and triple weaves are all handy tools for the handweaver.

The *technology* of manipulating textile fibers discovered in the Paleolithic era, when our hunter-gatherer ancestors wove containers, mats and rudimentary roofs using rigid or semi-rigid fibers and learned to make rope and twist and braid short fibers to form a long thread—what archaeologist and linguist Elizabeth Barber calls the *String Revolution*—is a continuum that goes to this day, a construction in which each new step builds on previous know-how, applying the latest technical and scientific advances. Despite the relentless flow of technological developments to produce more and more quickly and easily, the basic concepts that gave rise to the Neolithic inventions of spinning and weaving have remained unchanged over the centuries, until the *Industrial Revolution*, when manual processes were gradually replaced by mechanized spinning and weaving machines. Not forgetting that the *binary code* is found in the graphic representation of weaving structures, it was already applied to store information in the Jacquard loom (created in 1801–1804) and has become the means by which humans interact with machines. The development of textile technology has been a driver of innovation and reflects the evolution of human thought and the use of tools. Perhaps one of the most distinctive features of our time is the natural assumption of transversality between disciplines and knowledge embodied in the collaboration of designers such as Prada, Issey Miyake, Iris van Herpen and many others with artisans, engineers and scientists to push the boundaries of fibers and processes.

Conclusion

I believe it to be perfectly fair to end this paper with a quote from Ann Richards' *Weaving. Structure and Substance.* It is a great piece of advice for designer-handweavers:

> When designing, it is important to keep a balance between purposeful planning and a flexible attitude that can take advantage of any interesting, unplanned results that arise from the interplay of structure and material. Some of this back-talk may be both unexpected and unwanted, but it is wise to be cautious about rejecting such results as failures, since an undesired effect in one context may be successful in another—all results provide information. (Richards, 2021, p. 151).

References

Albers, A. (2000). *Selected writings on design*. Wesleyan University Press.

Collingwood, P. (1987). *Textile and weaving structures*. Batsford.

Dalgaard, L. (2012). *Magical materials to weave: Blending traditional & innovative yarns*. Trafalgar Square Books.

Dalgaard, L., & Adam, P. (2021). *Thread magic: Weaving for shape and texture*. Forlaget Mellemvaerk.

Richards, A. (2012). *Weaving textiles that shape themselves*. The Crowood Press.

Richards, A. (2021). *Weaving: Structure and substance*. The Crowood Press.

CHAPTER 24

A Story of Tradition

Spanish craftsmanship at Dior's cruise collection 2023 fashion show in Seville

*Paula Alegría Serrano Padilla**

ABSTRACT
Craftsmanship and design have gone hand in hand since their beginnings, resulting in fabulous creations in all fields of art. Many fashion designers today have chosen to delve into the roots of local crafts in order to rescue endangered processes and incorporate them into the creative fabric of their products. This paper analyzes a case of collaboration between the house of Dior and Spanish artisans; specifically, in the process of elaboration of the manila shawl of Ángeles Espinar. It is clear in this work the magnificent potential that the joint work between artisans and designers has not only in the final product, but also in the relevance, conservation and dissemination of local art, which otherwise would be destined to be lost in oblivion.

Keywords: Dior, craftsmanship, design, artisans

Craftsmanship, heritage of a tradition in danger of disappearing

To speak of crafts is to speak of history, and preserving it is a major challenge today. Today, many artisans fear for their craft because they cannot find the generational relay they need to pass on their legacy. UNESCO defines the cultural expressions of a given population or social group as "a form of expression of creativity that has Intangible Cultural Heritage (ICH) value" (UNESCO 2003, p.3). This characteristic feature of oral transmission of the craft makes it vulnerable and can often lead to its extinction when there is no relay. Amaya-Tellez points out that:

> This intangible cultural heritage, which is transmitted from generation to generation, is constantly recreated by communities and groups according to their environment, their interaction with nature and their history, infusing them with a sense of identity and continuity and thus helping to promote respect for cultural diversity and human creativity. Therefore, the work of the artisan is characterized

* Universidad Politécnica de Madrid.

> by rigor in execution and by the knowledge of the techniques of a trade, mastering them to perfection. (Amaya-Tellez 2015, p. 187)

At this point, it is worth asking ourselves: Is it possible that the figure of the designer allied with the artisan, is the answer to revive craftsmanship? Perhaps the products offered by some artisans are not demanded by today's society? Should we adapt craftsmanship to products that are more attractive to the final consumer?

To address this issue in greater depth and rigor, an analysis of the Dior fashion show in Seville in the year 2023, in which designers and artisans have worked hand in hand, is carried out.

Brief history of the house of Dior and Maria Grazia Chiuri's cruise shows

Since its founding by the young Christian Dior in 1946, the Dior house has had different designers. Each of them has reinterpreted in his own way the way of understanding the values of the Maison. Thus, some of the designers who have gone through this house are Yves Saint Lauren, Ralf Simon, or John Galliano, among the most prominent. Until February 2025, Maria Grazia has been at the helm of the firm, the first woman to take the reins of the house. The designer, who had previously been co-creative director of Valentino, has been studying embroidery and lace for more than 30 years.

Since she started as the Maison's designer in 2016, she has been cementing her idea of using local craftsmanship and resources from the cities where she does cruise shows. Other cities in which the designer has inspired her fashion shows are Marrakech, Chantilly, or Athens, thus trying to contextualize the craftsmanship taking into account the locations and cultures that make them possible (Rosellini, 2024). The fact that the crafts are rooted in a place significantly enriches the value of the designs. Maria Grazia is aware of this reality and that is why she decides to move her fashion shows to the cities of inspiration for the development and creation of the garments of the collection in question.

One of her stops has been in Seville. This parade has been the result of more than a year of work of the Dior house with different artisans in the area. There are 15 Spanish artisans or designers with whom the firm has worked to carry out the parade. According to the designer, she believed that it was time to pay tribute to the artisans of this country with so much wealth.

The Christian Dior fashion show in Seville

The fashion show took place in the Plaza de España in Seville, designed by the architect Aníbal González. It was one of the constructions made for the Ibero-American Exhibition of 1929. The parade was inspired by the dancer Carmen Amaya, known for being a revolutionary in her time and dancing with pants. Other inspirations of the fashion show are bullfighting or the religious tradition of our country: the virgins or the Holy Week.

The parade was composed of 110 looks that reinterpreted our culture. Some of them were made directly by local artisans, using their traditional techniques.

One of the most outstanding features of this fashion show is the collaboration between artisans and designers. Is it necessary to reinterpret certain crafts to make them respond to the new society? Is it perhaps the solution for craftsmanship to work with designers?

The figure of the artisan in this fashion show transcends the traditional concept of artisan, since his work goes beyond the mere manual elaboration of a product; he is part of the creative process together with the designer (Rosellini, 2024).

In this paper we analyze two of the 15 cases of collaboration between the house of Dior and Spanish artisans.

Case study: the Manila shawl by Ángeles Espinar for Dior

The Manila shawl is an article associated with Spanish culture since the seventeenth century. It arrived in our country from Canton, China, from the route of the Manila Galleon, which gave its name to this accessory, although over the years it has undergone a great evolution (Muñoz-Cárdenas & Díaz-Caro, 2024). According to Santamaría (2021), merchants bought these shawls from merchants in China, where the manufacturing process of this product was carried out, to use them for decorative purposes. Once they arrived in Seville, the bangs were added to the shawls and they were used for clothing rather than decorative purposes. Since then, the shawl has been a very valuable accessory for our society. Pérez-Galdós himself, in his novel Fortunata y Jacinta, spoke of this wonderful product:

> The Manila shawl, at the same time stately and popular, for it has been carried on the shoulders of the great lady and the gypsy. Wrapping oneself in it is like wearing a painting. Modern industry will not invent anything to equal the naive poetry of the shawl, splashed with flowers, supple, catchy, and matte, with that fringe that has something of the tangles of sleep and that brilliance of color that illuminated the crowds in the times when its use was general. (Pérez-Galdós, 1887)

The craftswoman chosen by the house to carry out this commission was Ángeles Espinar, a famous craftswoman recognized for her specialized work in shawls. There have been numerous collaborations with different designers in the national sphere, until this year the firm Dior noticed her work and made the leap to international level. Ángeles Espinar is one of the few artisans left in our country that preserves the traditional techniques of the shawl. She learned the craft from her mother, who in turn inherited the trade from her mother, making Ángeles the third generation in her family dedicated to embroidering shawls.

> My mother detected that most of the shawls that were being made did not use traditional techniques. Most of them were made in an industrial or semi-industrial way. My mother decided to preserve the forms of tailoring inherited from my grandmother, and we continue to do so. Our shawls are made as they were made in the old days. (Personal interview with María Ángeles Espinar)

Shawl design process. Collaboration with Pietro Ruffo

In order to know in depth what the design process has been, we asked Ángeles Espinar what material was provided by the Dior house as a guideline to create the shawl. She tells us that they provided her with a drawing that should be the guide to make that shawl. This drawing was created by the artist Pietro Ruffo, an architect based in Italy who has collaborated on numerous occasions in the design process of Maria Grazia. On the occasion of this work, we managed to have a personal interview through Zoom with Pietro Ruffo to explain the process of creating the shawl and his way of working with Maria Grazia.

Pietro Ruffo met Maria Grazia at the Academy in Rome. From here they felt a great synergy and today, much of Pietro Ruffo's work as an artist is to generate the visual universe of Dior for Maria Grazia.

Among some of Pietro Ruffo's most recurrent participations in Dior is all the design of drawings, both for prints of some of the garments and for the whole graphic universe of the Maison's perfumes.

Although this is the most important part of his relationship with Dior, he also works for the house creating "working drawings," as he calls them, to help some of the house's collaborators in their work.

In the interview, we asked him what his way of working with Maria Grazia is:

> Our way of working [Maria Grazia and Pietro Ruffo] is already practically only spoken. I don't need her to give me drawings. We just meet, have a conversation and we understand each other [...] All the drawings are always inspired by the original imaginary of Christian Dior himself, and we always keep that in mind when creating any drawing. (Personal interview with Pietro Ruffo)

We know that flowers are linked to the firm since the origins of its foundation. Le Rumbs, in Granville (France), was the house where Christian Dior grew up. In this village, part of his mother's passion was the cultivation of flowers, a taste that the designer inherited and that accompanied him throughout his career. Part of his floral imaginary are the varieties grown in other villas he acquired throughout his life, such as Le Moulin du Coudret in Milly-la-Forêt or his latest acquisition, Colle Noire in Provence. Some of the flowers that characterize the ideology of Dior's botanical garden are jasmine, wisteria, mimosas, and roses, the latter being one of the most characteristic species of the Maison.

Another lesser-known fact is his passion for Vilmorin-Andrieux catalogs. A series of gardening and horticultural magazines of the time that Christian Dior had at home, and whose covers served as inspiration for numerous drawings of his fabrics.

Analysis of the shawl

The order consisted of making two manila shawls. Both with the same drawing but with different colors.

We spoke with the author of the shawl, Ángeles Espinar. We asked her about the characteristic shape of the shawl, which we do not associate with the shawl tradition.

> It is a shawl in the shape of a toquilla or theater exit. It is an adaptation of the Victorian toquillas of the nineteenth century. It is not the most common but when Maria Grazia came to the workshop she noticed one we had in the workshop with this shape and liked it very much. They decided to adapt the drawing

> they had given us as a premise to follow this shape. (Personal interview with María Ángeles Espinar)

The base of the shawl is black, as is the fringe that surrounds the entire toquilla (see Figure 35). "The fabric was provided by the house of Dior. It is a black silk selected by the house itself." (Personal interview with María Ángeles Espinar).

The fringe is long and has a short lattice with a normal type knot. The length of the fringe is about 45 or 50 cm. We can observe a "false symmetry" in the drawing of the embroidery. The lateral elements are very similar without being the same. In the center we find a central motif that has the protagonism of the embroidery.

In the center of the shawl, we find a white sign that waves with the name of the house of Dior and a gold-colored sailor's cord that is intertwined in the sign. The sign is understood as a motif that is related to those traditionally used in Manila shawls. In this case, the Dior house wanted to mark its name as an innovative element within the tradition of shawls. The golden cord is associated with shawls of European origin. Thus, being an uncommon element in shawls, we can associate it to a type of traditional shawl, although not very abundant in the history of shawls. We asked Ángeles Espinar about the central motif, and the sign with the name of the house. Around this central and main motif, we find other elements that grow from this main one. The motifs used are flowers, birds, and butterflies, characteristic elements of Manila shawls. Next, we analyze each of the elements found and their relationship or dissociation with the traditional. The butterflies that we found respond to a motif and a way of understanding them in the content of the traditional shawl. We found two butterflies at the ends of the shawl forming a symmetry. These butterflies are in profile, showing only one of their wings. In the interior of the piece, we see some of smaller size and plan views.

Another of the motifs that we find in the piece and that are related to the butterflies are the dragonflies. These motifs are also associated with traditional shawls (see Figure 36). "Butterflies are very common elements in all shawls, as are dragonflies and birds." (Personal interview with María Ángeles Espinar). Butterflies and dragonflies are traditional elements of shawls since their Chinese origins in embroideries made in the city of Canton. Due to their good acceptance by European society, these traditional motifs were well received by other cultures.

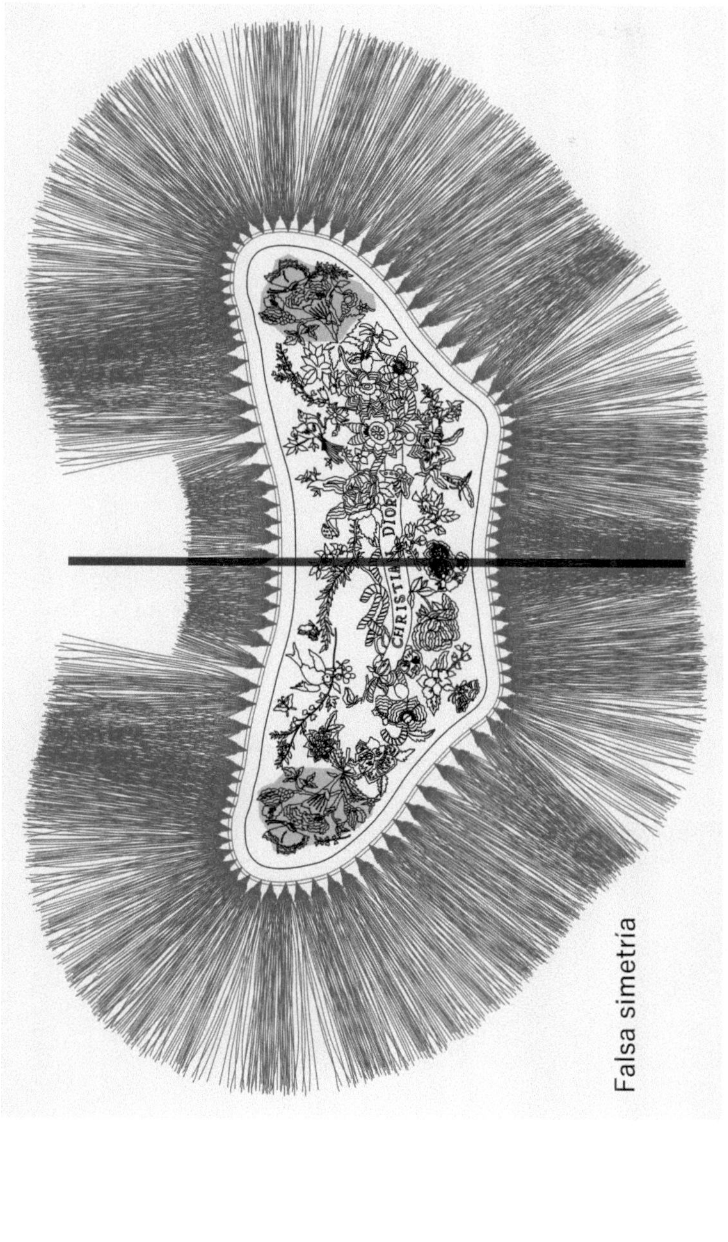

Figure 35. Drawing that depicts the shape of the shawl, the proportion of the fringe and the false symmetry in the embroidery drawing.
Image by the author.

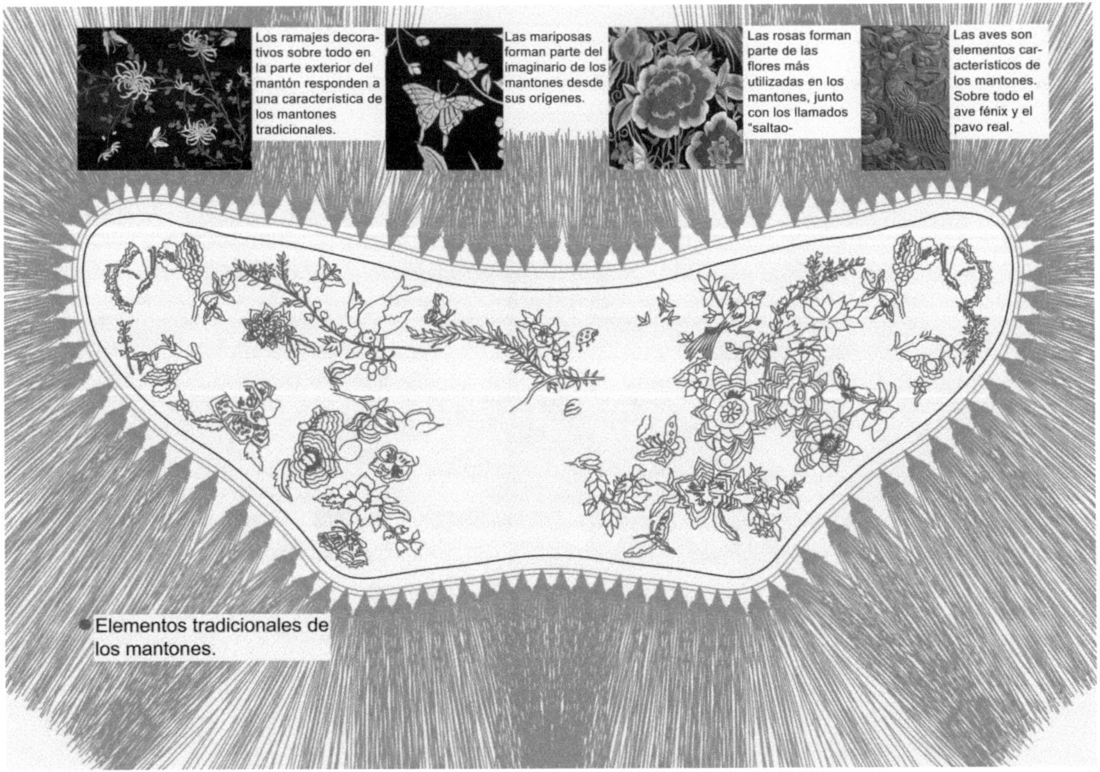

Figure 36. Image that marks the elements of the shawl associated with traditional Manila shawl motifs. *Image by the author.*

The most abundant motifs in this shawl are the floral ones. These motifs have been very characteristic of shawls since their origins. However, they are especially characteristic of traditional Andalusian shawls.

> All the flowers that are embroidered on the shawl belong to what they call *The botanical garden* which is the universe that has enveloped the entire collection. The selected flowers were present throughout the show. From the looks to the scenography, made with a large collection of red carnations. This whole floral universe that they call *Botanical Garden* has been drawn by Pietro, an artist who is a regular collaborator of the firm and author of the first preliminary drawings that gave us as a starting point for the shawl. (Personal interview with María Ángeles Espinar)

After the interview with Pietro Ruffo, we have been able to know first-hand what are the characteristic motifs of the imaginary of the Dior house from which they design all the iconography: certain similarities with the Vilmorin-Andrieux catalogs are observed. On the other hand, although dragonflies are part of the characteristic iconography of the shawls, they are also part of Dior's visual universe. As the central and most characteristic element of the shawl, we spoke with Ángeles Espinar about the central sign of the shawl and the cord that surrounds it (see Figure 37).

> We could say that the sign that puts Christian Dior and the cord that surrounds it are the most original part of the shawl. It does not respond to any element of the tradition of shawls, although it has always been something characteristic of shawls to customize them to the client's taste. That is why, despite the fact that there are characteristic and traditional motifs in our trade, you can find shawls with very diverse motifs. (Personal interview with María Ángeles Espinar)

The shawl analyzed in this article was versioned in two other shawls with different colorimetry, but with the same design.

Techniques used for the execution of the shawl

In the interview with María Ángeles Espinar, we also asked her about the execution of the embroidery and the techniques used.

> The same stitch has always been used. Type of stitch on top. If you want to know if a shawl is of quality, you have to see that the stitch on both sides is the same. There is no front and back in a good shawl. Machine-made shawls have a clear reverse. (Personal interview with María Ángeles Espinar)

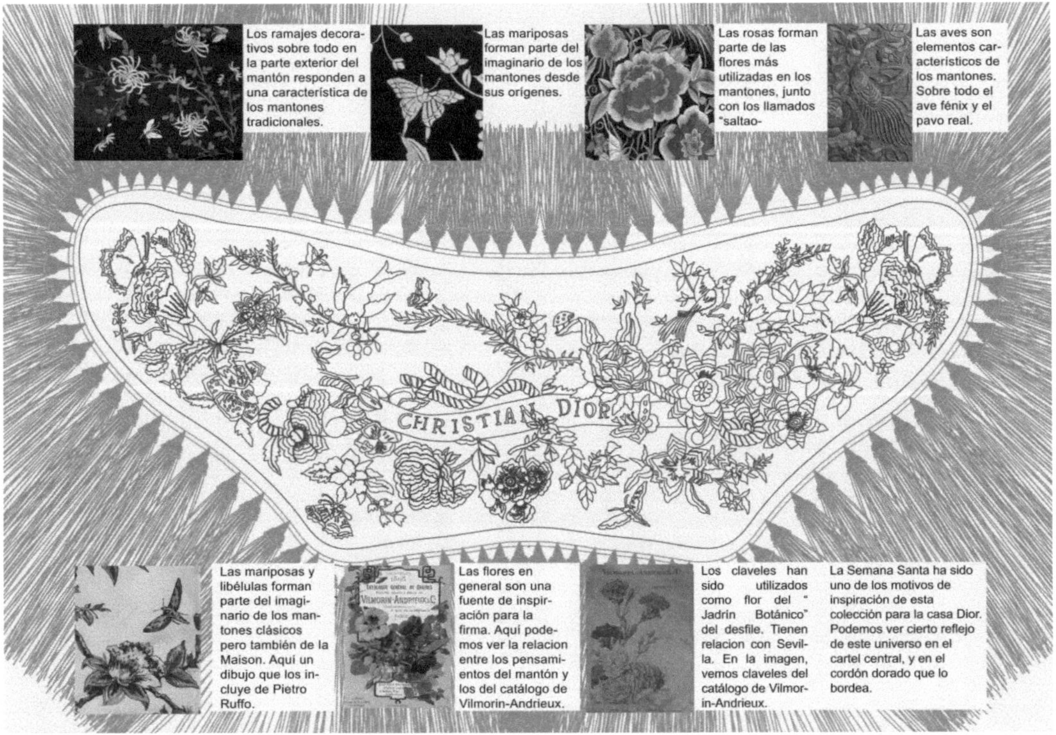

Figure 37. Image in which the traditional elements of the iconography of the shawls (in blue) and the most original or characteristic elements of the Dior house (in red) are compared.

Image by the author.

Ángeles Espinar's shawls are recognized nationally and internationally for their use of traditional techniques. She preserves the old ways of making shawls.

Conclusions

As a result of this work, the importance of preserving the handicrafts of different social groups is evident. Their conservation and economic support are essential for them to endure over time, since their role in cultural, economic, and socio-cultural development is decisive (Sandoval-Valle, 2021). This type of actions of great designers with artisans contribute positively to the dissemination and visibility of the work of artisans. Ángeles Espinar herself states that she has seen a considerable increase in the number of commissions from the Dior fashion show, especially at the international level.

Efforts to protect traditional craft techniques in modern design should be focused on respect for them not only with the aim of preserving craftsmanship for its rarity, beauty, or value, but also to encourage artisans to continue their work and to transmit their knowledge to young artisans in each community, who will be the ones who in the future can take over the baton of craftsmanship and must know how to make it coexist with the increasingly complex framework of today's design market (Amaya-Tellez, 2015).

As a complementary line of research, to explore this topic in greater depth, one could analyze other creators, such as the drawings of María Ángeles Vila Tortosa, among other artists.

References

Amaya-Téllez, H. (2015). Diseño y artesanía, un matrimonio con condiciones [Design and craftsmanship: A marriage with conditions]. *Actas de Diseño, 18*, 186–9.

Muñoz-Cárdenas, M., & Díaz-Caro, L. (2024). La cultura artesana y popular del mantón de Manila [The artisanal and popular culture of the Manila shawl]. *Centro de Estudios en Diseño y Comunicación, 235*, 109–29.

Pérez-Galdós, B. (1887). *Fortunata y Jacinta* [Fortunata and Jacinta]. Austral.
Rosellini, F. (2024). Proceso de diseño y artesanía [Design process and craftsmanship]. *Centro de Estudios en Diseño y Comunicación*, *237*, 49–58.
UNESCO. (2003). *Convención para la salvaguardia del patrimonio cultural inmaterial* [Convention for the Safeguarding of the Intangible Cultural Heritage]. Paris.

CHAPTER 25

Artists in the Design of Traditional Scarves for Louis Vuitton

*Sandra Barreiro Parguiña**

ABSTRACT

In their quest to bring originality and freshness to their proposals, various luxury brands have favorably valued their collaboration with artists with no previous experience in fashion. In the field of silk scarves, the imagination of the creatives has often been prioritized over the inconveniences that could arise in the translation of the work onto the textile surface.

Louis Vuitton is a firm recognized for its immersion in contemporary art and collaborations with artists over the last few decades, inviting various figures since the late 1980s to design its scarves.

Through the *LV Art Silk Squares* edition, five creative talents reinterpret the flower of the house's monogram through a limited edition of silk squares. These bring their own creative universe to each proposal, using digital and analog tools, as well as the combination of both media, exploring the intersections between craftsmanship and innovation.

Through this study, in the context of the turn of the millennium, we will see the contribution of the different styles and techniques used, in combination with the firm's artisanal approach.

Keywords: art, fashion, design, luxury, partnership, scarves

Introduction

When a Louis Vuitton accessory is mentioned, the handbag immediately comes to mind as its most representative element. Within this firm with a long artisanal tradition linked to the production of trunks and all kinds of luggage, the handbag has become a cult accessory, "the main attraction" (Thomas, 2008, p. 189), particularly in recent decades, whose graphics have been reinterpreted through different figures in the artistic scene, such as Yayoi Kusama or Takashi Murakami.

For this study, we propose to explore the scarf, another accessory involved in this *artification* [a term coined by Shapiro and Heinich (2012), used to refer to those products that, in a certain context, transcend their functionality and

* Universidade de Vigo.
(ORCID: https://orcid.org/0009-0002-6679-9137)

are elevated to an artistic status]. For years, the firm only marketed a simple brown square of fabric adorned with the monogram that harmonized with the design of its luggage; however, it was precisely its first edition of scarves entitled *The Silk Road,* which marked the beginning of a prolific activity in projects linked to contemporary art (Baseman et al., 1989, p. 18).

In his thesis, Yuli Bai identifies three periods of maximum activity in the relationship between art and fashion houses: surrealism in the 1920s, pop art in the 1960s, and the period after 1990 (2010, p. 12). Louis Vuitton has been in tune with the artistic aesthetics and movements of its time, although it was not until the last years of the twentieth century that these approaches to the artistic scene intensified (Gasparina, 2021, p. 44), a period in which several important changes took place within the firm, such as its acquisition by the leading luxury group chaired by Bernard Arnault.

Launched in 2024, the *LV Art series* is a limited edition of five silk squares that reflect today's design possibilities, in which the French firm has chosen to collaborate with artists whose technical approach ranges from the exclusively analog to the purely digital and the convergence of both modalities.

For the methodology and implementation of this study, the five collectives and artists participating in the collaboration were formally contacted and invited to participate in an interview. Of these, the German artist group eBoy (2024c), consisting of Kai Vermehr, Steffen Sauerteig and Svend Smital, and the Swiss artist Thomas Ott (2024b) accepted.

Louis Vuitton's collaborations with artists for scarf design

Sometimes, the foulard is used as a support for the guest artist's work, reproducing an existing work, and in other cases, we see how the creative reinterprets with his or her style a narrative concept, visual story, or emblematic object of the brand, as we discussed in a previous publication (2024a), where we explored the different creative figures involved in the creation of scarves for the case studies of the firms Hermès and Louis Vuitton. Regarding partnerships with external artists, we also find different typologies in the number of talents brought together in the same collaboration; the role in terms of whether it is the main accessory or, if it is one more within the products of a certain collection and whether it corresponds to a limited edition.

In Table 7, we collect those collaborations between Louis Vuitton and one or more guest designers that have resulted in the creation of some type of scarf. These include both editions focused exclusively on the accessory, as well as partnerships in which scarves have been produced together with other elements such as bags or leather goods.

The firm is interested in contemporary artists who are at the peak of their career or who have accumulated a certain recognition or prestige (Palmitessa, 2012, p. 12), such as Kusama or Murakami, a strategy widely analyzed by different authors such as Masè and Cedrola (2017). Although they can also surround themselves with a groundbreaking and experimental profile that Louis Vuitton finds in tune with the creative universe it advocates, in order to generate exclusivity and appeal to its younger audience, such as the collaboration with Stephen Sprouse. In fact, as Joy and Belk admit, "Sprouse was by any measure far from a safe choice as a collaborator for a luxury brand conglomerate" (2021, p. 315).

Wert Ortega, referring to all manifestations of street art, admits that they contain "a subversive, even challenging approach to the bourgeois order or the urban system" (2013, p. 53). Louis Vuitton likes this irreverence. His style plays on a constant contradiction between the traditional and the contemporary. He partners with street art and pop culture artists in order to connect with a younger audience, as we also see in the *Artist Scarves Street Art* editions of 2023 and 2024. In the words of Palmitessa, "Louis Vuitton has to be avant-garde in order to stay interesting, but at the same time be careful not to be too unconventional" (2012, p. 12).

In the *LV Art Silk Squares* series, launched in 2024, we see a collection whose focus is more on exploring the firm's possibilities in terms of its *savoir-faire* as artisans, than on collaborating with a transgressive or highly renowned artist.

Analysis of the LV Art Silk Squares series

All the artists in this edition previously collaborated with the French firm for another product, its *Travel Book*. In it, they invite different creatives to destinations unknown to them, with the aim of finding inspiration in the environment and expressing themselves through the format with illustrations. This concept, in tune with the universe of Louis Vuitton's *Art of travel*, is reminiscent of William Adjété Wilson's 1995 edition, who after a trip to

Arizona made a series of drawings that were captured in the form of silk squares (2024c).

This procedure of undertaking other projects prior to designing scarves is also common in other firms like Hermès, where many artists behind their iconic accessories explore other ideas. See, for example, Édouard Baribeaud, who created a *myriorama*, a card game that merges art and creativity, and worked as an illustrator for Hermès' Christmas campaign in 2016, as he expressed in a personal communication on March 14, 2022; also, Virginie Jamin, who designed a series of ashtrays prior to create intricate scarf designs for the brand (2023b).

When developing the format, the theme proposed by the Louis Vuitton team for the edition was the concept of the flower, understood as the four-petaled flower that forms part of its logo. We have two valuable contributions to the creative process: on the one hand, the eBoy collective, pixel artists, whose name already gives us a glimpse of a completely digital process; and on the other, the individual artist Thomas Ott, who uses the engraving technique through a dark and gloomy style.

Kai Vermehr from the eBoy collective admitted ironically during the interview that he no longer knew how to use his hand to work. Immersed in their digitalized artistic process, they use Photoshop as their main tool, and on more specific occasions they are accompanied by Blender or Sketch Up (2024d). Two of the members, Steffen Sauerteig and Svend Smital, work from Berlin while Vermehr resides in Los Angeles, a time difference of 9 hours that allows them to make the most of their projects. They work through a cloud platform that they feed, generating a library of components and from where they share their work dynamically. Their scarf design, *Maze Of Precious*, is a labyrinthine composition of geometric elements in isometric perspective, adorned with the company's logo in the form of flowers and clovers.

Ott's signature style was carried over into his piece titled *Urban Flowers*, developed using the technique of engraving on cardboard. During the interview (2024b), the artist expressed his surprise at the proposal of the French firm's team, as he stated that in his work he tries to "avoid elements such as flowers, sunbeams, and rainbows." For his project, he began by making a scientific drawing of a corpse from which flowers emerged, which he ended up reorienting into a more metaphorical and less realistic silhouette, as it was too sinister for the Louis Vuitton environment. When asked if he worked on any part of the process digitally, he only admitted to scanning the piece to intensify the contrast and correct the dust generated, but without changing anything with respect to the physical version. Ott delivered the project to the firm in digital format, keeping the original. An interesting fact, since unlike Louis Vuitton, other firms choose to keep the originals of their projects (Barreiro Parguiña, 2024a).

The interviewees were asked if Louis Vuitton had advised them on the composition of the format. In both cases, the answer indicated that they had complete creative freedom with several meetings aimed at exchanging impressions. Regarding the importance of the corners on the scarves, since it is the first area that is seen when it is worn by someone, Ott admitted that he naturally understood that if he left those spaces uncovered, it would detract from the interest of the design, so he continued to add details toward the edges and eBoy also reflected on this fact.

The Swiss artist took about three months to complete the design, while the collective needed about five months before presenting it to the firm's team, who in turn took charge of organizing the production arrangements.

In the cases of Ott and eBoy, we see great flexibility on the part of Louis Vuitton and a considerable margin of time for the artists to carry out their projects, although less than in firms such as Hermès, whose artists of the carré dedicate about a year to their graphic development (2023a).

In addition to the creatives with whom we maintained dialogue, the rest of the proposals in the series were made by Lorenzo Mattotti, Nicolas De Crécy and the duo of Icinori illustrators, made up of Mayumi Otero and Raphaël Urwiller.

Nicolas De Crécy is an illustrator and comic artist with a poetic and surrealist style. For his *Parfums de Méditerranée* proposal, he created detailed floral imagery in honor of the firm's perfumery tradition. In an article by *Runway Magazine* (Topi, 2024), a gallery of images of the edition's creatives is shared, where we can see that De Crécy paints the elements by hand with watercolor, some of them made separately. Another photograph shows a large-scale illustration of the design, with marks associated with the printing process, suggesting a mastery of digital tools that he has been able to rely on at some stages of his creative process.

Like De Crécy, Lorenzo Mattotti is a renowned illustrator and artist whose work explores dreamlike themes. For his *Iris Spring*, hand-drawn using colored pencils and pastels, he paid homage to a flower that decorates the windows of the firm's workshop in Asnières. The Runway images show various sketches of the stages of the process of composing his scarf and a drawing of the original design in a smaller format.

Although we have not heard their review directly, it is likely that digital tools have also been used for some part of the post-production in the proposals of these more analog artists. However, those who create a symbiosis between both disciplines are Otero and Urwiller, authors of the *Malles Monde* design. Inspired by the iconic trunks of the firm, different types of flowers emerge from its elements, represented in their characteristic style accompanied by the logo (Yang Shuen, 2024). Urwiller, during an interview with *Editions La Manufacture*, admits that, although they develop many parts by hand, the computer allows them a certain margin of reflection, even if in the end everything ends up being managed using traditional painting techniques (2022).

When we refer to firms that value collaborating with artists who have no previous experience in fashion in the making of scarves, we go back to Ascher, a British supplier that was very active during the 1950s and 1970s, which collaborated with talents such as Picasso or Matisse. The artists invited to design foulards for Ascher had complete freedom to create the composition and use the colors they needed, since they would then be in charge of managing the technical issues. This would cause Zika some headaches with proposals such as Topolski's, whose expressive stroke was difficult to translate onto the textile surface (Hlaváčková, 2019, p. 71–2). Also, the creative team at Hermès prefers that their silk squares be approached from an artistic perspective rather than from the field of design, a fact that we have learned through the interview with Shirley (2023a). Mentioning Louis Vuitton's collaboration with Sprouse, Monica Titton notes that "the label 'artist' is more associated with prestige than the label 'designer'" (2014, p. 64). Again, in our case study, eBoy and Thomas Ott had no prior fashion training, Ott noted: "I think that's really the idea of Louis Vuitton […] Items that are not made by designers, but by artists, that have a totally different approach" (2024b).

Conclusion

What sets the *LV Silk Art Squares* apart from the rest of Louis Vuitton's collaborations in the field of scarves is its approach to a more classic proposal, focused on the firm's *savoir-faire*, more aligned with its more traditional public. Despite the difference in atmospheres of each creative, in which we see a graphic and urban proposal in the case of eBoy, another with more transgressive content in the case of Ott, and more classic proposals in the other editing partners.

We see that the factor of analog or digital development is irrelevant as long as they create a piece of interest, given that nowadays even the most traditional artists commonly rely on digital tools at some stage of the process. However, they do seem to take into account the artist's lack of experience in the foulard industry.

During the same time frame, for its Pre-Fall 2024 collection, Louis Vuitton launched a campaign with the artist, featuring pop-inspired designs adapted both to the products in its collection and on silk squares. Once again, an image aimed at a younger and more urban clientele. Reaffirming its position as a brand that aims to engage with the public without confining itself to specific labels.

Table 7. Collaborations with artists for scarves by Louis Vuitton

Artist	Edition	Year	Name of the scarf
Arman	*The Silk Road*	1988	*Le Monogramme du Peintre*
Baldaccini, Cesar	*The Silk Road*[(a)]	1988	*Impressions Mêlées*
Chia, Sandro	*The Silk Road*	1988	*Les Fantômes de Montalcino*
Isozaki, Arata	*The Silk Road*	1988	*Repères dans la Ville I & Repères dans la Ville II*
LeWitt, Sol	*The Silk Road*	1988	*Rainbow, Undertow, The Earth is Round*
Rosenquist, James	*The Silk Road*	1988	*The Garden of Orchids*
Aulenti, Gae	-	1988	*Le Temps du Voyage*
Raynaud, Jean-Pierre	-	1988	*Printemps et Automne*
ZPutman, Andrée	-	1990	*Chemin Faisant*
Starck, Phillippe	-	1991	*The Winners*
Wilson, William Adjété	*Arizona Tour*	1995	Various designs

(Continued)

Table 7. (*Continued*)

Artist	**Edition**	**Year**	**Name of the scarf**
Sprouse, Stephen	*Graffiti* (2001), *Roses and Graffiti* (2009)	2001, 2009 (posthumous tribute)	Various designs
Wilson, Robert	-	2002	*Bandana Fluo*
Murakami, Takashi	*Monogram Multicolor* (2003), *Cherry Blossom* (2005), Monogramouflage (2008), *Louis Vuitton × Takashi Murakami* (2025)	2003, 2005, 2008, 2025	Various designs
Prince, Richard	*Monogram Pulp*	2008	*Monogram Pulp Square*
Kusama, Yayoi	*Infinitely Kusama* (2012), *Creating Infinity* (2013)	2012, 2023	Various designs
AIKO	*Artist Scarves, Street Art*	2013	*Giant Square 4 Seasons*
RETNA	*Artist Scarves, Street Art*	2013	*Étole Script*
Os Gemeos	*Artist Scarves, Street Art*	2013	*Mosaic Square*
Eko Nugroho	*Artist Scarves, Volume II, Street Art*	2013–2014	*Tropical Giant Square*
Ben EINE	*Artist Scarves, Volume II, Street Art*	2013–2014	*Neon Square*
eL Seed	*Artist Scarves, Volume II, Street Art*	2013–2014	*Giant Calligraffitti Square*
Kenny Scharf	*Artist Scarves, Volume III, Street Art*	2014	*Pop Cosmic*
INTI	*Artist Scarves, Volume III, Street Art*	2014	*Sun Giant Square*
André Saraiva	*Artist Scarves, Volume III, Street Art*	2014	*Monsieur A*
Koons, Jeff	*Masters*	2017	Various designs

(*Continued*)

Artist	**Edition**	**Year**	**Name of the scarf**
Wood, Jonas	*Louis Vuitton × Jonas Wood*	2019	Various designs
Israel, Alex	*Louis Vuitton × Alex Israel*	2019	Various designs
Yitian, Sun	*Animogram*	2024	Various designs
De Crécy, Nicolas	*LV Art Silk Squares*	2024	*Parfums de Méditerranée*
eBoy	*LV Art Silk Squares*	2024	*Maze of Precious*
Icinori	*LV Art Silk Squares*	2024	*Malles Monde*
Mattotti, Lorenzo	*LV Art Silk Squares*	2024	*Iris Spring*
Ott, Thomas	*LV Art Silk Squares*	2024	*Urban Flowers*

Note: Data compiled from Louis Vuitton: A Passion for Creation: New Art, Fashion, and Architecture (Gasparina et al., 2017). The data from this source covers information up to 2017; additional contributions include updates from more recent years, gathered from various online sources and other books.

[a] It has not been possible to confirm whether the author participated in The Silk Road edition or if the proposal was developed separately.

References

Bai, Y. (2010). *Fashion design and art collaborations: An investigation of the collaborations between fashion designers/brands and artists* [Doctoral dissertation, The Hong Kong Polytechnic University]. https://www.proquest.com/docview/849293360

Barreiro Parguiña, S. (2023a, May 19). Entrevista a Alice Shirley, artista y diseñadora de carrés para Hermès [Interview with Alice Shirley, artist and carré designer for Hermès]. *Entrevistas con diseñadores*. https://www.sandraparguina.com/_files/ugd/799627_fa09ba2e8d7a4e02983d077f38dcf2c0.pdf

Barreiro Parguiña, S. (2023b, May 28). Entrevista a Virginie Jamin, artista y diseñadora de carrés para Hermès [Interview with Virginie Jamin, artist and carré designer for Hermès]. *Entrevistas con diseñadores*. https://www.sandraparguina.com/_files/ugd/799627_b1dc284a80ca40c39259da5bbd8630db.pdf

Barreiro Parguiña, S. (2024a). El pañuelo de artista: Intersecciones entre el arte contemporáneo y la moda de lujo en el cambio de milenio [The artist's scarf: Intersections between contemporary art and luxury fashion at the turn of the millennium]. In E. M. Pérez, E. Martínez, & F. C. Silva dos Santos (Eds.), *VI Congreso Internacional de Investigación en Artes Visuales ANIAV 2024. EX±ACTO* (pp. 101–7). Editorial Universitat Politècnica de València.

Barreiro Parguiña, S. (2024b, September 25). Entrevista a Thomas Ott, artista y colaborador de Louis Vuitton para la serie LV Art Silk Squares [Interview with Thomas Ott, artist and collaborator with Louis Vuitton for the LV Art Silk Squares series]. *Entrevistas con diseñadores*. https://www.sandraparguina.com/_files/ugd/799627_a8e2099c8181410d851900932a97f021.pdf

Barreiro Parguiña, S. (2024c, October 2). Entrevista a William Adjété Wilson, artista y colaborador de Louis Vuitton para la serie Le Voyage en Arizona [Interview with William Adjété Wilson, artist and collaborator with Louis Vuitton for the Le Voyage en Arizona series]. *Entrevistas con diseñadores*. https://www.sandraparguina.com/_files/ugd/799627_56e5e46f99f94959b766a1781424c420.pdf

Barreiro Parguiña, S. (2024d, October 3). Entrevista a eBoy, colectivo de artistas y colaboradores de Louis Vuitton para la serie LV Art Silk Squares [Interview with eBoy, artist collective and collaborators with Louis Vuitton for the LV Art Silk Squares series]. *Entrevistas con diseñadores*. https://www.sandraparguina.com/_files/ugd/799627_f965d5a145204c178554affc8680b7e4.pdf

Baseman, A. (Ed.). (1989). *The scarf.* Tabori & Chang.

Editions La Manufacture. (2022, October 24). *Icinori* [Video]. *YouTube*. https://www.youtube.com/watch?v=Egl_JA6o98g

Gasparina, J. (2021). Art essay: *33 Colours by Jill Gasparina*. In I. Luna (Ed.), *Louis Vuitton: A passion for creation: New art, fashion, and architecture* (pp. 40–63). Rizzoli.

Gasparina, J., Hermange, E., Igarashi, T., Le Fort, M., Luna, I., Maertens, M., Mead, R., Morrisset, C., O'Brien, G., Saillard, O., Steele, V., & Trétiack, P. (2017). *Louis Vuitton: A passion for creation: New art, fashion, and architecture*. Rizzoli.

Hlaváčková, K. (2019). *The Mad Silkman: Zika & Lida Ascher: Textile and fashion*. Museum of Decorative Arts in Prague.

Joy, A., & Belk, R. W. (2021). Why luxury brands partner with artists. In P.-Y. Donzé, V. Pouillard, & J. Roberts (Eds.), *The Oxford handbook of luxury business* (pp. 309–30). Oxford University Press.

Masè, S., & Cedrola, E. (2017). Louis Vuitton's art-based strategy to communicate exclusivity and prestige. In E. Cedrola & B. Jin (Eds.), *Fashion branding and communication: Core strategies of European luxury brands* (Vol. 1, pp. 155–84). Palgrave Macmillan US. https://doi.org/10.1057/978-1-137-52343-3_6

Palmitessa, M. (2012). *The use of art for branding purposes: A study of Louis Vuitton's art collaborations* [bachelor's thesis]. Lund University.

Shapiro, R., & Heinich, N. (2012). When is artification? *Contemporary Aesthetics, Special Volume 4.*

Thomas, D. (2008). *Deluxe: Cuando el lujo perdió su esplendor* [Deluxe: When luxury lost its splendor] (J. Fernández de Castro, Trans.). Ediciones Urano.

Titton, M. (2014). Andy's heritage: Collaborations between fashion, art, and Louis Vuitton. In E. Gaugele (Ed.), *Aesthetic politics in fashion* (pp. 60–75). Sternberg Press. https://doi.org/10.21937/9783956790799.5

Topi, A. (2024, September 3). Louis Vuitton art silk squares. *Runway Magazine.* https://runwaymagazines.com/louis-vuitton-art-silk-squares/

Wert Ortega, J. P. (2013). Arte de la calle y gusto social [Street art and social taste]. In J. Díaz Sánchez (Ed.), *Arte, diseño y moda: Confluencia en el sistema artístico* (pp. 55–83). Universidad de Castilla-La Mancha.

Yang Shuen, K. (2024, October 22). Louis Vuitton scarves get an artsy spin in the hands of this duo. *Female.* https://www.femalemag.com.sg/fashion/louis-vuittons-art-silk-square-scarves-studio-icinori/

CHAPTER 26

Architecture as a Space for Innovation and Fashion Retail

*Ana Tinajero Cabrera**

ABSTRACT

In the words of architect Carl Elefante, the greenest building is the one that is already built (Elefante, 2007). In the case of clothing, are existing garments also the most sustainable?

While centuries-old buildings are listed as protected assets, others go unnoticed without even being a few decades old. There are costume museums, historical archives, and fashion institutes that preserve costumes for centuries and garments that disappear after several uses. These two worlds have similarities: a piece of great value is the result of a meticulous process that spans from its conception to its completion through specialized guilds and trades that have sometimes been forgotten.

A luxury item is defined by exclusivity, craftsmanship and know-how, high-quality design, innovation, and creativity. In a luxury fashion brand, the creative director sets the guidelines for new collections, and each team must ensure consistency of brand image, reflecting its values in every decision. The result is only possible through the work and coordination of multidisciplinary teams, responding to the problems that arise during the execution while obtaining an excellent result within the deadline.

Keywords: luxury brand, retail architecture, cultural heritage, innovation, creative concept

Introduction

This article examines case studies in which a former residence is restored to connect fashion, art, and history in a vibrant urban context; a factory becomes an atelier and academy to exchange skills and innovation training to the artisans of the future; and a historic archive is transformed into a traveling exhibition. The aim of analyzing these examples is to explore the commitment of luxury brands to the preservation of textile and architectural heritage, integrating new programs into protected historic buildings and maintaining their legacy, while adapting to new trends.

* Universidad Politécnica de Madrid.
(ORCID: https://orcid.org/0009-0004-2749-0238)

Methodology

This article is the result of the initial phase of a doctoral thesis in architecture, fashion, design, and society that explores the materialization of the creative concept of a luxury brand through architecture.

It analyzes built spaces that convey the values of the brand, specifically through innovation and implementation of new mechanisms, as well as proposals that combine past and future, tradition and avant-garde to connect with the customer.

To frame the theme of the thesis, numerous brands and their strategies in the field of luxury have been analyzed, observing their evolution and the strategies currently used to respond to the needs that appear, comparing them with the historical context of the brand.

Following the theme of the congress, three examples have been chosen according to brands that actively support and defend the arts and the dissemination of culture through different strategies in which antiquity, tradition, and heritage converge with modernity, new technologies, and innovation to reinvent themselves. The brands Prada, Bottega Veneta, and Gucci belong to the luxury category and carry intrinsic the values that the author Susana Campuzano has assigned to this categorization exclusivity, craftsmanship, and know-how, high-quality design, as well as innovation and creativity (Campuzano García, 2003 and 2019).

Craftsmanship is the foundation of Prada. It is recognized for the delicate production of handbags, footwear, and clothing using high-quality materials and traditional techniques, such as embroidery, with experimentation and the use of other innovative materials such as recycled fabrics adopting a more futuristic vision.

With tradition as a starting point, Prada redefines a new concept of luxury, being a pioneer in combining design with experimental processes using craftsmanship as a method of conceptual innovation.

Architecture is essential in the construction of the brand's identity. The prestigious architectural firm OMA, recognized worldwide, has signed numerous projects for the brand, not only stores and points of sale, but also fashion shows, window displays, and temporary pavilions until reaching the high point of its collaboration with the Prada Foundation in Milan.

The design of the spaces where the brand communicates with the customer reflects the innovation and craftsmanship intrinsic to the brand.

Architecture, in addition to showcasing the products, becomes a visual attraction by fusing tradition and contemporaneity. The combination of technology (design, installations, lighting) and the creativity of the objects on display creates a perfect intersection between fashion, art, and architecture. All spaces highlight the qualities and quality of the collections, accentuating their beauty.

Bottega Veneta combines traditional craftsmanship from the Veneto region of Italy with contemporary innovation and is one of the most recognized brands in the world of luxury, particularly in the silent luxury category. Renouncing to logos, its sophistication lies in emphasizing the quality of its products, the use of raw materials and the timeless vision of fashion.

Exceptional craftsmanship is the main value and hallmark of the brand, famous for leather work and the use of *intrecciato*, hand-braided leather that requires a great knowledge of the technique to ensure the highest quality in each of its unique pieces.

The use of exceptional high-end materials such as leather, wood, or innovative fabrics to transform them into luxury products ensures respect for the environment by investing in ethical production, with innovative production processes that minimize waste, without sacrificing quality. Through its practices, customers recognize the excellence of the brand's products beyond their visibility, refusing to associate the use of a logo with a status symbol.

Under the guidance of the latest creative director, Matthieu Blazy, innovation has also been present in the creativity of the designs, integrating contemporary fashion with traditional craftsmanship. The design of bags, shoes, and clothing reflects a balance between minimalism and modernity, creating new silhouettes without losing the classic spirit of the brand.

Architecture is part of the visual identity of the brand using noble materials such as wood, stone, or marble, creating an aesthetic aligned with Bottega's values, reinforcing the link between luxury design with durable materials, creating spaces in which the product interacts with its environment, without resorting to excesses in the design.

The famous Italian fashion house Gucci, one of the most prominent and recognized worldwide, also stands out for the fusion between traditional craftsmanship and contemporary innovation. Since its beginnings in 1921, its creations have featured leather work on bags and shoes, as well as hand-dyed and hand-woven high-quality materials. The brand has constantly reinvented itself, always maintaining a deep connection with its heritage, an example of which are the collections resulting from the creative direction of Alessandro Michele, mixing eras and styles, retro influences with contemporary ones, to reach a younger audience, a new generation of consumers.

Gucci has innovated by creating novel concepts, giving transparency to its processes and incorporating interactive fashion through digitization and the use of augmented reality to interact with its customers, exploring the future of digital fashion by working with blockchain and NFTs (Non-Fungible Tokens).

The brand particularly values traditional Italian heritage, the Florentine palaces that houses its collections reflect its commitment to culture. The essential architecture in Gucci's brand strategy is the visual language that reflects the values of luxury and avant-garde characterized by elegant and eclectic interiors that combine traditional materials such as marble, stone, or stucco with modern ones such as steel or glass.

Results

This is the first article belonging to the doctoral thesis in architecture, fashion, design, and society.

A first general analysis shows that the relationship between architecture and fashion goes beyond the similarity in the creative processes of both disciplines and that they work hand in hand, they are complementary, especially in retail architecture and have repercussions on other more global issues that affect the built heritage, the city, and the society that inhabits it.

This work has served as a reflection to organize the relevant points of the thesis topic that will be studied in the following phases. Although the thesis starts from the construction of the creative concept of a luxury fashion brand, focusing on the coordination of work teams, it is essential to analyze the scope of these processes and actions in the city and in society.

During the research process, the following sections will be studied:

1. The creative concept of a luxury brand, with the creative director as the main responsible and the role of fashion designers, architects, and other creatives in the process.

2. The real estate strategy, the place where the creative concept materializes. Why does a brand choose a certain place to establish a point of connection with the client and transmit its values in the urban context.
3. The complex management and construction process for the implementation according to brand design guidelines by coordinating multidisciplinary teams, different construction trades, designers, craftsmen, engineers, etc.
4. The format of the brand strategy, aligned with the size of the point of sale and materialized in the products and services offered.
5. The result, the object built as a way of brand communication, how this message is transmitted.
6. The impact of this process.

This thesis is a challenge due to the lack of scientific documentation on the subject, the rapid transformation that the fashion and luxury sector is undergoing due to new technologies, the speed of consumption, as well as changes in the profile of consumers (Rathinamoorthy, 2019).

It is noteworthy that, although the speed of consumption has increased, the processes of architecture and the opening of new stores have become more complex, because the decision-making process for the needs and unforeseen events that arise during the project is not immediate, as the brands themselves have specific departments for each of the branches of the project. Each decision must be aligned with each of the departments to ensure brand coherence.

On the other hand, the multidisciplinary nature of the thesis is novel, approaching the subject of study through the analysis of different sectors. Abstract concepts from artistic disciplines are studied, together with other technical ones such as construction or project management, or the economic impact generated in cities on a local and global scale without forgetting society, the people involved in these processes.

This article does not provide scientific results *per se* but structures the topics of analysis in the following phases of the thesis. It will unravel the complex process in which fashion and architecture converge, giving rise to unique spaces, highlighting the importance of people's work, craft techniques, and the use of technology to optimize these processes and innovation to be relevant in an industry that is constantly renewing itself.

Discussion

In the words of architect Carl Elefante, the greenest building is the one that is already built (Elefante, 2007). And in the case of fashion, are the garments that already exist also the most sustainable? In recent years the fashion industry is implementing strategies and new actions, good habits to improve its ecological footprint, because fashion is one of the most polluting industries, the second most polluting after the oil industry (Castro, 2021).

Due to the climate crisis, sustainability has become the term of our time, every action, every behavior, must be sustainable, also in the fashion sector. The actors involved in this sector have replaced traditional, commonly accepted practices with more respectful ones thanks to innovation. However, the concept of sustainability cannot be reduced to the environment, instead the result of this concept is the sum of three axes, social, environmental, and economic growth. If one fails, the concept is meaningless (Purvis et al., 2019).

This collective awareness has given rise to a consumer committed to global issues and demanding transparency in the brands they identify with, transparency in their practices and processes.

The following three specific examples were selected to showcase the actions that luxury brands have taken to connect with the customer. These actions include the use of new technologies to train in processes, improving working conditions, and sharing the stories of the people behind each unique piece. The importance of artistic heritage, cultural legacy, and tradition is also highlighted, as these elements remain alive through the incorporation of new techniques and adaptation to current demand.

Villa Rong Zhai—Prada

Prada has published a manifesto on its website in which it is possible to browse through each of the following areas:

1. Rethink the rules. Prada Group is synonymous with innovation, transformation, and independence.
2. Innovative tradition. The Group is firmly rooted in a century-old tradition being, at the same time, synonymous with research and innovation, attitudes at the core of its spirit since its origins.

3. Spirit of excellence. The Prada Group in every action is geared toward excellence. A mental attitude that leads its people to seek perfection in their work, always refining and surpassing the results previously achieved.
4. Uniqueness of talents. Passion, curiosity, obsession for details and expertise are the distinctive qualities of their employees.
5. Beyond boundaries. Art, philosophy, architecture, and cinema are just some of the cultural disciplines that provide continuous sources of inspiration for the Group.
6. Sustainable paths. The group is committed to sustainability leading economic growth and innovation in harmony with places, people, and the environment.

By clicking on each section, it allows access to more specific content. Thus, following the theme of the congress, the section *sustainable for culture* is very significant. The header image are some fragments of the restoration process of a 1918 villa in Shanghai, a project that was carried out by Prada in the Rong Zhai Villa with Baciocchi Associati as the architectural office responsible for the meticulous restoration process.

The result of this intervention is the fusion between the local culture of Shanghai and the global values of the brand, becoming a benchmark for art, design, and fashion in China.

In the luxury sector, brands look for strategic locations to implement their points of sale, often historic buildings, sometimes even protected by historical heritage. In the case of Rong Zhai, antiquity and modernity converge in a new space. The old villa is restored by craftsmen who know the traditional techniques, analyzing the existing spaces and materials to incorporate current devices and the technique of the twenty-first century to make the building work.

Lamps, sockets, and cameras, among other devices, are perfectly integrated without damaging or disturbing the original image. Without the integration of technology, it would not be possible to accommodate a new use. Far from falling into oblivion, the former villa has become a cultural hub in the world of the arts in Shanghai, hosting parties, openings, exhibitions (including architecture) as well as branded fashion shows.

Atelier and Accademia: Labor et ingenieum—Bottega Veneta

Bottega Veneta's philosophy is rooted in the Veneto region and the craftsmanship and production of leather products, for the brand it is crucial to be faithful to the origins of this land regardless of its international expansion.

Its workshops, the heart of handcrafted production, located in this region are the place where tradition and innovation converge, using traditional techniques and tools. They have been innovative by creating the *intrecciato* technique and adapting their production processes by reducing excess material in the manufacturing process. The handcrafted and customized production through small series guarantees the exclusivity and durability of its products, offering a lifelong repair service.

Under the direction of Mathieu Blazy and Massimiliano Bomba, the brand releases the video *Craft in motion* recorded in the workshops of Veneto to show its production process. The Montebello atelier, housed in an ancient Italian *palazzo*, is equipped with a modern workspace with the right furniture, air conditioning, and lighting systems to create optimal working conditions for handcrafted production. Past, present, and future go hand in hand.

The traditional *intrecciato* technique is passed down from generation to generation thanks to the *Labora e ingenium* academy, training the artisans of the future because this technique requires skill and dexterity to create unique objects of great beauty.

On the outside of the workshops, people and their scale blend with the sculptures of the palace, generating another order, highlighting the human scale.

The video highlights the importance of people in the process, the hands that cut and sew the materials appear, but also the faces of the artisans responsible for the production. In the video you can hear the leather, the high-quality materials being worked, while at the same time it is possible to hear the silence created by the commitment and concentration of the craftsmen during the experimentation phase.

Craft in motion conveys emotions, the sensorial characteristics of the space where the pieces are created and uses transitions in which the textures of the fabrics and products fade away to give way to architectural images, the texture of the traditional materials of the building.

Gucci Cosmos—Gucci

Alessandro Michele (Gucci, n.d.) introduces the term *Guccify*, during his time as creative director of Gucci, by recovering the tradition of the past, old objects come back to the Gucci family, to a place that preserves the past, but is really a bridge to the contemporary. An old building is full of life. Just like fashion.

The *Palazzo Settimanni* in Florence dates to the century and since its acquisition in 1953, the fifteenth century building has been factory, workshop and showroom until finally becoming home to the brand's historical archive, a place of preservation to keep the tangible cultural heritage alive in the present and in the future with the digitization of all the pieces.

It is possible to visit all the rooms through a virtual tour on the brand's website. The menu shows the floor plan of the palace with a click and a photo indicating the thematic room that can be visited. On the right side of the screen there is a list with the name of the other rooms. The names of these rooms are terms coined by the creative director to designate certain stages of a journey.

Through this digital tour it is possible to see the pieces of the Gucci archive, as well as the architecture, decoration, and furnishings of each of the rooms, showing the meticulous process of restoration of the palace, emphasizing and respecting heritage pieces in combination with other more modern elements.

These archives leave their home for the first time to bring the brand's creativity to life in a traveling exhibition, *Gucci Cosmos*, which opened in Shanghai to showcase 102 years of the brand's history, followed by exhibitions in London, Paris, and Kyoto.

With Maria Luisa Frisa as curator and Es Devlin as artistic creative, the exhibition is a cultural project launched by Gucci as part of a series of innovative and experimental exhibitions through which to explore the universe of the brand giving rise to a complex exhibition organism, exploring themes such as identity through iconic pieces, interactive installations, and collaborations with artists. This proposal broke traditional schemes with the use of changing scenography, light games, sounds, and visual stories.

The highlight of the exhibition is the *Duomo*, a replica of the dome of *Santa Maria di Fiori* in Florence, a project of technic innovation during the Renaissance period, designed by the Italian architect Brunelleschi. The *Duomo* is a symbol that reflects Italy's position in the world and a way of referencing the brand's excellence through architecture.

Conclusion

In the words of architect Richard Rogers (Elle Decor, n. d.) architecture is too important to be left to architects alone, it is a collaborative process that unites several disciplines for a common goal. This complex discipline requires the joint work of many professionals specialized in different fields, so it would be absurd to reduce the merit of an architectural project solely to the architect who came up with the idea behind it.

New stores and collections, finished projects, are often presented as inert objects, pristine as if they had been produced by magic, paying attention to the creator, designer, the person responsible for the creative concept, but the process, the intricacies that lie behind to reach that finished object, are not documented.

The purpose of this paper is to highlight the parts involved in the retail process, the opening of a store, or the creation of a new space for the brand and that technology and innovation are just another tool to improve the processes, that digitalization does not work if there is no support from a human team.

In the same way haute couture designs are not executed by the creative director of the brand, but there are numerous craftsmen behind them.

During the design and construction phase, adjustments are necessary, adjustments to the place where the project is inserted, but also to the project itself, because during the execution, new problems always arise and need to be solved.

In short, an architectural project is the result of the work of many professionals, it is the teamwork of many trades and disciplines as happens in a fashion brand. Here, and especially in the world of luxury, everything must be coherent. Every action must address the core concept of the brand and not just a superficial or traditional marketing aspect such as a logo or an attractive slogan (Wilson, 2023).

A brand is composed of different levels or layers of meaning, values, and emotions, ranging from the most superficial to the deepest, which are the beliefs, or the genuine experience offered by the brand. The brand must be authentic and transparent. If a brand focuses only on appearance, it runs the risk of coming across to the viewer as false or empty of content. This is why this work of transparency with the consumer is essential to build a solid foundation by creating an emotional connection with them and responding to their needs and expectations in a sincere way. Brands must be consistent and coherent in their actions and values in the long term based on authenticity and a genuine connection with the audience.

References

Campuzano García, S. (2003). *El universo del lujo* [The universe of luxury]. McGraw-Hill.

Campuzano García, S. (2019). *La fórmula del lujo* [The luxury formula]. Lid Editorial Empresarial.

Castro, J. (2021). La industria textil y de la moda, responsabilidad social y la agenda 2030 [The textile and fashion industry, social responsibility, and the 2030 agenda]. *Cuadernos del Centro de Estudios en Diseño y Comunicación, 100*, 66–84. https://dx.doi.org/10.18682/cdc.vi100.3986

Elefante, C. (2007). The greenest building is... one that is already built. *Forum Journal, 21*(4), 26–38.

Elle Decor (n.d.). *50 frases de arquitectos sobre arquitectura y urbanismo* [50 quotes from architects on architecture and urban planning]. https://www.elledecor.com/es/arquitectura/g20975706/frases-inspiradoras-arquitectos/

Gucci (n.d.). *Cosmos Shanghai: Making of.* Gucci. https://www.gucci.com/us/en/st/stories/videos/article/cosmos-shanghai-making-of

Purvis, B., Mao, Y., & Robinson, D. (2019). Three pillars of sustainability: In search of conceptual origins. *Sustainability Science, 14*(4), 681–95. https://doi.org/10.1007/s11625-018-0627-5

Rathinamoorthy, R. (2019). *Sustainable fashion: Consumer awareness and education*. Springer Nature Singapore.

Wilson, H. (2023). *A brand is an onion*. ODYSSEE.

Author Biographies

María Arcas Ruiz
ORCID: https://orcid.org/0000-0003-3773-5329
Maria Arcas (Jerez de la Frontera, 1976) holds a Ph.D. in Fashion Trends from Universidad Politécnica de Madrid (UPM) and a degree in Journalism. She began her career in 2000 as Naty Abascal's assistant and interned at Neil Barrett's atelier in Milan. After working at Agencia EFE, she collaborated as editor and photographer with outlets like Wallpaper, RBA, and Prisa. A professional trend hunter since 2003, she pioneered coolhunting education in Spain, teaching at numerous universities and earning her Ph.D. in the field. She has been a speaker at MIT (2014), Museo del Traje, and various institutions. Co-founder of Undernews Comunicación (2007), she has developed press and branding projects for clients like Jägermeister, Heineken, and Valentino. Her work has been featured by CNN, MTV, Monocle, and major Spanish media.

Sandra Barreiro Parguiña
ORCID: https://orcid.org/0009-0002-6679-9137
Sandra Barreiro Parguiña (Spain, 1995), a Textile Artist and Graphic Designer, specialized in conceptual expression through textiles and silk scarves. Her work has been exhibited at Museo de Pontevedra, Pazo da Cultura de Pontevedra Culturgal, Sede Afundación in Santiago de Compostela, Escuela Superior de Canto de Madrid, and Palacio de Villardompardo in Jaén.

She has participated in residencies such as *X Encontro de Artistas Novos and Encontros de Mariñán*. Her awards include *Novos Valores 2023*, finalist in

XV Certame de Artesanía Antonio Fraguas Fraguas, finalist in *Xuventude Crea 2024 (Plastic Arts)*, finalist in *Bolsa Ensaia 2024* and, finalist *XXVI Premio Fundación Unicaja de Artesanía*. As a researcher, she has presented at conferences like *Tech & Crafts* (UPM Madrid), *Jornadas Mujeres Creadoras* (US Sevilla), and ANIAV (UPV Valencia), and was an invited speaker at *Hilos de la Seda* (Valencia). After five years in the textile printing industry, she now designs silk scarves under her personal brand while pursuing a Ph.D. closely related to this field.

Carsten Behm
Carsten Behm is a professor of fashion design at Hannover University of Applied Sciences and Arts. He is an expert in digital pattern development and clothing simulation, with extensive experience in both industry and academia.

Sylvia Bossenz
Sylvia Bossenz is a teacher for special tasks at Hannover University of Applied Sciences and Arts, working in the intersecting fields of costume, fashion, media, and product design. The development of shapes in the design process and their changes over time are the focus of her work. Her research interests include digital tailoring, fashion history, and innovative approaches to teaching design.

Mónica Bueno Ortega
ORCID: https://orcid.org/0009-0006-2816-6274
Mónica Bueno Ortega is a fashion history specialist. Throughout her academic career, the history of costume has been one of her primary areas of interest, with studies focusing on the importance of fashion as a social element. She is currently pursuing her doctoral research on the evolution of personal ornamentation and decorative accessories during the Spanish dynastic transition through the Architecture, Design, Fashion & Society doctoral program at the Universidad Politécnica de Madrid.

She has participated in conferences presenting the results of her research, including in 2024, the International Congress, *¿Vestir a la francesa o a la española? La moda del siglo XVIII en España* and the First International Congress of Embroidery, *El Arte del Bordado: Historia, Tradición y Nuevos Horizontes*.

Adriana Cagigas Gil
ORCID: https://orcid.org/0009-0005-2700-337X
A doctoral student at UNED, Adriana is a lecturer and researcher at UDIT. She holds a degree in Fashion Design from Universidad Camilo José Cela in Madrid and a Master's in Cultural Economics and Management from the Universidad de Valladolid. She also has specialized training in textile artisanal techniques from NUA, Nanjing University of the Arts (China), complemented by courses on materials and circularity from Central Saint Martins. Currently pursuing her doctorate on textile rituals as a sustainability axis in the fashion industry, she also manages a project focused on the development of indigenous textile craftsmanship in China.

María Luisa Calvo Frutos
ORCID: https://orcid.org/0009-0000-5507-6916
Head of Research and lecturer at Centro Superior de Diseño de Moda de Madrid, Universidad Politécnica de Madrid (CSDMM, UPM), where she is also pursuing her doctoral studies. She holds a Master's in Pattern and Garment Technology from London College of Fashion, University of the Arts London (LCF, UAL), and a BSc in Telecommunications Systems Engineering from Universidad Carlos III de Madrid (UC3M).

Her research explores the intersection of design and technology, with an emphasis on programming applied to pattern cutting, the integration of contemporary textile craftsmanship with emerging digital technologies, virtual garment simulation, and AI applied to fashion design.

She has also taught at institutions such as Istituto Europeo di Design (IED Madrid) and Universidad Europea de Madrid (UEM), combining her academic focus with prior experience in the fashion industry as a studio manager, creative pattern cutter, and consultant for international fashion brands.

Caterina Cucinotta
ORCID: https://orcid.org/0000-0002-0572-6930
Caterina Cucinotta is Assistant Professor in the Communication Science Faculty in Rey Juan Carlos University in Madrid and was post-doctoral researcher at the Institute of Contemporary History of the New University of Lisbon. She holds a Ph.D. in Film Studies (2015) and has extensive experience in both teaching and costume design in film. She is the author of *Trip to cinema*

through costumes (LabCom, 2018), *Costumes and costume designers from Portugal, Concepts for new materialities* (Humus, 2023) and the visual essay *De la Femme* (2021), among other publications. In 2024 she coordinated the international workshop *Mediterranean Textures: Fashion, Media and New Research Routes.*

Rosa Deltoro Cremades
ORCID: https://orcid.org/0009-0007-9302-1781
Rosa Deltoro Cremades, degree in Art and Design specializing in Graphic Design, holds a master's degree in Design and Illustration and a master's degree in Artistic Production from the Universidad Politécnica de Valencia. Specialized in textiles, she has worked for international fashion brands designing prints. She is an associate professor and researcher at the Facultad de Bellas Artes de San Carlos, Universidad Politécnica de Valencia, and a Ph.D. candidate in the Art and Research program.

Elena Díaz Martín
Elena Díaz Martín holds a degree in Fine Arts from the Universidad Complutense de Madrid and a diploma in Fashion Design from IADE. In 2010, she completed a Master's in Teacher Training at the Universidad Complutense de Madrid, with her final master's thesis titled *Fashion as a Pedagogical Element in Secondary Education.*

In 2021, at the same university, she completed a master's in Design with the final project *Ciudad Real, Hidden Treasure. Design of a Fashion Collection and Its Subsequent Exhibition for the Promotion of the City's 600th Anniversary,* which earned her the 10th University Entrepreneurship Awards, recognizing outstanding master's theses.

In addition to her academic work, she has developed several personal projects as a fashion designer. She has been teaching fashion project courses for over 10 years at the Escuela superior de Diseño de Madrid.

Lala de Dios
Lala de Dios is Art historian and weaver. Co-founder and current president of the Asociación para la Creación Textil, ACT. Member of the Advisory Council of the European Textile Network, ETN. Independent researcher. Main interests: textile culture (heritage, education, art/design/contemporary

craft), the interaction of technology and crafts, posthumanism, networking, the hybridation of disciplines.

Latest publications: Arte Morbida no. 11 (2023), London Textile Tour; Arte Morbida no. 12 (2023), A Textile Tour in Canada; Arte Morbida no. 14 (2024), Weaving Futures; Bloomsbury Encyclopedia of World Textiles, Volume 1. Texts in exhibition catalogues: Ainda um elefante na sala (2024); Los hilos de la memoria, Josep Grau-Garriga (2024); A Fabric of Landscapes, Francesca Piñol (2024); Ultra Deep, Alexandra Knie (2024).

José Antonio Fernández Fernández
ORCID: https://orcid.org/0000-0002-8152-5284
José Antonio Fernández Fernández holds a degree in Art History from the Universidad de Granada. In 2023, he received his Ph.D. from the Universidad Politécnica de Madrid with the thesis *Indumentaria infantil en la corte española de los Habsburgo (1556–1621)* [Children's apparel at the Spanish Court of the Habsburgs (1556–1621)]. From 2013 to 2018, he served as a lecturer in Fashion Design at the Universidad Politécnica de Madrid and, since 2018, has held the same position at the Universidad Rey Juan Carlos. His research interests include the production processes of garments and Spanish clothing of the Modern and Contemporary Ages.

Gisela Beatriz Fortuna Mantellini
ORCID: https://orcid.org/0000-0002-6291-7979
Gisela Beatriz Fortuna Mantellini holds a Ph.D. in Architecture, Design, Fashion, and Society from the Universidad Politécnica de Madrid, where she is currently conducting research. She holds a master's degree in Advertising and Corporate Identity from the Universidad Camilo José Cela and a Postgraduate degree in Product Management for Fashion Companies. In addition, she has a bachelor's degree in Fashion and Textile Design from the Universidad de Buenos Aires.

She has authored the book *Dinamización del Proceso Creativo en las Empresas de Moda* (2014) and contributed to various book chapters on the teaching of sustainable design methodologies. She has led major international projects, such as *Europa Creativa Fashion Alive* and *Zero Waste Fashion Training*®, with the aim of promoting sustainable design in Europe.

She has been a recipient of several grants and international projects, including the European project *Europa Creativa Fashion Alive* (2022–2024). She has also coordinated the *Zero Waste Fashion Training®* project within the Erasmus Plus framework (2023–2025). She has worked as a lecturer and academic coordinator at ESNE (now UDIT) and has directed R&D projects in the field of sustainable fashion. She is currently the Executive Director of CREAMODITE, managing projects on digitalization, sustainability, and innovation in fashion and design sectors.

Guillermo García-Badell
ORCID: https://orcid.org/0000-0002-3990-2744
Guillermo García-Bardell is Dean of Centro Superior de Diseño de Moda de Madrid, Fashion Center at the Universidad Politécnica de Madrid (CSDMM-UPM). Clerk of the Committee for the UPM Ph.D. Program *Architecture, Design, Fashion, and Society*, and member of the UPM Research Group "*Analysis and Documentation of Architecture, Design, Fashion, and Society.*" Professor and Coordinator of *Design Fundamentals* in the BA Degree in Fashion Design.

Architect from the Universidad Politécnica de Madrid and Ph.D. in Marketing Research from the Universidad Complutense de Madrid. As a researcher, he is focused on synergies between design and other disciplines (such as Consumer Behavior or Marketing in general), and between different design disciplines themselves (architecture, product, and fashion design). As an architect and designer, he has been awarded prizes in several international competitions and has participated in various exhibitions.

Herbert González Zymla
ORCID: https://orcid.org/0000-0002-8578-3272
Herbert González Zymla holds a Ph.D. in Art History from the Complutense University of Madrid (2011) with the doctoral thesis *History and Art in the Royal Cistercian Monastery of Santa María de Piedra. 1195–1835*. He has been a fellow of the *Gabinete de curiosidades* of the Real Academia de la Historia. He was a professor at the Centro Superior de Diseño de Moda de Madrid, affiliated with the Universidad Politécnica de Madrid, between 2006 and 2017. Since 2008, he has been a lecturer in the Department of Art History at the UCM. Since 2014, he has been a Corresponding Academician in Ávila for

the Real Academia de la Historia, and since 2018, he has been an advisor to the Centro de Estudios Bilbilitanos. His main lines of research are: Monastic architecture, Cistercian architecture in the Crown of Aragon, Art and artistic patronages of the Ducal House of Alba, Classical and medieval iconography, History of fashion and textiles.

Paulina Grabowska
ORCID: https://orcid.org/0009-0007-0178-319X
Paulina Grabowska is an expert in sustainability and regenerative development. She runs NASDRA Institute, a company that develops urban farms and implements solutions for urban food systems and the circular economy in cities. Through her brand, mood.farm, she integrates biophilia, vertical farming, and health-promoting lighting into work environments, collaborating with global brands such as IKEA. mood.farm's solutions, incorporated into ARUP's Warsaw office, contributed to the project's recognition at the FRAME AWARDS 2023 and PLGBC Awards. She has also represented the Polish Cultural Institute in New York at Eco Solidarity, an event co-organized by Wanted Design Manhattan in 2021–2022 and again in 2024. Her research and development work has been showcased in Warsaw, New York, and Chongqing. She is an expert at the Warsaw Food LAB, a lecturer in bio-design at SWPS University, and a TEDxWarsaw speaker. She has led Science Now workshops on the future of food as part of the European Space Agency (ESA) initiative, Direction Earth/Space.

Venetia Koutsou
ORCID: https://orcid.org/0009-0001-6610-6401
Venetia Koutsou is a senior lecturer in Fashion Design, at the department of Creative Design & Clothing, school of Design Science, of the International Hellenic University (IHU). She teaches Fashion History, Style Semiology, Trends Forecasting and Fashion Design.

She has collaborated with the Hellenic Association of Knitwear and ready-to-wear companies (SEPEE), in the framework of lifelong educational programs for clothing industry employees. She has worked for Hellenic Organization of Small and Medium Sized Enterprises and Handicraft (EOMMEX) and has collaborated with the *Peclers* and *Carlin International* trend bureaus concerning Fashion Prognosis issues.

In collaboration with the visual artist Eleftheria Stoikou (PieTa Team), she has inspired and curated design projects such as, among others, *Endymatography: from home to journey*, *Wear is Art*, *Deconstructing Jeans*, for the promotion of the clothing culture.

Elisabeth Lorenzi
ORCID: https://orcid.org/0000-0002-9518-6666
Elisabeth Lorenzi is a lecturer in textile technology and materials at the Centro Superior de Diseño de Moda de Madrid, with a strong foundation in social sciences and humanities. As a professional, they have combined teaching activities with roles in consulting, cultural mediation, and cultural production. Their areas of expertise include collaborative design methodologies, textile electronics, material innovation, interactivity, and sustainability. Their research focuses on applying sustainability criteria to e-textiles, prototyping low-impact materials for the creation of wearables.

Daphne Mohajer va Pesaran
ORCID: https://orcid.org/0000-0001-5775-1487
Daphne Mohajer va Pesaran is an Iranian Canadian academic and designer. She is Senior Lecturer in the School of Fashion and Textiles at RMIT University in Melbourne, Australia. She spent ten years studying and working in Tokyo, where she learned about Japanese fashion and traditional craft practices. In her research and design practice she works with garments/products made from handmade paper and explores what materials and relationships can emerge in communities of human and nonhuman people. She is currently undertaking research fellowships for the British Museum, the Australian Museum, and the International Specialized Skills Institute to research the use of paper for clothing in Japan and the Pacific Islands, as well as recycling used clothing into paper. She is co-editor of *Radical Fashion Exercises: a workbook of modes and methods*, with Dr. Laura Gardner and published by Valiz. She co-runs a creative research practice called DNJ Paper which explores the use of paper for clothing and design objects.

Gianni Montagna
ORCID: https://orcid.org/0000-0002-5843-2047
Gianni Montagna holds a Ph.D. in Design by the Universidade de Lisboa since 2012, with a thesis on the application of smart systems to swim clothing,

teaches Fashion Design at the first academic year of the Masters in Fashion Design and often teaches other disciplines at the same institution, as in the case of accessory design, knit design, design methodologies and textiles for the architecture of the Ph.D. program in Architecture. In the textile development laboratory (D_TEX LAB) of the Faculty of Architecture of Lisbon, he is responsible for the area of Textile and Knit Design. From July 2024 he is a coordinator of the Fashion Design Master Course of the Lisbon School of Architecture, in Lisbon. He is the scientific coordinator of the International Congress on Textile Design *D_TEX _ Textile, Identity, and Innovation* which aims to bring together the different scientific domains around the textile area.

Lorraine Portelli

Dr. Lorraine Portelli, Ph.D., is a senior lecturer at the University of Malta's Faculty of Education, specializing in Fashion, Textiles, and Interior Studies. Her academic expertise lies in the historical progression of curricula in Home Economics and Textile Studies, with a particular emphasis on how these subjects have evolved over time.

Her research delves into diverse aspects of textile and fashion education, including the pedagogical approaches used to teach needlecraft during the nineteenth and twentieth centuries. She has also conducted extensive studies on the transformation of Maltese wedding attire between 1900 and 1950, analyzing how cultural, social, and economic factors influenced bridal fashion trends. Additionally, she explores sustainability practices within the fashion industry, examining how historical and contemporary methods contribute to ethical and eco-conscious design.

Currently, she is leading an EU-funded initiative under the Creative Europe program, titled *TRACtion – Tradition in Action – Traditional Costume Innovation*. This project aims to preserve and reinterpret traditional garments, blending historical craftsmanship with modern technology and innovative design practices to ensure the continuity and relevance of cultural heritage in contemporary fashion.

Martina Ponzoni

Martina Ponzoni (Ponz) is a 3D Fashion Specialist with a focus on digital craftsmanship techniques. As co-founder and director of d_archive, she collaborates with international institutions, such as the ModeMuseum in Antwerp, to make fashion archives more accessible and supporting preservation efforts by digital means. As Sessional Lecturer at RMIT's School of Fashion and Textiles, Melbourne, she develops and delivers innovative courses on digital fashion techniques and prototyping, focusing on technical aspects as well as reflecting and speculating about future applications and implications of such tools and practices in the broader cultural context of Fashion. Her freelance and consultant work includes collaborations with top global brands looking to integrate 3D tools in their workflow in a non-disruptive way. She holds a master's degree in Fashion and Accessories Design from Politecnico di Milano. She has recently been selected as a 2024 Fellow for the Italian Australian Foundation Sir James Gobbo Legacy Fellowship by ISS Institute.

Diego Prieto López
ORCID: https://orcid.org/0000-0002-7813-0097
Diego Prieto López holds a bachelor's degree in History from the Universidad de León and master's degree in Mediterranean Archaeology in Classical Antiquity from the Universidad Complutense de Madrid. Ph.D. from the Universidad Politécnica de Madrid within the program *Architecture, Design, Fashion, and Society.*

Head of Quality Assurance and Academic Coordinator at the Centro Superior de Diseño de Moda of the Universidad Politécnica de Madrid. In the academic field, he is a lecturer in Art History for the bachelor's Degree in Fashion Design and the Double Degree in Fashion Design and Commerce, both taught at CSDMM-UPM. He has also served as an adjunct professor in the Department of Art History at the Complutense University of Madrid.

Member of the Research Group *Analysis and Documentation of Architecture, Design, Fashion & Society* at the Universidad Politécnica de Madrid, and *The Medieval Image: Transversality and Cultural Projection* at the Universidad Complutense de Madrid. He has participated in national and international academic conferences such as DTex, CEHA, etc., and has also coordinated them. He is coordinator for the journal *Diseño de Moda: Teoría e historia de la indumentaria.*

Mercedes Rodriguez Sanchez
ORCID: https://orcid.org/0000-0002-9947-3865
Mercedes Rodriguez Sanchez holds a Ph.D. in Science of Communication and Media Studies from Universidad Complutense de Madrid. She is a professor at CSDMM, Universidad Politécnica de Madrid, where she teaches courses

on fashion design management and digital transformation. Her research focuses on the impact of digital technologies and sustainable innovation in the fashion industry, with a special interest in artificial intelligence, virtual fashion, and emerging business models. She has published academic articles and book chapters on digital fashion, and is the author of *Moda digital: transformación, negocio y nuevas tecnologías* [Digital Fashion: Transformation, Business and New Technologies]. She regularly collaborates with industry, cultural institutions, and media outlets.

Maialen Salcedo Berrueta
ORCID: https://orcid.org/0009-0005-9279-8359
Maialen Salcedo Berrueta is a Ph.D. student in Art History at the HiCSA laboratory of the Université Paris 1 Panthéon-Sorbonne. Under the supervision of Prof. Pascal Rousseau and Prof. Xosé Manoel Núñez Seixas, she studies the role of Spanish haute couture in the process of nation-building in Franco's Spain (1939–1975). This project is funded by a studentship from the Collège des Écoles Doctorales.

Fellow of the Casa de Velázquez, she has been a visiting researcher at Universidad Complutense de Madrid and the Museo del Traje. More recently, she was a visiting scholar at Columbia University, supported by the Alliance Doctoral Mobility Grant.

Her long-standing interest in the history of Spanish fashion and its links with the contemporary history of Spain has led her to participate in various seminars and conferences in both Spanish and French universities. In line with this commitment, she also serves as secretary of SARTORIA, where she is the project manager of the INHALab 2025 residency.

Timo Schnitt
Timo Schnitt is a professor of 3D animation, visual effects, and media design informatics at Hannover University of Applied Sciences and Arts. His research focuses on the application of digital technologies in creative fields, including cultural heritage preservation.

Paula Alegría Serrano Padilla
Paula Alegría Serrano Padilla is an architect and fashion specialist from the Universidad Politécnica de Madrid. Winner of the *Samsung Ego Innovation Project* presented at the *Mercedes-Benz Fashion Week* in Madrid in 2020. Her

work is characterized by mixing handmade techniques with high-tech ones, such as 3D printing or laser cutting, the organic and inorganic matter, the synthetic and the natural, the living and the non-living. She currently runs her own fashion firm, combining her work with teaching at the Centro Superior de Diseño de Moda de Madrid.

ELEFTHERIA STOIKOU

Eleftheria Stoikou is Assistant Professor of the department of Creative Design and Clothing of the International University of Greece.

She studied at the Aristotle University of Thessaloniki, Faculty of Fine Arts. She continued her postgraduate studies by means of her scholarship with the Melina Mercouri Foundation after having excelled at the School of Fine Arts in Barcelona (thesis: *Public Art and Public Space Renovation*).

She is a holder of a master's degree in Graphic Arts and Multimedia, EAP, a graduate of the University of Patras. She has taken part in numerous group exhibitions (Thessaloniki, Athens, Barcelona, Turin). She has also been awarded with various distinctions, and she has taken part in workshops (Yiannis Kounellis in Turin and with the sculptor Dani Caravan in Barcelona). She held nine solo exhibitions in Thessaloniki, Athens, Barcelona, and Istanbul.

She has organized a number of exhibitions for the students of the department of Creative Design and Clothing of the International University of Greece with the theme Artistic Cloth in Thessaloniki and Istanbul.

ANA TINAJERO CABRERA

ORCID: https://orcid.org/0009-0004-2749-0238

Ana Tinajero Cabrera is a Spanish architect graduated in 2016 at E.T.S.A.M.-UPM with international experience both academical and professional in several countries as Argentina, Mauritius, or Czech Republic among others.

Currently she is combining her professional practice as architect construction project manager with her studies as a Ph.D. student. Her scope of work in Cologne (Germany) consists of giving a second life to existing buildings, some of them protected by cultural heritage implementing creative concepts from luxury brands through construction while coordinating multidisciplinary teams. Her Ph.D. Research in Architecture, Design, Fashion and Society at CSDMM—UPM in Madrid (Spain), explores how the creative concept of a fashion brand becomes into reality through architecture in a retail space.

Both allow her to combine her creativity and passion for design and fashion with the technical part of her professional practice and formation.

Angelica Vandi
ORCID: https://orcid.org/0000-0002-3627-0059

Angelica Vandi holds a Ph.D. in Design and Post-Doc Research Fellow at the Department of Design is part of the faculty of the School of Design, Politecnico di Milano. Since 2019, she has been part of the *Fashion in Process* research lab of the Department of Design, Politecnico di Milano and, since 2021 of the Gianfranco Ferré Research Center. In 2018 she took part in the joint program in Fashion Design Management between the School of Design of Politecnico di Milano and Jefferson University, Philadelphia and in 2023 she was a Visiting Researcher at the *metaLAB* of Harvard University, Boston.

Her research interests focus on the relationship between Fashion Design, Cultural Heritage, and the integration of digital technologies. In particular, she delves into the topic of digital curation and the development of design scenarios geared toward the enhancement of fashion cultural capital through new modes of interaction.

Victoria Vásquez Pecile
ORCID: https://orcid.org/0009-0006-0703-3018

Victoria Vásquez Pecile, after completing several courses at the Chambre Syndicale de la Couture in Paris, teaches sewing, pattern making, and 3D modeling. She conducts research on the technical history of pattern making in Spain, designing and applying methodologies for the digitalization of clothing for its conservation. She works with institutions such as the Museo del Traje in Madrid, the Balenciaga Archive, the Alaïa Foundation, and the Yves Saint Laurent Foundation in Paris, applying these methodologies. Her work has been presented at forums such as the IFM in Paris, the Clo3D Summit in France, and Tongji University.

Maria Zoumaki
ORCID: https://orcid.org/0009-0006-8538-8754
Dr. Maria Zoumaki is an architect specializing in sustainable and creative design. She holds a Ph.D. from the Department of Mechanical Engineering at Aristotle University of Thessaloniki, focusing on sustainable ecological materials for industrial design and products. She is currently a faculty member in the Department of Creative Design and Clothing at the International Hellenic University.

Having worked as an architect, designer, VR developer, educator, and researcher on the sustainability of materials in various creative design industries, her research interests focus on sustainable design, the development of environmentally friendly techniques, alternative production methods, and the development of a new approach to sustainable fashion design.

Index

Note: Page references followed by "n" indicates a single note number and "nn" indicates a range or series of note numbers on the cited page.